The Survey
Research Handbook

The Irwin Series in Marketing
Consulting Editor   **Gilbert A. Churchill, Jr.**
University of Wisconsin, Madison

The Survey Research Handbook

Pamela L. Alreck
Robert B. Settle

both of
San Diego State University

Homewood, Illinois 60430

Library of Congress Catalog Card No. 84–80812

Printed in the United States of America

1 3 1 4 1 5 1 6 1 7 MP 2 1 0

Preface

Survey research is one of those activities that cut across a dozen different boundaries. Those in business and public administration, the social and behavioral sciences, professional and family studies, journalism and communications, education and health services, politics and law, and many other diverse areas all find an increasing need for information based on survey research. Fortunately, the same basic tools, skills and activities for doing surveys apply, regardless of the particular purpose or topics for any one survey research project.

As active survey research consultants for the past several years, we have designed and conducted projects in several areas for many different types of clients. Invariably, during the initial meeting with a potential new survey sponsor, those seeking the information will explain, with a good deal of sincerity and conviction, that their own particular organization, industry, or profession is unique—probably not much like any other we have encountered. This sometimes troubles potential survey sponsors because they wonder if they should seek out some survey consultant or agency that has worked in their own area of activity and has substantial experience with the special nature of their information needs. Their concerns are genuine, but they are also unfounded. It is certainly true that the institutions and organizations that depend on survey information are often very different from one another in their goals, objectives, and operations. Yet by applying the same basic principles and techniques described in this handbook, we have surveyed many thousands of different types of respondents for dozens of very diverse clients with uniformly positive and valuable results. Perhaps you are wondering if you should seek a research book devoted exclusively to your own discipline, profession, or activity to guide you in a survey project. You need not be concerned because you will find what you need here.

Fortunately, then, survey research *applications* cut across many institutional and disciplinary boundaries. Unfortunately, however, survey research also slices across many *technical* boundaries, as well. If you are going to do a complete survey project, from beginning to end, you will find the diversity of skills rather demanding. You will be working with people one minute and machines the next. At one time you may be concerned with how to phrase a question or word some instruction. A few days later you may be a little puzzled about some statistical method. You may have to deal with a printer who keeps telling you your work will be ready tomorrow or a computer that just does not seem to want to talk to you at all. Fear not!

Probably our most important objective in writing this handbook has been to bring together all of the various techniques and principles, skills and activities that are required to conduct a really effective survey project. As university instructors, we have both been faced with one, all too familiar situation far too many times. The stereotypical situation is simply this: A student comes to the office or approaches one of us after a class and declares with considerable gravity that he or she has decided to conduct a survey. Then comes the question: "Where can I find a book that will tell me what to do?" Often this same student has taken one or more university courses on research methods in their area of study. Occasionally, they will have a research textbook under their arm at the time. Yet we, and they, both know very well that neither the training they received nor the textbook they acquired was satisfactory to guide them through an entire survey research project, from start to finish. We sincerely hope that now, at last, we and they and you have the answer. This handbook is not devoted to any one, specific area, but it provides comprehensive coverage of the wide variety of things you will need to know to conduct effective survey research.

We have been guided by two criteria when judging whether or not to include material in the handbook: Is this sufficient, and is this necessary? We feel that both are important. When using a handbook or manual, there is, perhaps, nothing quite so frustrating as finding that it covers every conceivable situation *except your own*. Consequently, the breadth and scope of the handbook is, by necessity, fairly wide. It must be, in order to meet your own needs, whether you are a student who will conduct a single survey project to meet your academic requirements or a seasoned survey research professional seeking some new ideas or tools of the trade.

We have also avoided or eliminated substantial amounts of material that are ordinarily found in research textbooks. If we had never once used or seen the need for some technique, computation, or procedure in either academic or pragmatic survey research over several years time, we felt you probably would not need it either, and it could safely be excluded. Perhaps there will be some who feel the handbook lacks dignity because the practical and technical aspects of survey research take precedence over the conceptual and the theoretical aspects. To us, that is the whole idea, and it is a small price to pay for a handbook that is understandable and useful.

As you examine the handbook, you should find there is little that is likely to get in the way of understanding. Some aspects of survey research, especially those involving computers and statistics, are known for the use of buzz-words and obscure terminology. In our experience, the use of such vocabulary is intimidating and inhibiting, rather than helpful or enlightening. So we have deliberately avoided them in favor of plain, ordinary words and phrases. If you find more here than what you need, at least it will be understandable, and to the degree that we have been successful, you will find everything you need for survey research and very little else.

Pamela L. Alreck
Robert B. Settle

Contents

CHECKLISTS

GUIDELISTS

EXAMPLES

FIGURES

PART ONE
SURVEY PLANNING
AND DESIGN

1

Sponsorship and Topics

WHY SURVEYS ARE CONDUCTED

Individuals and organizations sponsor surveys to obtain information that is unavailable from other sources or would be more difficult and expensive to obtain otherwise. The sponsors may need a survey for one or more of three types of reasons: (1) They may want to influence or persuade some audience. (2) They may want to create or modify some product or service for a particular public. (3) They may focus directly on understanding or predicting human behavior or conditions because this is the focus of their academic or professional work.

Surveys of an Audience

Many sponsors would like to influence the beliefs or the behavior of their audience or persuade those in the audience to think in a certain way or to act in some particular manner. Certainly everyone often tries to influence and persuade others. This is neither unusual nor undesirable in most cases because those being influenced are not being exploited or harmed in any way. It is often in the best interest of those subject to these influences to respond to them. Parents try to influence their children, spouses seek to persuade one another, employees attempt to influence their supervisors, and buyers try to convince sellers to reduce their prices. When ordinary people try to influence others, those doing the persuading can usually see pretty clearly how successful their efforts have been. They know from conversation and from observation. Understanding the audience and gauging the effects are much more difficult for those who want to influence or persuade a large number of people simultaneously.

3

Business firms promoting their products or services; political parties and organizations promoting their candidates and issues; government bureaus and agencies promoting their positions; social service institutions devoted to education, public health and medicine, religious belief, or social welfare, promoting their doctrines and services: All of these organizations communicate with their publics in a variety of ways. But promotion is a one-way form of communication. The message to influence or persuade goes out from the sender to the audience, but how does the audience respond? Are the messages effective? Is there resistance? Do those in the audience even understand? Is the information what they need to know? Do the messages "touch a nerve" or evoke a need? When messages are directed to a large audience, survey research can be the other half of the conversation, so there is two-way communication between the message sender and those in the audience. Those who receive the messages ordinarily do not take the initiative to respond with their reactions. Even if they wanted to, there is often no real mechanism for them to respond. Those who sponsor a survey of their audience are taking the responsibility for both halves of the conversation and are providing a medium through which their audience can talk to them. This is no imposition on the respondents because nobody can be forced to respond if they do not wish to take the time or effort to do so. Most people welcome the opportunity to respond, to record their opinions and reactions, and to have some effect on the sponsor.

Surveys of a Clientele

The occupation of most people involves doing or making something for others and so do the operations of most companies, organizations, and institutions. Individuals and organizations often seek survey information to discover the needs, wants, and desires of those they serve, or the underlying human conditions that make their goods useful and valuable to others. The better the others are known and understood, the more able the providers of goods and services will be able to serve them economically and effectively. Commercial and industrial firms, political parties and candidates, governmental agencies and units, hospitals and clinics, schools and colleges, churches and religious groups, and those in professional practices all provide products and services to their own publics. In almost every case, there are many options and alternatives concerning *what* they provide, *who* they provided it to, *when* and *where* it will be provided, *how* it will produced, and the *cost* or charges to those who need the goods or services. Survey research is often designed to furnish information for making such decisions.

The producers of goods and services usually have to take the responsibility for learning and understanding the needs and desires of their public. The producers ordinarily have a fairly clear picture of what could be produced and delivered, but they are often very uncertain about the needs and desires of the public. Similarly, those in the public know what they need or want in a general way, but they seldom know what actually could be produced or by whom, among the many potential sources for goods and services. It is often desirable for those who produce goods for their public to take the initiative to learn about their clientele by sponsoring a research survey. Such a survey usually serves both the producers and the clients or customers who are the respondents. The better the producers understand their clientele, the more effectively they will be able to serve them.

Surveys of Other Populations

The reasons for surveys identified above are *practical* ones and the results are oriented toward decision making and executive actions. Sponsors may also be motivated by a desire for knowledge about people, in and of itself. People, themselves, are the subject matter and focus of attention for many academic and professional disciplines. Thus, students and professors, researchers and professionals within the social and behavioral sciences, the humanities and arts, business and public administration, and a wide variety of other professional studies very often focus exclusively or substantially on the behavior and conditions of the people in the society. The survey information is sought not so much to assist in decision making as it is to enhance the body of theoretical and conceptual knowledge of the discipline. Rather than information to be applied to practical problems and actions, *theoretical* research seeks information to answer research questions and to test hypotheses about the propensities and predispositions of people. The information gained from such survey research may not be directly applicable to existing conditions or potential actions at the present moment. Rather, it will be used to enhance the literature and the state of current thought within the discipline or area of the sponsor.

The criteria for judging the information needs differs between the two types of survey research, but the survey procedure itself is fairly standard, regardless of whether the purpose is practical or theoretical. Measurement tools are largely indifferent to what they are measuring. Those in many different occupations often use the same measurement tools. Carpenters, plumbers, and masons may all use a tape measure for lumber, pipe, or concrete, respectively. Similarly, surveys are measurement tools that can be used effectively by those in many occupations for a very wide variety of purposes and topics. But it is important to identify the general purpose of the survey project, not so much to indicate *how* the survey should be conducted as to show *what* information needs and survey topics should be considered.

EXPECTATIONS OF SURVEY RESULTS

Those who consider conducting a survey often wonder exactly what they can and should expect of the project. It may be difficult to assess the capabilities and limitations of survey research. Some potential sponsors may have overly ambitious expectations, while others may think that surveys are much more limited than they actually are. A survey's potential value depends a great deal on the amount of resources to be devoted to it, as well as how well or poorly the work is done. It is impossible to specify precisely what should and should not be expected of a particular set of survey results or to predict exactly what will or will not be accomplished in a given instance. However, some broad guidelines may be helpful to compare surveys with other techniques for obtaining information.

Surveys Are Comprehensive. Surveys can be designed to measure things as simple as respondents' physical or demographic characteristics, or as complex as their attitudes or preferences. Of course there are limits. There are some things that respondents will not answer, either because they do not *know* the answers, or because the information is so sensitive they are too embarrassed or threatened to give the information. For example, it is difficult to learn about issues that are associated with social taboos, such as sexual behavior, drinking habits, or drug abuse. Some such information may be obtainable with considerable expertise, effort, and ingenuity. But it is usually impossible to get survey information that will threaten a large part of the respondent group. For instance, questions about earnings and the amount of income listed on their tax returns are likely to elicit more heat than light from respondents.

Surveys Are Customized. When considering a survey, there are three questions that come up very quickly: (1) How much will it cost? (2) How long will it take? (3) How much will be learned? They often cannot be answered accurately at first. Much more specification is required, because survey research is not at all homogeneous. This is an important advantage of survey projects, because it means they can usually be customized to fit both the needs and the budget of those seeking information. A survey could cost only a few hundred dollars, or hundreds of thousands of dollars. It could be completed in a single day, or extend over many months' time. It might provide only a single piece of data or cover a huge range of information. In order to answer the three big questions above, the project must be matched to the needs and resources of the sponsor.

Surveys Are Versatile. Survey research can be designed to collect data by personal interview, telephone interview, or direct mail. Respondents can be reached with only visual contact, only audible stimuli, or both. They can be reached in their homes, at work, while shopping, or even during their recreation. They can be presented with a response task that requires only a few seconds, or one that takes nearly an hour. Thus, survey research is not confined to a single mode of inquiry.

Surveys Are Flexible. The volume of data collected and the degree of complexity are a matter of choice, depending on information requirements and resource availability. Simple surveys can be designed requiring only a few tally sheets and a pocket calculator to tabulate, and generating perhaps only a few pages of report. Complex and exhaustive surveys can employ highly sophisticated computer equipment and data analysis programs, making it possible to do computations and generate large volumes of precise information that was completely impossible to obtain only a decade or so ago.

Surveys Are Efficient. Because survey research uses sampling, information about an extremely large population can be obtained from a relatively small sample of people. Rarely do surveys sample more than a thousand or so people, even when the results are to be generalized to many millions. The vast majority of surveys include only a few hundred respondents, and there are some projects where a sample of only a few dozen respondents is completely adequate. The use of well-designed and organized instrumentation also contributes substantially to the efficiency of survey research. It is not at all unusual for survey questionnaires to capture the answers to a hundred or so different questions or items in only a few minutes of each respondent's time. Without this careful and often artful instrument composition, that many individual questions asked in random order and *ad hoc* fashion might take several hours to answer.

Surveys Do Have Limitations. Surveys should and often do generate information that is worth several times more than the cost of the project. But surveys take time, they cost money, and they require intelligent, well-directed effort. Survey research is extremely demanding in one respect: It requires very complete planning and very careful execution at virtually every step in the process. *One person* must take individual responsibility for the survey project. That person certainly need not do all of the work or make all of the decisions, but the person in charge has to monitor and supervise the project continually and diligently. The survey process consists of a series of interactive steps or phases that must ordinarily be done in sequence. The researcher may sometimes have to anticipate later phases and make decisions or commitments concerning them before completing the earlier steps. Unless the researcher has a fairly clear picture of the entire process, there is always the potential to do something at an early phase that will take the process down a dead-end street or have disastrous consequences at a later phase in the process.

Surveys Are Never Perfect.   As with any other kind of work, there will inevitably be mistakes, errors, and oversights along the way. These are not reasons to forego a survey project until it can be performed perfectly. It never will be. The objective of complete planning and careful execution is to avoid the *major* errors and oversights. So long as there is no serious jeopardy to the value of the survey information, minor mistakes can and must be tolerated. If minor errors show up during or after completion of the survey, they should be examined to see what effect they have on the survey information. It is never advisable to denigrate or discard survey results simply because some small mistakes were made during the process. Minor errors and inadequacies should not be allowed to throw a dense shadow of doubt over the entire range of survey results. Rather, they should be treated for what they are: things that may require some modification in the interpretation and reliance on the survey findings.

Surveys Never Dictate Decisions.   Even if no errors or omissions are discovered and the survey project goes precisely as planned, the results will not be definitive. They will not dictate decisions or contain the ultimate answers. Instead, survey results should be treated as another body of evidence or set of indications. Survey results have to be evaluated in the light of experience, common sense, and other information. Human perception and judgment will always be required. The reason that survey results are not definitive is simple but compelling: Respondents' answers are merely stand-ins for actual conditions or actions. It is usually very useful to know the answers to survey questions and understand the things they represent. Actions usually follow thoughts. On the other hand, survey responses are never precisely indicative.

THE ROLES OF THE PARTICIPANTS

Surveys that are relatively limited in scope may be initiated, sponsored, designed, and conducted by the same individual, but that is not ordinarily the case. Survey research often involves several people, and large surveys may require the services of a hundred or more people. Different aspects of the work each may have special roles and responsibilities to be performed by different people. During survey planning and initiation, the major focus is on the roles of (1) those who sponsor the survey and seek the information and (2) those who are to design and conduct the research.

The Sponsor's Role

Often those who sponsor a survey are unfamiliar with the survey process itself. They may be executives, managers, or professionals whose area of expertise lies elsewhere. They are likely to be quite familiar with the problems, decisions, actions, conditions, and perhaps the "conventional wisdom" of their own discipline, industry, or institution. Their understanding of the survey process may range from fairly accurate perceptions to only rather vague notions. Their role is to explain both what information is needed and also *why*. Some sponsors may expect the researcher to operate in a vacuum of information about the purpose for the survey. They may feel it is satisfactory merely to provide a few basic questions to be addressed by the survey and fail to provide sufficient background or prove reluctant to discuss frankly and openly the fundamental nature of the information needs or specific purposes to which the results will be devoted. Such a relationship between sponsor and researcher is virtually never advisable. The sponsor should indicate the ultimate purpose for the survey and also provide the researchers with fairly clear guidelines concerning the time requirements for the survey. They should also be prepared to indicate the general level of funding or resources that are allocated for the project. The role of the survey sponsor is outlined in Guidelist 1–1.

GUIDELIST 1–1

For Sponsors Initiating a Survey

1. Furnish the researchers with sufficient background information about the setting and operations.

GUIDELIST 1-1 (concluded)

2. Provide a description of the issues, problems, or uncertainties that lead to consideration of a survey.

3. Indicate the type of information that would solve the problem or reduce the uncertainty.

4. Describe what decisions, choices, or actions are to be based on the survey results or findings.

5. Estimate the value of the information, based on potential risks or opportunity costs.

6. Specify the time requirements for the project and the general level of funding or resource allocation.

The Researcher's Role

Those who are to conduct the survey must be thoroughly familiar with the capabilities and limitations of the survey research process. But in most cases, the research should not try to "educate" the sponsor concerning the survey process. Instead, the researcher should enquire thoroughly about the information needs, the nature of the decisions and actions to be based on the research results, and the general operation of the institution or organization sponsoring the survey. The researcher can then portray the alternatives and point out the survey procedures that might be used.

The sponsors must have a sense of trust in those conducting the survey. They should feel free to provide the information the researcher seeks from them. The researcher may have to explain that those conducting the survey stand in a fiduciary relationship with the sponsor. The researcher is ethically bound to do nothing to harm or endanger the sponsors. This relationship is no different than that of a physician and a patient, of an attorney and a client.

Unless it is otherwise stipulated in writing, the survey data, the information, the instruments, and even the knowledge that a survey is being conducted are all "proprietary" to the sponsor. In short, everything belongs to the sponsor. It would be highly unethical for those conducting a survey to discuss it with outsiders, reveal the sponsor, share the data, reports or information, or to dispose of these "properties" in any way that might prove undesirable to the sponsor. If the researcher intends to publish the results or promulgate the information in any form, it is the researcher's obligation either to obtain approval in advance and include it as a provision of the contract or to obtain written permission later, but *before* releasing the information. These and other aspects of the researcher role are outlined in Guidelist 1-2.

GUIDELIST 1–2

For Reseachers during Survey Initiation

1. Know the capabilities and limitations of survey research and indicate them to sponsors when appropriate.

2. Obtain background information concerning the operations, policies, and procedures of the sponsor.

3. Inquire about the nature of the uncertainty, problems, or issues to be the focus of the survey.

4. Ask what decisions, choices, or actions are to be based on the results of the proposed survey.

5. Make a preliminary assessment of the approximate value of the survey information to the sponsor.

6. Seek indications of the time requirements for the survey and the approximate funding and resources available.

7. Describe the type of cooperation and participation that will be required of the sponsors.

8. Explain the ethical responsibilities associated with a survey to sponsors.

9. Encourage the confidence and trust of the sponsors through candor and professional conduct.

The researcher also has some ethical obligations toward respondents. Reputable researchers respect and maintain the privacy and anonymity of the respondents, especially if they are promised it. When the respondents are promised they will not be individually identified, that promise must be carefully kept. Sometimes sponsors may request that individual respondents be identified. If this identification is to be provided to the sponsor, the respondents have to be advised of it in advance, so that they are free to decline participation if they prefer. If the respondents are to be assured of anonymity, only aggregate data or unidentified individual responses should be provided to the sponsor. There may be occasions when the sponsor will seek the identity of the respondents after learning the results of the survey. For example, an employer who sponsored a survey of employees may seek the identity of individual respondents for the purpose of reprisal for negative attitudes or behavior, or a company may wish to identify potential customers, based on their survey responses, and solicit them to purchase goods. When the respondents have been assured of their anonymity, the researcher is bound by ethical principles to keep that promise and to refuse the sponsor the information, even though the sponsor has initiated and funded the survey. If sponsors are so informed in advance, they have no legitimate claim to the identity of respondents.

Occasionally a potential sponsor will approach a researcher and propose a survey that is specifically designed to obtain certain results. In other words, the project is to *appear* to be an actual survey, but in fact the items are worded in such a way that they will obtain certain results, or the sample is designed to obtain responses from those who are most likely to be favorable to the position of the sponsor. Ordinarily, such motives and intentions become clear during specification of the information needs. They are totally unethical and the prudent researcher will both refuse the proposed project and also avoid any working relationship with the sponsor. These ethical considerations are outlined in Guidelist 1–3.

GUIDELIST 1–3

For Maintaining Professional Ethics

1. Maintain a fiduciary relationship, always seeking and protecting the best interests of the sponsor.

2. Treat all survey information, including the process and the results, as the sole property of the sponsor.

3. Obtain prior permission or approval before releasing, publishing, or using any survey information or data.

4. Refuse any project or relationship with a sponsor who seeks to bias the survey to get certain results.

5. Protect the privacy and anonymity of respondents if they are promised their identity will not be revealed.

6. Never permit the sponsor to identify individual respondents for reprisal for adverse survey results.

7. Do not identify respondents for solicitation unless they know they will be contacted before participating.

8. Recognize the legitimacy of withholding sponsor identification to respondents and others when appropriate.

9. Return all data, reports, or other materials purchased by sponsors to them on completion of the project.

Often a sponsor will want a survey to be conducted by an independent researcher because the sponsor does not want to be identified to the respondents. If the respondents know the sponsor, it might bias the results. It is legitimate to conduct a survey without identifying the actual sponsor. If potential respondents do not want to participate because the sponsor is not identified, they can refuse. The researcher is under no obligation to reveal the sponsor to the respondents or to explain the nature or reasons for the survey if it is against the wishes of the sponsor.

POTENTIAL SURVEY TOPICS

Surveys can be designed to capture a wide variety of information on many diverse topics. Eight basic topic categories are here: *attitudes, images, decisions, needs, behavior, lifestyle, affiliations,* and *demographics.* These categories are not perfectly distinct from one another. Some may overlap and some do not fit perfectly in one category. The topics do differ in many ways and they are often measured by rather different types of survey items. The most common methods for measuring the topics are also listed here to serve as a guide for survey planning.

Attitudes

Attitudes are very often the subject of surveys. They are psychological "predispositions," because they *pre*dispose people to act in a certain way toward the object of the attitude. The attitude comes *before* behavior and affects the way the person will act. Attitudes are fairly enduring and usually last for weeks, months, or even years. People change their mind when they receive additional information or experience, or perceive the object of the attitude differently.

Attitudes are always focused on some object. It can be a physical or material thing, a person or group, or an idea or issue. Attitudes are composed of three parts: what the individual knows or believes about the topic, how the person feels about the topic and how it is valued, and the likelihood that the individual will take action based on the attitude. These three parts of an attitude are often called the "knowledge" component, the "feeling" component, and the "action" component. When an attitude changes, any or all of the components may change. When attitudes are measured, the survey questions should include all three attitude components. For example, it would be necessary to ask if respondents know about the object, how much they liked or disliked it, and how they intend to behave toward it.

✳ GUIDELIST 1–4

For Measuring Attitudes

1. Be sure to include all three components of the attitude: knowledge, feelings, and action tendencies, in that order.

2. Begin with awareness and knowledge. Ignore feelings and action tendencies if knowledge is insufficient.

3. Use unaided recall to measure awareness, if possible, to avoid false reports of recognition.

4. Measure depth of knowledge with an index of the number of correct statements about the topic.

5. Use ratings scales to measure feelings, so that both direction and distance from neutral are revealed.

6. Consider a comparative scale where relative, rather than absolute levels of feelings are appropriate.

7. Do not ignore the intensity of feelings or assume intensity is the same as distance from neutral.

8. Measure intensity by asking how strongly respondents feel or how sure they are of their position.

9. Be sure to include the behavioral component of attitudes.

10. Past, present, and future behavior may indicate the strength of the behavioral component.

11. Specify hypothetical conditions and ask intentions if respondents lacked opportunity to act in the past.

Knowledge Component.   People base both their feelings and their actions on their knowledge of a particular object. So it is very important to learn what they know or believe about the topic. Respondents should be asked about their knowledge of the topic *first*. If they have never heard of it, there is no reason to ask about their feelings or actions. People often give an opinion, even though they have no notion whatsoever of what the thing is. Nobody likes to admit they do not know, so they pretend. To measure the knowledge component, begin by measuring *awareness*. There are two ways to ask about awareness: aided and unaided recall. With aided recall, the respondents are asked, "Have you ever heard of _____?" They would answer yes or no. The problem with such a question is that many will say they have heard of it, even though they have not. To avoid this problem, ask for more detail concerning the characteristics of the object or else use the unaided recall method.

With the unaided method of measuring awareness, the respondent is asked to name all the objects in a given group or to identify the object based on a description of its position or attributes. For example, people might be asked to name all the brands of a product they could recall. If they named the brand in question, they would have awareness. Or respondents might be asked, "Do you know the name of the member of Congress from this district?" Correct designation of the representative's name would indicate awareness. Another way to get more information about the knowledge component of an attitude is to ask a series of true/false questions about the topic. The number of correct answers is an index of each respondent's level of knowledge. Asking about the manner in which respondents learned of the object and the experience they have had with the topic is yet another indication.

Feeling Component.   People are seldom completely neutral about anything, if they are aware of it. An attitude receives its feeling component in one of two ways: through reward or through evaluation. In the first case, they learn to like or dislike the object because their experience with it was rewarding or unrewarding (punishing). For example, many have a negative attitude toward some food because they disliked the taste. The second way people obtain feelings about an object is by evaluation. People automatically and often unconsciously compare what they know or believe about a topic with their own, personal values. If their knowledge fits their values, they develop positive feelings, and if it is contrary to their values, their feelings are negative toward the topic. For example, suppose a person knows that a particular brand is very expensive, and this person places a high value on economy. This would lead to a negative attitude.

To measure the feeling component of an attitude, two sets of things often need to be measured: *position* on the positive/negative spectrum and level of *intensity* of feelings. The two are not the same. One person may feel that an attitude object is very good but may be rather unsure of this and may easily be convinced otherwise. Another person may feel very slightly negative about the object but may hold these feelings with great intensity and be extremely difficult to persuade otherwise. Measuring the position of feelings requires measuring both the direction and the distance of the feelings; to know if respondents liked or disliked the object and how much they liked or disliked it. This can be done by using either an absolute or a relative scale to indicate value to the person. So a linear, numeric scale with the extremes labeled "good" and "bad" could be used to give an absolute rating. For a relative rating, a comparative scale could be used, with some other object as the standard, and the ratings would be relative to that other object. The choice of an absolute or a relative measure depends on the situation, and neither can be identified as generally the most or the least effective.

It is easier to measure the direction and location of feelings than to measure intensity. Having respondents rate how *strongly* they feel about their evaluation or asking how certain they are of their good/bad or comparative rating provides a direct measure. Asking why they feel as they do or asking the likelihood of changing their opinion are indirect measures.

Action Component.   Even though two people have about the same knowledge about the topic of an attitude and share much the same feelings, they may behave differently toward the topic. For example, two shoppers who have the same knowledge and feelings about a certain brand may both find that the brand was out of stock at their favorite store. One may simply choose another brand, but the other may postpone purchase until the brand is available or seek that brand at another store. Why the difference in behavior? Because the attitudinal action components differ. Perhaps the best and most popular manner of measuring the action component is to measure past, present, and intended future behavior toward the object. This assumes the respondents have had or will have had the opportunity to act. If not, it may be necessary to specify a set of hypothetical conditions and ask questions about how the respondents would act under those circumstances.

Images

A person's image of something is exactly what the name implies: the "picture" the person carries in their mind of the object. But no picture is perfect. It may be very blurred, as though the lens of the camera were not focused, or it may be very sharp and resolute. It may be a real "close-up," showing every detail, or it may show only the most salient features of the object. It may be very accurate and precise, showing everything exactly as it is, or it may be badly distorted, as the image of someone looking at themselves in the curved mirrors of a fun house at the carnival. It may be very complete, including the entire object, or it may show only a portion or section of it. And it may be a blowup or a reduction, showing the object as bigger or smaller than it really is. Each person tends to see things a little differently from others. Thus, no two images are apt to be exactly alike, although some may be very similar and others distinctly different. But an image is likely to take on a different form from the "real thing." When people lack some information, they tend to fill in the picture.

Image Components.   To get a verbal picture of people's images, they might be asked how they would describe the object. They would be likely to name several characteristics and indicate their magnitude or the quality. These characteristics would be the components of the image. They are the features that define the image in the mind of the individual. There will be some variation from person to person, but many features will be included by nearly all of them, and some characteristics that could apply will be ignored by everyone. The tendency to define images with about the same attributes allows researchers to measure and compare images. The first step is to ascertain what attributes or characteristic features are most common and important to *respondents*. That can be done precisely the way described earlier, by asking for a description of the object from several typical respondents. Those seeking survey information must not be the *exclusive* source of ideas for identifying attributes, because respondents may not use some of the attributes to define their image and other attributes not specified by the sponsors may play an important role in defining images for respondents. The image profile is only accurate to the degree that it includes those attributes and only those that are the major ones for the responding sample.

The Image Profile.   The portrayal of an image requires the measurement of several attributes or characteristics in a configural sense. It is the constellation of ratings, rather than any single rating, that is ordinarily of interest. The individual attributes do not stand in any set pattern with one another, and the researcher must choose the order in which the items are listed. They may be in random order or according to some other system. Ordinarily, the most important ones are located among those in the middle of the list, rather than first or last. When some or all features have a good/bad connotation, about half should express "virtues" and half "vices." The two types should be scattered among one another. This controls for the tendency for some people to be globally positive or negative. Images can best be measured with an adjective check list, a semantic differential scale, or a Stapel scale, all described in Chapter 5.

Image Comparisons.   It is often desirable to compare images of different topics or objects in the same general class, such as different companies in an industry or brands of a given product. When the information needs call for comparison, each object must be rated

GUIDELIST 1-5

For Measuring Images

1. Use image profiles when several attributes or characteristic features of an object are to be measured.

2. Question some typical respondents concerning the objects to determine the attributes they use to define the image.

3. Do not depend on the sponsor to identify the relevant characteristics.

4. Include only those attributes that have meaning to respondents, limiting the number of items.

5. Randomly order the items, being sure that about half can be seen as positive and half negative.

6. Obtain ratings of more than one object in a class if comparisons of image profiles are of value. (This will increase the respondent task and quantity of data.)

7. Have respondents rate an "ideal" object if there is any uncertainty concerning positivity or negativity for many items.

8. Compare ideal image profiles for different respondent groups to reveal differences in preference patterns.

9. Plan to subtract ideal from actual ratings for each respondent to provide a "difference" profile.

10. Compare profiles of difference from ideal among the actual objects to assess positive or negative valences.

separately by each respondent. This allows the researcher to compare the profiles with one another after the data have been compiled. Sometimes there may be several image items that cannot be clearly identified as positive or negative. When the researcher is uncertain concerning the "valence" of such ratings, this can be ascertained by asking the respondents to rate their *ideal* entity. To obtain an indication of the good/bad valence of individual ratings or profiles, those for any actual object can be subtracted from those for the ideal object for each respondent. The closer the actual ratings to the ideal, the more positive the ratings. Negativity can be judged by the absolute value of the difference between actual and ideal. These differences between actual and ideal for each of the actual objects can also be compared. This indicates which are more positive and which more negative. Measuring both the perceptions of objects and the valences makes the image measurement scales very powerful devices.

Decisions

When decisions are the topic of research, the focus is not so much on the results of decisions in the past as on the *process* by which respondents evaluate things. Often people's choices require them to evaluate alternative courses of action. Their choices depend in part on their *information sources* and the *evaluative criteria* they use for judgment. Those seeking survey information are often keenly interested in these aspects of the decision process that people use to choose actions.

Information Sources. Decisions are conscious choices that are based in part on information. In some cases, the decision maker may already have all of the information required for the decision. In others, the person will need more information, and that will require an "information search." Survey research can measure both the information content on which a decision was based and also the nature of the information search process. Information can also be measured in terms of the source from which the decision maker obtained it. Generally, three different categories are useful: direct personal experience, social influence, and media sources.

Information obtained from nonpersonal sources is called "media" information. A survey inquiry might focus on several different "levels" of media effects. Respondents might be asked about mere *exposure* to some medium, such as whether or not they subscribe to a particular publication or listen to a certain radio station. They might also be asked how much *attention* they paid to a medium, such as whether or not they actually saw or read a particular advertisement. They may also be asked about their comprehension or recollection of *content* of a message presented through the medium. Lastly, the most detailed inquiry would measure the *impact* the message had on choices or actions.

Although valuable data on information acquisition can be obtained through survey research, a note of caution is required. The history of survey research indicates that most people are only vaguely aware of the information they actually apply to a decision and where they obtained it. Generally, direct experience is *over*stated and media influence is *under*stated. In general, people are likely to recognize that media influence other people's decisions, but they often will not admit they, themselves, are influenced.

Evaluative Criteria.   When someone evaluates something, the person is assigning a value to it. Consequently, it must be judged according to the attributes the decision maker feels are relevant. Any object

---

GUIDELIST 1–6

For Measuring Decison Making

1. Use when information requirements focus on the *process* of evaluation, not the results.
2. Determine how much the decision was based on pre-existing information and how much was directly sought.
3. Classify information sources as direct experience, social influence, or media effects.
4. Measure the appropriate level of media effects: exposure, attention, content, or impact.
5. Measure abstract, global values only when information is required concerning decisions about many different objects or those of profound importance to respondents.
6. Expect to identify only a very limited number of evaluative criteria for any one individual.

---

of evaluation can be viewed as a "package" of different characteristics. Ordinarily, the object to be judged has many more attributes or characteristics than people actually consider. Thought processes are limited to consideration of only a handful of things at one time, usually about six or eight at most. There is seldom the necessity for judgment of more than a few attributes, and research has indicated that in fact, people use only a few features to judge and select among alternatives, even for very important decisions.

The identification of the evaluative criteria people use to select among alternatives is a major task of survey research. There are several ways to accomplish it. One of the most common is simply to question respondents concerning why they made the choice they did. This requires composing a list of attributes of the object chosen and then asking respondents to rate the importance of each. Another method of detecting evaluative criteria is to present respondents with a hypothetical choice situation and ask what information they would seek about the alternatives. The attributes for which they seek information are those they would use for evaluation. This method does not require that they have previously made such a choice.

Needs

Sponsors are often concerned with *why* people behave as they do. Most behavior is directed toward the satisfaction of one or more

human needs. Thus, the answer to the question of "why" is often obtained by measuring the relationship between actions and needs, desires, preferences, motives, and goals. People generally act with intent. This does *not* imply that they know, consciously, what personal motives and needs lie beneath the surface of their actions. Consequently, it can be a difficult job to "dig out" the needs that underpin behavior and the motives that prompt action. The picture is often further complicated by the fact that (*a*) many different actions can serve the same motive or provide satisfaction for the same need and (*b*) several needs or motives may be served by one action or behavior pattern. To cope with these problems, the researcher must be willing to recognize the difficulties and to understand the nature of *needs, desires, preferences, motives,* and *goals.*

The Terms.   Needs can be viewed as categories of things that most or all people require for existence and contentment. They can be specified in terms of very basic things that must be provided to sustain human life. Such things as food, shelter, clothing, and the like are very basic human needs. Needs can also be classified according to the requirements for psychological and social conditions. For example, they might include love, affiliation, social status, prestige, or power. Finally, needs can be viewed in terms of very specific categories relating directly to different types of activity. Thus, the list might include such things as play, nurturance, achievement, recognition, and exhibition.

Desires are closely related to needs. When a person consciously focuses on some object, activity, or state of being that might provide satisfaction for a need, the person has a "desire" for that thing. The individual may not be aware of exactly what need is beneath the desire. Preferences are often treated as similar to desires that have less drive or energy behind them. In other words, both imply a conscious focus on something, but desires are stronger while preferences imply less vigor or pressure toward the object. Motives are also related to needs, but they are more closely associated with actions. Motives arise from unsatisfied needs, and they trigger behavior or energize the person to perform some action to get satisfaction. They might be seen as a "push" away from some negative condition or a "pull" toward some desirable situation. Goals or objectives are also related to needs. A person's goals represent some "end state," some destination or condition that the person seeks to reach through behavior. Goals are related to needs because the objective is often the satisfaction of one or more needs.

Measurement Techniques.   Several types of scales are commonly used to measure needs, desires, preferences, motives, and goals be-

---

GUIDELIST 1-7

For Measuring Need-Related Concepts

1. Determine the needs, desires, preferences, motives, or goals that are relevant to the information requirements.

2. Specify the items or categories in terms that will be easily understood by the respondents.

3. Use a fixed sum, comparative, or forced ranking scale in order to avoid *all* being rated as equally important.

4. Remember that multiple needs, etc., can be served by the same behavior, and different actions can serve the same need, etc.

5. Use projective methods when measuring or assessing motives that are likely to be "sensitive."

---

cause they "fit" the nature of the concepts being measured. Needs are often measured by first deciding on the types of needs that are relevant to the information requirements. Respondents are then usually asked to rank them in their order of importance or to rate them using a fixed sum scale. The researcher needs a way to obtain their *relative* importance. An ordinary, horizontal, numeric scale of importance is not advisable because many will rate most or all of the needs as equally important. The forced ranking scale, the fixed sum scale, and the horizontal, numeric scale are all described in Chapter 5.

Desires and preferences are often measured by identifying and listing the possible categories of "things" that might be desired or preferred. Horizontal, numeric scales can often be used because respondents are less likely to see all of them as equally important. To be safe, forced rankings or fixed sum scales can also be used to measure desires and preferences. Motives are relatively simple and easy to measure when they are obviously conscious and the respondents have no reason to conceal them. For example, they might be measured by a multiple choice item that listed the likely motives. Motives concerning "sensitive" behavior or opinions are more difficult to assess, and rather than using direct questioning, respondents might be asked to identify a close friend with similar views, and then the respondent might be questioned concerning how this person felt or behaved and why he or she would feel or act that way. This permits respondents to "project" their own motives onto another person. Goals or objectives are less sensitive than many motives. They can often be measured simply by listing alternative goals and having them

ranked or rated in the same manner as for assessing desires or preferences. Again, the researcher must take care to avoid obtaining equal ratings for all goals or objectives that might be regarded as generally or socially desirable by the respondents.

Behavior

The measurement of behavior usually involves four related concepts: what the respondents did or did not do; where the action takes place; the timing, including past, present, and future; and the frequency or persistence of behavior. In other words, it often means assessing "what, where, when, and how often." When research is used to establish which actions were taken by respondents, the alternative courses of action are usually listed in categories to be sure the responses are comparable. Simple multiple choice items can then be used, with either a single or a multiple response permitted.

The location of some particular form of behavior is often of interest. The places might be designated as geographic areas or by some other means, such as at home versus away. If only a few, specific, potential locations can be identified, a multiple-choice question can be used. Maps, graphs, or displays can also be shown to respondents to obtain their indication of the location. It is best to provide the respondents with a specific *set* of possible locations, rather than to depend on them to indicate a place in their own words, because there is a tendency for each respondent to use different terms to describe a location, and probably no two respondents will use exactly the same phrase to describe any one place.

Respondents may be able to indicate a location by using a designation that has been assigned to the places, such as the ZIP codes or political jurisdictions. Maps are often available to show such geographic areas. The researcher may have to translate these numbers indicating geographic areas into different categories than those used by the source of the designations. This is an effective means of measuring location, provided that the individual designations apply to areas that are about equal to or smaller than those required by the survey information needs. Areas can be combined if necessary, but they cannot be divided into smaller increments or blocks than those specified when the data is collected.

Respondents are often questioned concerning *when* they performed a certain action and whether or not they are presently engaged in such behavior. Future intentions to act can also be the subject of survey inquiry, but of course, these predictions by respondents may not be completely accurate. Individual predictions of future actions are less reliable than the collective or aggregate predictions of

GUIDELIST 1-8

For Measuring Behavior

1. Identify information needs in terms of "what, where, when, and how often."

2. Specify actions and locations in items or categories to make reports comparable to one another.

3. Determine if respondents might have engaged in only one or several categories of action, and use single or multiple response items accordingly.

4. Remember that frequency of behavior is often best expressed in terms of time, such as times per day or week.

5. Keep in mind that *individual* intentions or predictions are ordinarily not as reliable as they are in aggregate.

6. Be sure to use such items as verbal frequency or fixed sum scales when proportions or behavior policies are to be measured.

the proportions who say they will act in a certain way. Some may change their mind and do something else, but others may elect to do so when they did not intend to, so in the aggregate, predictions are often more reliable than any one expression of intent. Many actions are habitual, while others are performed routinely because a single decision has led to continuity until something changes the routine. Habitual or routine behavior of a respondent is often of great interest to sponsors. People might be questioned about their policies or practices concerning some action, such as their "favorite" place, their political party, or religious preference.

People also change patterns or deviate from them on some occasions. It is often important to determine just how consistent the respondents are or what proportion of the time they act in a certain way, given the occasion to act. In such cases, the researcher is often less interested in the *absolute* number of times the action is taken as in the frequency, *relative* to the number of occasions or opportunities to act. If so, it is inappropriate to ask how often the action is taken because it yields absolute values. The same number may correspond to half the time for one respondent and all the time for another, if the first had twice as many opportunities to take the action or perform the behavior. When the proportion of behavior, based on the number of opportunities, is the focus of the inquiry, or when the general policy of the respondents over time is sought, a fixed sum scale or a verbal

frequency scale can be used to obtain the proportion. Rarely can respondents be asked the percentage of times because they must know the exact proportion to respond accurately, and they usually will not. It is usually best to show proportions on scales with only a few scale points, rather than a hundred.

Lifestyle

Surveys can be used to determine the lifestyles of respondents. Lifestyle consists of the *pattern* of things people do, believe, and own. Groupings of the population by lifestyle can be used to identify an audience, constituency, target market, or other collectivity of interest to the sponsor. Often, those with different lifestyles will react differentially toward issues of key interest to researchers and sponsors. Different lifestyle patterns can be identified by several variables associated with respondents. Often four different types of variables are used: (1) activities, (2) interests, (3) opinions, and (4) possessions. Researchers interested in the measurement of lifestyle can obtain lists of lifestyle items from the literature on the subject. Most such libraries of items have been used successfully in the past and often define meaningful lifestyle segments or groups. Another alternative is to compose a family of lifestyle items to define lifestyle segments that are most meaningful and relevant to the information needs. Such lists must contain enough items to ensure that patterns are fairly reliable. No single item will define lifestyle adequately.

GUIDELIST 1–9

For Measuring Lifestyle Patterns

1. Seek out lifestyle libraries of items or compose items that are directly relevant to the information requirements.

2. Use multiple items to identify individual lifestyle patterns among respondents.

3. Choose questions concerning activities, interests, opinions, or possessions that are indicative of a particular lifestyle.

4. Keep in mind that lifestyle measurement requires many variables or items and may increase questionnaire size and response task time and difficulty.

5. Remember that lifestyle analyses focus on clusters to identify patterns and it requires much computation.

In summary, a given lifestyle is a collective or conglomerate item. The objective is to identify a pattern or profile. Consequently, respondents must be questioned about many items that relate to a given lifestyle or pattern of living. While this can be a potent method of identifying and distinguishing groups or segments, the measurement will often require many questions. In terms of questionnaire space and response time, this may be costly and in some cases, uneconomical.

Affiliations

Social contact and interaction are often the focus of survey research or bear heavily on other issues that are relevant to the survey. So the family setting, memberships, social contacts, reference groups, and communications of respondents are frequently measured or assessed within the survey research process. Those within the same nuclear or extended family often think, behave, and live similarly. Of all social groups, the family probably exerts more influence on individuals than those of other groups or units to which the person belongs. The most simple measurement is specification of family status, including marital status and children in the home. This method is discussed in the next section, on demographics. Other family issues, including the roles played by various family members, group decision making, and authority relationships within the family, can also be measured by surveys. The types of question and scale depend on what data are being sought. The researcher must select from among the available items and scaling techniques to obtain the most appropriate device.

Affiliations and both formal and informal relationships are often the subject of surveys. Their measurement ordinarily consists of the specification of the groups in terms that can be easily understood by the respondents, who are then asked to indicate any groups to which they belong. The importance of the group to the individual and the importance of the person to the group are also assessable through survey questioning. Leadership or officer status are often topics of inquiry.

Social integration can be measured by indications of the frequency and duration of contact and interaction with others. The propensity to interact with others can be assessed directly or indirectly. Direct measurement requires specification of the groups, and respondents are asked to indicate those with whom they interact. Such indirect measures as a series of statements accompanying a Likert scale might be used to reveal the importance of affiliation, or the importance of social interaction and affiliation might be measured with a compara-

GUIDELIST 1-10

For Measuring Affiliations

1. Membership in both formal and informal groups should be considered sources of influence for respondents.

2. Define groups clearly and concisely for respondents (e.g., such terms as "family" might include only parents and siblings, or more distant relatives as well).

3. Select the appropriate type of reference group for identification, either comparative or normative.

4. Consider both opinion leadership and key influentials when determining sources of influence on respondents.

5. Remember that identification of sources of influence is only approximate because people are often unwilling or unable to provide precise data.

tive, fixed sum, or forced ranking scale and then compared with the importance ratings of the value of other activities.

The *referents* or *reference groups* used by respondents are often of interest to the researcher. These terms refer to an individual or group that serves one or both of two major functions: normative or comparative. A normative reference group is one that establishes or provides norms of conduct or behavior that the individual is expected to follow. Normative reference groups tell one *what* should and should not be done. By contrast, a comparative reference group provides a standard or benchmark to show *how* an individual is doing in some respect. People often comment about "keeping up with the Joneses," and the Joneses are obviously the comparative reference group. Surveys often identify just who the Joneses are and why they serve as a referent. Comparative reference groups are often used whenever people lack an absolute, concrete standard by which to judge their own standing. Reference groups can be identified by using several techniques. The most common and direct method of identifying reference groups is to ask the respondent to identify them. A less direct means is to question respondents about affiliations with those in similar conditions or with similar opinions, so reference groups are specified only by inference.

Surveys may seek to identify opinion leaders and those within their sphere of influence. An opinion leader is one who has special

expertise, experience, or credibility in the eyes of others. The attitudes of the opinion leader are often amplified and extended to many others. Those known as "key influentials" occupy a special position or have special recognition that permits them to influence the attitudes of many others within a specific social setting. If key influentials can be identified prior to the survey, based on their position or office, the degree of influence or impact they exert can be measured. Respondents may rate the importance of the key influential, relative to other sources of information or influence. These data are useful, but they are never very precise because people are unwilling or unable to express influence patterns with much precision.

Demographics

Demographic factors often used in survey research include such variables as age, sex, marital status, family status, family life cycle stage, education, employment, occupation, income, and residential location and type, among others. Such data are often valuable to sponsors because (*a*) demographic groups often differ significantly on the issues of importance and (*b*) demographics can be used to identify segments, groups, audiences, or constituencies of people who are both identifiable and behave in similar ways.

GUIDELIST 1–11

For Measuring Demographic Status

1. Include all demographic items that may be systematically associated with other items of importance in the survey.
2. Specify categories clearly and concisely for respondents.
3. Choose categories and items that will be comparable with other, external, secondary data or information.
4. Use sample demographic items where possible and make only necessary modifications to avoid risk.

The key to accurate measurement of demographic status is the clear, concise statement of the categories or dimensions. This depends on clarity and meaningfulness to respondents and degree of precision required by the information needs. Several examples of demographic items are shown in Chapter 6. They include some items that are broad

and comprehensive, and others that are relatively precise and fine-grained. Select among these items and modify them as required, because items that have been previously tested have less inherent risk than newly composed items, scales, and formats.

Conclusion

The topics discussed here represent only one scheme that might be used to classify items or subjects. The list of topics is not intended to be comprehensive or all-inclusive. Other topics might arise that could not easily be classified into the categories provided. This does not preclude their use. There are two purposes for including this outline of topics: (1) They help those seeking survey information to recognize the range and type of information that can be obtained from survey research, and (2) they assist the researcher to classify information needs and make tentative, preliminary plans for the survey process to follow.

SUMMARY

Survey Sponsorship and Potential Topics

A. Evaluate survey potential. The same measurement methods are useful for many occupations and needs.

B. Maintain realistic expectations. Survey research is neither impossibly difficult nor precisely definitive.

C. Expect and evaluate errors. Minor mistakes may affect some results, but seldom ever invalidate them all.

D. Recognize the potential topics. They indicate what can be measured and suggest ways to obtain information.

E. Allow for other topics. The list provided here is not all-inclusive, and others might be used productively.

F. Consider suggestions carefully. The methods of measurement noted here are thoroughly tested.

2

Project Planning

THE SURVEY PROCESS

A survey project is a process with a series of steps that are linked with one another. The decisions made during the early stages affect the choices open at later stages. The information needs specified at the first stage indicate what type of sample will be required, what type of measurement instruments will be needed, what data collection methods will be most appropriate, and more. This forward linkage among the steps is shown in Figure 2–1 by the solid lines running downward and to the right, on the left side of the diagram. If there were only these forward linkages, the researcher could take one step at a time, performing each set of tasks in turn. Only the effects on subsequent steps would have to be considered at each step. But this would assume there are no limitations on the options available at the later steps. In reality, this is seldom so. In most cases, data collection and data processing resources are almost always limited. These limitations restrict the alternatives that are open at the *earlier* stages. So there are *backward* linkages in the survey process. They are shown by the dashed lines running upward and to the left in Figure 2–1, on the right side of the diagram. If the researcher ignored these limitations during the earlier steps in the process, it may lead to a dead-end when the limitations are encountered later.

Figure 2–1 shows that the backward linkages in the survey process run from the data collection phase and the data processing phase, back up to the sampling design and instrumentation steps. Major decisions concerning data collection must always be made *prior* to designing and selecting a sample or composing and constructing the questionnaire and other materials. Some information needs can be

FIGURE 2-1

Linkage in the Survey Process

Major steps in the process

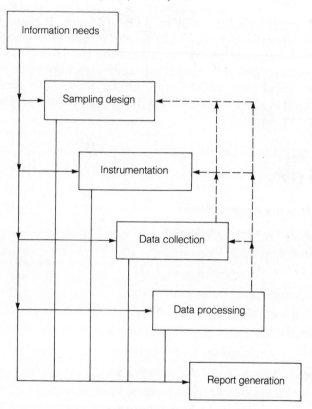

satisfied more effectively with one method of data collection than with another. Yet data collection is often the most expensive phase of the process. It would not make sense to design a sample without first having selected the data collection method and estimated the cost of collecting the data, because different data collection methods will require different sampling designs and questionnaires. The availability of data processing facilities also influence the early stages of the process. It is important that the data processing methods be anticipated, so that sampling and instrumentation will be compatible with both the capabilities and the limitations of the data processing method.

The Project Outline

The project outline is designed to guide, direct, and coordinate the tasks required to initiate the survey. It should be written by the researcher after conferring with the sponsor, the individual or organization funding the survey project and seeking the information. The project outline is used to estimate costs and time requirements, to identify resource needs, and to guide the survey process. When someone other than the researcher is the sponsor, they should inspect and approve the outline before continuing the project. The project outline is more important than it may seem. It is even more important for less experienced researchers than for those with considerable background in survey research. The 10 elements of the project outline are listed in Figure 2–2.

FIGURE 2–2

Elements of the Project Outline

1. Specify the information needs.
2. Estimate the information value.
3. Assess internal resource availability.
4. Choose the data collection method.
5. Select the data processing method.
6. Measure the scope of the response task.
7. Determine sample size and design.
8. Specify the instrumentation and costs.
9. Describe the type of reports required.
10. Summarize final costs and the timetable.

The elements of the project outline are not in the same sequence as the steps of the survey process shown in Figure 2–1. This is because the backward linkage in the survey process requires consideration of some of the later phases prior to making decisions about those that come earlier. It may be necessary to make several passes through the list, making only tentative decisions about each element at first and making modifications as they are required with each subsequent pass until the outline is complete.

SPECIFYING INFORMATION NEEDS

The specification of information needs plays a key role in the survey process. Accurate and effective specification of information needs is one of the most difficult of all the tasks associated with a survey. It often receives too little attention and effort. Errors or inadequacies in the specification of the information required from the survey will be amplified during the later stages of the survey process.

Sponsor—Researcher Dialogue

Sponsors who are not researchers are seldom aware of the capabilities and limitations of survey research. Consequently, the researcher must be completely familiar with the potential topics that can be measured effectively with survey methods, as well as the techniques for measuring them. The dialogue between the researchers, on the one hand, and the sponsors, on the other, ordinarily begins at the point where information needs are to be identified and specified. This is best accomplished in conferences among the participants, rather than by telephone or correspondence. The initiation stage will require considerable involvement and cooperation from the sponsors, and they should be advised of the demands on their time and effort. At later stages of the survey process, the researchers will carry the major responsibility and perform most of the tasks. Ordinarily, the sponsors will need only examine the preliminary questionnaire drafts, study the explanations of how the items relate to the information needs, suggest or recommend additions, deletions or modifications, and provide their approval for the final instrument. Finally, both researchers and sponsors resume their dialogue at the completion of the process, during the reporting of the project results and findings.

Survey Capabilities and Limitations. The researcher must have a clear understanding of both the capabilities of survey research and also the limitations to this form of inquiry. Those who sponsor surveys are often unaware of the remarkable potential of a well designed and conducted survey. Sponsors usually underestimate the feasibility and power of surveys, but in fewer instances, sponsors may overestimate the ability of a survey. The researcher will more often have to explain capabilities, rather than identify limitations. Often, the needs for information can be satisfied by a fairly wide variety of data, obtained from several different forms of questions and scaling techniques. Sponsors usually have a series of questions they would like answered, but they are seldom in a form that can be asked of re-

spondents directly. Thus, the specification of information needs is an *iterative process*. It begins with the identification of a set of questions in the minds of the sponsors. The researcher may provide suggestions concerning how the data might be obtained and the information provided, to respond to the questions. The original questions may then be refined, and additional suggestions offered, until there is agreement that the procedures suggested will, in fact, satisfy the needs for information. During the process, the researcher should both reveal the capabilities inherent in survey research and also advise the sponsor of the limitations that might restrict certain avenues or approaches.

Decisions and Action Potential. Survey research information should always be directly related to decisions and have specific action potential. The information generated by a survey should suggest or preclude specific actions to be an adequate basis for making decisions. The academic survey project is the one major exception to this general principle. Professionals and students in universities and other institutions of learning who conduct surveys to provide data for theses, dissertations, the advancement and testing of theory, or the publication of scholarly works should base the specification of information needs on the specific research questions and hypotheses. In those cases, the researcher must be sure the survey information provides an adequate test of the hypotheses or that it measures the specific phenomena that are to be described. Academic researchers must certainly be familiar with the scientific process and it need not be discussed here. But the specification of information needs and the other aspects of the survey process are quite similar, regardless of whether the research is devoted to practical or theoretical purposes. An outline for guiding the communications process between sponsors and researchers is provided in Guidelist 2–1.

GUIDELIST 2–1

For Maintaining a Dialogue with Sponsors

1. Researchers must be completely familiar with potential survey topics, as well as the survey process.

2. Sponsors may articulate questions without being familiar with potential topics or the survey process.

3. Conference discussions are a far more effective format than telephone or written correspondence.

4. Information specification is an iterative process that may require several meetings among participants.

5. Sponsors participate and contribute most at the beginning and again at the end of the survey process.

6. Information needs should always be directly related to potential decisions or specific actions or policies.

7. Survey results may suggest choices or actions, but may never *dictate* them because results are only within a specific range of confidence and never entirely perfect.

8. The remaining guidelists and discussion should guide the information specification process.

Occasionally, either the researchers will tend to be overly ambitious regarding the results of survey research, or the sponsor will have exaggerated expectations of the results. Survey information should not and does not *make* decisions or *dictate* actions. There are several reasons why. Survey data are almost always obtained from a sample of the population of interest and not from a complete enumeration of all those in the population. Thus, the results are only estimates of the actual parameters and should be used only to make inferences about the population as a whole. Both the researchers and sponsors must fully understand that there will never be complete certainty about the results. On the other hand, the degree of uncertainty must be within a tolerable range. There must be some confidence interval around each specific result, so the sponsor is assured that there is only a very small probability that the actual parameters would lie outside the range.

Another reason that survey results are not entirely indicative of decisions or actions results from the nature of inquiry itself. No survey is completely free of factors that introduce bias in the results. It is important to note that information needs should be specified to provide *evidence,* rather than conviction. The information should serve as a partial basis for decisions and it may suggest the choice of particular actions. The actual decisions and choices must be tempered by the awareness of other facts, as well as by the judgment, experience, training and background of the sponsoring executives, managers, or professionals. To avoid overconfidence or dogmatic perceptions of the survey results, the researcher should ask the sponsor what the various possible results would *suggest* or *support* in terms of decisions and actions. No survey, no matter how creatively conceived, artfully designed, and expertly conducted, will ever substitute adequately for

common sense, good judgment, background, and experience. Survey results can and usually are very valuable; however, they are never absolutely perfect.

Priority, Value, and Funding

The specification of information needs should do two things: It should include all of the information that is genuinely required or highly valued, based on priority, and it should exclude any items that are overly redundant or any information that is not actually of worth or value. Some sponsors may want to include items that merely satisfy curiosity, rather than serve any legitimate information need. They may lack awareness of the cost of each additional item of information. It is the researchers responsibility to be sure that every survey item is required for making decisions, choices, selections, or judgments. The information should have action potential.

Assignment of Priority. The priority of information needs should be based on the consequences of the actions they indicate. Information for decisions that have major consequences has a higher priority than that for decisions with relatively minor consequences. Information can usually be classified into about three levels of importance: (1) Items that are absolutely essential because they constitute the main reason for the project. (2) Information that would be valuable for making decisions of a substantial nature. (3) Information that would provide supportive data or enhance the understanding of decision makers and clarify the picture portrayed by the survey results. Items of lesser value should be culled from the list.

Classifying information by priority is important because time and resources are always limited. Inevitably, it will be necessary to eliminate items or reduce the number of questions. Such deletions can more readily be made when there is a clear indication of item priority. The least valuable items can be discarded and all of the most valuable questions will be retained as the plans are modified. The priority of information items or survey questions has another function as well. When those who design and conduct the survey and compose the questionnaire or survey instrument have a clear indication of the importance of the various items, they will be able to place greater time, effort and emphasis on the most critical and valuable items of information. When the structure and sequence of items within the survey questionnaire require some degree of compromise, the least valuable items, those with the lowest priority, are more likely to be moved or adjusted. In that way, the most crucial questions will maintain the most prominent place within the instrument, where they are

likely to receive the greatest attention and more accurate response from those completing the questionnaire or interview. The major considerations for assigning priority are shown in Guidelist 2–2.

GUIDELIST 2–2

For Classifying Information by Priority

1. There are two basic objectives to be met:
   a. To obtain *all* of the essential information.
   b. To obtain *only* what is directly applicable.
2. Information items can be classified into three categories:
   a. *High priority.*   Items that are essential or the main reason for conducting a survey.
   b. *Medium priority.*   Items that are of substantial value for decisions or actions.
   c. *Low priority.*   Items that provide supporting information or background.

Assessment of Value.   The value of survey information depends on the size of the sponsor's potential gains or losses from decisions or choices. When a tentative list of information needs has been specified and the information classified by priority, the value of the information should be assessed and compared to the funds and resources allocated to the project. The potential value of the information should be at *least* two or three times the entire cost of the survey project, and preferably even greater. This is because the estimate is only the *potential,* and not the actual value. It may prove to be of greater or lesser value than estimated. Rarely if ever can the value be precisely determined. The estimate of the information value will sometimes turn out to be too conservative and sometimes it will turn out to be too liberal. It is almost impossible to obtain an accurate estimate of what actual costs for the project will be. In almost every case, there will be "cost overruns," so the actual costs nearly always prove to be greater than anticipated, even when there is an allowance or "safety factor" built into cost estimates. There are always some "hidden" costs associated with survey research as well. These are things that have costs which are not measured, such as the time and efforts of sponsoring executives or managers.

The value of information from *academic* survey research can only be estimated by scholars familiar with the concepts that are being tested by a survey. Estimation of information value depends on expert judgments concerning the value of the potential contribution of the research to the scholarly literature. Information from those research projects that make substantial contributions in critical areas of interest would be more highly valued than that which has more finite implications or deals with more trivial issues. The value of information from *applied* survey research depends on its potential to avoid two types of decision errors that might be labeled "go" errors and "no-go" errors. *Go* errors are more obvious, while *no-go* errors are often more obscure. A *go* error results when a decision maker takes a course of action and it proves to be costly or unsatisfactory. A *no-go* error results when the decision maker either fails to take some action that would have positive results, or ignores the alternative that would be most positive, in favor of some less positive course. (In some areas, the possibility of *go* errors is referred to as "down-side" risk, while the chances of *no-go* errors are viewed as potential opportunity costs.)

The greater the potential gains or losses inherent in a decision or set of decisions, the greater the cost of uncertainty. Surveys that promise to reduce very costly uncertainty have commensurately more value. The evaluation of survey information comes down to two basic questions: (1) How much might the uncertainty cost, in terms of both *go* and *no-go* errors? (2) How much is the uncertainty likely to be reduced by the survey information? When a great deal rests on the quality of the decision because there is much to be gained or lost, survey research information would have greater value. In many cases, only the sponsor will know the facts pertaining to *go* and *no-go* errors. The research designer may have to question them carefully to ascertain the potential value of the information. The factors that would indicate relatively high and low information value are listed in Figure 2–3.

FIGURE 2–3

Factors Determining Value of Information

Factors Indicating High Information Value

1. The cost of selecting a "bad" alternative (*go* error) or failing to select the best alternative (*no-go* error) would be relatively high.

2. There is a very high degree of uncertainty about which alternative to choose, based on existing information.

3. Survey research information is likely to reduce a substantial portion of the uncertainty.

4. There is high likelihood that survey research will be effective at reducing the uncertainty.

Factors Indicating Low Information Value

1. The cost of making either a *go* error or a *no-go* error would be relatively small.

2. There is relatively little uncertainty about the decision, based only on existing information.

3. Survey research information will remove only a small portion of the uncertainty about the decision.

4. There is no way to be sure that survey research information will be effective at reducing uncertainty.

Resource Availability and Costs

At this point, the researcher should make an accurate estimate of the costs for each phase of the work. This requires fairly concrete specification of the actual tasks to be performed, the labor costs, the services needed, and materials and incidental items that will be needed. It may be necessary to check with potential vendors or service organizations who will work on the project to obtain their estimates or bids for the goods or services they provide. Some allocations of "overhead" costs for the project and for overall supervision are also ordinarily applied.

The two areas where availability and cost are likely to be most critical for most surveys are data collection, and data processing. Data collection often needs support from either special data collection agencies or from mailing houses, depending on the method to be used to collect the data. Data processing and analysis may also require external services for computer hardware and software. When estimating costs, the survey designer must pay special attention to resource availability when making choices in these two key areas. It is important to discover the external services that might contribute to the project and to make effective use of these services. It is absolutely vital to be sure that external services anticipated in the project outline are, indeed, available in the community at an acceptable cost. The steps in the process of estimating costs for data collection and data processing are listed in Guidelist 2–3.

GUIDELIST 2-3

For Assessing Resources and Costs

1. Select the data collection and data processing method, based on the following discussion in this chapter.

2. Refer to the appropriate chapter on data collection to determine resource requirements and external services.

3. Examine the chapters devoted to data processing and statistical analysis to assess resource requirements.

4. Investigate potential, external services in the community for availability and costs.

5. Consider the internal resources that are currently available or that might be acquired.

6. List the resource requirements, particularly for data collection and data processing.

7. Identify those that are available internally and those that must be provided by external vendors.

8. Provide external service providers with descriptions of the tasks they are to perform.

9. Obtain cost estimates from alternative vendors and make a tentative selection of those to be used.

10. Determine what additional, internal resources will be required for the project.

11. List all resources and their costs in the project outline.

ALTERNATIVE COLLECTION METHODS

The choice of a method for collecting the data depends on the information needs and value, as well as the budget and resources available for the project, as well as the timing. Collecting the data requires contact with respondents, and that can be accomplished by speaking with them in person, by reaching them on the telephone, or by mailing them a questionnaire to be completed and returned. Thus, personal interviewing, telephone interviewing, and direct mail surveys are the three principal methods of data collection used in survey research. The selection of the most appropriate method for collecting the data is a key decision for the researcher. Each of the three basic methods of data collection has its own special capabilities and limita-

tions. There are some types of information that can only be obtained by one method, but often the researcher has a choice between two methods, while the third lacks the capability required.

The fundamental difference among the three data collection methods consists of the intensity of contact between the researcher and the respondents. The closest contact and the greatest opportunity for two-way interaction between those collecting the data and those providing it are provided by the personal interview method. The most remote contact is obtained with the direct mail survey, while telephone interviewing falls between the other two methods on this spectrum. The three methods of data collection are likely to differ markedly in their resource requirements, as well. One may require much more time than the other. One particular method may be far more or far less expensive than the others. Each demands a different type of expertise from the field data collection team. The physical facilities that are needed differ for each method of data collection. Travel and media requirements differ from one method to the next. The degree of control over data collection differs widely.

In summary, the data collection method that is selected is likely to result in a *very* different survey project from that which would ensue if another method were chosen. The contact and interaction requirements, the nature of the inquiry and information sought, and the timing and geographic circumstances of respondents determine the choice. Figure 2–4 provides a sketch of the major factors.

FIGURE 2–4

Comparison of Data Collection Methods

	Personal	Telephone	Mail
Data collection costs	High	Medium	Low
Data collection time required	Medium	Low	High
Sample size for a given budget	Small	Medium	Large
Data quantity per respondent	High	Medium	Low
Reaches widely dispersed sample	No	Maybe	Yes
Reaches special locations	Yes	Maybe	No
Interaction with respondents	Yes	Yes	No
Degree of interviewer bias	High	Medium	None
Severity of non-response bias	Low	Low	High
Presentation of visual stimuli	Yes	No	Maybe
Field worker training required	Yes	Yes	No

Personal Interview Collection

The size of the survey sample may vary from a few dozen to several thousand respondents. Personal interviewing usually requires a field force of interviewers. The field workers may be recruited and trained by the researcher or outside field data collection agencies may be hired to collect the data. If the interviewers work directly for the researcher, they must be trained in both the general procedures for selecting respondents and interviewing them and also the specific characteristics and requirements of the project. When field data collection agencies are used, they need only be instructed concerning the specific nature of the task. This data collection method requires the most interviewer training in order to avoid the most common sources of interviewer bias. It aslo requires a substantial amount of supervision in the field, and there is still substantial possibility of bias because field workers fail to adhere to instructions. The project supervisor has less control than with other methods.

Personal interviewing provides the most complete contact with respondents because with face-to-face contact, there is both audible and visual contact with respondents. They can examine, touch, handle, or try objects that are relevant to the questions. The interviewer can present visual materials, such as rating cards and the like, and physical objects can be presented to the respondents for them to see, feel, hear, taste, smell, handle, and even consume. Personal interviewing is often able to win respondent cooperation and hold it for a substantial period. Non-response bias is minimal, and this method is quicker than mail surveys for small samples. This method is usually the most expensive per respondent, because of the travel expenses and interviewer costs, especially if the respondents are dispersed over a wide geographic area or difficult to locate. But personal interviewing can reach respondents at home, at work, or at special locations, such as intercepts at polling places, the shopping mall, or some other place in close proximity to the location of an activity that might be the topic of the survey. So the advantages often outweigh the disadvantages of this method, and the flexibility of this data collection method sometimes makes it the only choice for projects that demand direct contact, a special location, or special selection of respondents who qualify for the survey.

Telephone Interview Collection

With telephone surveys, the interviewers need not go into the field, and the interviewing can either be done from one or more central locations or perhaps from the homes of the telephone interviewers. Much depends on the location of the respondents and the

toll charges for the calls, as well as the degree of trust in the interviewers and the need for supervision. While personal interviews may take weeks or months, telephone interviewing is usually completed much more quickly. But there are some important distinctions between the two methods. Telephone interviewing allows only audible contact, not visual. The interviewer cannot see the respondent and must gauge the mood and demeanor of the person providing the data merely by the tone of voice, vocabulary, and so forth. Nor can the respondent see such visual materials as rating scales or the color, size, shape and texture of some object. They cannot try some device or touch, taste, smell, or handle it.

There are also important psychological differences, as well as physical. Eye contact and the physical presence of another person affect a respondents attitude, mood, and cooperation. It is often more difficult for the interviewer to build as much rapport on the telephone. Physical presence helps to build trust and confidence in most cases. There are also some situations and topics for which telephone interviewing leads to *greater* cooperation than personal interviewing. Telephone respondents feel they have greater anonymity when they respond to the inquiry, so in some cases they may be more confident and at ease if asked to reveal information that is personal or sensitive. There are also some respondents, such as the elderly or handicapped, who may be physically fragile or psychologically vulnerable, and might be threatened by the physical presence of a stranger asking questions, but they may be willing and able to respond on the telephone.

Usually the telephone interview must be shorter than a personal interview, and considerable resistance or premature termination of the interview by the respondent can result from interviews of more than 15 or 20 minutes. Without the physical presence of the field worker, interviewer bias is likely to be less with telephone interviewing, because physical appearance, dress, facial expressions, gestures, and other visual aspects are not a consideration. The interviewers ordinarily require less training and instruction, and if the telephone work is done from a central location, there is a greater opportunity to monitor interviewer performance and more control by the supervisor. Of course, this method is much more limited in its ability to reach respondents at special locations, and because they must be near a telephone, respondents to telephone surveys are usually at home or at work.

Direct Mail Collection

Mail survey data collection differs from interviewing, either in person or by telephone, in many important respects. The "cosmetic"

aspects of the mailing piece must be considered carefully because its form and appearance will affect the rate of response and the quality of the data. The composition, production, printing, and mailing of the questionnaires can often be done by one researcher and a small staff or with external services. The researcher usually has much greater control with a mail survey than with interviewing. Contact with the respondents is least intense with mail surveys, and in one respect, this method is the "reverse" of the telephone interview survey. The telephone provides for audible, but no visual contact, while mail provides visual, but no audible contact. Interviews often vary greatly, and any differences may be reflected in the responses, as error or bias. With the mail survey, the time of day and day of the week and the location where respondents complete the questionnaires may differ from one respondent to the next, but the questionnaires are identical to one another. Each respondent is presented with *exactly* the same instructions and tasks, eliminating the chance of serious interviewer bias.

Interviewing is ordinarily more expensive than collecting data by mail, although direct mail often takes longer because respondents must have time to complete and return their questionnaires. For a given budget, mail surveys usually yield a much larger sample size than interviewing, providing the response rate is satisfactory. Perhaps the greatest advantage of the mail survey is its ability to reach widely dispersed respondents inexpensively. Mailing costs are identical whether the respondent is three blocks or three thousand miles from the mailing point. The geographic dispersion of respondents is often the compelling reason for selection of this data collection method, although respondents can ordinarily be reached by mail only at home or at work, and the amount of data than can be collected from each respondent is usually more limited than it is when interviewing is used.

The mail surveys do not permit interaction with the respondents, except through the medium of the questionnaire, so the mailing piece must be constructed very carefully, the instructions must be clear to virtually all potential respondents, questions or sections that are contingent on an earlier question (known as "branching") must be kept to an absolute minimum. Normally, the questionnaire should be pretested to insure its effectiveness and clarity, unless the researcher is thoroughly experienced and knows well what to anticipate from the particular group to be surveyed. While the standardization of the communication to respondents eliminates bias due to variance among interviewers, the demand for covering all possible contingencies "up front" is a heavy responsibility with this form of data collection.

Mail Surveys and Non-Response Bias. The single most serious limitation to direct mail data collection is the relatively low response rate. Mail surveys with response rates over 30 percent are rare. Response rates are often only about 5 or 10 percent. That means that over 9 out of 10 people who are surveyed *may not respond!* If so, the cost of each completed response will be about 10 times the cost of preparation, printing and mailing for each questionnaire that was originally sent. The reliability of the data depends on the size of the sample that is *obtained,* and not the number of surveys sent, so the researcher must make an estimate of the response rate and mail enough questionnaires to yield the approximate number of responses required. But the most important consequence of a low mail response rate is the non-response bias that is likely to result. If respondents *randomly* complete or fail to complete and return the questionnaire, there will be *no* non-response bias, but that is seldom the case. Usually the persons characteristics, attitudes, opinions, and interest in the topic determine, in part, whether or not a questionnaire recipient will complete and return it or discard it. Thus, some groups tend to be *over-*represented and others *under*represented in the sample received, creating biased results.

There are some general principles regarding non-response that help the researcher gauge the degree of non-response bias, but they do not provide a definitive solution to this problem. Ordinarily, those who are highly involved with the topic are more likely to respond than those who are not. That includes those who feel strongly *positive* about issues or topics and those who feel strongly *negative* as well. The more neutral the respondents or the less experience they have with the topics or issues, the more often they will discard the questionnaire. Then, too, certain demographic groups are more likely to respond than are others. Those with more leisure time, such as the very young or the elderly, the unemployed, or those outside large urban areas are more likely to respond.

Non-response is a *very* important factor when there is a direct connection between the purposes of the survey and the information needs, on the one hand, and likelihood to respond, on the other. For example, if the survey seeks to measure the proportion of people who own a certain product, and owners are more likely to respond than are nonowners, the results will be worse than useless; in fact, they will be *much* worse. The tendency to respond would be directly effected by the very thing to be measured. To avoid such bias and error, the researcher must judge the degree to which non-response will interact with the topics or issues of the survey. If the interaction is likely to be too strong, the data must be collected in interviews. Even if this

interaction is negligible, over- and underrepresentation of some segments of the population may preclude a mail survey.

Collecting Data from Panels.   There are a few large, commercial firms, such as Consumer Mail Panels, Inc., Market Research Corporation of America, and National Family Opinion, Inc., that recruit and maintain national "panels" consisting of individuals, families, or households among the general public. They provide data on their panel members and access to them for survey data collection, on a fee basis. Thus, they use an entire panel or some segment of it as an option for direct mail, telephone, and personal interview survey data collection. Typically, the panel members are recruited by the company offering the panel and either paid a fee for their participation on the panel, or given a gift of substantial value to win their cooperation. Usually they are surveyed with an initial inquiry to measure and record their demographic status and other relevant background data. They may remain on a panel for a few weeks, months, or even a few years.

Such panels are especially valuable when the *same* group of respondents must be surveyed more than once, such as when the information needs seek a measurement of change among respondents over time. They can also be used for a single, nonrecurring survey. They are particularly useful and economical when only a very small proportion of the public are qualified to respond to a survey. In such cases, only those qualified might be singled out from the entire file of panel members, based on either initial panel data or on data from a special "qualifying" question included in an earlier survey of members. The advantages of using such panels include economy, in some cases, and a reduction in the demands on the researcher, since many aspects of sampling and data collection may be simplified or eliminated. The possibility that the panel members may not be closely representative of the population is probably the major disadvantage of using a sample from an ongoing panel.

Factors Determining the Selection

The basic characteristics of the major data collection methods have been identified and compared. To select the most appropriate method, the researcher should decide whether or not interviews are required. If not, a mail survey is indicated. If the mail survey must be ruled out in favor of interviews, the second step is to decide whether personal or telephone interviews would be most appropriate. The factors that influence the first decision most heavily are outlined in Checklist 2–1.

CHECKLIST 2–1

To Choose Interviews versus Mail

1. Does the task require interaction with the respondents? If there must be a two-way conversation, or if there are several "contingencies" where the question to be asked depends on a previous response, interviews will be required and direct mail collection is not feasible.

2. Is there the likelihood of interaction between the tendency to respond and the issues or topics being measured or assessed? If such interaction is present, serious non-response bias precludes the use of mail and the survey requires interviews.

3. To what degree are accurate, timely mailing lists of *qualified* respondents available? Lacking one or more mailing lists that: (*a*) include a full representation of the population to be surveyed, and (*b*) exclude unqualified individuals, interviewing will be necessary.

4. Must the survey be conducted in a *specific* location, such as a store or polling place, or at a *specific* time such as in the morning or on a particular weekend? If so, interviews are needed.

5. Can the respondents provide and *record* their own responses, or must the recording be done by a field worker? The more complex and intricate the recording of the data, the less likely a mail survey will provide satisfactory data.

6. Is it more important to collect a large amount of data from each of a limited number of respondents, or to obtain a more limited amount of data from each of a very large number of respondents? In general, the larger the sample required, the more appropriate a mail survey becomes.

7. Are the respondents widely dispersed over a broad geographic area or concentrated in groups in a confined area? The more widely dispersed, the less appropriate interviewing becomes, because of the cost of travel or of long distance telephone calls.

8. Would respondents be more embarrassed or threatened by talking to someone than merely recording their own responses? Is complete anonymity very necessary? The higher the degree of psychological threat and need for anonymity, the more appropriate the mail survey becomes.

If a direct mail survey proves to be less appropriate than interviewing, the researcher must choose between telephone interviewing and interviewing in person. Again, the choice is based on comparison of the information needs and interviewing task with the attributes

and characteristics of the two types of interviews. Checklist 2–2 lists the major considerations in outline form. For some surveys, one method will be completely precluded and the other will be absolutely necessary. In most cases, the decision will not be dictated and the

---

CHECKLIST 2–2

To Choose Telephone versus In-Person

1. Must the data be collected at some special location outside the home or workplace, such as a shopping center, polling place, meeting, or event? If so, personal interviews will be required.

2. Does the interview task require showing the respondent something? If so, telephone interviewing is precluded and personal interviews are required.

3. Must the respondent be seen to judge if they are qualified to respond? If there is a quota based on the physical appearance or observed behavior of respondents, personal interviews will be necessary.

4. Are interviewers likely to include or exclude certain types of people, based on their appearance or visible characteristics, contrary to quota specifications? If such selection bias is likely, telephone interviews are more appropriate.

5. Is there a likelihood of psychological threat or intimidation in a personal encounter with an interviewer? If so, the more remote telephone interviewing method is indicated.

6. Is there a likelihood of "contamination" of responses by the respondents companion's during the interview session? If so, telephone interviewing is more appropriate because others are less likely to overhear the conversation or interrupt it.

7. Will the interview take an exceptionally long time? If so, personal interviews are preferred because greater rapport and cooperation can be achieved with personal presence.

8. Does the telephone directory or other telephone number list serve as an adequate sample frame? If not, telephone interviews are precluded.

9. Are the respondents spread throughout a wide geographic area? If so, time and travel costs for personal interviews are likely to be prohibitive and long distance telephone interviews are advisable.

10. Is there the necessity for very rapid data collection? If so, telephone interviews can normally be completed much more quickly than interviewing in person.

advantages and disadvantages of each must be weighed against one another.

While there are times when the information needs or availability of resources clearly dictate one particular data collection method, there is usually a choice to be made. Selection must come after specification of information needs, but there may be times when the data collection method chosen may necessitate changes in information needs. This might be either because some data cannot be obtained, or because more is available than originally anticipated. Nonetheless, information needs should be the predominant consideration.

DATA PROCESSING AND THE COMPUTER

The data processing methods are largely determined by the availability of computer hardware and software. Hardware refers to the physical equipment and software refers to computer programs of various types. Computers come in different sizes and the size of the machine affects what it can and cannot do. For survey data processing, computers can probably best be divided into two main groups: (1) large computers that are ordinarily accessed by a remote terminal and (2) small computers of the table-top variety, that are used directly. Those within each category are not all the same size, but they can often be treated that way. Ordinarily, the larger the computer, the more capacity it will have. If there is a choice, it is certainly better to process data with a computer that has more capacity than to use those with less capability. Surveys generate a large amount of data, and even the smallest and most limited computer will be extremely helpful, even though there may be no statistical programs at all, because simply the ability to sort and count is a tremendous help to those processing survey data.

Computer Hardware

Surveys of very limited scope, with few respondents and very few items or questions, may require nothing more than a tally sheet and a pocket calculator. The vast majority of surveys generate enough data to make it worthwhile to check on the availability of a computer for processing. The large computer usually offers more capacity than the smaller, table-top computers. Consequently, in most cases it will be advisable for the researcher to seek availability of large computers first. Then if none are available, the researcher may turn to the smaller models.

Large Computers.   Computers are very prevalent and visible to everyone, but not all computers are available for analysis of survey data. The companies or organizations sponsoring the survey may have an in-house computer. Researchers should not automatically expect that the computer will be available to process survey data. Surveys are nonrecurring projects, while the major work of the computer within the organization is likely to be continuous processing of data for the organization's information system. The researcher must check with those responsible for computer operations to ascertain availability and capability. They should be advised of the nature of the project and the volume and type of data that are to be processed. If the computer is not available at all, then the researcher must turn elsewhere. If the computer is available, those responsible for the computer operations will want to know more details about the data and the processing routines and tasks that are to be used. If a large computer is not available from the sponsor, it may be possible to obtain external computer services.

Small Computers.   A small computer will often provide the researcher with substantial help processing survey data. While they are generally much more restricted in their ability to do statistical analysis than are the larger machines, they are often adequate for survey data processing, depending on the size of the project and the complexity of the information needs. Small computers vary greatly and they are often not very compatible with one another. They also require fairly thorough familiarity by the operator. If the researcher intends to acquire a small computer for survey data processing, it will require substantial time and study to learn to use it effectively. If such a machine is rented or borrowed for analysis, it may be advisable to hire or borrow the skills of a trained and experienced operator, as well.

Computer Software

The programs used for survey data analysis may be as important as the machines, themselves. Either custom programs or library programs might be used. Custom programs are written specifically for the purpose at hand, while library programs are those that are written to do a certain type of task and are available from those who provide software. Ordinarily library programs are used for survey analysis, but experienced programmers are often able to write small, simple routines for either large or small computers quickly and inexpensively, and they may be quite useful. Some library programs will also require additional programming of instructions.

Statistical Analysis Programs. Some computer programs are designed specifically to do statistical analysis. They are ideal for processing survey data. They vary greatly in their versatility, complexity, and range of application. Some are designed to do only one type of analysis or use one statistical tool, and others include a family of different procedures that perform different analyses and generate different statistics. Some cover the entire range of statistical manipulation, including many different tasks, procedures and tools, while changing or recoding the data and selecting only certain records or subsamples. The types of reports they produce also differ widely, and may be limited to reporting only one or a few numeric values, while other statistical packages can generate complete reports, including hundreds of tables and graphs, if needed. These more comprehensive packages allow each table to be very thoroughly labeled by the program, so that the print output indicates what survey items were analyzed, what responses the codes or values represent, what procedures were used, and what coefficients were computed. The information on such labels must be included by the researcher in the instruction program, but these report generation routines may be extremely useful for large surveys. After writing such label information just one time within the instruction program, they may be printed many hundreds of times on the report to make it more readable and understandable. Usually, the more sophisticated the analysis programs, the more expert the user must be to get the most from the software, but some complex programs can be used for only limited tasks without extensive user training and experience. All statistical programs require some instruction from the operator, but their demands differ substantially.

General Purpose Programs. There are a wide variety of programs available for many different computers, large and small, that were designed for purposes other than data processing and statistical analysis. Yet, many can be used effectively for the more simple, straightforward types of survey data analysis. Electronic spreadsheets, editor programs, and word processor record managers can sometimes perform common arithmetic operations repetitively and selectively, for limited analysis of survey data.

Software Documentation. Special descriptions and instructions are almost always written to accompany computer software. This documentation may be internal, producing menus and instructions at the terminal, or external, in the form of books and manuals. The documentation is important, yet the amount, quality, and clarity of pro-

gram documentation varies widely, and it will probably never be entirely adequate. When picking survey analysis software, it is important to check both the programs and the internal and external documentation carefully. The more user-friendly the program and the more thorough the documentation, the better. For those with no computer experience or training, it will very likely require a considerable amount of time, effort, and patience to acquire enough skill to process survey data without help from others. It may appear that the manuals and instructions for the hardware and software will be of sufficient help, but that is doubtful. Those who lack computer skills tend to err in one of two different directions: either they assume that computer analysis is too difficult and arduous to undertake and abandon it, or they assume they can process the data on a computer by themselves, if they just devote a little time and effort to it. Both assumptions are wrong. Even those who are well-trained and experienced with computers depend more heavily on one another than on external documentation or instructions. The researcher lacking computer expertise should seek the advice and help of those who know computers. They were all once just as puzzled and they are usually quite hospitable to those who share their interest.

Computer Services

There are three sources of computer services that are available to most researchers: computer networks, service bureaus, and data analysis firms. All three are designed to take responsibility for some or all of the details of processing. Use of any of these facilities will reduce the need for the researcher to become familiar or expert in the use of both computer hardware and the software. In effect, the researcher "buys" this freedom from the necessity to cope with the detailed aspects of processing, but this is often an acceptable trade-off if the service fees are reasonable and the survey budget has sufficient resources to pay them.

Computer Networks. There are several large computer networks that can be reached by telephone from any location, using a small computer with communications ability. The researcher must arrange for access and payment of the fees, to gain access to the network. Often the network will allow the user to access one or more computers, and each may have a wide variety of programs that might be used for analysis. The survey data will be keyed to a special file to serve as an independent data base. The researcher may need skill and experience in the use of computer software and hardware. Even when the

researcher has the required experience or training to use such a system, it is advisable to allow for a substantial amount of trial-and-error time and expenses, in order to become familiar with the system and programs.

Service Bureaus. The typical service bureau is a firm that has one or more large computers and provides computation services to clients on a fee basis. Many service bureau offices may be connected to the same computer, forming a large, time-sharing system that may cover the entire country. Most service bureaus offer both remote and on-site access. If the sponsor uses a service bureau on a regular basis, it would be advisable for the researcher to contact the service bureau to check on the availability of processing and consulting services. If the sponsor is not affiliated with a service bureau, the researcher may be able to use the facilities of a service bureau that are at the local bureau office or through a terminal or small computer with communications ability. It will be necessary to initiate a contract and obtain an individual account with the bureau before beginning the work. It is important to be sure that both the nature and extent of the services and the costs are well described and anticipated by both the bureau and the researcher, before continuing with the survey project.

Data Processing Firms. Most major metropolitan areas will have one or more firms that will take complete responsibility for processing survey data. Some such firms may specialize only in data processing and computer report generation. Others may also provide field data collection services, or they may be a "full service" market research or survey research company. Such firms may provide only data processing and analysis services to those who require it, even though they themselves do not conduct the survey or generate the data. Such data processing firms are more often listed with companies providing marketing research than among the firms engaged in data processing or computer services and equipment. When such a firm is used, they will ordinarily take full responsibility for the data analysis. They may provide the researcher with examples of the range of analysis they are prepared to do and the types of reports they are capable of generating. They will also provide guidance concerning the requirements for coding and data input formats. They may even accept the completed questionnaires as source documents and furnish the operators to key the data to computer files. While individual firms do differ from one another in the services they offer, the typical characteristics of the three types of external processing services are shown in Figure 2–5.

FIGURE 2–5

Comparison of Computer Service Facilities

	Computer Networks	Service Bureaus	Analysis Firms
Requires computer expertise..........	Yes	Maybe	No
Trial and error practice needed.......	Yes	Maybe	No
Degree of analyst involvement........	High	Moderate	Low
Consultants available	No	Maybe	Yes
Type of assistance provided	On-line	Verbal/written	Verbal
Equipment required for use...........	Yes	Maybe	No
Available from any location...........	Yes	No	No
Permits remote operations............	Yes	Maybe	No
Special programs available...........	Maybe	Probably	Certainly
Cost of services.....................	Low	Moderate	High

Processing Alternatives

The researcher should make an overall assessment of the data processing resources and the capabilities and limitations for the survey project at hand. The first step is to assess the in-house computer facilities of the sponsor. Next, check the external computer resource availability, including both large and small computers and software. Finally, investigate the availability of the three computer service organizations identified above. The potential options to be examined are listed in Figure 2–6. The researcher should first eliminate from con-

---

FIGURE 2–6

Outline of Computer Processing Alternatives

I. Small computers.
    1. Statistical analysis programs.
        a. Numeric data description.
        b. Category data description.
        c. Cross-tabulation or breakdowns.
    2. General purpose programs.
        a. Arithmetic operations.
        b. Electronic spreadsheets.
        c. Other analysis routines.

II. Larger computers.
   1. Statistical library programs.
      a. Individual library programs.
      b. Statistical program packages.
   2. Programming requirements and features.
      a. Complete, custom programming.
      b. Data recoding and case selection.
      c. Item, code and task labeling.
III. Processing services.
   1. Computer networks.
      a. Access requirements.
      b. Hardware availability.
      c. Software availability.
   2. Service bureaus.
      a. Access and connection details.
      b. Consulting services offered.
      c. Software and reports options.
   3. Data processing firms.
      a. Range of services available.
      b. Data requirements and transfer.
      c. Consultation and reports available.

---

sideration those options that are either not available or clearly not satisfactory to process the data from the survey to be conducted. Next, the remaining alternatives must be evaluated in terms of their advantages and disadvantages. The three criteria for judging alternatives are listed and described in Guidelist 2–4. Finally, a choice must be made and then the constraints on the survey design must be specified in the project plan.

GUIDELIST 2–4

For Evaluating Data Processing Options

1. Consider the information value and the amount of resources available for data processing.
   a. The survey information is critical and substantial funds have been allocated.
   b. The survey information is valuable but the funds are relatively limited.
   c. The survey information is merely supplementary and funds are strictly limited.

GUIDELIST 2–4 (concluded)

2. Consider the information requirements and the degree of data processing that will be needed.
    a. Simple descriptions of continuous numeric or discrete category data.
    b. Measures of association among items, such as crosstabulations or breakdowns.
    c. Recoding of survey items and/or selection of subsamples or certain cases.
    d. Computer generation of large reports with items, codes, and tasks labeled.
3. Consider the degree of research analyst expertise, experience, training and/or interest and involvement.
    a. The analyst has extensive experience and interest in computer processing.
    b. The analyst has limited expertise and interest in computer hardware and software.
    c. The analyst is principally concerned with statistical results, rather than computers.

The value of the information to the sponsor and the amount of funds allocated for data processing are gauges to judge the type of facilities to be used and the amount of researcher involvement and participation. The information needs and the degree of data processing that will be required to meet them are more important indicators of the type of computer (small or large) and the type of programs (statistical analysis or general purpose) than they are of the means of obtaining computer facilities (researcher or external service provider). When only simple data description, and perhaps a few crosstabulations of category data are needed to meet information needs, general purpose programs and small, table-top computers will often suffice. If they are not available, such analysis can be done by hand tabulation, though it is laborious and time-consuming. On the other hand, if the information needs demand more elaborate data description, and/or breakdowns, recoding of items, subsample selection or elimination of some cases, or large reports that must be well-labeled, then special statistical programs or a program package will be needed. Such programs ordinarily require a large computer, though either an in-house computer or an external service provider's computer might be used for such data processing. The researcher's expertise, interest, and motivation may determine whether or not an external data processing service provider is required.

CHECKLIST 2-3

To Select a Data Processing Method

1. Do important decisions hinge on the survey results, where risks or opportunities may be substantial? If so, external service providers with greater expertise and more elaborate facilities should be considered.

2. Are results valuable, but funds limited? The analyst may take more responsibility for processing and in-house facilities may be required in lieu of external services.

3. Will the survey provide only supplementary information with strictly limited funds? If so, a small computer and general purpose programs or hand tabulation may suffice.

4. Are the information requirements met by simple description of few items, mostly in categories? Hand tabulation or a small computer, general purpose program may do.

5. Do the information needs require a large number of items and/or respondents, many measurements of association among items, recoding and/or subsample selection, or large, well-labeled reports? A large computer with a data processing and analysis program package may be needed.

6. Is the analyst well-experienced and interested in computers? External services may not be needed or they may provide computers and programs without consultation.

7. Is the expertise, background and motivation of the analyst limited in the area of computer operations? It would be advisable to use a data processing and analysis firm or service bureau with competent consultants.

SAMPLING, INSTRUMENTATION, AND RESPONSE

The actual selection of a sample and development of a questionnaire come later in the survey process. Only the basic strategy must be chosen at this point and included in the project outline, to guide the project.

Sampling and Response

Survey research strategy tends to lean in one or two directions: Obtain a large amount of data from a small sample, or obtain a small amount of data from a large sample. Usually the resources are quite limited, while the information needs tend to be insatiable, so there is

a trade-off between the amount of data to be obtained from any one respondent and the number of respondents to be surveyed. The more data to be collected from an individual, the greater the costs per respondent, and the larger the sample, the greater the expense. The choice of which strategy to take depends on the information needs. When very precise estimates are needed, larger samples are usually required and that limits the amount of data that can be collected from any one respondent. When the information needs depend heavily on the *relationships* among the survey questions so that patterns can be detected, a large amount of data must be collected from each respondent. This limits the number of respondents that can be sampled at a given cost.

It is important to estimate the amount of data required from each respondent at this point in the survey process. This will determine the duration and difficulty of the response task and that will affect the estimate of cost per respondent. High cost per response will require a precise and perhaps elaborate design for a small sample. Low cost per response will permit sampling of a larger proportion of the population. The next step is to decide the approximate size of the *responding* sample; that is, the number of respondents who provide complete responses. The general considerations indicating the size of the sample and the size of the response task are listed in Figure 2–7, while sample size and design are discussed in Chapter 3. Once the approximate sample size and the cost per respondent have been estimated, approximate data collection costs can be estimated and listed in the project outline. This is vital to the budgeting process, since data collection is often the single, most costly phase of the survey research project.

FIGURE 2–7

Factors Determining Sampling Strategy

Indications for Large Sample, Small Response Task

1. Very precise estimates of numeric values are required and there must be a high degree of confidence in them.

2. Individual survey items are of more interest than are patterns of response among many survey items.

3. The range and volume of information required from each respondent is fairly limited.

4. The data are to be collected by mail, so that a simple response task will tend to increase the response rate.

Indications for Large Response Task, Small Sample

1. Estimates of numeric values for the population need only be approximate, within a fairly broad range.

2. Focus of information needs is more on patterns or configurations among responses to items than on the items taken individually.

3. The range and/or volume of information required from each respondent is relatively large.

4. The data are to be collected by telephone or personal interview rather than by mail.

Instrumentation and Topics

The information needs are expressed in terms that are appropriate to the sponsor. They are also listed in the order of their priority or importance to the user of the information. It will now be necessary to translate the information needs into survey topics. Doing so will provide fairly clear indications of the tasks, resources and costs for instrumentation, including the composition and production of the survey questionnaire and the cover letter and mailing materials or the rating cards and display materials that might be required. Depending on the nature of the survey project, it may be necessary to compose a rough draft of the survey instruments to be checked and approved by the sponsor. In many cases, however, the questionnaire and other materials need only be described in sufficient detail to indicate their nature.

Classification of the information needs into survey topics serves two purposes: It groups items that are similar to one another into the same topic categories and it suggests the type of questions and scales that will be needed to obtain the information. When the information needs have been expressed as topics, the entire task of inquiry is expressed in terms that are more appropriate and meaningful to the researcher. This process also assembles the items into groups, so that items that require about the same kind of task from the respondent are listed together. This is the first step in arriving at a sequence that will facilitate response and assure more reliable, accurate data.

To classify the information needs into topic categories, each question specified in the list of information needs must be identified as relating to one or more of the seven topics identified in Chapter 1. At times, the topic that is inherent in the question will be obvious. Where more than one topic is implied or where the identification of one particular topic is ambiguous, careful thought and judgment may be required. The translation of information needs into survey research

topics should meet two important criteria: Every important information need should be classified into one or more topic categories and expressed in the terms of the topics, and redundancy should be limited and deliberate, so there is no accidental overlap. Nothing should be neglected or it will not be collected, and the exact same information should not be sought more than once unless that is intentional.

When the information needs have been classified into survey topics, the researcher should be able to estimate the size and scope of the questionnaire and other materials that will be required for recording responses. It may be advisable for the researcher to examine Part Two of the handbook, devoted to survey instrumentation, for a more thorough view of the questionnaire requirements.

The approximate number of survey items or variables should be noted in the project outline. It is also important at this point to estimate the costs for composition and production of the survey instruments. Thus, it may be necessary to obtain cost estimates or bids from internal or external sources, such as typesetters, printers, and the like. When these costs have been obtained, they should be listed in the project outline, together with the other information that is relevant to instrumentation.

Reporting and Approval

If the researcher is providing the research services for others who sponsor the survey, it is often useful to deliver draft copies of the questionnaire and other materials as they are prepared. Ordinarily, such materials might be submitted two or three times, as the sponsor suggests additions, deletions, or modifications. It will often be necessary for the researcher to explain the relationships between the questionnaire sections and the various information needs, when they are not evident to the sponsor. The final draft of the instruments may require approval before actual data collection begins. The more informed individuals who check and edit the work, the fewer the errors, omissions, or mistakes that are likely to escape notice. It is always well worth the time and effort required to do so.

The nature and format of the reports to be provided to the sponsor must be specified and the costs of reporting must also be estimated in advance. A wide variety of report mechanisms and formats are used for survey projects, depending on sponsor preferences and information needs. Both report composition and production can often be more expensive and time consuming than might be anticipated. It is important to consider the size of the reports and also the number of copies of written documents, as well as conference time for reporting results. The options and alternatives are identified and described in Chapter 12.

THE FINAL PROJECT PLAN

The final element of the project outline is the cost schedule and the timetable for the project. Since the costs for the various steps and tasks in the research process have been estimated individually for each element of the project outline, they need only be totaled and summarized, together with the estimated time requirements for each step.

The important factor for the researcher to note when completing the survey project plan is the necessity for an integrated project. Each element must fit together and be compatible with the others. When inconsistencies or incompatibilities are discovered, the elements must be changed. It is always advisable for the researcher to express the elements of the project plan in written form. This plan will serve as the basis for subsequent decisions and choices as the work is performed and the project continues to completion. It may also be necessary or desirable to edit and refine the project outline and append any questionnaire drafts or other relevant materials. The project outline should be submitted to the sponsors, with whatever annotation they might require. When approved, it serves as the basis for an agreement or contract for the survey project work to be performed by the researcher. For those projects where the researcher sponsors the survey, it is advisable to submit the project outline and obtain comments and suggestions from others who might provide insight by virtue of their training or experience.

SUMMARY

Completing the Project Plan

A. Consider first things first. The survey objectives and information needs should be the basis for selecting instrumentation, data collection, and processing methods.

B. Value control very highly. The chance of catastrophic error increases dramatically with the number of people involved in survey data collection.

C. Communicate with others. Maintain a dialogue with the sponsor and obtain comments from those who can assist.

D. Evaluate options thoroughly. Questionnaire, data collection, and processing alternatives must all be identified and examined to make the best choice.

E. Choose alternatives carefully. If there is doubt about data instru-

mentation, collection, or processing, turn to the later chapters on these issues for detailed discussion.

F. Place trust in sampling. Inexperienced researchers tend to demand large samples when careful sampling design will obtain precise information from smaller numbers of people.

G. Budget *very* carefully. Instrumentation, collection, and processing always cost more than anticipated and the budget should have a safety factor to allow for error.

H. Match costs and information value. Revise the project tasks or increase allocation of funds so that there is an adequate margin of safety between costs and benefits.

3

Sampling Design

THE PURPOSE OF SAMPLING

Nearly every survey uses some form of sampling. The concept of sampling is easily understood. It simply means taking part of some population to represent the whole population. The alternative to sampling is enumeration; counting the entire population. The census of the U.S. population conducted each decade and political elections where all qualified citizens who register and vote are "counted" at the polls are both examples of enumeration. Sampling is much more often used. Even though the Census Bureau uses enumeration for the decennial census, they generate a gigantic volume of data about citizens, industry, and other subjects by surveying only a sample of the population under study. The news media, political parties and candidates generate predictive data using sampling, prior to the actual election. Sampling is a key factor for virtually any survey project.

The major reason for sampling is economy. To survey every individual in a population using enumeration is ordinarily much too expensive in terms of time, money, and personnel. There is really no need to survey every individual. Only a small fraction of the entire population ordinarily provides sufficient representation of the group as a whole and enough accuracy to base decisions on the results with confidence. While sampling is extremely practical and economical, it must be done correctly or it will introduce bias or error in the results. The sample must be selected properly, or it will not represent the whole. It must be large enough to meet the requirements for reliability, but not too large or it will waste resources.

Reliability and Validity

The reliability and validity of survey data depend in part on the sampling design used. Sampling is not the *only* procedure or factor that affects reliability and validity, so it is important to understand the concepts of reliability and validity in general, and the affect that sampling has on them, in particular.

The Meaning of Reliability. Reliability means the freedom from random error. The most fundamental test of reliability is "repeatability;" the ability to get the same data values from several measurements made in a similar manner. For example, if a survey question obtained the same response, time after time, from one particular respondent who was asked that same question several times in one month, that would mean that there was high reliability *over time.* If the answers varied in a random pattern, the reliability over time would be low. If a survey item yielded the same data from one respondent to the next when they did, in fact, hold identical positions on the issue, that would indicate high reliability *over respondents,* and if there were random differences, reliability over respondents would be low. Similarly, if a survey yielded the same distributions of data from one sample of a given size to the next when they were drawn in the same way, there would be relatively low "sampling error" and high reliability *over samples.* The greater the random error, the lower the reliability.

Random error can occur as the result of "happening" to sample a particular group of people, and when it does it is referred to as "sampling error." But random error can result from other measurement factors, as well. For example, if a survey item used a term that was completely unfamiliar to many respondents, they would be likely to guess at the meaning, even though they had no idea what it really meant. They might give answers that were merely a *random* guess, and the reliability of the data for that item would be reduced.

The Meaning of Validity. A survey is valid to the degree that it measures what and only what it is supposed to measure. To be valid it must not be affected by extraneous factors that systematically "push" or "pull" the results in one particular direction. To the degree that things other than those being measured affect the results by introducing a systematic bias, the results are less valid. Unfortunately, there are many factors that can bias the results of a survey, including the effects of sampling. Later chapters will identify and discuss other sources of bias and their affect on validity.

The Reliability/Validity Picture

The concepts of reliability and validity can be shown more clearly with the use of an analogy. Figure 3–1 shows four different patterns. Each of the four pictures shown there might represent a target, such as the "bull's eye" on a dart board. In this example, that bull's eye is the actual average of some value among a whole population of people. The small circles on the diagram are the marks of the darts thrown at each target. These marks are analogous to the averages that might be obtained from several measurements from sets of people in the same population. Each of the rows and columns on the diagram are labeled to show what they represent. The first column shows the results when reliability is high, and the second column shows low reliability. The top row contains the pattern for high validity, and the bottom row shows low validity.

High versus Low Reliability. In the left-hand column of the diagram, the marks from the darts are all closely clustered. In other

---

FIGURE 3–1

The Reliability/Validity Diagram

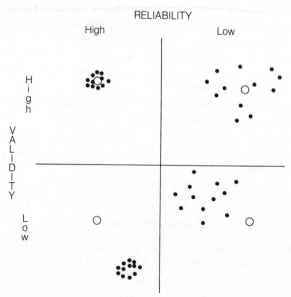

words, the person throwing the darts managed to place them all in very nearly the same place on the target. If the marks are taken to represent averages obtained from different measurements from the same population, the reliability is quite high because the results are very similar. In other words, there is very little "random error" in the data. By contrast, the marks on the two targets in the right-hand column are spread over a wider area, rather than being clustered closely together. The dart thrower in these cases was not doing exactly the same thing with each throw, and the darts were randomly scattered on the targets. By analogy, if the marks were results from different survey measurements, they are not very good "replicates" or representations of one another. Thus, the reliability is fairly low and the random error is quite high.

High versus Low Validity. Both targets on the top row of the diagram contain marks that are centered on the bull's eye. Despite the fact that the marks on the right-hand target are spread over a wider area, they are in a random pattern, centered around the center of the target. Nothing is "pushing" or "pulling" all of the marks in one direction. By contrast, the patterns on both targets in the bottom row of the diagram are off the mark; all are toward one direction. It appears that the person throwing the darts at the target on the lower left had a steady hand, but consistently threw the darts below and to the right of the bull's eye. The player who threw the darts at the target on the bottom right tended to be less steady and consistent and also to persistently throw too high and to the left. Thus, the effect of *systematic bias* is to push or pull the results in one or another specific direction. So the lower row of the diagram represents the results of survey data typical of low validity.

The pattern of marks on the upper right-hand target of the diagram are identified as low in reliability but with high validity, because the pattern is *centered* on the bull's eye. Technically, no data can be more valid than it is reliable, because validity means hitting the bull's eye consistently, and in this case, many miss the mark, due to low reliability. Thus, the degree of reliability limits the degree of validity.

Sampling Error and Sampling Bias

There are many factors that can produce error and bias in survey results, decreasing both reliability and validity. Error and bias resulting from sampling are the focus here, while other sources are discussed later.

Sampling Error. No sample is likely to produce results that are pre-

cisely the same as those for the entire population from which the sample was drawn. There is always some chance that those who are included in the sample are not perfectly representative of the whole population. It is always possible to pick, strictly by chance, a particular group who happen to be higher or lower than the population as a whole. If such differences between the sample data and the population data results purely by random chance, this is known as *sampling error.* Smaller samples are more likely to be different from the population than are larger ones, so smaller samples have more sampling error. The higher the sampling error, the lower the reliability, so the smaller the sample, the lower the reliability of the data.

It is ordinarily very impractical to measure the entire population. So usually the researcher knows nothing about the whole population except what is learned from the sample, itself. Thus, researchers and statisticians usually think of sampling error in terms of comparisons between similar samples. Data from a sample is relatively free from sampling error and is reliable if another sample of the same size, taken from the same population with the same selection technique is very likely to provide results that are the same or very similar. If another identical sample provided very different results, then there would be a considerable amount of sampling error and the data from the original sample would be seen as unreliable. There is always some chance that a sample will include many individuals who are atypical; who are different from the most typical members of the population. The degree of sampling error is a function of both the size of the sample, relative to the population as a whole, and also the degree of variation from one individual to the next, within the population. The larger the proportion of the entire population included in the sample, the lower the sampling error will be; and the more similar the individuals in the population, the less the sampling error for a sample of any given size.

Suppose only 5 people out of 10,000 were interviewed on some subject. There is a fairly high chance that they might happen to hold a view that was not typical of the whole group. By comparison, it would be very unlikely that a sample of 1,000 people would happen to contain all or mostly people who were quite different from the other 9,000 in the population. Thus, the larger the sample, the lower the sampling error.

Variation among individuals in the population also affects sampling error. Assume that all the individuals in the population are exactly alike in every way. If each individual member were precisely the same as every other, a sample of only one person would be needed. If there is some variation among individual units in the population, so that they are very similar to one another but not exactly identical, then a sample of only a few units would provide fairly

low sampling error. If no two units are very much alike and there is a lot of variation in the population, it would be necessary to select a fairly large sample to represent the whole population with a high degree of reliability.

When a sample is drawn from a population with a great deal of variation among the individuals, the sample is more likely to differ from the whole population than it would if there were very little variation in the population. There is more sampling error when the variance in the population is large than when it is small. The higher the sampling error, the lower the reliability of the data. Thus, the larger the variance in the population, the lower the reliability of the data for a sample of any given size.

Sampling Bias. Extraneous sampling factors that affect survey results produce systematic bias and reduce the validity of the data. Systematic bias is often called just plain "bias." The word "systematic" simply means that it is not random; that the effect is to push results in one or another specific direction. Suppose a survey were conducted to measure how satisfied or content people are. If all the field workers were quite shy and would only interview people who looked like they were very friendly, the data would reflect two things: How satisfied people in general really are, and also the positive effects of picking people who look friendly and happy. Selecting only friendly people to interview would produce a bias in the direction of greater satisfaction. The greater the bias, the less validity of the data.

Controlling Sampling Error and Bias. The degree of sampling error depends on the sample size. The smaller the proportion of the entire population that is included in the sample, the greater the sampling error. So, to control or reduce sampling error, the researcher need only obtain a larger sample. In order to be accurate and useful, survey data must not only be reliable, but also valid as well. Consequently, the researcher must control sampling bias effectively. Systematic bias results when extraneous factors push the results in one specific direction. The researcher can control sampling bias and improve validity by the careful selection of a sampling design. Some sampling designs are far superior to others in this regard.

Random Sample Attributes

The most desirable sample for almost every survey is a *random* sample. When the respondents are picked from the population at random, the probability of any one person being included in the sample is precisely equal to the probability of including any other

---

GUIDELIST 3-1

For Controlling Sampling Error and Bias

1. Sampling error results because those in the sample are not *perfectly* representative of the average for the entire population.

2. Any sample of less than the entire population will have some sampling error.

3. Sampling error is "random" error and it affects both the reliability and validity of the data.

4. The greater the sampling error, the lower the reliability and validity obtained.

5. The less the variation among individual members of the population, the smaller the sampling error.

6. The larger the proportion of the population included in the sample, the smaller the sampling error.

7. Survey data cannot be more valid than it is reliable, because reliability limits validity.

8. Survey data can be highly reliable, but still be low in validity because of systematic bias.

9. Like sampling error, systematic bias can never be eliminated completely.

10. Systematic bias can best be controlled by identifying the things that are most likely to exert bias and eliminating them or protecting from them in the sampling design.

---

individual. (In a technical sense, the probability of inclusion need not necessarily be equal, so long as the probability is known. A random sample is merely a special case of what is sometimes called a "probability sample.") The random sample is best because it is most representative of the entire population, and because it is least likely to result in bias. Such a sample has statistical properties that allow the researcher to make *inferences* about the population, based on the results obtained from the sample. Random samples permit the researcher to compute and report *confidence intervals* indicating the probability that the population average is within a certain range around the sample average. With random sampling, the researcher can calculate and report the *statistical significance* of relationships between survey items, based on the probability that such relationships would result only from sampling error.

Without random selection, none of these statistical coefficients or values would be accurate or legitimate. This is not to say they cannot be computed. They can be. The analytical computations can be performed for *any* numeric data, regardless of how it was obtained. On the other hand, the resulting values and coefficients would have little or no real meaning or legitimacy, and they could be very misleading, indeed. The more the sample deviates from purely random selection the less representative it is likely to be, and the less legitimate the results of statistical computation will be.

IDENTIFICATION OF THE POPULATION

The actual specification of a sampling design begins with identification of the *population* to be surveyed. This may appear to be a simple task, but it seldom is. Suppose a survey is to be conducted to measure community attitudes toward a municipal, political issue. Then the population to be surveyed would include all those within the city. Are those who are temporarily living outside the city to be included or excluded? Should only registered voters be included in the population? Must respondents be 18 or 21 years of age or older? What about those who own property in the city but live elsewhere? Should business be included, or only individuals?

It is important for the researcher to anticipate the inclusion decisions that are likely to arise during actual sample selection. Respondents must be qualified to respond on the basis of two criteria: first and foremost, they must possess the information, and secondly, they may also need to have certain attributes or characteristics to make their responses meaningful.

GUIDELIST 3-2

For Identifying Populations

1. Be sure the population consists of those people who actually possess the information sought by the survey.

2. Identify all of the major factors that would otherwise "qualify" respondents and make their responses meaningful to the sponsor.

3. List the criteria for inclusion and exclusion of respondents, together with the decision rules to be used.

Specification of Sample Units

A sample unit is the smallest entity that will provide one response. Ordinarily, survey sample units consist of individual people. Each person in the population might be a sample unit. This is not always the case. For some surveys, the appropriate sample unit might be a "household," consisting of all those living in one housing unit. For another, the sampling unit might be a "family," consisting of parents, their children, and relatives. Some surveys may require sample units that are individual business firms or companies. Others may use organizations or institutions as sample units.

The specification of a sample unit must be neither too broad nor too narrow. If it is too broad, it will not be the smallest single unit. For example, it would not be appropriate to use the family as a sampling unit for a survey of political attitudes because different family members may hold different opinions about the issues. If the specification of a sampling unit is too narrow, it would produce redundancy or be misleading. For example, a survey designed to discover the methods charitable institutions use to solicit contributions could not effectively use individual employees as the sample units. Each would be reporting on the same institution, and all but one would be redundant. There is one other factor that must be considered when specifying sample units. There are times when the data to be generated by a survey are to be compared with existing survey data; secondary data from some source other than a survey. If so, it is important to be sure that the specification of the sample unit for the survey is the same as that for the data to which the survey results will be compared, to insure comparability.

GUIDELIST 3-3

For Specifying Sample Units

1. The sampling unit should be specified so that it is the smallest single entity from which the data can be obtained.

2. If the unit contains several individuals who might provide different data, the specification of the unit is too broad and should be narrowed.

3. If responses from individuals would be redundant or overrepresent some entities, the specification is too narrow and should be broadened.

4. If the survey data are to be compared with existing survey or secondary data, the same sample units must be used for the survey or the data will not be comparable.

Sample Frame Selection

The sample frame is a list or a set of directions indicating all the sample units in the population. Individual respondents will be selected from the sample frame when the survey data are to be collected. The sample frame might be a list of names and telephone numbers for a telephone survey, a map showing a specific residential area for in-home, personal interviews, or a list of names and addresses for a mail survey. There are other types of sample frames that are used for special types of surveys or data collection methods. Assume that interviews are to be conducted at some location such as a store. The sample frame might consist of all those who enter the store during the sampling period.

It is seldom possible to identify or obtain a perfect sample frame. The more complete and accurate the sample frame, the better the sample data will represent the population as a whole. There are three criteria that should be used to select a sample frame for a survey: the frame should be all inclusive, it should be exclusive to the population under study, and the units identified in the frame should be defined in exactly the same way as the sampling units. An all-inclusive sample frame is one that includes every member of the population to be surveyed. The frame should be exclusive in the sense that it includes *only* those from the population to be surveyed. The frame must list or identify the same entities in the same way as the specification of the sampling units. There are times when it is necessary or desirable that the sample frame contain other detail as well.

RANDOM SAMPLE SELECTION

Selecting sample units from the sample frame on a random basis may appear to be simple and easy, but it is often difficult to select the units on a *purely* random basis. No systematic patterns must evolve. Any factors that would change the probability of any one unit or type of unit being selected must be ruled out. There are several techniques for random selection.

Nth Name Sampling.   When the sample frame consists of a list of sample units, the most common method of selecting a random sample from the list is to select every "*n*th" name, where *n* is calculated by dividing the number of units in the sample into the number on the list. If a sample of 100 were to be drawn from a list of 1,000, every 10th name would be picked. Strictly speaking, this is systematic sampling, rather than purely random, but it requires the use of one form of random selection.

GUIDELIST 3–4

For Selecting a Sample Frame

1. The sample frame is required to identify the entities or units to be surveyed.

2. The sample frame should be all-inclusive, so that every unit in the population to be surveyed is included.

3. The frame for the sample should exclude any units that are not part of the population being surveyed.

4. The entries listed in the sample frame must be specified in exactly the same way as the sampling units were specified.

5. When the sample is clustered, stratified, or both, the sample frame must indicate cluster boundaries and/or strata membership for the individual units.

When nth name sampling is used, the researcher should *not* begin counting with the first name on the list. Often those who happen to be the first on a list, such as the first name on the page of a telephone directory, are contacted much more frequently than others, because of their position on the list. In the example, the researcher should begin with one of the first 10 names or units. The actual starting point should be picked *randomly*. If the number drawn happened to be 7, the first unit for the sample would be the 7th name on the list, the second, the 17th, etc.

Random Number Generators. There are several computational routines and computer programs that generate lists of random numbers. When a random number generator is used, the generator will often be able to discard duplicate numbers and order the numbers in a sequence from lowest to highest value. The researcher would then pick those units to be sampled from the list or sample frame according to the random list.

Tables of Random Numbers. Many books on statistics and mathematics or books of tables contain an appendix with a list of random numbers. The researcher should follow the instructions provided there very carefully when picking the numbers. The list is then used in exactly the same way as computer-generated random numbers.

Physical Selection Methods. When the units in the frame can be listed individually on small cards of the same size, the cards can be

mixed in a container and the sample drawn from it with "blind" selection. Mechanical devices to select numbers randomly can be obtained or created simply and easily when needed. One such device is commonly used to select "Bingo" numbers, and others use small balls, cubes, key tags, and the like.

GUIDELIST 3–5

For Selecting a Random Sample

1. For *n*th name sampling, divide the number in the population by the number to be sampled for the value of *n*.

2. Randomly pick the first unit for an *n*th name sample from the first one through *n* entries of the frame.

3. Random number generators often produce near-perfect random lists, often without duplicates and ordered from lowest to highest.

4. When a "seed" number is required by a random number generator program, it should be picked at random.

5. Statistics texts often contain random number tables and the instructions for their use must be followed carefully.

6. When units from the sample frame can be identified on small, physical objects, mechanical devices can be obtained or created to make random selection.

Sample Selection Bias

When random selection is used to pick a sample from a sample frame, the probability that any one unit or type of unit will be selected is exactly equal to the probability of selecting any other unit. For example, if the sample consists of 10 percent of the population, then the probability of randomly selecting any one unit is 1 in 10, or 10 percent. Any factor that alters that probability, either increasing or decreasing it for one unit or type of unit, will create bias in the selection process. It is important to protect against factors that bias random selection. The reliability of the data and the statistical inferences about the population depend on random selection and the equal probability of selecting each sample unit. There is a danger that the presence of serious, unrecognized biases may lead to inaccurate estimates and errors when making interpretations and drawing conclusions. The most common sources of selection bias identified here

do not constitute an exhaustive list, and every survey is subject to other, specific sources of bias. There is no substitute for careful consideration of the process, itself, to identify any additional bias factors.

Visibility Bias.   Often some types of units in the population are more visible than others. The sample frame may fail to identify one or more classes of units. If the telephone directory serves as the sample frame, those who have unlisted or unpublished numbers and those without telephones would not be included. The researcher must be sure that such frames or lists are complete and also be careful that the selection system does not pick the more visible units at a higher rate than those which are more obscure.

Order Bias.   Most sample frames contain sample units that are listed or appear in an orderly pattern. A telephone directory lists names in alphabetical order. A list of credit card holders may be in sequence from the earliest to the latest applicants. The selection routine must take into account any such order in the sample frame. The sequential order of the units must not be allowed to increase or decrease the probability that any particular unit or block of units are selected for the sample.

Accessibility Bias.   For many surveys, the actual selection of units takes place in the field, rather than at the survey headquarters. If so, some respondents may be more accessible than others. Field workers tend to pick the most accessible respondents; those that are most easily reached. When all units are not equally accessible, the researcher must provide controls and incentives to insure that there will be no over- or underrepresentation of some types of respondents.

Cluster Bias.   Some sampling designs include clusters of respondents, rather than individuals. Cluster sampling is legitimate and often very practical, and the technique is discussed later. Cluster bias occurs when the clusters are specified too closely. If respondents from 10 households that are next door to one another were interviewed, this design is likely to lead to bias because of two things: membership and interaction. People of the same type or status tend to live and work near one another. Those who live near one another are likely to interact, sharing their attitudes and opinions with one another. This tendency for consensus formation would bias the survey results because units within one cluster would provide redundant responses and there would be less variance among those in one cluster than among the population as a whole. Respondents in geographic or sequential clusters must not be too close to one another or be

directly interconnected. The responses from each individual must be completely independent of those from all others. To obtain that independence, cluster designs must be specified so that there is sufficient distance or no connection between individuals within a cluster.

Affinity Bias.   When the selection of individual respondents is performed according to a set plan within the field and by interviewers, there may be affinity bias. This is especially true if the plan fails to identify *precisely* which individuals are to be picked, so that there is some choice on the part of the field workers. Interviewers tend to select certain types of respondents because they have an affinity for them. For example, they will ordinarily ignore those who appear to be very hurried, those who look crabby, grouchy, or unpleasant, those in groups or in the company of others, adults who are caring for small children, and those who are otherwise different in any way, such as the physically handicapped or those wearing unusual or bizarre dress. By contrast, they tend to approach and include people with the same demographic characteristics as the interviewers. They may more often interview those who are of the same age and sex as they are, as well as those who are more leisurely in their movements, or appear to be more friendly, cooperative, or attractive. When respondents are selected on the basis of their affinity to the interviewer, bias is introduced into the process. This affinity bias can be avoided by very precise specification of who is to be selected and contacted and by strict supervision and enforcement of the instructions to field workers.

Self-Selection Bias.   Some sampling designs permit the self-selection of respondents. The most common type of self-selection occurs with a mail survey, where respondents can easily refuse or fail to respond. Such bias is called "non-response" bias, and it is considered separately below. Aside from non-response bias, self-selection can occur when a sample frame is being constructed or when respondents have a choice of attending or participating. To avoid self-selection bias, the researcher may need to reduce or remove the choice on the part of the respondent. While people cannot be forced to participate, their degree of choice can often be markedly decreased.

Non-Response Bias.   Non-response may be "independent" of the survey content, or it may "interact" with the survey content. If people decide to respond to a survey or not to respond, *purely* on a random basis, then the non-response will be independent of the survey content and there will be no non-response bias. In such a case, the

---

CHECKLIST 3-1

To Avoid Sample Selection Bias

1. Are some units in the population more visible than others? If so, be sure the more visible units are selected in the same proportion as the more obscure units.

2. Are the units in the sample frame presented in systematic order? If so, the sequence must not alter the probability of selection of some units over others.

3. Are some respondents more accessible than others? When they are, controls and incentives must be used to obtain equal proportions of those with high and low accessibility.

4. Are sample units clustered, either deliberately or accidentally? When clusters exist, there must be no more interaction or similarity within clusters than between.

5. Will field workers have more affinity for some respondents than others? If so, incentives and controls must be used to avoid over-selecting those with greater affinity.

6. Is there an opportunity for respondents to select themselves or decline? If so, the opportunity should be reduced or concealed from potential respondents.

7. Will there be a high proportion of non-respondents? If so, there should be as little interaction as possible between non-response and the issues being surveyed.

8. Are some types of respondents *both* more or less likely to respond *and* likely to respond in a certain way? If so, the non-response bias must be reduced or controlled.

---

response rate need only estimate and include a sufficient number to be contacted, so that the data collection yields an adequate number of respondents to satisfy the sample size requirements. The selection of respondents would remain a random selection.

Unfortunately, non-response is almost never completely independent of the survey issues. Interaction between survey issues and non-response can be direct or indirect. With direct interaction, the very things to be measured affect whether or not people will respond to a survey. Suppose a survey were conducted to measure purchase probability for a new consumer product. Those who have a need for the product are more likely to respond to the survey than are those

who see no need for it. The latter group is likely to notice the topic, conclude that they have no interest, and discard the questionnaire or refuse the interview. The survey results would portray the product as much more popular and with much greater potential for acceptance than actually exists in the population as a whole.

There may also be indirect interaction, mediated by the demographic or psychographic status of some respondent groups. For example, those in some demographic categories have more time than others. Elderly, retired respondents often feel less time pressure than younger people who are fully employed. They may respond in greater numbers than others. There may not be a direct interaction between the issues measured by the survey and the willingness to respond, but there is an indirect interaction. If those who are retired, are *both* more likely to respond *and* more likely to answer in a particular way, this would be a serious source of non-response bias.

It is almost impossible to avoid non-response bias entirely, and so some such bias must usually be tolerated. It is the researcher's responsibility to assess the degree of direct and indirect interaction that may exist between the survey issues and topics, on the one hand, and the propensity to respond, on the other. At times, it may be virtually impossible to predict the "direction" of the effect; whether a particular attitude or opinion would tend to increase or decrease the response. When there are no clear indications of the direction of the bias, it may be advisable to conduct a pretest or pilot study that focuses directly on the issue of non-response. Another alternative is to use dual data collection methods. Because non-response is likely to be very high and the effects quite severe for mail surveys, some survey projects use a mail survey to obtain a sufficient number of respondents within the budget or resource constraints, but also do a limited number of interviews. By comparing the results from the two types of respondents, the mail response results can often be adjusted or modified to compensate for the non-response bias that is detected and measured.

SPECIAL SAMPLING DESIGNS

The random sample is the most straightforward form of probability sampling, but there are also systematic designs that yield a sample where the probability of inclusion of units is equal or known to the researcher. Stratified and clustered samples are the most common of these systematic sampling designs, and they have special advantages and applications.

Stratified Sampling

There are times when it is useful to divide a population into two or more segments or strata and sample a different proportion of each. The selection of sample strata is most often based on some demographic characteristic, but other variables might also be used for dividing the population into strata and the sample into subsamples. A stratified sample is ordinarily practical when one or both of two conditions exist: it may be necessary or desirable to sample a much larger or smaller proportion of some strata than others, or there may be very little variance in the population within a strata, but great variance between them. Each condition can be exemplified.

Assume that the industrial relations department of some company would like to measure the preferences and evaluations of employees concerning several various types of fringe benefits that might be included in a labor contract. Some of the employees belong to a union whose contract with the employer will expire soon, and negotiation of a new contract is to begin shortly. Another group is represented by a different labor union that very recently signed an agreement, so that it will be many months before that contract could be changed or modified. The sponsor may need to be very precise and accurate about the opinions and attitudes of the first group. They may wish to obtain only a general overview of the attitudes of those in the second, to anticipate reactions some time in the future. Under such circumstances, the population of employees might be divided into two, mutually exclusive groups or strata, based on their union affiliation. A large proportion of those in the first strata would be surveyed and a smaller proportion of the second strata would be included. If simple, random sampling were used without stratification, the result might be less confidence than desired for the first group, while the views of the second strata would be overrepresented and resources would be wasted, generating much greater reliability for that group than was required.

Another case can be used to exemplify a situation where the use of stratification dramatically increases the reliability and confidence obtainable from survey data. Suppose a political survey were to be conducted on a particular issue, and the population is sharply divided or "polarized" on the issue. Assume that the men in the population very often tend to hold one position very strongly, and that the women are likely to maintain an opposing view with equal vigor. On the other hand, there are indications that there is very little variation among the men concerning the issue, and the women also tend to agree fairly closely with one another. If the sample were not stratified

---

CHECKLIST 3–2

To Choose a Stratified Sample Design

1. Is there a requirement for greater reliability and a larger sample for some strata than for others? If so, stratification would be practical.

2. Are there indications that there is little population variance *within* strata and large variation *between* strata? In such cases, stratification is recommended.

3. Is it possible to obtain or create a sample frame indicating strata membership for individuals? If not, stratification is difficult or impossible without quota sampling.

4. Can respondents' strata memberships be determined in advance by observation or questioning with a quota system? If they cannot, stratification is not feasible.

---

on the basis of the sex of the respondents, a very large proportion of the population as a whole would have to be surveyed to provide the degree of certainty required. That is because the degree of reliability is partly a function of the variance in the population, and the variance would be large because of the polarization. Alternatively, the researcher might divide the population into masculine and feminine strata. Because the variance within the strata is likely to be small, a

---

GUIDELIST 3–6

For Designing a Stratified Sample

1. Select the variable(s) or characteristic(s) on which to base or define the strata.

2. Obtain or create a sample frame that indicates the strata membership of each unit in the population.

3. Estimate the variance that is likely to exist among individuals within each strata and the variation to be expected between strata.

4. Decide on the level of confidence required for each strata, based on the information requirements.

5. Specify the sample size for each strata to provide the desired confidence level for each.

---

much smaller proportion of each strata need be surveyed to furnish the necessary reliability and confidence intervals.

With stratified sampling, the sample frame must indicate strata membership on the variables used to define the strata. In the first example above, the union affiliations of employees would have to be indicated in the personnel records. The strata membership of respondents must also be identifiable in advance, or a quota system must be used with stratification.

Cluster Sampling

The population to be surveyed is often physically or geographically separated or dispersed. This is of little concern for mail surveys, because postage is ordinarily the same, regardless of whether the respondent is across the street or across the nation. The concentration of the population is important for personal interview surveys because often field workers will spend more time and effort traveling from one respondent to the next than they do on the actual task of interviewing. Similarly, the toll charges can be very high for telephone interviewing over a wide geographic area. Cluster sampling is a method for reducing costs and time requirements by surveying groups of respondents who are geographically close to one another.

An example of a typical situation where cluster sampling can be used effectively may clarify the technique. Suppose a company would like to survey potential buyers of their product within a single metropolitan area. The sample units are households, and a detailed street map of the entire area will provide the sample frame. Three hundred consumers are to be interviewed. Individual households might be selected at random based on their location on the map. With such a design, even the two respondents who are nearest to one another may be several blocks or miles apart. Some outlying respondents may require many miles of travel.

To reduce travel time and cost markedly, the researcher may decide on a clustered, random sample. The design might specify that each cluster will contain 10 respondents, all from the same neighborhood. The location of each such neighborhood would be chosen at random from the map, just as an individual respondent might be selected. The interviewers would then be instructed to begin with a particular household, then move five household units in a specific (randomly determined) direction, and obtain a second interview from the sixth household. They would continue until all 10 interviews in the cluster were obtained, then travel to the next cluster location. With the use of the cluster sampling design in this example, the driving time and travel costs would be reduced by nearly 90 percent.

Cluster sampling can also be used effectively to reduce costs for telephone interviewing. Rather than placing a very large number of long distance calls with relatively high toll charges, clusters can be specified within particular, randomly selected communities, area codes, or exchanges. Interviewers within those communities can then place local calls that have only small toll charges or none at all.

CHECKLIST 3-3

To Choose a Cluster Sample Design

1. Is the data to be collected by personal or telephone interviewing? If not, clustering is not necessary.

2. Are the respondents spread over a wide physical or geographic area? If so, clustering may be appropriate.

3. Will travel time and costs be high, relative to the actual interviewing? If so, cluster sampling will be economical.

4. Is the total sample size large enough to permit selecting many clusters? If not, clustering should not be used.

Cluster sampling is not *limited* to geographical clustering, although that is most often the reason for using such a design. Clusters might also be selected on some other basis, such as groups of consecutive records from a namelist file, rather than an nth name sampling design. This might be done to save time and costs associated with "passing" every individual record to select a sample from a very large file contained on different physical devices. Another such situation that is not based on geographic areas or distance is the case of cluster sampling *over time*. For example, if visitors to a certain location were to be surveyed over an extended period of time, the total time might be divided into clusters, such as four hour periods, and the cluster periods during which sampling were to occur could be selected randomly. This would reduce the amount of time required of interviewers and thus might reduce data collection costs substantially.

It is important to note that those within one cluster must *not* be too close to one another or very similar to one another by virtue of the fact that they share the same location or position in space or time. If there is substantial interaction among those in the same cluster, or if those within a cluster are markedly more similar to one another than are those from different clusters, responses within a cluster

would be redundant. Estimates of population variance would be erroneous and statistical inference would be illegitimate. The clusters should also be small enough so that many "areas" are surveyed. If only 3 clusters of 100 respondents each were specified, the design would be faulty and the data likely to be biased. If 30 clusters of 10 households each were specified, there is much less chance that most or all would be atypical of the entire region than if 3 clusters of 100 were used.

GUIDELIST 3-7

For Specifying a Cluster Sample

1. Determine the degree to which those within one area are likely to be similar to one another or to interact.

2. Decide on the number of units to be "skipped" between individual units, based on similarity and interaction.

3. Consider the degree of variance that is likely to exist from one area to another.

4. Specify a minimum number of clusters that would still be large enough to "sample" the entire region adequately.

5. Divide the total sample size by the minimum number of clusters to obtain the number to be within each cluster.

6. Select the first or "key" unit in each cluster on a random basis.

7. Determine the procedure for moving from the key unit to others within the cluster, maintaining random selection.

Quota Sampling

There are often situations where a stratified sample would be most desirable, but the sample frame does not indicate the strata membership of the sampling units. If the data can be collected with interviews, a quota sample may be the best solution to this problem. When a quota sample is employed, it is advisable to use a random sampling technique and to specify a stratified sample, as described above. The major factor that distinguishes a quota sample from those without quotas is the necessity for "qualification" of respondents. When the sample frame does not indicate strata membership, the interviewers do not know the stratum or group to which any one potential respondent belongs. Thus, interviewers are assigned a "quota" of a

given number of people from each strata. The interviewers then contact the potential respondent and before beginning the inquiry itself,
they first determine the stratum to which the person or unit belongs.
If the interviewer needs a respondent for the stratum to which the
person belongs, based on their remaining quota, they would then
continue with the interview and collect the data in the usual fashion.
If they do not need a respondent for that particular stratum, they
politely terminate the interview with an explanation to the person, then continue to contact the potential respondents until they
identify one belonging to one of the strata that still requires another
respondent.

Interviewers can identify the strata membership of respondents in
one of two ways: they may be able to identify membership when they
see or hear the respondent, or they may ask one or two questions to
ascertain the group to which they belong by their response. For example, when the quota is based on sex, both telephone and personal
interviewers need only see the person or hear their voice. With such
stratification variables as age, employment status, occupation, and
the like, interviewers will probably need to ask the potential respondents about their status before they are accepted as qualified.
Quota sampling can also be based on observation or questioning
about some incidence of behavior. For example, a survey design might

---

GUIDELIST 3–8

For Designing a Quota Sample

1. Select the variable(s) or characteristic(s) on which to base or define the quotas, just as with stratification.

2. Use combinations of variables to define quotas carefully and be sure it is economical to locate such respondents.

3. Estimate the variance that is likely to exist among individuals within each quota category and the variation to be expected between quota categories.

4. Decide on the level of confidence required for each quota category based on the information requirements.

5. Specify the sample size for each quota category to provide the desired confidence level for each.

6. Provide instructions for interviewers to qualify respondents by strata membership and assign individual or group quotas to interviewers.

---

require interviewing only those who make a purchase over a certain value or only those who regularly buy and use a particular product. The strata and quota specifications might be based on virtually anything that can be observed by the interviewer or ascertained quickly with a few questions.

Economy is the principal advantage of quota sampling designs. This technique can often be nearly as economical as stratified sampling where the sample frame indicates strata membership. On the other hand, if the sample is not designed properly, quota sampling can become exceedingly expensive. This is because it may require an extremely large number of contacts in order to identify those in the most obscure strata. For example, telephone interviewers may have to call virtually millions of people before finding "a black, Protestant woman over 70 who drinks more than a pint of sour mash whisky a day." Such an example may sound bizarre, but such strange combinations can arise by combining quotas on race, religion, age, and consumption habits. Combined quota variables must be used with care.

Special Sampling Designs

There are many very acceptable variations of the sampling designs discussed above. Such special sampling procedures are designed to cope with problems or achieve special objectives. Researchers are encouraged to handle such unusual problems by combining some of the techniques or devising new ones that will be effective. There are no hard and fast rules, so long as the sample is random and sufficiently free from sampling error and bias.

Some examples of special sampling designs may suggest solutions to particular problems or provoke ideas about coping with unique situations. One such technique consists of random sampling over time. Suppose a supermarket is going to survey shoppers who visit the store during a certain period. One design might be to obtain a set number of interviews each hour the store is open throughout the week. Such a design would not be effective unless an equal number of shoppers visit the store each hour and day. That is certainly not the case for supermarkets, since fewer people shop early in the day than later, and more customers will visit the store during the weekend period than earlier in the week. To cope with these differences in traffic patterns, the sample designer might first estimate the approximate total number of shoppers during the week. All such shoppers would constitute the "population" for the survey. For an nth name sample over time, the sample size would be divided into the total number of shoppers to determine the value of n. Then, each nth shopper to visit the store would be interviewed. With such a proce-

dure, heavy and light traffic times would be proportionately represented in the sample.

Clustering over time might be an additional refinement to the design exemplified above. While there are no travel costs for interviewers to move from one respondent to another, the design would require interviewers to be present for a very long period of time to cover the entire week. To reduce such time requirements and the costs associated with waiting, the researcher might divide the store's work day into short periods of time, such as an hour or so. The "time clusters" in which shoppers are to be interviewed could then be selected at random and a larger proportion of shoppers could be interviewed during those hours. No interviews would be conducted during the other hours and interviewing time and costs would be reduced.

Another example of a special design and data collection technique might be the case where a telephone survey that is especially sensitive to exclusion of unlisted numbers is to be conducted. In such a case, the telephone directory would not make an adequate sample frame, and other listings of the population, including telephone numbers, might not be available. In such a case, the researcher might revert to random digit dialing of respondents. The three-digit telephone number prefixes for the area would first be ascertained and the number of residential units within each determined or estimated. The sample size would be *proportionally* divided among the prefixes. A large number of four-digit, random numbers might then be generated and interviewers or calling machines would first dial the prefix, then the random number. If an unused number, a commercial business, or a nonqualified respondent were reached, the call would be properly terminated and the next number dialed until the appropriate number of responses were obtained for each prefix.

Special designs can be created for mail surveys, as well as for interview surveys, when they are required. Assume that a mail survey of those residing within some geographic area is to be conducted, but no mailing list with names and addresses can be obtained. The designer of the survey might use typical clustering design described earlier, and select a sufficient number of clusters defined by zip code area. The surveys might then be mailed to "occupant" or "resident" at each address occurring within the zip code area, rather than to individual residents by name. Such a mailing would result in a very high percentage of non-response, but that might be tolerable in some cases.

With selecting or creating special sample designs, the researcher should continually seek the answer to two questions: Will the design being considered violate random selection and produce bias? Will it

seriously distort the inferences and estimates of variance among the population? If either is likely to result, the design should be abandoned in favor of another or modified until these two prime requisites are met.

GUIDELIST 3-9

For Devising Special Sampling Designs

1. Inspect the conventional designs to determine if any might be modified or extended for the special case.
2. Attempt to combine designs, such as clustering and stratification, to meet special needs.
3. Remember that random sampling can be done over time, entities, or occurrences, as well as over sample units.
4. Be certain that any special sampling design does not violate random selection or distort variance estimates.

SAMPLE SIZE DETERMINATION

The sample size depends on the budget and degree of confidence required. For any survey task and population, the researcher can "buy" higher reliability, lower sampling error, and more confidence. Ordinarily, though, there is some minimum sample size below which the data are useless.

Confidence Level.   Surveys ordinarily include several items or variables, and occasionally they may have as many as a few hundred. Despite this multiplicity of variables, the specification of information requirements and assignment of priority will ordinarily identify only a few *key* variables that are the most important and constitute the major reason for the survey. The researcher must obtain a sense of the level of confidence desired for these key variables. This can be assessed by asking a series of "what if" questions about various levels of confidence and error. For example, the sponsor might be asked, "What if the average value for this item is off by 1 percent?" Usually the answer will be that it would make no real difference; that it would not matter. The next question might be, "What if it were off by 5 percent?" The researcher should soon discover both the consequences of basing decisions on estimates that are somewhat inaccurate for the

population, and also the "critical point," below which the error would not be important, and above which it would have very negative consequences. These estimates of the desired confidence level will serve as target values during sample size determination.

Variance in the Population.   The more the respondents are likely to differ on the key items of the survey, the larger the sample must be in order to reach a given level of confidence. If all responses are almost identical, fewer respondents need be surveyed. If responses vary widely among respondents, there will be a greater chance of selecting people who are not typical and a larger sample will be needed. The researcher must make an estimate of the amount of variance that is likely to exist in the population for the key survey variables. These estimates might be based on the previous experience of the researcher or sponsor. Casual observation of the population may provide some indications. Data from previous surveys or from other secondary data may be available. If there is no indication whatsoever of the population variance for some key items, a simple pilot survey on only those items for a fairly small number of respondents from the population may be necessary to obtain an estimate.

After identifying the key variables, assessing the tolerable error for each and making an estimate of the amount of variance among those in the population for each one, the next step is to combine this information. This process will require some judgment and perhaps just plain guesswork. The objective is to identify one, or at most, two or three items that will require the *largest* sample size in order to provide adequate confidence. If there is one item for which there is *both* a very high need for confidence *and* a high level of variance in the population, that is obviously the determining variable for selecting the sample size. Any sample large enough to meet the confidence requirements for that item will be sufficiently large for all the others. If the key items requiring the most confidence are likely to have the least variance in the population, and vice versa, the items must be considered as a group or the researcher must make a "judgment call" and pick one or two as a guide.

The Outside Limits.   Before determining the actual sample size to be used, the researcher should be aware of the maximum and minimum practical sample sizes that apply to virtually all surveys. Ordinarily, a sample of less than about 30 respondents will provide too little certainty to be practical, and usually experienced researchers regard 100 or so respondents as the minimum sample size when the population is large. The exception would be the case where the survey

contained only a few items, and there is likely to be very little variance in the population. The reason survey samples seldom contain fewer than a couple of hundred respondents is related to the cost structure for survey research. Part of the cost is "fixed" and will be incurred regardless of sample size. Information requirements must be determined, survey topics identified, a data collection method selected, questions written and scales chosen, a questionnaire composed, and so forth, no matter how many or how few units are surveyed. Thus, the additional or "marginal" cost of including at least 100 or so more respondents is often very small, compared to the fixed costs that will automatically result.

The maximum *practical* size for a sample is about 1,000 respondents, under ordinary conditions. Contrary to popular belief, the maximum practical size of a sample has *absolutely nothing* to do with the size of the population, provided that it is many times greater than the sample. This fact may be difficult for a novice to accept, but it is statistically sound and virtually indisputable. A simple analogy can be used to make this fact intuitively understandable. Suppose you are warming a bowl of soup for yourself and you want to know if it is hot enough. You would probably *sample* it by stirring the soup, then trying a spoonful. The sample size would then be *one spoonful*. Now assume that you are to warm a hundred gallons of soup for a large crowd, and you want to test it to see if it is hot enough to serve. You would probably stir it and take a sample of *one spoonful*, even though the "population" of soup was hundreds of times larger than when only one serving was sampled. Thus, the size of the population does not determine the size of the sample that is required.

It is seldom necessary to sample more than 10 percent of the population to obtain adequate confidence, providing that the resulting sample is less than about 1,000 and larger than the minimums noted earlier. Thus, for a population of 1,000 units, the experienced researcher would probably consider a sample size of about 100 or so. For a population of 5,000 units, the minimum practical sample would be 100 or so, and the maximum would be approximately 500, or 10 percent. For populations of 10,000 or more, most experienced researchers would probably consider a sample size between about 200 and 1,000 respondents.

Maintaining the Size of Subsamples.   Some survey samples may be divided into subsamples and analyzed separately. When that is the case, the size of each subsample must be determined separately as well. In the vast majority of cases, the entire sample will be used for analysis and interpretation, to estimate the values and distributions in

the population. Ordinarily, though, most survey data is "implicitly" divided into what might be called subsamples during analysis. Thus, it is necessary for the researcher to anticipate the types of analysis that will be used and the size and number of the implicit subsamples that might be created.

The two most common techniques used for data analysis that implicitly create subsamples are cross-tabulation and breakdowns of averages. For example, respondent age might be broken down to show the average for men and for women, or the sex of the respondents might be cross-tabulated with their response to a yes/no question. In the first case, two subsamples would be created: males and females. In the second, four implicit subsamples would result: men responding positively, men responding negatively, women responding positively, and women responding negatively.

The reliability and confidence that results from these types of analyses depend in part on the size of the implicit subsamples. The size of the subsamples depends, in turn, on both the nature of the variables or items used for cross-tabulation or breakdowns, and also on the distributions of response obtained from the survey. Items with only two alternatives or "levels" create fewer and larger subsamples than those with many response options or levels. Thus, the size of subsamples or cells within the analysis is of less concern when there are fewer categories for the item, providing that respondents are about equally divided among the levels or subsamples. This is certainly not the usual case. For example, on a simple, dichotomous, yes/no question, only 10 percent or less may fall in one category. That would create a very small subsample. This problem is confounded even further by the fact that cross-tabulation creates individual "cells" which may become even smaller. For example, suppose the item cited above was to be cross-tabulated with another, similar variable. Assume that it also has a distribution of 10/90 as well. If there were no relationship between the two items, only 10 percent of 10 percent, or 1 percent of respondents would reside in the smallest cell of the cross-tabulation.

Certainly the researcher designing a sample and determining the appropriate size cannot fully anticipate all of the breakdowns and cross-tabulations that will be used for analysis, nor can the researcher predict accurately the distributions of response that will result for items with response categories. On the other hand, the researcher must be aware of the implicit creation of subsamples. In addition, those designing a sample must anticipate the potential for subsamples inherent in the survey task. If the analysis is likely to generate many, small subsamples, the total sample size must be relatively large to insure adequate numbers within them.

Judgment and Determination. Most surveys do not clearly call for a particular sample size. Thus, the researcher must use study and judgment of the conditions listed in Figure 3–2. If most or all of the factors indicating a large sample size are present, the researcher would choose a sample size very near the maximum practical limit for the population, as noted earlier. By contrast, if most or all of the conditions indicating a small sample size applied to the survey, the sample size selected would appropriately be very near the minimum

---

FIGURE 3–2

Factors Determining Sample Size

Factors Indicating a Large Sample

1. The decisions to be based on the survey data have very serious or costly consequences.
2. The sponsors demand a very high level of confidence in the data and estimates.
3. There is likely to be a high level of variance among the units in the population to be sampled.
4. The sample is to be divided into relatively small subsamples during analysis and interpretation.
5. Project costs and timing vary only slightly with increases in the size of the sample.
6. Time and resources are readily available to cover the costs of data collection.

Factors Indicating a Small Sample

1. There are few if any major decisions or commitments to be based on the survey data.
2. The sponsors require only rough estimates concerning the parameters of the population.
3. The population to be sampled is very homogenous, with little variance among units.
4. The analysis and interpretation will be based on the entire sample or only a few, large subsamples.
5. A large proportion of total project costs are for data collection or costs increase dramatically with sample size.
6. Budget constraints and/or time requirements limit the volume of data that can be collected.

---

limit noted above for the particular population to be sampled. When there are factors that indicate a large sample but others indicating a small one, the actual sample size must be in the mid-range between the maximum and minimum values suggested. It may be advisable for the researcher to consider each of the factors listed, to determine the importance of each for the particular survey task at hand. Obviously, the most salient and important factors for the project would be the determining ones and would be weighed most heavily in the decision.

Pilot Surveys and Sequential Sampling

In order to make the necessary decisions concerning the appropriate sample size for a survey, the researcher must somehow anticipate at least two types of results before hand: Variance in the population for the key variables to be measured, and distributions of response for items that will form implicit subsamples during analysis. There may be cases when it is virtually impossible to anticipate one or both of these two types of results. If so, the researcher has two options, either of which might provide the data necessary to the decision. One option would be to conduct an informal pilot survey to obtain responses to only the key variables. These results would be tabulated to reveal the degree of variance and confidence intervals that might be expected from the actual survey, as well as the percentage distributions of response to categorical items. The advantages of a pilot survey are simplicity, speed, and economy. Only a small number of respondents and a few questions are required. The pilot survey need not even use the same data collection method as that for the main survey, and such pilot surveys can often be completed easily, quickly and inexpensively.

Another alternative open to the researcher in doubt about the most appropriate sample size is known as "sequential sampling." With this technique, the researcher proceeds with the project just as though a sample size had been determined. Any quotas are expressed as percentages, rather than numbers of respondents. The necessary analysis routines are obtained or created in advance, and the survey initiated without precise determination of when termination should occur. As the data are obtained, they are submitted to analysis, the confidence intervals around estimates computed, and the size of the implicit subsamples recorded. By observing the decrement in the confidence intervals and/or the increases in subsample sizes as data are added to the file, the researcher may be able to predict quite accurately the point at which the values will be adequate. If so, that number of respondents would be determined as the limit at which data collection would be terminated. If prediction is not feasible, the

data collection would continue until the results were satisfactory, then terminated at that point.

The disadvantage of sequential sampling, compared to a pilot survey, is that this method takes more time, effort, and resources. It is more cumbersome and complex, and requires analysis routines to be available during data collection. Nor does it permit testing of other survey decisions, such as the questions wording or scaling techniques, while these can be tested in a pilot survey. The major advantage of sequential sampling is its precision and accuracy. As the cliche says, "What you see is what you get!" Extra data obtained after adequate certainty or subsample size have been reached will enhance the values, but they cannot be less than what is required.

SCIENCE AND ART OF SAMPLING

The researcher should be advised that there are statistical formulas for the computation of a specific sample size to yield a given level of confidence for a single variable. Unfortunately, they are of little value, even to experienced, practicing researchers, for several reasons. The computations require fairly accurate estimates of population variance, and that is seldom known in advance. In addition, most surveys include dozens or even hundreds of items or variables, and it would be virtually impossible to complete the calculations for each. If such computations were performed for each item and the largest required sample size were used for the survey, the sample would very likely be much larger than that required for all but a few survey items. Lastly, sponsors usually know and can verbally express the degree of confidence in the data and estimates that they desire, but rarely if ever will they be able to express these requirements numerically, in terms of confidence intervals.

While there are some scientific principles and procedures associated with sampling, the design of a sample and the selection of a sample size remain largely an art. The researchers designing survey samples should follow the guidelines and apply the recommendations, but ultimately they must be somewhat creative and willing to trust their own judgment.

SUMMARY

Sampling Design and Determination of Size

A. Strive for reliability and validity. Check each decision to deter-

mine if it will increase sampling error or introduce a systematic bias into the data.

B. Depend upon random sampling. The greater the deviation from random selection, the less legitimate and accurate the statistical analysis and reports will be.

C. Identify components quite precisely. The population, sample units, and sample frame must be described with clarity and precision.

D. Identify sources of bias. Be aware of the major sources of bias, but constantly inspect the design to be sure additional sources of bias are not introduced.

E. Evaluate design refinements. Use stratification, clustering, quota sampling, and special designs to increase reliability and decrease costs.

F. Determine sample size carefully. Consider confidence required, population variance, analysis techniques, and the resources available for the project.

G. Use trial when necessary. A pilot survey or sequential sampling will indicate the appropriate sample size if it cannot be determined in advance.

H. Be creative and confident. Sampling design and size determination is more of an art than a science!

PART TWO
SURVEY INSTRUMENTATION

4

Question Composition

THE CORE OF THE SURVEY

The questions that are asked of respondents are the ultimate core of the survey project. The entire effort is directed toward inquiry, and the questions, themselves, are the elements that perform the actual interrogation. The reliability and validity of survey results depend on the way that every aspect of the survey is planned and executed, but the questions that are addressed to the respondents are the most essential component. Their performance ordinarily has a more profound effect on the survey results than has any other single element of the survey. Thus, it is vitally important that this fundamental task of composing the questions be done carefully and properly.

This and the following two chapters form a trio because they are all devoted to the broad topic of asking questions and obtaining answers. The more general principles and practices regarding question composition will be discussed first in this chapter, because they apply to virtually all types of questions that might be asked in a survey questionnaire. The most common mistakes and threats to reliability and validity are identified and recommendations for avoiding them are provided here. Several more technical aspects of writing questions are also discussed here, and a wide variety of examples are presented. The scaling techniques that are used in conjunction with many survey questions are presented and discussed in the following chapter. Chapter 6 contains guidelines for construction of the survey instrument, including question sequence, the questionnaire structure and format, and the introduction and instructions to respondents. While studying the material concerning question composition presented here, it may be useful to refer to the following two chapters to see how

the questions relate to the scales and how they fit into the question-naire as a whole.

Basic Attributes of Questions

Effective survey questions have three important attributes: focus, brevity, and simplicity. The questions should focus directly on the issue or topic specified in the statement of information needs. They should be as short or brief as possible while still conveying the meaning. The questions should be expressed as simply and clearly as they can be.

Focus.   Every question on a questionnaire should focus directly on a single, specific issue or topic. This appears to be very obvious, but in practice it is not as easily achieved as it might seem. Example 4–1 shows three sets of questions. The first of each set lacks focus and the second is focused directly on the issue or topic in each case. In the first set, the researcher seeks to measure purchase preference. It would be a mistake to ask which they liked best, because they may *like* a very elegant and expensive brand, but be unwilling to buy it because of its price. In the second example shown, asking when the respondent usually goes to work also lacks the necessary focus. It does not indicate the point from which the respondent "goes" to work, nor does it ask for a time of day. Thus, some respondents might say, "Just as soon as I get to the shop" or respond that "It depends on how much traffic I run into." The third example listed is supposed to determine voting preference for a particular office. The first question of the set is focused on party preference, rather than the individual choice of a candidate. The two things need not necessarily be the same.

EXAMPLE 4–1

The Focus of the Question

Wrong: Which brand do you like the best?

Right: Which of these brands are you most likely to buy?

Wrong: When do you usually go to work?

Right: What time do you ordinarily leave home for work?

Wrong: Are you going to vote Democratic or Republican?

Right: Which candidate will you vote for on election day?

The best way to be sure that a question is focused directly on the issue at hand is to ask as precisely as possible exactly what the sponsor needs to know. Each of the correct examples shown is a direct expression of the information need; they focus directly on one issue.

Brevity.   There are several reasons for keeping survey questions as brief as possible. The longer the questions, the more difficult the response task will be. Short questions are less subject to error on the part of both interviewers and respondents. When questions become too long and cumbersome, respondents are likely to forget the first part of the question by the time they read or hear the last part. Also, long questions are more likely to lack focus and clarity. In Example 4–2, the brief form of each question is more likely to provide reliable data than is the longer form.

EXAMPLE 4–2

The Brevity of the Question

Wrong: Can you tell me how many children you have, whether they are girls or boys, and how old they are?

Right: What is the age and sex of each of your children?

Wrong: If you own one or more automobiles, please list the year and the make of each one, starting with the newest one?

Right: Please list the year and make of each car you own?

Wrong: When was the last time that you went to the doctor for a physical examination on your own or because you had to?

Right: How many months ago was your last physical examination?

If a person is asked the brief form of the first question, the respondent might reply, "I have a nine year old boy and a four year old girl." The interviewer would know the age of the boy and that of the girl. If the longer version of the first example were used and the respondent could remember everything that was asked, the response might be, "I have two children. A boy and a girl. They are four and nine years old." The interviewer might either assume the boy was four and the girl nine, or else the field worker would have to ask which child was which age. In the second set of questions, there is no need for the respondent to put the cars in sequence because that can

be done by the analyst later. The item does not have to be conditioned on car ownership because those who have no car will leave it blank. For the last pair, the brief form is more straightforward and the longer form would receive answers in weeks, months, years, or by date.

Clarity. The meaning of the question must be completely clear to all respondents. Clarity demands that virtually everyone interprets the question in exactly the same way. In Example 4–3, the correct version of the question in each pair has only one interpretation while the incorrect version has two or more.

EXAMPLE 4–3

The Clarity of the Question

Wrong: What do you have to say about the charities that your church contributes to?

Right: How much influence do you, yourself have on which charities your church contributes to?

Wrong: About how much of the storage space in your home do you and your spouse use?

Right: What proportion of the storage space in your home is used for your things and what is used for your spouse's?

Wrong: Ordinarily, do you take aspirin when you feel some discomfort or when you feel actual pain?

Right: Do you usually take aspirin as soon as you feel some discomfort, or only when you feel actual pain?

In the first incorrect example shown, the phrase, "What do you have to say . . ." can be interpreted in different ways. The phrase might be perceived as asking, "What do you have to say (to me, right now,) . . ." If that were the case, the respondent is likely to indicate how much he or she agreed with the selection of charities, rather than indicating his or her own degree of influence.

In the second example, the researcher intends to measure the proportion of storage space used by each head of household. The correct version of the question makes that clear, but the incorrect version does not. There is nothing in the wording to indicate that the proportion of each person's space should be indicated, and the respondents

are likely to assume the question concerns the use of storage space by both spouses, combined. Thus, they are likely to respond with such a statement as, "We use all of the storage space we have!"

The third example is supposed to present a dichotomy. It assumes that the respondent does use aspirin, and that the individual *either* takes aspirin at the first sign of discomfort *or else* waits until there is the perception of actual pain. The dichotomy is lost in the unclear version of the question, and respondents might simply respond with, "Yes, I do." The researcher would not learn at which point the aspirin were consumed, and such data would be useless.

When constructing questions, the researcher must ask again and again: Does this question *focus* precisely on the issue? Is this as *brief* as the question can be stated? Is it completely *clear* what is being asked? If the researcher returns several times to questions that were written earlier, he or she will ordinarily detect some defects and find several questions that can be improved. It is also advisable to have one or more other people check each question for focus, brevity, and clarity. Checking one's own work is difficult because the writer knows what is intended, but others can only approach the questions strictly on their content and wording.

CHECKLIST 4-1

To Construct Effective Questions

1. Does the question focus directly on the issue or topic to be measured? If not, rewrite the item to deal with the issue as directly as possible.

2. Is the question stated as briefly as it can be? If the item is more than a few words, it may be too long and should be restated more briefly.

3. Is the question expressed as clearly and simply as it can be? If the meaning will not be clear to virtually every respondent, the item should be reformed.

Expressing the Questions

Survey questions are, of course, expressed in words. To obtain meaningful answers, questions must be expressed with the appropriate words. In addition, the words must be combined and arranged in a way that is appropriate to the respondents. Thus, both vocabulary and grammar are important when forming survey questions.

Vocabulary. If the words used in a question are not in the vocabulary of some respondents, they will not understand what is being asked. This will introduce error or bias in the data. For any individual, there are three levels of vocabulary. Respondents have a *core* vocabulary of words with which they are very familiar. These are words they use in common speech. They also have a wider vocabulary of words that they recognize when they hear or read them. They seldom, if ever use such words in common speech, but they have a fairly good understanding of what they mean. Then, of course, there are many other words in the language that the individual does not recognize or understand. Such words have little or no meaning to the person.

The researcher should use words that are in the *core* vocabulary of virtually *all* respondents. The reason can be explained very logically. *Comprehension of very pedestrian vocabulary is universal, while that of sophisticated vocabulary tends to be peculiar to the elite.* The reader may well understand the last sentence, but most respondents from the general public would not! Nor would anyone use such a sentence in common speech. The sentence should have been expressed this way: *Everybody understands common words, but only very well educated people understand words that are seldom used in speech.* The conclusion is obvious. If common words from the core vocabulary of the least sophisticated respondents are used in the questions, everyone will understand. If bigger words or words that are seldom used in speech are used in the questions, many will not know what they mean or what is being asked. The researcher has everything to gain by using simple, core vocabulary and avoiding difficult wording, as shown in Example 4–4.

EXAMPLE 4–4

The Use of Core Vocabulary

Wrong: Are you cognizant of all the concepts to be elucidated?

Right: Do you know about all the ideas that will be explained?

Wrong: With what frequency have you experienced this of late?

Right: How many times have you had this happen recently?

Wrong: What emotions were evoked by perceiving the spectacle?

Right: What kinds of feelings did you have when you saw it all?

Sometimes people who write survey questions unconsciously want to appear well-educated or sophisticated, so they use fancy words and complex sentences. Also, many people were taught as students to use a special vocabulary or sentence structure for writing; one different from their speech. In either case, there is a temptation to use a vocabulary that is beyond the core vocabulary of many respondents. The researcher should keep firmly in mind that the ultimate measure of sophistication in survey research is to generate data that is reliable and valid, data that is free from error and bias. That can best be done by using simple, core vocabulary.

Grammar.   When writing survey questions, arranging the sentences in the right way is just as important as using the right vocabulary. There are four basic kinds of sentence structure: simple, compound, complex, and compound-complex. Simple sentences have a subject and predicate, and sometimes an object or complement. Compound sentences are just two simple sentences linked together by a conjunction. Complex sentences are simple sentences with a dependent clause taking the place of a word, and compound-complex sentences are a combination of the two. The most effective questions are simple sentences. When a simple sentence cannot be used, a complex sentence may be required. Compound sentences and compound-complex sentences should be broken down into simple and complex sentences. Three examples of effective and confusing questions are shown in Example 4–5. The correct phrasing in the first example broke the compound sentence into three simple ones. In the second pair, the correct expression of the question uses different wording to avoid the compound-complex sentence structure. The third, correct example eliminated several superfluous words.

EXAMPLE 4–5

The Use of Compound Sentences

Wrong: What would you do when you had only a few things to buy and there were a lot of people in the checkout line?

Right: Suppose you have only a few things to buy. There are a lot of people in the checkout line. What would you do?

Wrong: How do you work it out when you want one thing and your spouse wants another and you both feel very strongly about it?

Right: How do you settle disagreements with your spouse when you both have strong feelings about it?

EXAMPLE 4–5 (concluded)

Wrong: If you didn't have a reservation ahead of time and you found out that the only seats that you could get were at the very top of the upper balcony, what would you do?

Right: What would you do if the only seats available at show time were at the top of the upper balcony?

GUIDELIST 4–1

For Expressing Questions Correctly

1. Use only *core* vocabulary; the words and phrases that one would use in casual speech.

2. Limit the vocabulary so that the least sophisticated respondent would be familiar with the words.

3. Use simple sentences where possible, and complex sentences only when they are actually required.

4. Use two or more short, simple sentences rather than one compound or compound-complex sentence.

5. Change long, dependent clauses in sentences to words or short phrases where possible.

INSTRUMENTATION BIAS AND ERROR

The manner in which questions are expressed can all too often introduce systematic bias, random error, or both. Even questions expressed with focus, brevity and clarity may jeopardize reliability and/or validity. Use of the proper vocabulary and grammar does not guarantee that they will be free from bias or error. Consequently, several specific types or forms of instrumentation bias and error and the means of avoiding them must be noted.

Unstated Criteria.   If the criteria by which respondents must judge some issue or respond to some question are not completely obvious, the criteria must be stated in the question. If an item might be judged by multiple standards and the criteria are not explicitly stated, some respondents will use one set of criteria and others will use another.

In Example 4–6, there is no clear indication of the criterion in the incorrect question. Thus, some people may respond based on their own needs and others may consider what the stores need to do to win customers in general. The correct question clearly indicates the criterion to be the personal preferences of the respondent only.

EXAMPLE 4–6

The Use of Unstated Criteria

Wrong: How important is it for stores to carry a large number of different brands of this product?

Right: How important is it *to you* that the store you shop at carries a large number of different brands?

Inapplicable Questions. The questions must be applicable to all respondents in the sense that they can reply, based on their own experience or condition. In Example 4–7, those who walk to work, ride a bike or motor cycle, take a bus or cab, would often indicate that parking was no problem to them. The researcher in this case wants to include only those people who drive to work. Thus, to include those who do not drive would provide biased results. The data obtained from the incorrect question would indicate a less severe problem or need than actually existed among those who drive.

EXAMPLE 4–7

The Use of an Inapplicable Question

Wrong: How long does it take you to find a parking place *after* you arrive at the plant?

Right: *If you drive to work,* how long does it take you to find a parking place *after* you arrive at the plant?

Example Containment. When the question contains an example that consists of a response alternative or identifies a class or type of response alternative, it is likely to interject a bias. Because the exam-

ple brings that particular response or type of response to mind, many may choose or include it but fail to include others. In Example 4–8, the incorrect question would lead many to identify toasters, mixers, or blenders. At the same time, they are likely to exclude such appliances as vacuum cleaners, power tools, or hair dryers. It is important to identify the entire class of alternatives and avoid examples that are among the possible choices for the respondents.

EXAMPLE 4–8

The Use of Examples in Questions

Wrong: What small appliances, such as counter-top appliances, have you purchased in the past month?

Right: Aside from major appliances, what other smaller appliances have you bought in the past month?

Overdemanding Recall. The researcher must not assume that respondents will recall their behavior or feelings over an extended period of time. Often the topics or issues of the survey are very important to those conducting the project, and so the researcher assumes that they are equally as important and memorable to respondents. That is seldom ever the case.

The first question in Example 4–9 assumes that respondents would remember the actual number of times they had gone out with their spouse, prior to their marriage. Very few would recall that. Yet, many would not want to admit that they did not remember, so most respondents would probably estimate the number. Thus, there would be a large amount of error in the data. By contrast, most married

---

EXAMPLE 4–9

The Use of Overdemanding Recall

Wrong: How many times did you go out on a date with your spouse before you were married?

Right: How many months were you "dating" your spouse before you were married?

---

respondents are likely to have good recollection of both the day when they had met their spouse and the date of their marriage. These are fairly important anniversaries for most married couples. Thus, virtually all could report the number of months they were "dating" prior to their marriage.

Overgeneralizations. There are times when it may be appropriate and acceptable to ask respondents for generalizations. When a survey question seeks a generalization, it should represent a policy, strategy, or habitual pattern of the respondents, rather than specific behavior. Whenever specific incidents can be identified, the survey question should be specific. In Example 4–10, the incorrect item asks the respondents to generalize about their behavior. The question is much too general, as well. It does not state whether the respondent is to use the immediate past as a frame of reference, go back well into the distant past, or indicate expectations for the future. By contrast, the proper wording of the item includes the past 10 incidents of the action. They would ordinarily be easily recalled by virtually all respondents, and the data are far more precise and accurate, so error is reduced and reliability improved greatly.

EXAMPLE 4–10

The Use of Overgeneralizations

Wrong: When you buy "fast food," what percentage of the time do you order each of the following types of foods?

Right: Of the last 10 times you bought "fast food," how many times did you eat each type of food?

Overspecificity.   A survey question is overly specific when it asks for an actual or precise response that the respondent is unlikely to know or unable to express. In Example 4–11, virtually all respondents will be able to indicate their *policy* concerning the action in broad terms. Few respondents could report an exact number of times they had behaved in that way. In addition, the incorrect example would be of little value in many cases, because there is no *base* number of opportunities. Two people might both report they read 30 such explanations. One may have visited only 30 exhibits, and read the plaque on each, while the other may have visited 300 and only read 1 in 10. They would appear from the data to be identical, yet their policies

---

EXAMPLE 4-11

The Use of Overspecificity

Wrong: When you visited the museum, how many times did you read the plaques that explain what the exhibit contains?

Right: When you visited the museum, how often did you read the plaques that explain what the exhibit contained? Would you say always, often, sometimes, rarely, or never?

---

toward this issue would be very different, indeed. If the information needs were concerned with the policies, the data would lack validity.

Overemphasis. If the wording of a question is overemphatic, it is likely to introduce bias by calling for a particular type of response. When it is necessary to describe some condition in the question, it is advisable to use words that lean toward understating, rather than overstating the condition. Respondents are then free to reach their own conclusions about the degree of severity. If the condition is described in overemphatic terms, a judgment or conclusion is imposed on the respondents. Such words as "catastrophe" or "tragedy" suggest that a potent remedy is required, while words such as "predicament" or "mishap" do not. An example of such a case is presented in Example 4-12.

EXAMPLE 4-12

The Use of Overemphasis

Wrong: Would you favor increasing taxes to cope with the current fiscal crisis?

Right: Would you favor increasing taxes to cope with the current fiscal problem?

The correct and incorrect examples are identical except for the last word in each: crisis versus problem. The use of the word "crisis" implies a conclusion on the part of the researcher. In addition, it is always desirable to avoid or to end a *crisis* as quickly and completely as possible. On the other hand, a *problem* is not necessarily something that requires immediate or dramatic action. Each question must be examined carefully to avoid wording that overemphasizes or overstates the condition. Words that are overly dramatic or constitute a conclusion must be avoided.

Ambiguity of Wording. There are many words and phrases that designate different things for different people. Often those who write questions are totally unaware of the fact that others may have a completely different understanding of the term. In Example 4–13, the researcher is referring to the evening meal. Those from the eastern or western areas of the country eat breakfast, lunch, and *dinner*. In many areas of the midwest, people eat breakfast, *dinner*, and supper. A researcher native to New York or Los Angeles might be shocked and surprised by the results, if the incorrect example were used in a national survey. To avoid such ambiguity, virtually every questionable word or phrase must be checked carefully to be sure that it has a common meaning for everyone in the survey sample.

EXAMPLE 4–13

The Use of Ambiguous Words

Wrong: About what time do you ordinarily eat dinner?

Right: About what time do you ordinarily dine in the evening?

Double-Barreled Questions. When two questions are both contained within one item, the item is known as a double-barreled question. In Example 4–14, the incorrect item actually asks two questions: Do you take vitamins and if so, do you take them to avoid sickness? Those who take vitamins regularly but for some reason other than to

---

EXAMPLE 4–14

The Use of Double-Barreled Questions

Wrong: Do you regularly take vitamins to avoid getting sick?

Right: Do you regularly take vitamins? Why or why not?

---

avoid sickness would be in a quandary as to how to respond. To obtain the required data, the researcher should first ask if the respondents take the action. A second question might be expressed as in the correct example, or it might be *conditioned* on an affirmative response to the first item. In other words, it might be stated: "If so, why do you do so?"

Probably the most common form of the double-barreled question includes both the action and the reason or motive in the same item. This is certainly not the only form of double-barreled question, however. Simply asking about two things at one time also creates a double-barreled item. For example, "Do you often get headaches and stomachaches?" Those who get one but not the other would be puzzled with that item. Consider the question, "Do you and your family often go to the movies?" Singles who enjoy the movies could not answer accurately, nor could respondents who do one thing when their family does another. The key to detecting double-barreled questions is to determine if part of the item might be true and part false.

Leading Questions. When questions lead the respondents to a particular answer, they create a very strong bias and often result in data that are completely invalid. The incorrect question, in Example 4–15, would result in the identification of much greater danger than would the use of the correct form. Respondents are actually being led to identify dangers, while the information requirements seek only to measure the degree to which respondents, themselves, perceive danger.

EXAMPLE 4–15

The Use of Leading Questions

Wrong: Don't you see some danger in the new policy?

Right: Do you see any danger in the new policy?

There are many situations where those conducting the survey are hired by a sponsor. Some sponsors may underwrite the survey in order to "prove" a point or to obtain certain kinds of results that are in their own best interests. Such sponsors may try to insert leading questions or insist on such wording to produce data that are favorable to their position or in their own best interests. Survey data that purport to be "independent and objective" when such leading questions are used are actually fraudulent. This applies as well to other deliberate sources of bias, such as the use of "loaded" questions. Thus, the researcher who would maintain an honest reputation through ethical behavior must not allow the deliberate "rigging" of survey results. When sponsors insist on such unethical practices, the researcher is best advised to resign the sponsor, no matter how attractive the project might otherwise appear to be.

Loaded Questions. While leading questions direct the respondents attention to a specific type of response or suggest an answer, loaded questions are less obvious. The loaded question includes some wording or phrase that constitutes a more subtle form of influence. Often loaded questions take the form where a "reason" for doing something is included in the item. Notice the phrase, ". . . to save human lives," in the incorrect question shown in Example 4–16. Saving lives is, of course, a very desirable goal. The question is phrased in such a way that those who would respond in the negative would appear not to value human life. The correct version of the question in this example is more objective. It deals directly with the issues and avoids weighting one response with the feelings or emotions associated with "life saving" policies.

EXAMPLE 4–16

The Use of Loaded Questions

Wrong: Do you advocate a lower speed limit to save human lives?

Right: Does traffic safety require a lower speed limit?

The most common sources of bias and error resulting from the composition of questions have been identified and described. Some introduce a systematic bias, "skewing" the answers in one particular direction. Others lead to random error because they result in answers that might "go in any direction." Some create both bias and error. The greater the amount of error or bias that is introduced, the lower the reliability and/or validity of the survey results will be. Probably no survey question is completely free of error and bias, but the goal is to approach that as closely as possible.

SOURCES OF RESPONSE BIAS

When the questionnaire instructions, questions, scales or response options introduce bias, it is called "instrumentation bias," and the major forms of such bias were discussed in the preceding section. When bias is introduced because of the mentality or predispositions of respondents, it is called "response bias." Those composing survey questions must consider this type of bias as well, because it can be reduced or controlled in part by the wording and sequence of questions. There are many different sources of response bias and they can be classified in a variety of ways. Ten of the major types are listed and identified in Figure 4–1. Each of them will be discussed briefly below.

FIGURE 4–1

Sources of Response Bias

1. *Social desirability.* Response based on what is perceived as being socially acceptable or respectable.

2. *Acquiescence.* Response based on respondent's perception of what would be desirable to the sponsor.

3. *Yea- and nay-saying.* Response influenced by the global tendency toward positive or negative answers.

4. *Prestige.* Response intended to enhance the image of the respondent in the eyes of the others.

5. *Threat.* Response influenced by anxiety or fear instilled by the nature of the question.

6. *Hostility.* Response arises from feelings of anger or resentment engendered by the response task.

7. *Auspices.* Response dictated by the image or opinion of the sponsor, rather than the actual question.

8. *Mental set.* Cognitions or perceptions based on previous items influence response to later ones.

9. *Order.* The sequence in which a series is listed affects the responses to the items.

10. *Extremity.* Clarity of extremes and ambiguity of midrange options encourage extreme responses.

Social Desirability. When personal preferences, opinions, or behavior deviate from what is socially prescribed, respondents are *very* prone to report what is socially acceptable, rather than their true answers. This is a serious problem, and even the most experienced researchers find it a difficult problem to overcome. Some issues, such as sexual deviation, drug or alcohol abuse, or tax evasion, may require some other form of investigation because survey data would be useless.

The wording and the format of the question may increase or decrease the degree to which it will evoke a socially desirable response, rather than the true answer. For example, if the spouses of working women were asked, "Do you earn more than your wife?" nearly all would respond that they do, because of the social role prescription that the male be the main "breadwinner." The same question can be expressed in a way that is less likely to obtain a socially desirable response: "Are your wife's monthly earnings usually somewhat more, about the same, or somewhat less than your own?" The first version states the social norm and in effect, asks if the respondent conforms. Most will indicate they do. The second version provides all three alternatives without stating the norm, and it "softens" the phrasing by using the words "somewhat" and "about."

CHECKLIST 4–2

To Avoid Instrumentation Bias

1. Does the question state the criterion for answering? If not, the criterion must be clearly indicated.

2. Is the question applicable to all respondents? If not, it must be reworded or some respondents exempted by using a detour around it for those to whom it does not apply.

3. Does the item contain an example that is also a possible answer? If so, change or discard the example.

4. Does the question require respondents to remember too much detail or recall distant events? If so, it must be modified or generalized to make recall easier.

5. Is the question as specific as it can reasonably be? If the item is too general, state it more specifically.

6. Is the item more specific than the way respondents think? If so, it should be expressed in more general terms.

7. Does the question overemphasize some condition? If so, it must be stated in less dramatic terms.

8. Are some of the words in the item ambiguous? If so, reword it using more commonly recognized phrasing.

CHECKLIST 4–2 (concluded)

9. Is the question as free from threat to respondents as possible? If not, change it to reduce the threat.

10. Does the question include only *one* issue? If it is a double-barreled item, it must be split or modified.

11. Will yea-sayers or nay-sayers always choose one answer? If so, revise the item to include both "yes" and "no."

12. Does the question lead respondents toward a particular answer? If so, the leading phrase must be removed.

13. Is the question "loaded" with a reason for responding in a particular way? If so, the reason *must* be deleted.

Acquiescence. People are generally cooperative. The fact that they have agreed to respond to a survey indicates their tendency to cooperate. If they feel that a certain response will be more welcome to the sponsor, researcher, or interviewer, then many will almost automatically provide it. There are two things the researcher can do to reduce such bias: First, assure respondents that candid, honest answers are much more helpful than purely favorable ones. They must understand that cooperation requires honesty, not flattery. Second, provide no indications of which answer is "positive." If questions are worded so that the respondent cannot detect what answer is positive in the eyes of the sponsor, researcher, or interviewer, their tendency to cooperate will not affect their responses.

Yea- and Nay-Saying. Some people have a more or less global tendency to agree or answer positively, and others to disagree or respond negatively. When an entire series of survey items or scales seek responses on a positive/negative dimension, yea-saying or nay-saying may become a source of bias. One method of controlling such bias is to avoid yes/no or positive/negative options. For example, rather than asking the question, "Would you prefer to go?" it might be expressed, "Would you prefer to: (*a*) go to that place, or (*b*) remain where you are." In the second version, there are no positive or negative options. When many questions must be answered on a positive/negative basis, this form of bias can be partially controlled by "reflecting" roughly half of the items. For example, if attitudes toward some issue were to be measured by listing a series of statements and asking about agreement or disagreement, then half the statements might be negative toward the issue and half positive. Thus, yea-saying or nay-saying would, in effect, automatically compensate or "equal out."

Prestige.   Virtually everyone likes to "look good" in their own eyes and in the eyes of others. When respondents inflate their income, shave a few years off their age, or amplify the importance of their job on a survey questionnaire, their desire for prestige becomes a source of bias. If every aspect of the survey shows respect and admiration for people of all walks of life, the likelihood of this type of bias will be reduced. This bias can be reduced further by avoiding questions that invite respondents to seek prestige. Asking, "How would you rate yourself on self-reliance?" would invite a high rating and introduce serious bias. The same information could be obtained by seeking a rating along the continuum from: "Depend entirely on myself" to "Depend mostly on others." Assigning the lower numbers to self-reliance and the higher to dependency would also help to compensate for the remaining bias from the pursuit of prestige.

Threat.   Survey questions can constitute a psychological threat to respondents when they deal with issues and outcomes that have very negative consequences for them. Most people do not like to think about such things as their own death, disease, serious accidents, the loss or separation of a loved one, and the like. When the survey requires information concerning such issues, it is important to avoid the more graphic words and phrases, in favor of euphemisms. It is less threatening to speak of having a "hearing impairment" than to talk about being "partially or totally deaf." Other means of reducing threat bias are either to "depersonalize" the issue either by referring to it in the abstract or by "projection," referring to the experience or condition of some other person. For example, rather than asking what the *respondent* would do if he or she lost their job, it may be necessary either to ask about how people might cope with unemployment (the abstract) or what they might suggest if a friend (another person) were temporarily unemployed.

Hostility.   There are some situations where either the topics or issues included in the survey or the response task, itself, may engender strong hostility or resentment in some respondents. Once these strong feelings have been evoked, they do not tend to be concentrated exclusively on the thing that evoked them, or to dissipate very quickly. In such cases, the respondents who feel hostile may "generalize" these feelings to other questions that follow. They are, in effect, responding more to a previous item than to the ones that follow. One way to avoid this form of bias is to word questions in a manner that is less likely to create feelings of hostility in the first place. When it is not possible to avoid evoking some hostility, or where these negative emotions must be measured by the survey, there are two ways to keep them from contaminating the items that follow. One is to allow the respondents to dissipate these feelings as fully as possible, directly on the issues that created them. If respondents are allowed adequate opportunity to express these feelings, before continuing, they are more likely to "get them out of their system," and then to relax and continue. Another helpful technique is to provide some means of separating one section very distinctly from the next. If respondents clearly understand that the next set of items deals with an issue or topic that is completely separate, they are less likely to carry their hostile feelings over to this new area.

Auspices. When respondents know in advance who is sponsoring the survey, their feelings toward the sponsor may bias their answers to the questions. For example, a survey of employees sponsored by the company may generate very different answers than if it were sponsored by the labor union. To avoid such auspices bias, many surveys are conducted by an independent agency or research team. There is often no necessity to tell respondents in advance who is sponsoring the survey. When information about the sponsoring organization must be obtained or when respondents might easily infer the identity of the sponsor from the questions, such questions should come as late in the questionnaire as possible. Such bias can also be avoided by "clouding" or "smoke-screening" the identity of the sponsor. For example, if the survey focused on the sponsoring company's brand of products, the same questions might also be asked concerning some other brands as well. That way, respondents would not be sure which company was seeking the information and auspices bias would be controlled.

Mental Set. When respondents are asked to perform some mental task, they develop a set of perceptions and assumptions that serves as a frame of reference for responding. Usually, they will maintain that same frame of reference or mental set until they realize it no longer applies. For example, the survey might include two questions: "How many times have you moved in the past five years?" and "How many times have you owned the home in which you lived?" Their frame of reference for the first question would cover only the past five years. When responding to the second question, many would use the same frame of reference, considering only the past five years when they answer, even though the question does not limit the history to that period. If the researcher intended the second question to include the entire residential history of the respondents, rather than only the past five years, the obsolete mental set of the respondents would create a bias. This bias can be avoided or controlled by making it perfectly clear to respondents when they are to shift their frame of reference or make a new set of assumptions in order to respond. That can be done by beginning a new section with new instructions or by stating the new assumptions or frame of reference as a preface to the next question.

Order. The order or sequence in which survey questions or scaled items are listed will often affect the response, even though respondents are to respond to each one in turn. There are three things that might induce order bias in these cases: *initiation, routine,* and *fatigue.* With the first item or so, initiation requires that respondents learn how to handle the response task. "Samples" or items of little importance should be listed first, so that any bias from initiation will not affect the most important items.

When several similar items appear in sequence, the routine nature of responding may lead to a response strategy or policy. If that happens, each item will not be viewed or evaluated independently, as they should be. Bias from routine response can be reduced by varying the list to make individual items distinct and to require separate consideration of each. Rather than composing all items on a list to "ascend" in one direction, the list should be composed so that some items ascend in one direction while others descend in that direction. For example, a list of statements might consist of a random mix, so that some are positive about the issue and others negative. Recognizing this, respondents would then have to read and evaluate each one independently, rather than developing a "policy" of agreeing or disagreeing with all of them.

When respondents must rate or respond to a long list of items, the rote nature of the task may cause fatigue. In short, they get tired of the process. If that happens, they may respond carefully to the earlier items and carelessly to the later ones on the list, causing error, bias, or both. This form of bias can be controlled by keeping any one list or sequence short enough so that even the least motivated respondents will not be affected by fatigue when responding to that section.

When responses are required for each and every item on a list, initiation, routine, and fatigue may cause order bias. Two different kinds of order bias apply when respondents are given a list of alternatives and asked to pick one from the list: *primacy* and *recency* effects. People usually tend to remember the first item or so of any list, simply because they are first. This is called a primacy effect. They also tend to recall the last item or so more readily than others, because they have been presented more recently. Thus, this is called a recency effect. Usually, both apply for any list of substantial length, but not necessarily with equal strength. In any case, the general principle indicates that people are more likely to recall the first and last things that are presented in sequence than they are those which come in between. Consequently, there is a bias toward respondents picking the first or last alternatives from a group, simply because they are more easily remembered.

There are two methods for reducing or controlling order bias from primacy and/or recency effects. One way is to be sure any such lists are fairly short. This is especially important for interview surveys, where respondents are read the list and must keep the whole set of alternatives in mind while they choose one. Ordinarily, only four or five such options can be recalled at one time. When a longer list of alternatives must all be evaluated relative to one another, it is usually advisable to provide a scale and have *each* item rated. Ratings can be compared during analysis and the most preferred can be identified by its highest rating.

CHECKLIST 4-3

To Control Response Bias

1. Is the question subject to any of the 10 sources of response bias listed in Figure 4–1? If so, consider each of the methods for control noted below.

2. Can the question be reworded to reduce or eliminate the bias? Compose a few alternate forms of the question and substitute the version that is least likely to be subject to bias.

3. Might the instructions be changed so that the item is not subject to the bias? Examine and substitute instructions for the question, section, or scale to reduce bias.

4. Does the source of bias arise from the choice or form of a scale? Consider alternative scales from the examples in the previous chapter or modify the scale to reduce bias.

5. Does the structure of the section or questionnaire induce or encourage bias? Try reforming the section or moving it to another location in the questionnaire.

6. Do the presence or nature of preceding or following questions or items make the question subject to bias? Tentatively rearrange the items in the section or move the question to another section to control the bias.

7. Do the modifications in the question or questionnaire to reduce one form of bias make it more subject to another? Check the revised item against the sources of response bias to be sure the changes have not created another problem.

Another method of controlling order bias resulting from primacy and recency effects is to vary the order or sequence of items from one respondent or subsample to the next. This is ordinarily not feasible for mail surveys, because more than one form of questionnaire would be required and that would be costly. It may be more feasible to instruct interviewers to read a list in random order (checking off each as it is read) for each respondent. This method should be used only when such order bias is regarded as a *serious* threat to the validity of the data, because it puts a burden on the interviewers and requires that they be instructed and monitored carefully.

Extremity.   This form of bias is similar, in some respects, to primacy and recency effects. When scales are used, there is sometimes a tendency on the part of respondents to "dichotomize" the scale by picking only the extremes. Thus, if a scale contained numbers from 1 to 10 with the extremes labeled "Extremely good" and "Extremely bad," some people may answer only with a 1 or a 10. In effect, they are refusing to make a more fine-grained discrimination. It is easier to think in terms of black and white than to distinguish between shades of grey. (Ironically, the result is the exact opposite of "fence-riding" or picking a neutral, middle value so that the respondent actually avoids making a choice entirely.)

The careful choice and composition of scales will help to reduce or control extremity bias. Such bias may result because the scales have too many numbers or points. The number of scale points should be about the same as the number of categories in the respondents' mind. For example, when looking at a product, buyers may think in such terms as: terrible, unacceptable, poor, fair, good, and excellent. A scale of five, six, or even seven points would be appropriate, but one with a hundred points is not. It is also important to label the ends of the scale with the *ultimate extremes.* In the example above, if the extremes were labeled "poor" and "good," rather than "terrible" and "excellent," a bias would result because the midrange would cover only products that were viewed as fair.

QUESTION FORMAT

There are two basic formats for survey questions: unstructured and structured. Unstructured questions are sometimes called "open-end" questions because only the question is expressed and no alternative answers are listed for the respondent. Structured survey items do two things: they ask a question and they list the alternative answers the respondent might choose. Experienced researchers prefer to use structured questions whenever they are feasible because they have many important advantages.

The Dimension of Answers. Unstructured questions often do not clearly indicate the dimension along which respondents are supposed to respond. In Example 4–17, an unstructured item is listed in the top section together with seven verbatim answers from different respondents. Notice that some respondents are selecting reasons for visiting *that* particular store, while others are indicating why they visited *today,* rather than another time. The unstructured version of the item does not indicate the range along which respondents should answer, while the structured version clearly indicates it.

EXAMPLE 4–17

Structured versus Unstructured Questions

Unstructured Item

Q. Why did you visit this store?
A1. "I happened to be in the neighborhood."
A2. "I didn't have anything better to do."
A3. "I like the merchandise they have here."
A4. "I have an account at this store."
A5. "I always shop on Wednesday."
A6. "A friend recommended the store."
A7. "It's fun to shop. I enjoy it."

Structured Item

Q. What is the one *major* reason you visited this store?
A1. ____ The price of the goods.
A2. ____ The selection of merchandise.
A3. _X_ The location of the store.
A4. ____ Friendly, helpful staff.
A5. ____ Availability of credit.
A6. ____ Some other reason. Specify what below:

_____

A7. ____ No particular reason, don't know.

In the structured form of the item used in the example, the list of alternatives clearly indicates to respondents that they are to base their answer on the attributes or characteristics of the store. In effect, they know more precisely what is being asked or what information is sought. The researcher with considerable experience probably knows through some unpleasant experiences that respondents seldom answer the way they are expected to respond, if they are free to provide any answer they wish. Even when it appears to the researcher that the dimension along which respondents are to answer is plainly evident, respondents are likely to be in a different frame of mind; and therefore, to respond along some completely different dimension.

Comparability of Data. Unstructured items often produce data that is not directly comparable from one respondent or group to the next. When structured items are used, the data are comparable among respondents. Thus, data processing and analysis can compare and contrast the answers of various individuals or subsamples.

In Example 4–17, there may be as many different verbatim responses as there are respondents in the sample. It would be necessary to "group" answers into categories when editing and postcoding the data, after it was collected. This can be a laborious and time-consuming process. In addition, the editor or analyst must make many judgments about the meaning or intent of the respondents when grouping the responses into categories. On the other hand, when a structured item is used, this process of selecting categories is done in the field, at the time the data was collected. Futhermore, the judgments are made by the respondents, themselves, rather than by another person who must interpret their meaning or intentions.

There may be times when an interviewer may be instructed to read only the question, but not the alternatives, and then select the category to check. Even in such cases, when the selection of the category can be done while the interview is in progress, the field worker can question the respondent further if there is uncertainty. If, on the other hand, the categories are to be selected during editing and postcoding, there is no way to obtain additional information if it is needed.

Recording Accuracy. It is difficult and time-consuming for either the interviewer or the respondent to record verbatim responses to questions. The answers listed in the top section of the example are quite short, but in actual practice, respondents might provide two or three sentences to explain why they visited the store. If the structured version of the same item listed in the bottom of the example were used, the respondent or field worker would only have to check the appropriate category. There is much less likelihood of error in recording.

The Response Task. When a self-administered questionnaire is being used, or when the alternatives are listed for the respondent, the response task is much quicker and easier with structured items. Thus, there is likely to be greater cooperation, a higher response rate, less missing data, and fewer "random" responses when structured items are used.

Inappropriate Reasons. There are several reasons why unstructured survey questions are often used when structured items would be superior. It takes time and effort in the beginning to compose structured questions effectively. It takes only a few minutes to write an unstructured question. There is a tendency for the researcher to hurry the composition task and worry about the editing and coding later, after the data has been collected. Thus, the work is both amplified and procrastinated.

Another reason for the frequent and inappropriate use of unstructured questions comes from the sponsor. Often those who sponsor a survey feel that the use of structured items will limit the "richness and variety" of people's answers. This is, of course, quite true. Such untrained and inexperienced sponsors fail to recognize the enormity of the task of interpretation. Invariably, when presented with several hundreds or thousands of such verbatim responses, they are overwhelmed by the volume and abandon the data by necessity. The researcher has the responsibility to explain the problems associated with verbatim answers and provide assurance that structured items will obtain the required data.

GUIDELIST 4-2

For Using *Unstructured* Questions

1. Structure the question *whenever* it is possible to do so, even though it requires substantial time and effort.

2. Resist requests by sponsors for verbatim response, explaining the difficulty of interpretation.

3. Be sure the dimension or range of alternatives is *crystal* clear to respondents when an item is unstructured.

4. Be sure the interviewers or respondents can record verbatim responses to unstructured items accurately.

5. Estimate the degree to which using an unstructured question will increase the response task.

6. After all is said and done, go back and see if it may not be possible to use a *structured* item, anyhow.

Composing Categorical Items

When a structured question is to be used, it is often necessary to choose the categories or response alternatives to be used by respondents. Such items are called "discrete, categorical" items because all responses must fall into a particular category. (Alternative forms of structured items using conventional categories or numeric scales, are presented in the following chapter.) It takes considerable time and effort to compose a categorical question and select the proper categories. On the other hand, if the task is done carefully and thoroughly, it will save substantial time and effort later and it will also increase the reliability and validity of the data.

Stating the Question. Typically, a categorical item asks a question, followed by a series of alternative answers. When composing the question itself, all of the principles and guidelines discussed earlier apply. In other words, the same things are required of the question itself, when it has structured response categories, as would be needed for an unstructured item. The only important difference between the two is that structured questions receive some "help" when the alternatives are listed for respondents. Aside from that, the task of expressing the question remains the same.

An All-Inclusive List. The categories used form what is sometimes called a "taxonomy" or system of classification. The responses are being "classified" into categories. There are three "rules" or principles to be observed when choosing the categories for an item: (1) the list must be all-inclusive, (2) the categories must be mutually exclusive, and (3) there should be more variance in the meaning *between* categories than within them.

The first rule is that the list must include every possible response. Every answer a respondent might possibly give must fit into a category and there must be no conceivable answer that does not fit into a category.

In Example 4–18, the incorrect classification scheme shown in the top section does not meet the requirement of an all-inclusive set of categories. Suppose some respondents had actually seen the new clinic building. There is no category for recording that means of learning of the clinic. By contrast, the correct version, shown in the lower section of the example, includes an "other" category so that those responses that do not fit into any of the first six categories can be recorded and identified in the seventh. It is very advisable to include such an open, "other" category in such lists. Even though the questions are pretested in a pilot survey, there are likely to be a few

---

EXAMPLE 4–18

Structured Category Questions

Incorrect Classification

Q. How did you *first* learn about the new clinic?

A1. ___ From a friend or co-worker.
A2. ___ From a relative or family member.
A3. ___ From a newspaper or magazine.
A4. ___ From the radio or television. .
A5. ___ From a news story.
A6. ___ By seeing a sign, billboard or poster.
A7. ___ By some other announcement or advertisement.

Correct Classification

Q. How did you *first* learn about the new clinic?

A1. ___ From a relative or family member.
A2. ___ From an associate or acquaintance.
A3. ___ From a newspaper or magazine *advertisement*.
A4. ___ From a radio or television *advertisement*.
A5. ___ *Read* a news story in some publication about it.
A6. ___ *Heard* a news story about it on radio or TV.
A7. ___ Some other way. Specify how below:
_____

---

exceptional or unusual responses that will not fit into any category listed.

When an "other" category is used, the nature of the "other" may or may not be specified, depending on the information requirements. There are times when those seeking information may be interested *only* in a few certain categories, but answers might range widely beyond them. When that is the case, the answers that do not fit into the categories of interest may all be "lumped" into an "other" category without specification of just what the other things are. For some situations, the nature of the "other" responses may be useful or required by those seeking the information. When they are, they should be specified so that they can be identified, categorized, and post-coded when the completed questionnaires are being edited.

A Mutually Exclusive List. There must be a *unique* association between any given answer and one category or alternative. In other words, no response should fit into two or more categories. In Example 4–18, the incorrect version of the item has "overlapping" categories.

Those respondents who first learned of the clinic through a news story could be recorded in that category *and/or* as having gained awareness from newspapers or magazines or from radio or television. The correct version of the item in the lower portion of the example makes a distinction between broadcast and print media, but also makes a distinction between a paid advertising and publicity through news articles. Thus, no answer would fit into more than one category and the requirement for a mutually exclusive list has been met.

Meaningful Clusters.   When answers are recorded in categories, the alternatives used should cluster together responses that are similar to one another. Those answers that are substantially different from one another should fall into separate categories. Lacking such a classification system, the data would not be especially meaningful or at least some value will be lost. In Example 4–18, the categories used in the improper example do not make a distinction between print media publicity and broadcast media publicity. "News stories" consist of one category, and both types would be clustered together, although they might be regarded as having significantly different meaning for the sponsors. Also, the incorrect version makes a distinction between "signs, billboards, and posters," and "some other announcement or advertisement." Such a distinction does not appear to be especially valuable or meaningful.

The incorrect list of alternatives in the example would result in too much variation in meaning in the category for news stories and too little meaningful variation in the last two categories. There are no set rules for forming categories with more variance in meaning between than within them. The task requires a thorough understanding of what distinctions will and will not be meaningful to the sponsors. The choice also depends on what would be meaningful to *respondents*. Thus, the task is something of an art, requiring judgment and perhaps a pilot test.

Size and Number of Categories.   The researcher composing a structured, categorical item must also make a decision about the number of categories to be used and how broad or narrow each should be. The simple, dichotomous question with only two categories is the lower limit on the number of categories. The upper limit is ordinarily about six or eight categories. With more than that, the response and recording task increases greatly and it is seldom necessary or advisable to exceed that limit. The choice of the number of categories between these two extremes depends on how "fine-grained" the sponsor would like the data to be. The general rule should be to have no more categories than are actually required. The reason for minimizing the number of categories lies in statistical processing. When the analysis seeks to measure the relationships between survey items, it is often necessary to cross-tabulate two items or break down one item by the various levels of another. If the categories are quite narrow and there are several of them, some are likely to contain very small numbers of responses. Thus, they may have to be combined with others during analysis to obtain adequate "cell" sizes, defeating the purpose of many, narrow categories.

There is one *very important* precaution when determining the size and number of categories for a discrete, structured item. If there is some doubt in the mind of the researcher composing the item, concerning how precise or fine-grained the data must be, the researcher should elect to use the larger number of more narrow categories. The reason is simple, but compelling: categories can easily be *combined* during processing, if necessary. On the other hand, if they prove to be too broad, so that a large majority of respondents fall into only one or two categories, there is *no way* to disaggregate the broad categories into smaller ones after the data have been collected. In other words, once clustered, the answers must remain so.

GUIDELIST 4–3

For Composing Categorical Items

1. For composing the question itself, the same rules and principles apply to structured, categorical items as to unstructured questions.

2. The categories must be "all-inclusive," so that there is an appropriate category for any conceivable response.

3. If all possible answers cannot be anticipated or when some types are of no interest, exceptional responses should be clustered into an "other" category.

4. The categories must be "mutually exclusive," so that no answer would fit into more than one category.

5. There should be more variance in meaning *between* categories than within them, so that answers are clustered into categories on a meaningful basis.

6. Ordinarily, there should be no more than six or eight categories for any one question.

7. Categories should be broad enough to capture a substantial number of responses, to provide adequate frequencies during processing and statistical analysis.

8. The categories should not be more "fine-grained" than required by the sponsors.

9. When in doubt, choose the more narrow categories because they can always be combined later but they cannot be "split" apart after data collection.

Verbal and Numeric Scaling

The discrete, categorical, structured survey item is but one type of verbal "scale." Several thoroughly tested and commonly used verbal and numeric scales are presented and discussed in the following chapter. They should, of course, be used where appropriate. It is *always* advisable to use an ordinary *numeric* scale when it is feasible to do so. There is sometimes a tendency on the part of less experienced researchers to use categorical items in place of numeric scales. They may feel it will facilitate the analysis or it might be the mistaken notion that respondents would prefer the categorical type. Neither is so, and the question should seek a number, not a category.

In Example 4–19, discrete categories are used in the incorrect example. The categories are inappropriate because the data can readily be obtained in numeric form, as shown in the correct item. In addition, the categories are too broad and the data cannot be disaggregated after data collection. Ordinarily, it is important to distinguish between those who had "some high school" or "some college" and

---

EXAMPLE 4–19

Numerical versus Categorical Items

Incorrect Categorical Item

Q. What level of education have you attained?
A1. ___ Elementary school only.
A2. ___ High school only.
A3. ___ College education.
A4. ___ College postgraduate.

Correct Numeric Item

Q. What is the last year of education you have completed?
[For example, high school graduate equals 12 years.]

A. ___ years of formal education.

---

those who completed the course of study and obtained a degree or diploma. That discrimination is forever lost with the categorical form of the item.

By contrast, the numeric data can easily be grouped into categories if required by those who seek the information. Those with 8 years of school or less would be grouped into the "elementary only" category, those with 9 to 11 years into "some high school," those with 12 years into "high school graduate," etc. In addition, the correct version of the item is less threatening and it presents the respondents with a much simpler and easier task than does the categorical item.

SUMMARY

The Composition of Survey Questions

A. Focus very precisely. Every item should zero in very directly on one, specific issue or topic.

B. Keep each item brief. The longer the question, the greater the response task and the more error and bias.

C. Strive for clarity. Every respondent must know exactly what is being asked.

D. Use "core" vocabulary. Use the same words as the least sophisticated respondents would use in common speech.

E. Use "simple" sentences. Two or more simple sentences are far preferable to one compound sentence.

F. Avoid specific sources of bias or error. Be sure items are free from the factors that create bias and error.

G. Use structured questions. Unstructured items ordinarily provide large quantities of poor quality data.

H. Classify answers carefully. Observe the three rules for an effective classification system.

I. Choose appropriate categories. Be certain they are neither too broad nor narrow, too many nor too few.

J. Use scaling effectively. Refer to the following two chapters for guidance on numeric and verbal scales and to combine survey items into groups.

5

Scaling Techniques

WHY SCALES ARE USED

Answers to survey questions are typically a choice of "position," either within some category or along some continuous spectrum. A response scale is merely a representation of the categories or continuum along which respondents will arrange themselves. When scales are used, reports provide a description of the distribution of respondents along the scale or in the categories; and the positions of various individuals or groups can be compared with one another. Scales can be coded with numbers. The numeric codes that represent answers to questions are more easily manipulated than words. The use of a numeric data base saves time and money and helps to insure accuracy, reliability and validity. Scales can be arranged so that they capture answers to many questions quickly and in very little space. They are both efficient and practical.

SPECIFICITY OF SCALES

Scales are used to obtain responses that will be comparable to one another. All of the responses should be expressed in the same terms. Sometimes the scale will be obvious to the respondent, and sometimes it will be necessary only to name the scale. There are also times when the scale will have to be clearly portrayed. For some questions, the scale already exists in the minds of the respondents. For example, when someone is asked their age, they will respond with the number of years. There is a common understanding between the questioner and the respondent, concerning the scale to be used. This is an *im-*

plicit scale because it is implied by the question. Weight, height, eye color, distance between cities, and simple, dichotomous questions such as "yes/no" questions are other examples.

At other times, the common understanding between the questioner and the respondent is lacking. If people were asked, "How long has it been since your last visit to a physician for treatment?," some might respond in days, some in months and some in years. A few may even say, "Oh, its been a long time" or "I go whenever I'm sick." Such answers are difficult to manipulate or compare to one another. It would be better to ask, "How *many months* has it been since . . ." rather than "How long has it been since . . ." Thus, the scale is *explicit.* All responses will be expressed in calendar months and they are comparable.

For common denominations, such as months, pounds, dollars, degrees of temperature, or the number of a certain thing, such as trips taken during a given time, virtually everyone will be familiar with it if it is named in the question. When this is the case, and the question can be asked by merely specifying the scale in the question, it should be done that way, so long as the respondents understand the scale specified.

When scales cannot be specified within the question, they must be *depicted* as response options, verbally, numerically, or graphically. For example, if the question was, "Where are you going when you leave here?", answers would not be comparable. There is no scale that can easily be specified within the question, so the response options must be listed or depicted following the question: home, work, shopping, recreation, etc. When seeking qualitative evaluations, preferences, images, perceptions, or judgments, the scale dimensions may be depicted in the form of rankings, ratings, graphic figures, or some other set of response alternatives. In the examples that follow, several of the most popular scaling devices are shown.

The scale should be depicted only when necessary. Implicit scales should be used when respondents are sure to understand them and are as willing to respond to an implicit scale as to a depicted one. This is usually the case. When specification is required, common, simple dimensions should be used. Some researchers tend to specify age *groups* when it would be more simple and accurate to ask, "What is your age?" Four words in the question and one number for the answer; what could be simpler? No specification was necessary, and the scale is implied.

The question concerning level of education is another example. Here, the scale must be explicitly specified, but many researchers will list an elaborate set of categories, including: elementary only, some high school, high school graduate, some college, college graduate, some postgraduate school, or postgraduate degree. A simpler way to ask would be, "How many years of formal education have you completed?" The researcher can safely assume that 8 years means elementary school, 12 means high school, etc. Where an underlying dimension is commonly understood by both questioner and respondent, it should be used without elaboration.

CHECKLIST 5–1

To Select the Scale Category

1. Will the respondents clearly understand the dimensions they are to use? If so, dimensions need only be *implied*.

2. Will the respondents be familiar with the scale dimensions if they are named, such as years, times, or miles? If so, the dimensions need only be *explicit*.

3. Will the respondents be uncertain or unfamiliar with the scale? If so, scale must be *depicted*.

MULTIPLE CHOICE QUESTION

Multiple choice questions are very common because they are simple and versatile. They can be used to obtain either a single response, or several. Multiple choice questions of both single response and multiple response are shown in Example 5–1.

EXAMPLE 5–1

The Multiple Choice Item

Multiple Response

Please check *any* type of newspaper you regularly read for business news.

___ Local, morning paper	11
___ Local, evening paper	12
___ Local, weekly paper	13
___ Regional, weekly paper	14
___ National, daily paper	15
___ National, weekly paper	16
___ Other (What kind?_____)	16–18

EXAMPLE 5–1 (concluded)

Single Response

What kind of newspaper do you *most often* read for business news? (Check only *one*.)

(1) ___ Local, morning paper
(2) ___ Local, evening paper
(3) ___ Local, weekly paper
(4) ___ Regional, weekly paper   19
(5) ___ National, daily paper
(6) ___ National, weekly paper
(7) ___ Other (What kind?_____)   20

The Multiple Response Item. In the multiple response case, the respondents can indicate one *or more* alternatives, and they are instructed to check *any* within the question, itself. In this case, *each* alternative becomes a "variable" to be analyzed. Thus, this one item actually asks seven questions. They could be expressed individually, one at a time: "Do you regularly read the _____ paper for business news?" for each of the six, and "What other papers do you regularly read for business news?" That would take much more time and space, and so this one item is very economical.

GUIDELIST 5–1

For Using a Multiple Choice Item

1. The entire range of response should be classifiable into a *limited* number of discrete categories. About 8 or 10 are usually the maximum.

2. The category names should define a set of discrete alternatives, so that there is a clear distinction between them in the minds of interviewers and/or respondents.

3. The named categories should be mutually exclusive, so that no possible answer could fit into more than one of the categories used.

4. There should be certainty that the labeled alternatives will capture over 90 percent of all answers that are likely to be given to the question.

5. An "other" category should be listed last to include any answers that do not fit into the named categories, unless there is no possibility of other answers.

The Single Response Item. When only one alternative is to be singled out from among several by the respondent, the item is a multiple *choice*, but a single *response* item. No "ties" are allowed, and the respondent is supposed to pick only one. Respondents do not always follow instructions if they are unclear. Consequently, single response items can be used only when: (1) the choice criterion is clearly stated and (2) the criterion actually defines a single category. Notice that the words, "most often" and "one" are underlined in the item shown in the lower section of the example. This clearly states that only one option is to be designated. Note also that few if any respondents are likely to read two or more publications with exactly the same frequency, so "ties" are unlikely and there is a *unique* answer to the question. The selection of a single response, rather than a multiple response item, depends on the researcher's needs and the respondents ability to identify one answer.

It is important to note, once again, that the multiple choice item is ideal for responses that fall into "discrete" categories. On the other hand, multiple choice items should *not* be used for numeric data. When the answers can be expressed as numbers, a direct question should be used, and the number of units should be recorded. If it is desirable to "group" responses into categories within certain ranges, that can easily be accomplished during computer processing.

CONVENTIONAL SCALE TYPES

The types of scales that are most commonly used in surveys are described below. While all of them have been thoroughly tested and used extensively, some are much more common than others. Nearly every information need or survey question can be scaled effectively with the use of one or more of the scales described in this chapter. Some special scales, less conventional than these, are presented in the following chapter as well. Thus, the researcher's scaling decisions are more a matter of *choice* among the conventional scales than of invention of scaling devices.

The "Likert" Scale

There are times when it is necessary to obtain people's "position" on certain issues or conclusions. This is a form of opinion or attitude measurement. An unstructured or "open-ended" question might be used for this purpose, but that type of question has many problems associated with analysis and interpretation. Answers are seldom comparable. The Likert scale, named for its creator, states the issue or opinion and obtains the respondents' degree of agreement or disagreement. This scale provides answers in the form of coded data that are comparable and can readily be manipulated.

When a Likert scale is used, the "question" is stated in the instructions, above the scale. The question becomes, "How much do you agree with this statement?" The actual items are not questions, but statements that represent particular opinions. Respondents indicate their agreement or disagreement to each one, so that responses are on a single dimension or continuum. The instructions for such a scale, the scale itself, and 10 item statements are shown in Example 5–2.

EXAMPLE 5–2

The Likert Scale

Please pick a number from the scale to show how much you agree or disagree with each statement and jot it in the space to the right of the item.

Scale

1 = Strongly agree
2 = Agree
3 = Neutral
4 = Disagree
5 = Strongly disagree

A man should never cry in public. . . . . —   11

Higher education is more important for men than women . . . . —   12

Women should receive equal pay for equal work. —   13

A man should not resent a woman supervising his work . . . . —   14

A woman's place is in the home. . . . . —   15

A man should help and protect a woman in public. . . . . —   16

Women should pay their share when dating . . . . —   17

The husband should make the major family decisions. . . . . —   18

Women should never put career before family . . . . —   19

Men should always take the lead in sexual matters . . . . —   20

Likert scaling is very popular with researchers because of the power and simplicity of the format. The principal advantages of this type of scale include flexibility, economy, and ease of composition. The procedure is flexible because items can be only a few words long, or they can consist of several lines. Vocabulary can be technical and sophisticated or it can be very simple and primary, depending on what is appropriate to the population to be surveyed. The method is economical because one set of instructions and scale can serve many items, and once the respondent understands what is required, he or she can complete the items very quickly and easily. Likert scaled items can often be composed by the researcher quickly and easily, especially when the issues have been articulated in advance as statements.

GUIDELIST 5–2

For Using Likert Scale Items

1. The Likert scale should be used for several items, rather than just one or two, to obtain the inherent economy.

2. The researcher should be able to identify or compose statements that are opinions "typical" of a global issue.

3. The items should be sufficiently diverse, so that they represent an adequate range of the global issue.

4. There must be reasonable certainty that a large number of respondents will not pick only a neutral value.

5. If a summated score is to be computed, about half the items should be "inclined" toward the pro side of the issue and half toward the con side, to avoid "yea-sayer" or "nay-sayer" bias.

A major advantage of this scale is the ability to obtain a summated value. In the example, the research is measuring attitudes toward sex role prescriptions. Some of the statements prescribe something for one sex, but not the other, and some others state that no distinctions should be made between the sexes. Besides obtaining the results of each individual item, a total score can be obtained from this set of items. Some of the items would have to be reflected by reversing the numeric scores, so that all items ascend toward either pro or con. Then, the total value would be an index of attitudes toward the major issue, as a whole. This ability to measure a more general construct is a major advantage of the Likert scale.

The Verbal Frequency Scale

The format of the verbal frequency scale is fairly similar to that of the Likert scale, with a couple of important exceptions: Rather than strength of agreement, the verbal frequency scale contains five words that indicate *how often* an action has been taken. Rather than statements about issues, the items of the verbal frequency scale indicate some action the respondents might have taken. Example 5–3 contains 10 items to measure the degree of political activism of respondents.

EXAMPLE 5–3

The Verbal Frequency Scale

Please pick a number from the scale to show how often you do each of the things listed below and jot in the space to the right of the item.

Scale

1 = Always
2 = Often
3 = Sometimes
4 = Seldom
5 = Never

Seek out information about candidates and issues.	—	11
Actually vote during a strictly local election	—	12
Actually vote during a state and national election.	—	13
Vote along strict party lines.	—	14
Contribute money to a local political campaign	—	15
Contribute money to a state political campaign	—	16
Contribute money to a national political campaign	—	17
Volunteer to work on a local political campaign.	—	18
Volunteer to work on a state political campaign.	—	19
Volunteer to work on a national political campaign.	—	20

There are times when it might be necessary to know the frequency of some action or behavior by respondents. Under some conditions, the question to measure this might simply ask, "How many times in the past _____ have you _____?" Such a simple, straightforward question is recommended when the *absolute* number of times is appropriate and required. But there are many occasions when the absolute number is of little use, or when the respondent would be unable to specify an absolute number. In the example provided, the absolute number of times would *not* be of very much interest or value. Suppose there had been three or four elections in the districts of some of the respondents, and none in the districts of others. In that case, some groups would *appear* to be very inactive, based on the absolute level of participation. But this inactivity would not be the *choice* of the respondents. It merely reflects the fact that there was no opportunity to participate. In this case, the researcher wants to know the proportion or percentage of activity, given an opportunity to perform it. The verbal frequency scale provides this more meaningful measure.

For some measurements, the respondents might not be able to say with any precision of recollection exactly how many times they have behaved in a certain way. For example, respondents could be asked, "What percentage of the time did you vote for a political candidate who was a member of your own political party in the past six elections in which you voted?" Aside from the fact that this is a long, protracted question, there are other difficulties. To answer accurately would require substantial powers of recollection. Most respondents would be reluctant to try to recall each election and to complete the tedious computations to obtain an accurate percentage. With the use of the verbal frequency scale, this difficulty is avoided.

In the example and in many real situations, the focus is on the *policies* of the respondents concerning the frequency of certain actions, rather than the actual number or percentage of performance. Thus, the item that seeks to measure how often the respondent votes along strict party lines provides an overall measure of loyalty to a political party. The general policy and underlying motivation are more important and valuable than the actual number or percentage of times the respondent has voted in that way in the past.

The advantages of the verbal frequency scale include the ease of assessment and response by those being surveyed. The number of opportunities to perform the action is automatically assumed within the question and serves as the basis for picking the frequency category. The ability to array levels of activity across a spectrum of only five categories for data description and the ease of making comparisons among subsamples or among different types of actions for the same sample of respondents provides a strong incentive for the use of the verbal frequency scale.

Perhaps the major disadvantage of this type of scale is the fact that it provides only a gross measure of proportion. For example, "sometimes" can mean anywhere from about 30 to 70 percent of the time. Also, different groups may assign different "breakpoints" between categories.

In the example shown, the research could "reflect" all items, so that the values ascended toward political activism, and then sum the values for all 10 items. This would provide an overall index of political involvement. In this case, the researcher would be *assuming* that seeking out information about a candidate is as much a contribution to overall political action as contributing money or volunteering to work on a campaign. To the degree that this assumption is appropriate, such an overall index has considerable value in many research areas. Thus, the ability to obtain an overall measure of a construct is an advantage that the verbal frequency scale shares with the Likert scale, but individual weighting of items may sometimes be necessary.

GUIDELIST 5-3

For Using Verbal Frequency Scale Items

1. The verbal frequency scale should be used for several items, not just one or two, to obtain the economy.

2. The researcher should be able to compose items that assume the opportunity to perform the action.

3. The items should be used when only an approximation of percentages is required, with limited precision.

4. These scales are most appropriate when respondents are unable or unwilling to compute exact percentages.

5. If a summated score is to be computed, each item should have approximately equal "weight" in determining the overall index, or a weighted average should be computed in place of a "total" score.

The Ordinal Scale

The ordinal scale is actually a multiple choice item that shares some of the arithmetic characteristics of a Likert scale or a verbal frequency scale. But there is an important difference in the response categories. With the multiple choice item, the response alternatives do not stand in any fixed relationship with one another. With the ordinal scale item, the response alternatives define an ordered sequence. Thus, the choice listed first is less than the second, the second less than the third, and so forth. The scale might be reversed so that each choice alternative is greater than the one that follows. The item is ordinal because each time category listed comes *before* the next one.

Example 5-4 contains two items intended to measure when in the day the family first turns on the television set. They might have been phrased, "About what time do you or someone in your family *first* turn on the television set in your home on weekdays?" Then, the respondent would simply record a time of day. While the simple, direct question would obtain an absolute time of day, it would not

EXAMPLE 5–4

The Ordinal Scale

Ordinarily, when do you or someone in your family *first* turn on a television set in your home on a *weekday*? (Please check *only one*.)

(1)	___	The first thing in the morning
(2)	___	A little while after awakening
(3)	___	Mid-morning
(4)	___	Just before lunch
(5)	___	Right after lunch
(6)	___	Mid-afternoon
(7)	___	Early evening, before dinner
(8)	___	Right after dinner
(9)	___	Late evening
(0)	___	Usually don't turn it on.

11

Ordinarily, when do you or someone in your family *first* turn on a television set in your home on *Saturdays*? (Please check *only one*.)

(1)	___	The first thing in the morning
(2)	___	A little while after awakening
(3)	___	Mid-morning
(4)	___	Just before lunch
(5)	___	Right after lunch
(6)	___	Mid-afternoon
(7)	___	Early evening, before dinner
(8)	___	Right after dinner
(9)	___	Late evening
(0)	___	Usually don't turn it on.

12

indicate the time, *relative* to waking or eating. Thus, if this relationship between TV viewing and other daily activities were important, the typical time for each of the other activities would also have to be obtained.

The principal advantage of the ordinal scale is the ability to obtain a measure *relative* to some other benchmark. For example, the position of a child *relative* to his siblings within the family is often regarded as more important than just the child's age. The assumption is that a child of a certain age will be treated differently if he or she is the first child of the family than if there are older siblings. The *order* is the major focus, and not merely chronological age.

Note that in the example provided here, if two respondents both indicated they turn on the television a little while after awakening,

---

GUIDELIST 5-4

For Using Ordinal Scale Items

1. The ordinal scale should be used when a direct question concerning a quantity or value would not be sufficient.

2. This scale is appropriate when the researcher seeks to include some benchmark to obtain a *relative* measure.

3. The researcher should be aware of the statistical limitations of ordinal versus interval or ratio data.

4. The response alternatives must stand in a meaningful sequence, based on some order of magnitude.

5. The interval between categories must be of little or no interest, and the order should be of major concern. In that sense, the researcher must be willing to sacrifice some information.

---

they would be regarded as identical on this question. They would be seen as the same, even though one individual or family may arise at five o'clock in the morning and the other, not until nine o'clock. Thus, the item obtains a *relative* measure, but some information is lost concerning the distance or span between categories. The ordinal scale should *not* be used when an absolute, numeric value can be easily obtained and when it is most meaningful. In other words, there is no reason to use the less economical and more complex ordinal scale when a direct question concerning a quantity will serve as well.

The Forced Ranking Scale

Forced rankings of items produce ordinal values, just as the verbal frequency scales and the ordinal scales do, only the items are *each* ranked relative to one another. In Example 5-5 the brand most preferred is ranked first. The forced ranking scale obtains not only the most preferred, but also the sequence of the remaining items.

With forced ranking scales, the "relativity" or relationship that is measured is among the items. This is one of the main advantages of this scaling technique. People are often faced with choices among goods, services, ideas, individuals, institutions, or actions. They are constantly making choices among a limited set of options. The forced ranking scale indicates what those choices are likely to be, from an "ever shrinking" number of alternatives. While the parallel between the actual life choice situation and the measurement format is an advantage of forced ranking, this scale has several disadvantages. The

---

EXAMPLE 5–5

The Forced Ranking Scale

Please rank the colas listed below in their order of preference. Jot the number 1 next to the one you prefer most, number 2 by your second choice, and so forth.

___ Pepsi-Cola		11
___ Coca-Cola		12
___ Royal Crown Cola		13
___ Like Cola		14

---

major limitation is the fact that the *absolute* standing and the *interval* between items is not measured.

Suppose two respondents to the sample item both rank Coca-Cola first and Pepsi-Cola second. This suggests that given a choice among all four, they would choose Coca-Cola. It also suggests that if Coke were not available and the others were, they would both select Pepsi. This may or may not be the case, however. While the two appear identical, they may differ. One of the two hypothetical respondents may regard Coke and Pepsi as almost identical in their preferability. The other one may see Coca-Cola as far preferable to any of the others, including Pepsi. Thus, the first individual may subsititute Pepsi with little sacrifice, if Coke were not available. The second person may refuse a cola beverage if his or her favorite were not available. In effect, then, the forced ranking reveals the *order* of preference, but the *distance* or *interval* between ranks for different respondents or between different pairs may differ markedly. That information is lóst with ranking, but it can be obtained by direct ratings of each item. If ratings of items are obtained, the absolute value, interval between items, and relative standing are all easily computed and reported.

The number of entities or items that can be ranked is also a limitation with this type of scale. Respondents must first go through the entire list and identify their first choice. They must then go through the list again, eliminating their first choice, and selecting the alternative they would rank second, and so forth. To rank 20 items, respondents would have to make 19 "passes" through an ever decreasing list of alternatives, until only the last choice remained. Consequently, forced ranking scales are limited to only a few items, and if too many are included, the response task becomes too tedious and time-consuming. This problem can also be avoided by the use of ratings, rather than rankings. Ratings do not require several "passes" through the list, and each item need be considered only once.

GUIDELIST 5–5

For Using the Forced Ranking Scale

1. The number of things to be ranked should be less than 10, to avoid making the response task too difficult.

2. The major focus should be on the *relative* standing of the entities, not their absolute position.

3. The researcher must be willing to forego measurement of the "distance" between ranks.

4. A *single* judgment criterion must be clearly stated, so that all entities are arrayed on the same dimension.

5. As with other scales yielding ordinal data, analysis is confined to a limited set of statistical procedures that do not require equal intervals.

The Paired Comparison Scale

There are times when a researcher may want to measure simple, dichotomous choices between alternatives. The paired comparison scale is appropriate to such a need. Basically, the same assumptions apply to paired comparisons as to forced ranking scales. That is, the focus must be almost exclusively on the evaluation of one entity, *relative* to another. In this sense, paired comparisons can be regarded as a special case of ranking, where only two items are ranked at a time. The same brands of cola beverages which were used to exemplify the forced ranking scale are also used in Example 5–6. In this case, each brand is compared with each other brand.

There is a major problem with paired comparisons when several pairs are ranked, known as "lack of transitivity." Logically, if a respondent prefers A to B and prefers B to C, then he or she should obviously prefer A to C. It is not unusual when paired comparison scale data are analyzed, to find that many respondents fail to provide this transitivity.

If "ties" or equal rankings can be tolerated, and especially if the determination of absolute distance or interval between pairs is useful, it is advisable to use a numeric rating scale. Virtually all of the limitations and problems inherent in paired comparisons are avoided by using ratings, rather than rankings of items taken two at a time.

Despite their limitations, paired comparisons can be useful when only certain comparisons are sought and the relative distance between rankings is unimportant. When only *one* item must be compared with

---

EXAMPLE 5-6

The Paired Comparison Scale

For *each pair* of soft drinks listed below, please put a check mark by the *one* you *most prefer,* if you had to choose between the two.

(1) ___ Pepsi-Cola		11
(2) ___ Coca-Cola		
(1) ___ Royal Crown Cola		12
(2) ___ Pepsi-Cola		
(1) ___ Royal Crown Cola		13
(2) ___ Like Cola		
(1) ___ Royal Crown Cola		14
(2) ___ Coca-Cola		
(1) ___ Coca-Cola		15
(2) ___ Like Cola		
(1) ___ Like Cola		16
(2) ___ Pepsi-Cola		

---

several others, and no direct comparisons among the others are required, a simple comparative scale can be employed, using the one item as the standard by which all of the other items are judged.

GUIDELIST 5-6

For Using Paired Comparisons

1. The number of things to be compared should be less than 10, to avoid making the response task too difficult.

2. The method is most effective when actual choices in the real situation are always between two things.

3. The researcher must be willing to forego measurement of the "distance" between items in each pair.

4. A *single* judgment criterion must be clearly stated, so that all entities are arrayed on the same dimension.

5. The less sophisticated and careful the respondents, the greater the lack of transitivity will be, and the researcher must always expect some failure of transitivity.

The Comparative Scale

In those situations where the researcher is most interested in the comparison(s) between one object and one or more others, the comparative scale is most appropriate. With this type of scale, one entity can be used as the standard or benchmark by which several others can be judged. In Example 5–7, the previous management group is the standard by which respondents are to judge the new management group.

EXAMPLE 5–7

The Comparative Scale

Compared to the prevous management group, the new one is ... (Check one space.)

Very Superior		About the Same		Very Inferior
				11
1	2	3	4	5

There are two very important advantages to the use of a comparative scale. Note that with this method, no *absolute* standard is presented or required, and all evaluations are made on a *comparative* basis. Ratings are all *relative* to the standard or benchmark used. Thus, where a relative measurement is of greatest interest, or where no absolute standard exists, the comparative scale approach is applicable. Researchers are frequently most interested in comparisons of only "their own" sponsor with other, competing stores, brands, institutions, organizations, candidates, or individuals. The comparative scale meets the requirements for such measurement.

Unlike such methods as ranking or paired comparisons, the comparative scale does *not* produce ordinal data, even though a relative measure is obtained. The scale actually consists of a *rating*, rather than a ranking of items. Thus, the results indicate *both* the rank or relative position, and also the interval between the standard and the item being compared to it.

Another advantage of the comparative scale is its flexibility. The simple example shown here can be extended in two ways: The same two entities can be compared on several dimensions or criteria and several different entities can be compared with the standard. For example, by listing several scales with different labels beneath them, such as "Much more progressive" and "Much less progressive," etc., an entire "profile" of the new management could be obtained, with the perceptions of the previous management team serving as the standard for judgment.

A second type of modification would be to list the same scales, but include several different entities. Each would be judged against the same standard. In the example, the question would read, "How would you rate each management group, compared to the present one? Compared to the present one *this group* is . . ." Then, each management group would be listed with a scale beside or below it. Each group could be compared with the present, and indirectly, with one another.

GUIDELIST 5–7

For Using Comparative Scales

1. The major research emphasis should be the comparison of a single, standard entity with one or more others.

2. The actual rating scale should have an *even* number of alternatives, if "fence-riding" is likely.

3. The researcher must be sure the respondent is *very* clear about which is the standard and which is to be rated.

4. This method is advisable *only* if all or nearly all respondents are very familiar with the standard.

5. The method is particularly applicable when interval data are desired, but a *relative* measure is required. Both ranking and distance between entities are generated.

In general, rankings are used much too often, and the comparative scales are not used as much as they should be. The comparative scales are more powerful in several respects: They present an easy, simple task to the respondent, insuring cooperation and accuracy. They provide interval data, rather than only ordinal values, as rankings do. They permit several things that have been compared to the same standard to be compared with one another, and economy of space and time are inherent in them.

The Horizontal, Numeric Scale

When items are to be judged on a single dimension and arrayed on a scale with equal intervals, a simple, horizontal, numeric scale with the extremes labeled appropriately is the most advisable method of scaling. Example 5–8 provides a sample of the way that this common scaling method is used.

EXAMPLE 5–8

The Horizontal, Numerical Scale

How important to you is each of the public issues listed below?

If you feel the issue is extremely important, pick a number from the far right side of the scale and jot it in the space beside the item. If you feel it is extremely unimportant, pick a number from the far left, and if you feel the importance is between these extremes, pick a number from someplace in the middle of the scale to show your opinion.

Scale

Extremely Unimportant	1	2	3	4	5	Extremely Important

The protection of endangered species of animals. . . . . ___ 11
The improvement of the quality of the air. . . . . ___ 12
The discovery of additional petroleum reserves. . . . . ___ 13
The development of "renewable" sources of energy . . . . ___ 14
The reduction or elimination of water pollution . . . . ___ 15
The development of additional nuclear power . . . . ___ 16
The protection of overall ecological balance. . . . . ___ 17
The industrial and technical growth of the nation. . . . . ___ 18
The provision of social services to those in need. . . . . ___ 19
The improvement of national defense and security . . . . ___ 20

In the example, the question is listed first, and the indented instructions are quite detailed; perhaps more so than would be necessary for most adult respondents. If those in the responding sample are fairly sophisticated, the instructions might simply say: "Pick a number from the scale to show your opinion and jot it in the space beside each item, below."

In the example provided, the researcher seeks to measure the "importance" of 10 public issues. In effect, the respondents' values are being tapped and compared. Notice that this scaling technique is very economical, since a single question, set of instructions, and rating scale apply to many individual items. It is also important to note that the linear, horizontal, numeric scale provides *both* absolute measures of importance and also relative measures, or rankings, if responses among the various items are compared. (Of course, there is the possibility of identical ratings, yielding "tied" ranks.) Yet, even though ranking is available, the rating scale is an equal interval scale and provides data that is relatively unrestrictive, compared to ordinal data from forced rankings or paired comparisons.

There has been considerable controversy among researchers, concerning whether or not the intermediate points on the scale should be labeled with words, such as "Somewhat important" or "Slightly important." In most cases, it is *not* advisable to label the intermediate levels of the scale. There are several reasons: First, consensus concerning the meaning of such words as "very" or "slightly" is less likely than for the interpretation of only a series of numbers. Second, the graphic spacing and the common understanding of the equal "distance" between numbers form a conceptual "mapping" of the underlying evaluation. Third, with only numbers, there is no possible mistake about the fact that there is a single dimension or continuum. The bulk of the research on this issue indicates that in most cases, labeling of intermediate values is no more effective, and doing so can sometimes produce undesirable results, in the form of scale points that are not of equal interval from one another. Extensive experience indicates that most surveys of the general public do *not* require labeling of intermediate points, and there is practically no confusion or misunderstanding using only numbers.

GUIDELIST 5-8

For Using Horizontal, Numeric Scales

1. This method is most applicable where evaluative responses are to be arrayed on a single dimension.

2. The scale is most economical where several items are all to be rated on the same dimension.

3. Scale extremes should be labeled, "Extremely _____," to define the dimension and the words used must be bipolar opposites.

4. In the vast majority of cases, the intermediate scale values should *not* be labeled with words, and only numbers should be used, spaced at equal intervals.

Simplicity, clarity, economy and productivity are all certainly among the major advantages of the horizontal, numeric scale. The format is clean and straightforward. Respondents have little or no difficulty understanding the task they are to perform. The same question, instructions and scale can be used for many items. Rankings can be computed with the use of this scale, but it provides equal interval data for statistical analysis and an absolute level of measurement.

The horizontal, numeric scale has few limitations, compared to other scaling methods. Of course, it is not applicable to all situations. For example, it is less effective than the verbal frequency scale for measuring approximate frequency, and not applicable when direct comparison with a particular standard is required. On the whole, this scale is a powerful device and it has become very conventional and popular among many researchers.

The Semantic Differential Scale

Researchers would often like to learn the *image* of an entity in the minds of the public. The most commonly used device for measuring such images is shown in Example 5–9. Using this scaling device, the image of a brand, store, political candidate, company, organization, institution or idea can be measured, assessed, and compared with that of similar topics.

To use the semantic differential scale, the researcher must first select a series of adjectives that might be used to describe the topic object. This can be a difficult task. It is very important to select the adjectives specifying attributes that are important to the respondents. The attributes used in the survey should be the major ones respondents actually use to judge and evaluate the topic being rated. The actual attributes and adjectives most relevant in the minds of respondents are seldom obvious to the researcher. If there is any uncertainty, a preliminary inquiry can be used to identify the most appropriate terms. If important attributes are neglected, an incomplete picture is developed. If unimportant attributes are included, some aspects of the profile that result will be relevant.

Once the attributes and the adjectives associated with them have been selected, the polar opposites of each adjective must be determined. This, too, can be a major problem, and some substitutions to the list may be necessary. For example, is the opposite of "good" the word, "poor" or the word, "bad?" Once the attributes have been identified and descriptive adjectives and their polar opposites have been chosen, the semantic differential scale can be composed. About half the items should list the more positive adjective first and the

EXAMPLE 5-9

The Semantic Differential Scale

Please put a check mark in the space on each line below to show your opinion of the *pizza* served here.

	1 : 2 : 3 : 4 : 5 : 6 : 7		
Hot	__ : __ : __ : __ : __ : __ : __	Cold	11
Bland	__ : __ : __ : __ : __ : __ : __	Spicy	12
Expensive	__ : __ : __ : __ : __ : __ : __	Inexpensive	13
Moist	__ : __ : __ : __ : __ : __ : __	Dry	14
Soggy	__ : __ : __ : __ : __ : __ : __	Crisp	15
Good	__ : __ : __ : __ : __ : __ : __	Bad	16
Unattractive	__ : __ : __ : __ : __ : __ : __	Attractive	17
Fresh	__ : __ : __ : __ : __ : __ : __	Stale	18
Small	__ : __ : __ : __ : __ : __ : __	Large	19
Natural	__ : __ : __ : __ : __ : __ : __	Artificial	20

others, the more negative first. Items are ordinarily listed in random order on the actual scale.

The major advantage of the semantic differential scale is its ability to portray images clearly and effectively. Because several pairs of bipolar adjectives are used, the results provide a profile of the image of the topic or entity being rated. When a series of semantic differential scales are used to measure the image of several topics or entities, entire image profiles can be compared with one another. Still another advantage of the semantic differential scale is the ability to measure "ideal" images or attribute levels. In the example provided here, the researcher seeks to measure the image of pizza served at a particular restaurant. If another semantic differential scale were used to measure the image of a competing establishment, the two could be compared. Yet, additional information might be extremely helpful.

For most of the items used in the example, the "positive" and "negative" adjectives can easily be identified. For example, it is better to be "good" than "bad" and "fresh" than "stale." On the other hand,

---

GUIDELIST 5–9

For Using the Semantic Differential Scale

1. This method is most effective for measuring image profiles, people, things, organizations, or concepts.
2. Adjectives must define a single dimension and each pair must be bipolar opposites labeling the extremes.
3. Precisely *what* the respondent is to rate must be clearly stated in the introductory instructions.
4. No more than about 20 items should be used, and about half should begin with the most positive word.
5. If the same scale is used for several topics and/or for rating an "ideal" entity, image profiles can be compared among real entities and between real and ideal ones.

---

if the researcher learns that the sponsor's pizza is more moist or more spicy than a competitor's, is that good or bad? Where several scales cannot be identified as positive or negative, respondents can be asked to rate their ideal _____; whatever the topic. It is often very useful to compare only ideal images among respondent groups, to determine differential preference patterns. Images of real and ideal topics can also be compared, and the closer a real image corresponds to the ideal image, the more positive the profile.

The requirement for adjectives that are bipolar presents a serious limitation to the use of the semantic differential. The adjectives must be on the ultimate extremes of the spectrum and they must define a single dimension. It is sometimes difficult to identify antonyms. For example, is the opposite of spicy "bland" or "mild," in the minds of potential respondents?

The Adjective Check List

It is sometimes necessary to ascertain just how a topic is viewed by respondents and what descriptive adjectives or phrases apply to it. This can, of course, be measured with the semantic differential scale, but such an application may not be appropriate. The semantic differential technique is limited in the number of items that can be used, and requires the specification of bipolar opposites. The adjective check list is a very straightforward method of obtaining information concerning how a topic is described and viewed. In Example 5–10,

---

EXAMPLE 5–10

The Adjective Check List

Please put a check mark in the space in front of any word or phrase that describes your job.

——	Easy	——	Safe	11–12
——	Technical	——	Exhausting	13–14
——	Boring	——	Difficult	15–16
——	Interesting	——	Rewarding	17–18
——	Low-paying	——	Secure	19–20
——	Strenuous	——	Slow-paced	21–22
——	Routine	——	Enjoyable	23–24
——	Dead-end	——	Rigid	25–26
——	Changing	——	Pleasant	27–28
——	Important	——	Satisfying	29–30
——	Demanding	——	Degrading	31–32
——	Temporary	——	Risky	33–34

---

the instructions ask respondents to check any of the adjectives that describe their jobs. There are 24 adjectives listed, but because of the economy of space and time and the ease with which respondents can complete the task, many more could have been included. Simplicity, directness, and economy are the major virtues of the adjective check

---

GUIDELIST 5–10

For Using the Adjective Check List

1. This method is appropriate for measuring images.

2. The instructions and response task are quick and simple, and a large number of adjectives can be included.

3. Precisely *what* the respondent is to rate or judge must be stated very clearly in the instructions.

4. The scale yields a profile, but only in terms of discrete, nominal data indicating a dichotomous choice.

5. If several topics and/or an "ideal" entity are rated, using more than one adjective check list, profiles among real entities and between real and ideal can be compared.

---

list. A very wide variety and a large number of adjectives can be listed, and even short, descriptive phrases can be used. This is especially valuable for exploratory research work. The greatest disadvantage of the adjective check list is the dichotomous data it yields. There is no indication of "how much" each item describes the topic.

The "Stapel" Scale

The major advantages of the adjective check list, discussed above, are simplicity and economy, but the "profiles" that result are in terms of only nominal data. In other words, the values only name categories indicating whether or not the item was checked. There is no measure of how *well* or how *poorly* the adjective described the topic. On the other hand, the semantic differential scale technique *does* measure this "distance" between the descriptive adjective and the thing being rated. Yet, the semantic differential requires bipolar adjectives and is limited in the number of items that can be used because the response task is more difficult than with the adjective check list. Example 5–11 shows a scale that combines the best of both.

EXAMPLE 5–11

The Stapel Scale

Please pick a number from the scale to show how well each word or phrase below describes your job and jot it in the space in front of each item.

Scale

Not at all	1	2	3	4	5	6	7	Perfectly

___ Easy	___ Safe	11–12
___ Technical	___ Exhausting	13–14
___ Boring	___ Difficult	15–16
___ Interesting	___ Rewarding	16–18
___ Low-paying	___ Secure	19–20
___ Strenuous	___ Slow-paced	21–22
___ Routine	___ Enjoyable	23–24
___ Dead-end	___ Rigid	25–26
___ Changing	___ Pleasant	26–28
___ Important	___ Satisfying	29–30
___ Demanding	___ Degrading	31–32
___ Temporary	___ Risky	33–34

GUIDELIST 5-11

For Using the Stapel Scale

1. This method is appropriate for measuring images.

2. A relatively large number of words or phrases can be included.

3. Precisely *what* the respondent is to judge and rate must be stated very clearly in the instructions.

4. The scale yields a profile indicating "how much" each phrase describes the topic, with continuous data.

5. If several topics and/or an "ideal" entity are rated, using more than one Stapel scale, profiles among real entities and between real and ideal can be compared.

The Stapel scale, named for its creator, is very similar in appearance to the adjective check list. The major distinction is that the Stapel scale includes a horizontal, numeric scale below the instructions and above the descriptive adjectives or phrases. Rather than merely checking or not checking an item to indicate whether or not it applies to the topic, the Stapel scale requires that the respondent provide a *rating* of *how much* each item describes the topic. In that way, the data generated by the scale is interval "distance" from the item to the topic. This interval data is similar to that obtained by the semantic differential scale.

Just as the semantic differential scale and the adjective check list can be used to provide an image profile, so too, can the Stapel scale be used to portray an image. The major advantage of the Stapel scale, over the semantic differential, is that the adjectives or descriptive phrases that are used need not have polar opposites. The researcher could specify "dry" without being concerned if the opposite is "wet" or "moist." The advantage of the Stapel scale, compared to the adjective check list, is the quality of the data provided by the former. Stapel scale data is interval data, rather than nominal data indicating only discrete, yes-or-no categories. Consequently, it can be manipulated and statistically processed with all of the facility associated with any other interval scale data. Greater complexity is the major disadvantage of the Stapel scale, compared to the semantic differential or adjective check list. The respondent task is more difficult to explain.

All of the same capability inherent in the semantic differential and the adjective check list is included with the Stapel scale. Profiles can be compared among real topics, an ideal entity can be rated, and ideal profiles of preference can be compared among different respondent subsamples or respondent groups. Of course, real entity profiles can be compared with ideal profiles, by subject, if computer analysis is used, and the degree of correspondence will indicate the overall "favorability" of the real ratings.

The Fixed Sum Scale

There are times when it is important to learn what *proportion* of some resource or activity has been devoted to each of several possible choices or alternatives. The fixed sum scale is an excellent device for this purpose. It would be possible to simply ask, "What percentage of the time do you do each of the following?", but the respondent is likely to have great difficulty with such a question. The data from many respondents are not likely to total to 100 percent. Example 5–12 shows a more effective format. The scale is most effective when it is used to measure actual behavior or action in the *recent* past. Ordinarily, about 10 different categories is the maximum, but as few as 2 or 3 can be used. The number to which the data must total has to be *very* clearly stated.

The major advantage of the fixed sum scale is its clarity and simplicity. The instructions are easily understood and the respondent

---

EXAMPLE 5–12

The Fixed Sum Scale

Of the *last 10 times* that you ate lunch or dinner at a casual or fast food restaurant, how many times did you have each of the things listed below?
(Please be sure to make the total equal 10.)

___	Hamburgers	11
___	Hot dogs or sausage	12
___	Chicken	13
___	Pizza	14
___	Chinese food	15
___	Fish or seafood	16
___	Deli sandwiches	17
___	Hot sandwiches	18
___	Mexican food	19
___	Other (What?_____)	20–21

Total = 10

---

task is ordinarily easy to complete. It is important to list an *inclusive* set of items for this type of scale. If there are several options missing, respondents would be faced with the task of listing several "other" alternatives and there would be no provision for obtaining the number of times each was exercised.

GUIDELIST 5-12

For Using the Fixed Sum Scale

1. The scale is used to measure proportions, rather than absolute values.
2. The occurrences must be apportioned into not more than about ten categories.
3. The instructions must state *very* clearly the value to which the responses must total.
4. The scale provides continuous data so that proportions can easily be compared among alternatives.
5. The data can be converted to percentages by dividing each value by the actual total, so every case will total a hundred percent and be comparable.

SCALE CREATION CRITERIA

There is seldom a single, clear-cut choice of a scale for any given question or information requirement when composing a questionnaire. Thus, it is impossible to list a set of rules that dictate exactly what scale should be used in each situation, even if every circumstance could be anticipated. On the other hand, some scales are easily identified as potential tools for some common information needs and questions, and there are often other scales that are clearly inappropriate.

The criteria and considerations listed in the summary are merely guidelines, but there are no ironclad rules that would limit the creativity and effectiveness of the researcher. Some examples of special scales, created to meet the special needs of the researcher and respondents, are described in the following chapter. While the conventional scales are almost always adaptable, others should be invented for special needs and circumstances.

SUMMARY

How to Create Effective Scales

A. Keep it simple. Given a choice between a very short, concise scale and a more elaborate, sophisticated one, the less complex scale should be used. Even after identifying a scale to be used for an item, ask, "Is there an easier, simpler scale or way of asking this question?"

B. Respect the respondent. While respondents are ordinarily cooperative and helpful, response is a favor. They have little involvement with the task. Select scales that will make it as quick and easy as possible for them. That will reduce nonresponse bias and improve accuracy.

C. Dimension the response. In what dimensions do respondents and sponsors think about the issue? They will not always be the same, so some commonality must be discovered. The dimensions along which the respondents are to answer must not be obscure or difficult, and they should parallel respondents' thinking.

D. Pick the denominations. Always use the denominations that are best for respondents. The data can later be converted to the denominations sought by information users. Feet and inches can be changed to metric or time converted to a 24 hour clock during processing.

E. Decide on the range. Categories or scale increments should be about the same breadth as those ordinarily used by respondents. Normally, respondents classify things into a range from about 2 to about 7 or 8 categories, and seldom more than 10. Respondents often cannot be as precise as researchers would like.

F. Group only when required. Never put things into categories when they can easily be expressed in numeric terms. People think in years, not decades or centuries. Data can always be grouped during processing, but if obtained in broad categories, it cannot be disaggregated later, no matter how badly one might wish to do so.

G. Handle neutrality carefully. If respondents *genuinely* have no preference, they will resent the forced choice inherent in a scale with an even number of alternatives. If feelings are not especially strong, an odd number of scale points may result in "fence-riding" or piling on the midpoint, even when some preference exists.

H. State instructions clearly. Even the least capable respondents must be able to understand. Use language that is typical of the respondents. Explain exactly what the respondent should do and the task sequence they should follow. List the criteria they should judge by and use an example or practice item if there is any doubt.

I. Always be flexible. Scaling examples provided here are only that. They can and should be modified to fit the task and the respondents. The instructions, format, vocabulary and number of scale points can all be changed to suit the needs of the survey. Scales should fit the task, not conform to the original authors specifications.

J. Pilot test the scales. When there is any doubt about the ability of respondents to use the scales, a brief, informal pilot test is quick, inexpensive insurance. Do not wait until the entire questionnaire is written. Individual parcels can be checked with a few typical respondents.

6

Questionnaire Construction

FUNCTION OF THE QUESTIONNAIRE

The composition of individual survey questions and the scaling techniques used in conjuction with them were discussed in the two previous chapters. It is time now to bring these elements together into a complete, finished survey instrument. When the survey is self-administered, such as for a mail survey, the instrument is called a questionnaire. Technically, the measurement and recording instrument for surveys using interviewing is called an "interview schedule." All survey instruments will be referred to here as questionnaires, just as they ordinarily are by most researchers. Generally, the same principles and practices apply to the construction of both types of instruments. In those few instances where the mode of data collection requires distinctions in the construction of the questionnaire, the differences will be noted.

The questionnaire has several functions or objectives. It is the "package" that presents the questions and ultimately contains the record of response for an individual respondent. The first section of the questionnaire introduces the survey to the respondents. The internal sections contain the items and scales relating to the survey topics, in a logical and necessary sequence. The final section ordinarily contains questions to measure the characteristics of the respondents, so that they can be grouped and compared. The questionnaire also contains several other elements that facilitate data handling. These include the spaces to record the data and the codes that identify particular responses. The questionnaire also shows the column and record of the data file into which each data point will be keyed.

Other instrumentation devices to accompany the questionnaire are also identified and discussed in this chapter. They include such things as the mailing piece for mail surveys or rating scale cards for interviewing.

Survey Introduction

Research surveys ordinarily depend very heavily on the *voluntary* cooperation of respondents. Research experience consistently indicates that nearly all who refuse their cooperation do so within the first few seconds after initial contact, whether that contact is in person, on the telephone, or by mail. The general principle is this: if the potential respondent agrees to participate promptly when the survey is introduced, only a very small percentage will withdraw their cooperation later. Once they *begin,* they almost invariably continue and complete the response task, except under the most unusual circumstances. Consequently, it is absolutely essential that the introduction be composed and delivered effectively. If the survey is introduced properly, the response rate will be increased and the reliability and validity of the survey enhanced. If it is done poorly, refusal and nonresponse will increase data collection time and costs. Error and bias will be introduced and the reliability and validity of the data will be diminished.

Questionnaire Organization

The cover letter or interviewer greeting serves as the introduction to the questionnaire and response task. It is very useful to view the questionnaire, itself, in three main parts: the initiation, the "body" of the questionnaire, and the conclusion. Each plays a different role. The composition of cover letters is discussed in Chapter 7. In Chapter 8 the initial greeting is considered in detail.

The first part of the questionnaire initiates the task for the respondent. It "sets the stage" and suggests what kinds of questions will follow. It indicates the type of information sought, and provides some indications concerning the response task. Usually, this first part contains the most general questions that will be asked of respondents. It is important to include only questions that are applicable to all respondents and are fairly quick and easy to answer in the initiation portion of the questionnaire. It is especially important to avoid any questions or issues that may be threatening to respondents. This is *not* the place to ask "delicate" questions or seek "sensitive" information.

The body of the questionnaire is the middle portion. It is ordinarily much larger than the initiation or conclusion. It contains the questions or items that deal with the substance and detail of the survey topics. The specific organization of this part of the questionnaire is discussed below. The general rule is that the items should be in a sequence that appears to be logical and meaningful to respondents. There should be a smooth transition from one issue or topic to the next, with no sudden breaks or dramatic changes in the respondents' frame of reference.

GUIDELIST 6-1

For Organizing the Questionnaire

1. Picture the questionnaire in three major parts: initiation, body, and conclusion.

2. Begin with the most general questions and avoid those that might be threatening or difficult to answer.

3. Remember the initial portion sets the stage and influences the respondents' expectations about what is to come.

4. Be sure the body of the questionnaire flows smoothly form one issue to the next.

5. List items in the body in a sequence that is logical and meaningful to respondents.

6. Save the most sensitive issues and threatening questions for the concluding portion, when rapport is greatest.

7. List demographic or biographic questions last, so that if some respondents decline, most data is still usable.

The final or concluding part of the questionnaire is best reserved for two kinds of questions: Those that deal with the most sensitive or delicate issues or topics, and those that measure the attributes or characteristics of the respondents. The "demographic" or "biographic" questions and variables are almost always contained in the final portion of the questionnaire. The reasons for reserving these questions until the end of the response task are simple but compelling. First, the respondent has become familiar with the inquiry and rapport should be maximum at this point. Thus, they have more trust and are less likely to be skeptical or uncooperative. Second, some respondents may terminate at this point or refuse to answer some of the items. Nevertheless, they have provided the bulk of the data and their responses to these items may still be usable.

CREATING QUESTIONNAIRE SECTIONS

For most surveys, the questions can be grouped into smaller sections than the three main parts described above. Some surveys may include only a dozen or so questions, but typically a survey will have 50, 100, or more individual items. Grouping the items into sections will simplify the task of asking the questions. It will both make the task appear simpler and easier for the respondent, and actually make it so. The more effectively the items are grouped into sections, the more efficient the questionnaire will be.

Grouping Items by Topic. One of the most common criteria for grouping items is by topic. For example, a marketing research survey may contain questions about three different topics: past, present and future purchase *behavior*, the *image* of one or more retail stores, and the *lifestyle* of the respondents. One section of the questionnaire might be devoted to each of these topics. Each section would contain all of the individual items devoted to that particular survey topic. This would be an effective means of organizing the items, providing that it appears logical or makes sense to the respondents. For example, it would make sense to ask all about the products they have purchased from various stores in one section, then about their perceptions or images of several different stores. This might be followed by a section containing several items that would define their lifestyle in terms of the respondents' activities, interests, and opinions. This would be a much more meaningful organization than if all the various topics and kinds of questions were intermixed with one another.

Grouping Items by Content. Survey items can also be grouped logically by the content of the questions. For example, it would make sense to the respondents if all items about job satisfaction were asked in one place, all items about relationships with co-workers were contained in another, and all questions concerning occupational history were listed together in a third section. It would not be appropriate to "jump around" from one of these areas of inquiry to another. After the first question or so about a particular area, the respondents' minds will have turned to that issue. They can easily respond to additional items about the issue, but it would be difficult to shift abruptly to another issue, then turn their attention again to the first.

Grouping by Scaling Technique. Often many survey questions can be answered using the same scale. When that is the case, it is most economical and efficient to list them together in one section of the questionnaire. For example, all of the items composed as statements and using a Likert Scale (Strongly agree, Agree, Neutral, Disagree, or Strongly disagree) can be listed in one place and the scale shown only once at that point in the questionnaire. Another section might contain all of the items that use a Verbal Frequency Scale (Always, Often, Sometimes, Rarely, or Never). Such a grouping saves time and space and makes the response task easier as well. The respondents need only read the instructions and learn to use that scale one time, and they can then proceed through the list of all such items.

Grouping by Multiple Criteria. Items can often be grouped by two or by all three of the criteria listed above. In other words, the items are often such that a set of them are devoted to the same topic, contain similar content, and require the same scaling technique. This is, of course, the ideal situation because there is both a logical sequence and a very high degree of time and space economy. Several of the examples of scaling techniques shown in the previous chapter contain items grouped by type of scale and by topic or content as well. When

---

EXAMPLE 6–1

The Multiple Rating Matrix

Several savings or investment vehicles are listed below. Please indicate how safe or risky you feel each one is by circling a number beside it. If you feel it is very safe, circle a number toward the left. If you feel it is very risky, circle one toward the right, and if you think it is someplace in between, circle a number from the middle range that indicates your opinion.

	Extremely Safe					Extremely Risky		
Banking savings account	1	2	3	4	5	6	7	11
Savings and loan savings account.	1	2	3	4	5	6	7	12
Money market account.	1	2	3	4	5	6	7	13
Certificates of deposit.	1	2	3	4	5	6	7	14
Treasury bills	1	2	3	4	5	6	7	15
Corporate common stocks	1	2	3	4	5	6	7	16
Corporate preferred stocks	1	2	3	4	5	6	7	17
Corporate bonds	1	2	3	4	5	6	7	18
Municipal bonds	1	2	3	4	5	6	7	19
U.S. government bonds	1	2	3	4	5	6	7	20
Foreign government bonds	1	2	3	4	5	6	7	21
Credit union shares	1	2	3	4	5	6	7	22
Commodity futures.	1	2	3	4	5	6	7	23
Corporate stock futures.	1	2	3	4	5	6	7	24
Precious metals	1	2	3	4	5	6	7	25
Precious gems	1	2	3	4	5	6	7	26

a group of items can be included in one section, meeting two or three of the criteria, special scaling methods can be devised to gain even further facility and economy. Example 6–1 shows one such combination. One set of instructions and one horizontal, numeric scale serve all 16 items. Respondents need only circle a number on each row of the matrix, rather than jotting it down, so the task can be completed very quickly and easily. Another example of a grouping of items in an even more condensed format is shown in Example 6–2. In that example, nine items are each rated four times on a horizontal, numeric scale. Thus, 36 data points are obtained with sufficient ease and very little space.

EXAMPLE 6–2

The Multiple Rating Grid

The grid shown below lists four types of "PRO" brand baseball equipment along the top, and several characteristics of sports equipment along the left side. Please take one product at a time, and working down the column, pick a number from the scale indicating your evaluation of each characteristic, and jot it in the space in that column to the right of the characteristic. We would like your rating for each product and characteristic.

Scale

Very poor   1   2   3   4   5   6   Excellent

	Bats	Balls	Gloves	Shoes	
Price..............	——	——	——	——	11–14
Design............	——	——	——	——	15–18
Selection..........	——	——	——	——	19–22
Durability..........	——	——	——	——	23–26
Appearance.......	——	——	——	——	27–30
Availability.........	——	——	——	——	31–34
Service............	——	——	——	——	35–38
Packaging.........	——	——	——	——	39–42
Construction.......	——	——	——	——	43–46

The questionnaire is an outline of a "conversation" between the researcher and the respondents. The respondents do not expect the conversation to switch abruptly from one topic, issue, or format to another. Each section should be integrated and consistent, and there should be a "bridge" leading from one section to the next, to insure proper flow of the dialogue.

GUIDELIST 6-2

For Grouping Items into Sections

1. Group items into sections in order to save interviewer time or space on a self-administered questionnaire.

2. Always group items in a way that is meaningful to the respondents or facilitates answering questions.

3. Items that deal with the same survey topic can often be clustered into meaningful sections.

4. When items have similar content or deal with the same issues, they may form a single section.

5. Items that use the same scaling technique may be grouped together into a coherent section.

6. Often grouping of items can be based on two or three of the criteria listed above.

7. When items use the same type of scale and have similar content, special scaling formats can be composed.

8. It is very efficient and practical to group items so that many share the same scale and instructions.

Conditional Branching

Often there are survey items that apply to some respondents but not to others, depending on their answers to a previous question. When that is the case, the questionnaire writer must use a "branch" or "go to" statement so that those for whom the items do not apply will skip them.

Four slightly different methods of branching within a questionnaire are shown in Example 6-3. The instructions might be expressed a little differently, depending on whether the data collection was by mail and the questionnaire self-administered, or by interview in person or on the telephone. In any case, the basic concept is the same. Assume that in the examples shown, the researcher intends to ask one or more questions about the Sunday newspaper. It may not make sense to ask such questions of those who did not subscribe. Consequently, the questionnaire must *first* establish whether or not the respondent subscribes. If so, the question(s) would be asked. If not, they would not be asked and the process would move on to other issues and questions.

EXAMPLE 6-3

The Use of Conditional Branching

Implied Branch or Subquestion

Do you subscribe to the Sunday newspaper?	___ yes	___ no
If so, do you read it regularly?	___ yes	___ no

Explicit Branch with a Single "Go To"

Do you subscribe to the Sunday newspaper?	___ yes	___ no
[If not, go to Question 30]		

Explicit Branch with "Skip"

Do you subscribe to the Sunday newspaper?	___ yes	___ no
[If not, skip Question 20]		

Explicit Branch with Multiple "Go To's"

What Sunday newspaper do you *most* often read, if any?

___ Times	(Go to Question 30)
___ Tribune	(Go to Question 35)
___ Dispatch	(Go to Question 40)
___ Chronicle	(Go to Question 45)
___ none	(Go to Question 50)

The first example shown is an "implied" branch because there are no specific branching instructions. The second question begins with the phrase, "If so, . . ." to indicate that if not, the question need not be answered. This is the most simple form of branching around a question that may not always apply. It is often used in self-administered questionnaires because it is simple, quick and easy for the respondent to understand. Even if some respondents who need not answer the question do so, little time and effort is lost and the data for such cases can be ignored when it is transferred and processed.

The second example is very typical of an explicit branch. It contains instructions directing the interviewer or the respondent to go to a particular question, and any items between the instruction and that point would be ignored or skipped. Alternative forms of the instruction might specify a different page of the questionnaire, or some other mark or indication might be used in place of the question number. For example, interviewers might be instructed: "IF *NO,* go to the * below," or some similar designation.

The third section of the example shows a similar branch with an explicit instruction, but rather than directing the interviewer or respondent to a particular place, it indicates what must be skipped. It

---

CHECKLIST 6-1

To Organize and Group Items

1. Does the initial section "set the stage" for respondents? If not, only general, nonthreatening items that apply to everyone should be retained in the first section.

2. Is each section in the body of the questionnaire organized around one topic, set of issues, or scaling technique? If not, items must be regrouped into meaningful sections.

3. Does the "conversation" flow smoothly from one section to the next? Rearrange the sections or insert a "bridge" between sections when necessary.

4. Have threatening or "sensitive" questions been retained for the latter sections of the questionnaire? If so, they will more often be answered because rapport is greater.

5. Are the demographic or biographic items contained in the concluding section? Placing them there increases response and obtains the most data in case of refusal.

6. Does the entire dialogue flow smoothly in a manner meaningful to respondents? If not, any abrupt shifts or discontinuities should be identified and removed.

---

is ordinarily advisable to use this form only when one or two items are to be skipped. It becomes too complex and difficult when several items to be skipped must be listed in this way. It is also important to note that the question(s) to be skipped should be *immediately* following the instruction. The interviewer or respondent will not remember to skip the items if they come later in the questionnaire.

The last example shown consists of an explicit, multiple branch. In this case, the researcher needs to ask a *different* set of questions, depending on which paper is most often read. (Note that the item seeks only one newspaper. If it asked about subscription, more than one might be identified and the branching would become extremely complex and intricate.) This type of branching instruction is acceptable for interview surveys, but it is ordinarily too complex for mail surveys that are self-administered by respondents. Notice, also, that this format will require a second branch after the set of five questions about any one newspaper. Presumably, an unconditional branch instruction would be used to direct the questioning process to item 50, where a new set of questions or issues would be addressed.

As with the single "go to" branch statement example, the designation of where to go need not be listed as a question number. The instruction might refer to "Part A, B, C, etc." to "Section I, II, III, etc." to a page number, or to any other meaningful designation. The researcher constructing the questionnaire may wish to use color coding or shading of pages or sections, or any other device that would help make the place to which the process should move distinct and clearly identifiable.

Unconditional Branching

The conditional branches just described are so called because the branch is made "on condition" that a certain answer is given to the preceding question. An *un*conditional branch directs the questioning process to another place for all respondents who reach that particular location on the questionnaire. In the example of a branch with multiple "go to" instructions used earlier, some respondents might indicate they most often read the Sunday Times. The interviewer would then move to Question 30, as shown in Example 6–4 and ask the next five questions. Because Questions 35 through 49 apply to other newspapers, the process would then branch over them and go to the next section, beginning with Question 50. A similar such branch instruction would follow Questions 39 and 44, but obviously if the branch was to Question 50, none would be required after Question 49. As in the case of conditional branch instructions, unconditional branches need not necessarily use a question number, and any other clearly identifiable means of designating the location to which the questioning process should move would be acceptable.

EXAMPLE 6–4

The Use of an Unconditional Branch

30. Do you *regularly* read the:	Magazine section?	___ yes	___ no
31.	Sports pages?	___ yes	___ no
32.	Editorials?	___ yes	___ no
33.	Religious news?	___ yes	___ no
34.	Home directory?	___ yes	___ no

(Go to Question 50)

Branching Limitations

Branching instructions within the questionnaire can be very useful and helpful, and at times, some form of branching will be inevitable. On the other hand, the use of branching is strictly limited. Each branch adds greatly to the complexity of the interviewing or response task. Thus, too many branches or use of the technique too extensively tends to introduce bias and error and thus, to reduce the reliability and validity of the results. With the use of a self-administered mail questionnaire, the least sophisticated respondents will often become confused or bewildered by the instructions and fail to follow them correctly. The respondents are voluntarily doing the task for the researcher, and if it becomes too complex or difficult, many are likely to give up and fail to return the completed questionnaire.

While the researcher is somewhat more free to use branching instructions with personal or telephone interview surveys, the use of branches is still very limited. Those who construct questionnaires commonly, if not universally overestimate both the ability and the willingness of the interviewers to follow instructions. In addition, it is often difficult for those building the questionnaire or interview schedule to appreciate the conditions under which the field workers or interviewers must ask the questions and record the responses. Needless to say, it is often extremely difficult to hold the respondents attention and maintain their interest, and at the same time, to record answers, read branching instructions, find the correct location to which they direct the flow of questions, and continue with the interview. An occasional branch over one or a very few items is almost always acceptable. When many branches are required and the task is very complex, it would be advisable to prequalify respondents and use alternative forms of the questionnaire for different groups of respondents.

CHECKLIST 6-2

To Use Branching Instructions

1. Are the data to be collected with a self-administered questionnaire? If so, branching must be strictly limited.

2. Does only one question immediately following another need to be skipped by some respondents? In that case, use an implied branch instruction, such as "If so . . ."

3. Must some respondents skip an entire set of questions? If so, a conditional branch with "go to" should be used.

4. Do several different answers to an item require going to several different sections that must be completed? If so, a multiple, conditional branch and an unconditional branch after each such section will be needed.

5. Is the location to which each branch is to be made clearly designated and easily identified? If not, shading, color coding, or some other designation should be included.

6. Is it absolutely certain that the least sophisticated or least motivated interviewers or respondents can and will branch correctly? If not, modifications are necessary.

7. Are there more than a few branches required within the questionnaire? If so, multiple forms of the questionnaire should be considered.

8. Are there several branches that are based on the same basic "condition" or response? If so, the conditioning question should be used as a "qualifier" in the greeting and multiple forms of the questionnaire used.

COMPOSING INSTRUCTIONS

Whether the questionnaire is self-administered or administered by an interviewer, there are likely to be many places where instructions are required or where they would be helpful. Instructions are really not part of the actual questions or items. Rather, they tell the interviewer or respondent how to present or respond to one or more questions. Most often the instructions will apply to an entire set of items or questions. For example, several items may use the same scale for response, and the instructions indicate how the scale is to be used.

The indented paragraphs above the items listed in Example 6–1 and Example 6–2 presented earlier in this chapter, are typical examples of instructions. They apply to all of the items listed below them. Many other such examples of instructions relating to scales are shown in the previous chapter. Most scaling techniques require some instruction, at least for the first time they appear in a questionnaire, and these are the most common instructions found in questionnaires. On the other hand, these are only one instance of the use of instructions within a questionnaire, and several other types of instructions may also be required or useful. Some of these other types of instructions will be considered later, after discussing those used with scales.

Instructions for Using Scales. The more complex the scaling technique and the less sophisticated the responding population, the more elaborate the instructions must be. For example, the very common Likert scale with five categories ranging from "Strongly agree" to

"Strongly disagree" ordinarily requires very simple instruction. Typically, it would be sufficient merely to say, "Please pick a number to show how much you agree or disagree and jot it in the space beside each statement below."

The Semantic Differential Scale, shown in Example 5–9 in the previous chapter, requires very brief instruction because of its visual or graphic nature. On the other hand, the Stapel Scale, shown in Example 5–11, requires a little more elaboration because it is less graphic and depends on a horizontal, numeric rating scale from which numbers are selected and recorded. The Fixed Sum Scale shown in Example 5–12 of the previous chapter is even more complex because the answers should total to a given, constant sum. Thus, that example provides the basic instruction at the top, an additional, parenthetical note just above the items, and yet another "cue" at the bottom indicating the total to which the numbers should sum.

The degree to which instructions should be simple and brief or elaborate and complete depends as much on the sophistication of the respondents as on the complexity of the scales. Example 6–1, shown earlier in this chapter, contains very thorough and complete instructions. It assumes that the respondents are relatively naive or unsophisticated. If this same scaling technique and set of items were to be used for a survey of Certified Public Accountants, rather than the general public, the instructions might read as follows: "Please circle a number for each investment vehicle to show your perception of financial risk." The general rule is to compose instructions that meet the requirements of the least sophisticated respondents.

Instructions on how respondents from the general public should use scales should ordinarily contain several elements. They should say: (a) what items or elements are to be rated; (b) what criterion or standard should be used for judgment; (c) how the scale is to be used; and (d) exactly how and where the responses are to be reported or recorded. In Example 6–5, the correct version contains all elements while the incorrect version contains none.

The incorrect example does not indicate that respondents should rate each and every item. Typically, many respondents would rate only some of them and ignore others or would rate all of them collectively, as a set. More importantly, this version of the instructions does not indicate the basis, standard, or criterion to be used when rating the items. The correct version indicates that importance of *ownership* should be rated. Many, if not most respondents would agree that it is vitally important to have a refrigerator or a kitchen range available, and in the incorrect version, these appliances would almost always be rated as highly important. On the other hand, many who

---

EXAMPLE 6-5

Correct and Incorrect Scale Instructions

Wrong: Please rate the importance of the following.

Scale

Unimportant   1   2   3   4   5   Important

___ Dishwasher
___ Kitchen range
___ Refrigerator
___ Washing machine
___ Clothes dryer

Right: Please rate how important it is for *you to own EACH* of these household appliances. If it is not at all important to own it, pick a low number from the scale and jot it in the space in front of the item. If it's very important, pick a high number, and if it's somewhat important, pick a number from the middle range and jot it in the space.

Scale

Unimportant   1   2   3   4   5   Important

___ Dishwasher
___ Kitchen range
___ Refrigerator
___ Washing machine
___ Clothes dryer

---

rent homes where such appliances are provided would not regard it as important to own those appliances.

The incorrect version does not indicate how the scale is to be used. Note there are five points on the scale and five items to be rated. Many respondents could be expected to *rank* the items, when the researcher's intention was clearly to obtain ratings where two or more may be rated the same. Lastly, the incorrect version does not indicate how or where the answers are to be recorded. Thus, some respondents could be expected to check a space, others to circle scale numbers, and still others to write in the words "unimportant" and "important." To the inexperienced researcher, such responses might seem to be absurdities that are highly unlikely. They are not. Extensive experience demonstrates all too well that a surprisingly large proportion of respondents will provide very bizarre responses if the instructions are not crystal clear.

GUIDELIST 6-3

For Composing Scale Instructions

1. Clearly indicate which items are to be rated and if only one is to be picked or an answer recorded for all items.
2. Say what criterion or standard should be used to judge the items or answer the questions.
3. Describe how the scale is to be used and include an example if the task is complex or difficult.
4. State how the responses are to be reported or recorded, such as a check mark, number, circle, etc.
5. Use brief instructions for simple, easy tasks and more elaborate instructions for more difficult response tasks.
6. Make the instructions clear and complete enough to be sufficient for the *least* sophisticated respondents.
7. The less sophisticated the responding sample, the more complete and thorough the instructions must be.
8. Write instructions so the most sophisticated respondents need only read the first part and can skip the remainder.

It is ordinarily better to error in the direction of providing instructions that are too thorough than too brief. If the instructions are well written, the more sophisticated respondents who quickly understand will need only read the beginning, while others have complete direction when needed.

Special Instructions

There are times when the respondents must be given special instructions on how to respond to one or more survey items. The need for such special instructions depends on the particular situation. Some examples of them are shown in Example 6–6.

In Section A of Example 6–6, respondents are instructed to read each item only once and not to study or compare the items. The instructions in Section B of the example list an "unconditional inclusion." The favorite brand is to be rated, *regardless* of whether or not other brands are sometimes purchased. In Section C, the respondent is instructed to respond for his or her spouse, rather than for him- or herself. The instructions in Section D list a "conditional exclusion."

EXAMPLE 6-6

Special Respondent Instructions

A. Please read each item *one time*, then indicate your opinion. Remember, it's your *first impression* that counts.

B. Please answer the following questions about your *favorite* brand, even though you may sometimes buy others.

C. Please pick a number from the scale to show how often *your spouse* does each of the following things.

D. Please rate how satisfied or dissatisfied you are with each appliance that *you now own.* Leave the space beside the item blank if you do not now own one.

E. Let's assume that you have decided to buy a new car in the next few weeks. What brand would you be most likely to consider *first.*

F. If one of your children suddenly needed emergency medical treatment during the daytime, where would you be most likely to take the child?

Since the respondents do not rate appliances they do not own, these are *implied,* miniature branches around such items. The last two sections list *assumptions* that the respondent is to make when answering the questions. In Section E the assumption is explicitly listed in the first sentence. The example in Section F implies an assumption with the use of the conditional clause, "If one of your children . . ." These are but a few such special instructions that might be needed for some survey items. Special instructions such as these are needed whenever the respondents are to make an assumption, answer for another person, base their responses on a special criterion, or otherwise act or respond in some extraordinary manner. The same rules of grammar, vocabulary and style that apply to composition of survey items, themselves, also apply to the composition of special instructions. They must be crystal clear, and the key words or phrases should be underlined or highlighted to insure recognition.

Interviewer Instructions

When a telephone or personal interview survey is to be conducted, it will often be necessary to include instructions for the interviewers within the survey instrument. These are designed for the interviewers only, and they are not read or shown to the respondents. Several such instructions are shown in Example 6-7.

EXAMPLE 6-7

Instructions for Interviewers Only

A. [If yes:] What store did you purchase it from?

B. [If respondent is male, skip to page 5.]

C. [If respondent is married, return to * above and ask each question about his or her spouse.]

D. [Hand respondent the pink rating card.]

E. [Check appropriate category below but do NOT read alternatives to respondent.]

F. Are there any other reasons? [Probe for all others.]

G. [Record ethnicity of respondent below. DO NOT ASK!]

_____ White	_____ Black
_____ Oriental	_____ Hispanic
_____ Other (Specify what: _____)	

Sections A, B, and C are samples of branching instructions for interviewers. Branching was discussed in detail earlier in this chapter, but it is important to note here the exceptions that apply for an interview survey. First, the instructions should be enclosed in brackets or parentheses, written in upper case letters, or otherwise distinguished from the items, themselves. The questionnaire writer should use *one* convention throughout the entire instrument to indicate to the interviewers that these phrases are not to be read to respondents. Any easily recognizable markings will do, so long as the same ones are used throughout and all interviewers know what they mean.

It is also important to note that branching must be limited and very clearly indicated. Some researchers are inclined to assume that the field workers are more sophisticated and better motivated than they are actually likely to be. The branching can be *somewhat* more elaborate or *slightly* more complex for interviewers than if the questionnaire is self-administered, but not much. While interviewers receive training and instruction before going into the field and can examine the questionnaire thoroughly before using it, it is advisable to assume they are no more sophisticated than are the responding sample.

Section D of the example is merely an instruction to give the respondent a visual display of a rating scale. Such supplementary materials will be discussed more fully later in this chapter. In Section E, the field worker is instructed in how to record the responses and reminded not to list the alternative for the respondent. Similar instructions can be used to indicate that the alternatives *should* be read to respondents, when that is required. Notice that the word "not" is both entirely upper case and underlined, to be sure the interviewer sees this is a prohibition.

Section F of Example 6–7 shows a question followed by a general instruction for the interviewer to probe for more reasons. The use of probing is discussed more fully in Chapter 8. Interviewers are instructed on the methods for probing when they are trained or before going into the field, so they need only be told in the survey instrument when to do so and they need not be told exactly how to do it each time a probe is required.

In the final example, Section G, the interviewers are conducting a personal survey so that they can visually identify the respondents' ethnicity. They are instructed to record it without asking the respondent, so that any potential threat might be avoided. Note the use of uppercase letters and underlining, so that the interviewer will not fail to see that part of the instruction.

These are only a few such special instructions for interviewers. Many other types might be used, as they are needed. The same general rules about clarity and simplicity apply to these instructions as to all others.

GUIDELIST 6–4

For Composing Special Instructions

1. Keep the instructions as clear and simple as possible.

2. Use upper case letters, bold face type, italics or underlining to highlight important words or phrases.

3. Set instructions slightly apart from actual items.

4. Use some convention, such as brackets or parentheses, for instructions to interviewers only.

Interview Rating Cards

Surveys often require respondents to rate items using a scale. With self-administered questionnaires, the scales can be printed directly on the survey instrument. If personal interviewing is used, the various scales must be printed on cards that can be handed to the respondents, so that they can see the scale and select their choice for each item as it is read. Three such samples are shown in Example 6–8.

EXAMPLE 6–8

Respondent Rating Cards

A.   *Horizontal, Numeric Scale Card*

> *Scale*
>
> Unimportant   1 2 3 4 5   Important

B.   *Verbal Frequency Scale Card*

> 1 = Always
> 2 = Often
> 3 = Sometimes
> 4 = Rarely
> 5 = Never

C.   *Annual Family Income Indicator*

> R = Under $10,000
> G = $10,000 to $19,999
> L = $20,000 to $29,999
> W = $30,000 to $39,999
> F = $40,000 to $49,999
> Q = $50,000 & Over

In each case, the questionnaire would contain an instruction to the interviewer to hand the respondent the rating card. The cards should be color coded by printing each on a different color card stock, or they can be labeled with a name, letter, or number to distinguish the various types. When such identification is used, the labels should be printed on *both* sides of each card, to facilitate their recognition and use. It is usually not advisable to include more than one such scale on the same card. Ordinarily, the contents of the cards are printed in large typeface, or the cards can be prepared with large type by using "dry transfer" numbers and letters or lettering stencils.

In the first two examples, in Section A and B, two frequently used scales are shown. They are basically the same as those used for a self-administered questionnaire, shown in Chapter 5. The same type of instructions are given respondents and they are used in the same way as described earlier. The last example in Section C shows a rating card for obtaining an indication of annual family income. This is a "sensitive" item. Many respondents are likely to refuse, those with high incomes tend to understate and those with low incomes tend to overstate income if asked the dollar amount. Thus, using random letters obtains more reliable data. Respondents are asked simply to report what letter indicates their annual family income.

GUIDELIST 6–5

For Creating Respondent Rating Cards

1. Put only one rating scale on each card to make identification easier and facilitate handling.
2. Color code the cards or label them with a name, letter, or number on *both* sides so they are easily recognized.
3. Have the cards printed, use dry transfer letters and numbers, or a letter stencil using a large typeface.
4. Compose instructions using the same rules as for scales on self-administered questionnaires.

GRAPHIC AND PICTORIAL SECTIONS

The survey items and scales that have been discussed and shown in examples earlier have all contained verbal and numeric content. There are some situations where graphic or pictorial survey items must be used to obtain the data. For example, with a survey of young children, the respondents' ability to read or to understand numeric scales may be very limited. It may not be feasible to measure the children's evaluations or reactions with the scales described earlier. One solution might be to use a pictorial scale, such as one shown in Example 6–9.

In Section A of the example, the interviewer would first ask the child to point to the face that is very happy, then to the one that is very sad, to be sure the child understands the pictures. The children would then be asked to point to the face that shows how they feel when they do each of the things listed in the items, such as going to school or watching TV cartoons.

EXAMPLE 6–9

Children's Pictorial Scale Cards

A. Happy and Sad Faces

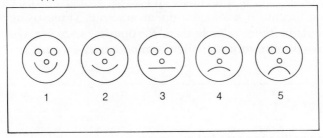

B. The Bottle Scale

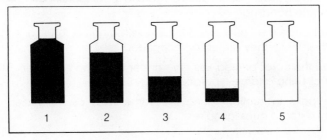

C. The Stair-Step Scale

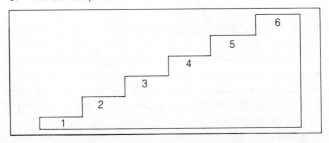

The sad faces and happy faces work well for very young children. Even though they may have very little experience with letters, numbers, and other symbols, they have learned to recognize facial expressions very early in life. For older children, The Bottle Scale, shown in Section B of the example, may be more acceptable to the respondents and it provides smaller increments for a more fine-grained measurement. The Stair-Step Scale, shown in Section C works effectively both for older children and for adults with little education or with impairments that limit their ability to respond to verbal and numerical scales.

These are but three of many such graphic or pictorial scales that might be created and used in questionnaires. Other such possibilities include pictures of ladders, thermometers, or geometric figures of various size or height. Any such pictorial scales should be easy for the respondents to understand, they should be based on some phenomenon with which the respondents would be very familiar, and they should be easy to draw or create. Scales of this type are most often used for personal interview surveys, but they can also be included in self-administered questionnaires for some respondent groups.

Example 6–10 shows one example of using a diagram to capture several pieces of data. This item obtains a complete "picture" of the family. Asking the respondent to circle his or her own age after listing it in the diagram has an additional advantage. Respondents are less likely to lie about their age because they ordinarily list the correct age with the others in the family and are reluctant to change it afterward.

EXAMPLE 6–10

The Diagrammatic Scale

Please list the ages of all those in your family living at home in the spaces below. Jot the ages of the women and girls in the *circles*, and the ages of the men and boys in the *squares*. Use as many spaces as you need, listing them in order from oldest to youngest in each row.

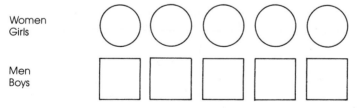

Now draw a big circle around the space with *your own age* in it.

Other types of diagrammatic scales or items include simple line drawings depicting geographic areas, buildings, housing complexes, malls, or shopping centers. They can be used to measure traffic patterns or locational preferences of respondents.

GUIDELIST 6–6

For Creating Pictorial Scales

1. They must be very easy for respondents to understand.
2. They should show something respondents have often seen.
3. They should represent the thing that is being measured.
4. They should be easy to draw or create.

The Demographic Section

Almost every survey contains items indicating the status of the respondents. These are called "demographic" items. They are used in three ways: First, the profiles portray the nature of the sample. Second, the demographic profile of the sample can be compared to that for the population as a whole, when these parameters are known. Third, the items can be used to divide the sample into subsamples by age, sex, etc. The data for the other survey items can then be compared among the demographic groups to determine the effect of demographic status on other responses.

Figure 6–1 contains a fairly exhaustive list of demographic items. Not all of them will be required for any given survey, and some other items, such as travel history or residential history might also be included with demographics. For some surveys, demographic data for only the respondent would be necessary. For others, it may be valuable to obtain demographic data for both heads of household. (In years past, surveys sought data for *the* head of household, assuming the person was a male. In contemporary American society, that often creates resentment and data for both heads of household are invariably more valid.)

FIGURE 6–1

Commonly Used Demographic Variables

A. Sex of respondent.

B. Sex of family members.

C. Age of respondent.

D. Age of each head of household.

E. Age of family members.

F. Age of youngest child in the home.

G. Education of respondent.

H. Education of each head of household.

I. Employment of respondent.

J. Employment of each head of household.

K. Occupation of respondent.

L. Occupation of each head of household.

M. Annual income of respondent.

N. Annual income of each head of household.

O. Annual family income.

P. Racial or ethnic identity of respondent.

Q. Race or ethnicity of each head of household.

R. Religious preference of respondent.

S. Religion of each head of household.

T. Type of family dwelling.

U. Zip code, or location of residence.

V. Time of residence at present location.

W. Self-designated social class membership.

The age of the youngest child is often included because it can be used with marital status and occupation to determine the stage in the family life cycle. There are several different classifications of family life cycle, but the most common scheme is described in Figure 6–2. In many cases, the stage in the family life cycle is more likely to influence response than merely the age of the respondent. For example, a 35-year-old single male may respond in a manner more similar to a 20-year-old single male than to a 35-year-old who is married and has children in the home.

Demographic items are ordinarily clustered together in a single section and included at the end of the questionnaire. Doing so facilitates response, and respondents are less likely to refuse or terminate the process if they have been cooperating for some time. Notice that income, ordinarily the most sensitive and threatening demographic item, has been listed last. Similarly, if racial or ethnic identity or religious preference were to be included, they would be listed just prior to annual income. Even if a small proportion should decide to

---

FIGURE 6–2

Family Life Cycle Stages

1. Young Single:
   Under 45 years of age, not married and/or living with a spouse, no children in the home.
2. Young Couple:
   Under 45 years of age, married, no children in the home.
3. Full Nest I:
   Single or married parent with the youngest child in the home less than six years old.
4. Full Nest II:
   Single or married parent with youngest child in the home from 6 to 15.
5. Full Nest III:
   Single or married parent with the youngest child in the home between 16 to 23.
6. Empty Nest I:
   Over 44, married, no children in the home, one or both in the work force.
7. Empty Nest II:
   Over 44, married, no children in the home, retired, neither in the work force.
8. Single Elder I:
   Over 44, not married, no children in the home, still in the work force.
9. Single Elder II:
   Over 44, not married, no children in the home, retired, not in the work force.

---

refuse further cooperation, data obtained earlier in the questionnaire may still be usable and valuable.

A typical demographic page, obtaining five pieces of data for each head of household, is shown in Example 6–11. It would, of course, be necessary to include an additional item to learn the sex of the respondent, if that were not to be recorded by an interviewer. If family life cycle stage were to be computed, the age of the youngest child at home would also be required.

In the example, age, education, and income are to be obtained in

EXAMPLE 6–11

Demographic Questionnaire Section

Please check or fill in the items below for *each* head of household present.

MALE Head of Household	*FEMALE Head of Household*	
Age.................... ___ years	Age................. ___ years	11–14
Formal education....... ___ years	Formal education.... ___ years	15–18
(For example, high school graduate = 12 years)		

Employment Status: *Employment Status:*

(1) ___ company employed	(1) ___ company employed	
(2) ___ government employed	(2) ___ government employed	
(3) ___ self-employed	(3) ___ self-employed	
(4) ___ seeking employment	(4) ___ seeking employment	19–20
(5) ___ military	(5) ___ homemaker	
(6) ___ retired	(6) ___ retired	
(7) ___ student	(7) ___ student	

Occupational Status: *Occupational Status:*

(1) ___ professional (med, law, etc.)	(1) ___ professional (med, law, etc.)	
(2) ___ managerial, executive	(2) ___ managerial, executive	
(3) ___ administrative, clerical	(3) ___ administrative, clerical	
(4) ___ engineering, technical	(4) ___ engineering, technical	21–22
(5) ___ marketing, sales	(5) ___ marketing, sales	
(6) ___ skilled craft or trade	(6) ___ skilled craft or trade	
(7) ___ semiskilled occupation	(7) ___ semiskilled occupation	

Annual Income: *Annual Income:*

Approximately $___,000.00	Approximately $___,000.00	23–26

continuous, numeric form. They can be grouped into appropriate categories during data processing if that is required. Employment and occupation are listed in categories. Different categories, more or fewer in number, might be used, depending on the nature of the survey and the information requirements. The categories listed have proved to be both meaningful and easily understood in many surveys of the adult, general public.

The format in the example is typical of one for a self-administered questionnaire. Respondents can complete it quickly and easily. If only one head of household is present, the other column is simply ignored. This or a similar format would, of course, work effectively for an interview survey, with appropriate interviewer instructions included.

PRECODING AND FORMATTING

The survey questionnaire should contain two kinds of numbers that are included for data transfer and processing, rather than for respondents. When a questionnaire is "precoded," it contains a number (or letter) code for each alternative. Notice that in Example 6–11 the employment and occupation categories are numbered from one to seven and the numbers are in brackets. These are the code numbers that will later be keyed to a data file or transferred to a work sheet for processing. Listing such codes on the questionnaire before data collection avoids the extremely laborious and time-consuming task of "postcoding" the alternatives. In fact, one of the major reasons for using structured questions is the ability to precode the alternatives.

Notice that in the example, age, education, and income are not and cannot be precoded. Nor do they need to be. The numeric values that respondents record would be keyed directly to file, so no precoding is required for these and other numeric items. Similarly, some of the scales shown in the examples in the previous chapter contain no precodes, or the codes are a part of the scales, themselves. On the other hand, where the scale is formed by categories, such as the Likert Scale, the categories must then be precoded with a letter or number. Numbers are far preferable to letters because they can be keyed and handled more easily during data transfer and processing.

The second type of numbers that are printed on the questionnaire can be seen in the far right-hand margin of Example 6–11 and in the examples shown in the previous chapter. These numbers specify the "record format" that will be used for the data. While the precodes are *what* will be keyed, the record format numbers indicate *where* in the record the data will appear.

The codes for item categories are ordinarily listed as the questions are composed. By contrast, the listing of the record format in the far right-hand column should *never* be done until the *entire* questionnaire has been assembled. During the final questionnaire construction, space in the margin should be allowed, but no numbers listed. The reason is simple, but compelling. Any change, such as adding or deleting an item, or even changing an item, is likely to require that all of the following record format values must be changed.

Each survey questionnaire that is completed will constitute one "case" for analysis. Thus, if a survey has 200 respondents, there will be 200 cases for analysis. Each case will include one or more "records." A record is simply one data card or one line of a computer file or record sheet. A data card contains 80 columns. A single line in a file to which the data is keyed directly may contain from one column to as many as 200 or 300 columns or spaces. Ordinarily, very "long" lines or records are difficult to read and manipulate, so it is advisable to limit the length of a record to only 70 or 80 columns.

GUIDELIST 6–7

For Precoding Survey Items

1. Use numbers, rather than letters, because they are more easily processed.
2. Codes are not required for "dichotomous" items that need only be checked if they apply.
3. Numeric items and scales containing numbers to be checked or circled require no precoding.
4. Enclose codes in brackets or parentheses, or print them in very small typeface so respondents ignore them.

Listing the record format numbers on the questionnaire may seem to be a little difficult for an inexperienced researcher. Actually, the process is quite simple and easy, but it must be done *precisely* and with *extreme care*. It is *very* difficult to cope, later on, with any errors that might occur. Such errors are usually not discovered until the questionnaires have been printed and the data collection completed. Often such errors require that a new set of record format numbers must be listed on *each* and *every* questionnaire, from the point the error occurred to the end of that particular record or to the end of the questionnaire, itself. It is a very tedious, and time-consuming process. It can be avoided by using great care in formatting.

Determining Maximum Record Size. The first step in record formatting is to determine what the maximum size of any one record should be. If data cards are to be used, the maximum record size will be eight spaces or "columns." If the data is to be keyed directly to a computer file, such as on a disk, diskette, or magnetic tape, it is advisable to establish a maximum record size of about 60 or 70 columns. (Many video display screens on computer terminals show only 70 columns per line.) Once the maximum size has been determined, no record format numbers greater than that value will be listed on the questionnaire.

Identification of Cases. Each questionnaire should be assigned a unique number, either before or after data collection. This "case number" is then keyed to the data file. The reason is quite simple. If an error is discovered or a problem encountered after the data has been transferred, the case number indicates from which completed questionnaire, known at that point as a source document, the data was keyed. The researcher can then return to the source document and make any corrections that might be required. The researcher should decide if the case number is to be listed at the beginning or at the end of each line or record in the data file. It is often advisable to list the case number at the beginning of each record, because this facilitates any sorting that might later be required. The highest case number determines the number of columns that must be assigned. Thus, if less than 100 questionnaires were to be numbered, two spaces would be required for the case number, if less than 1,000, three columns, and so forth. Note that it is *always* advisable to allow too many, rather than too few, if there is any doubt. If too many are assigned, one or two columns may not be used. If too few are assigned, there is no way to "shrink" the size of the number, and serious problems are likely to result.

Identification of Records. If a survey has only a fairly limited number of questions, so that the data can obviously be listed in fewer columns than the maximum record size, each case must be identified, but individual records need not be identified within the file. On the other hand, if each case (questionnaire) will contain more than one record (line), then *both* the case and the record must be identified in the file. Ordinarily, only one column is required for the record number, because surveys seldom obtain more data than can be keyed on nine records or lines. Suppose the largest case number is 250. This is a three digit number and so three columns would be assigned to the case number. Assume that there will be four records for each case. The record number will require only one column. The researcher might then assign the case number to the first three columns of *each* record and the record number to the fourth column. The less experienced researcher might wonder why the case number need be listed on each record. This is because order of data files can easily be disturbed. If the case number is not keyed on each record and the data cards are dropped or the order changed, or some records are misplaced or deleted from the file, it would be virtually impossible to locate or replace the missing records and insert them in the proper place in the file. If each record contains a case number, followed by a record number, as noted above, then any such misplaced or lost records could merely be inserted into the proper place in the file. (The cases could also be added anyplace in the file and the records or cases numerically sorted on the first four columns, to insure that the data file was in proper sequence.)

Identification of Data Fields. A data "field" is merely the *maximum* number of columns that might be required to key one survey item or "variable." For example, age and education in Example 6–11 would each require a field width of two columns (assuming no centenarians are included in the responding sample). The field width for income in the example might be three columns if some respondents reported an income greater than $99,000. (Notice that the extra zeros to indicate thousands need not be keyed.)

Listing the Record Format. Assume that the entire questionnaire has been constructed and all items finalized. The case number requires three columns, and there will be four records so the record number will be listed in the fourth column. The researcher has decided on a maximum record size of 70 columns. To facilitate reading and handling the records, six columns are to be left blank following the case and record numbers. Thus, the first actual data point is to be keyed to column 11 and the last data point will never be beyond column 70. It is time to list the record format on the questionnaire for this hypothetical survey.

The researcher would begin with the first item on the questionnaire. If the maximum field width for the item were one column, then the number 11 would be listed at the far right, opposite the space where the datum is to be recorded on the page. If the field width for the *next* item were two columns, the numbers 12–13 would be listed in the margin, etc. In this way, the person keying the data to file would: (1) key the case number in the first three columns; (2) key the record number, number 1 for this first record, in the fourth column after the case number; (3) leave columns 5 through 10 blank; (4) key the data for the first item in column 11; and (5) key the data for the second item in column 12 and 13, etc. In other words, the key operator knows exactly where in the record each piece of data is to appear. If the number to be keyed is actually less than the field width, the "leading" zero(s) may be keyed or the leading columns left blank.

The researcher would continue to list the record format numbers in the margin until reaching column number 70. At that point, a *new* record would begin and the numbering would start again at column 11, the first column where actual data is to appear. The same case number would be keyed in the first three columns, when the data is transferred, and the number 2 for the second record would be keyed in column 4, while columns 5 through 10 would be left blank, as

---

GUIDELIST 6–8

For Listing the Record Format

1. Do not begin listing the format until the entire questionnaire draft is complete.

2. Determine the maximum record size or number of columns to be used in the data file.

3. Determine the maximum likely value of the case numbers.

4. Assign the appropriate number of columns at the beginning of *each* record for the case and record number.

5. Determine the *first* column in which actual data will be keyed and begin listing with that number.

6. Determine the field width for each item, in turn, and list the columns for the field in the right margin.

7. Remember that each alternative of a multiple response item constitutes one variable and requires a field.

8. Allow a field of sufficient width for any "other" or open-ended items to be postcoded.

9. *Never* "split" a single data field between two records.

10. Begin a new record at the beginning of a new section to facilitate data transfer, even if some records are short.

11. *Always* perform the acid test, filling in maximum values, checking all options, and keying to a test file.

---

before. The process is fairly simple and straightforward, but there are some exceptions that deserve attention.

When listing the record format on the questionnaire, a single field must *never* be "split" between two records. If the field is too wide to fit entirely at the end of a record, a new record should begin at that point. For example, suppose the next available column were column 69 in the example used above. Assume that the next survey item had a field width of three columns. It would not fit into columns 69 and 70, and it *must not* be split so that the first two digits are at the end of one record and the third at the beginning of the next. Rather, this record would end at column 68, column 69 and 70 would be blank, and the data for the next item would be keyed to column 11 of the next record.

It is advisable to go to a new record at the beginning of a section of the survey. It makes it easier to key the data to file. All records need not be the same length. When listing the record format column numbers on the questionnaire, it is best to look ahead at each section. If the record is nearly full, begin a new record with a new section, even though a few columns at the end of the previous record remain unused.

Experience indicates that it is all too easy to make mistakes when listing the record format in the margin of the questionnaire. One of the most common mistakes is to fail to recognize "multiple responses" to an item and allow columns for each alternative. To clarify this point, refer to Example 5–1—The Multiple Choice Item, in the previous chapter. Notice that in the section containing a multiple response item, the alternatives are not precoded. This is because respondents can check any or all alternatives. *Each alternative becomes a survey item or variable.* The number one would be keyed for that item if it were checked, and a zero if it were not. Notice also that *each* alternative has been assigned a column in the record. The problem is that it is extremely easy to glance at the item, assume it is a single response item, and assign only one column to it. If the mistakes were not discovered until it were too late to correct it, all of the remaining record, and perhaps the remaining records, as well, would be five columns "off."

In the bottom section of Example 5–1, the item allows for only one response; one alternative must be selected. Thus, only one column is required for that item. If the person listing the record format made a mistake and assigned each a column, five columns would be "wasted" and data transfer would be a little less convenient, but no serious harm would be done. Thus, the basic rule, "better too many than to few," holds true.

Notice how the "Other" category is handled in Example 5–1. In the top section, with multiple responses, one column was assigned if any "other" were checked and another column also listed to accommodate the postcoded identity of the other newspaper specified in the blank space. Similarly, in the single response section of the example, a single column was designated for recording what "other." This assumes that no more than nine "other" publications will be listed by respondents. When deciding on the number of columns for items such as this that must be postcoded, remember the basic rule: Better too many than too few.

The Acid Test. Testing the codes and record formats is absolutely required for inexperienced researchers and highly recommended for even the most experienced. It takes only a few minutes to do so, and the testing can be expected to return many, many times its cost in time by catching errors before the data is collected. To test the codes and record formats, the researcher should make a copy of the final questionnaire draft. Then, the researcher should complete the questionnaire, listing the *maximum* value for each item. *Every* alternative on each multiple response item should also be checked. When that has been done, the data from the test questionnaire should actually be keyed to cards or a computer file. Lacking that availability, a work sheet must be composed showing the columns and records. More often than not, one or more errors will be discovered.

SUMMARY

The Construction of the Questionnaire

A. Emphasize the introduction. Most refusals will come immediately and once respondents begin, they seldom terminate prematurely.

B. Check sequence carefully. Simple, interesting, informative items should come first and sensitive or threatening items as late as possible.

C. Group items into sections. Combine items that use the same scales or treat the same topics into sections to facilitate response and simplify the task.

D. Limit and control branching. Make branch instructions simple, clear and concise and avoid complex branching or multiple branches as much as possible.

E. Use ample instructions. An instruction should be included if there is any doubt and they must be simple enough for the least sophisticated respondents.

F. Do not overestimate interviewers or respondents. Sophistication and motivation are always less than the researcher is likely to expect.

G. Make good use of rating cards. For personal interview surveys, good rating cards will simplify the response task and increase reliable, valid responses.

H. Always precode items and list record format. Precoding and record formatting must be done very precisely and accurately and must always be tested.

PART THREE
DATA COLLECTION AND PROCESSING

7

Mail Data Collection

MAIL SURVEY CHARACTERISTICS

Direct mail surveys are distinct from interview surveys in a variety of ways. There are many aspects of data collection for the mail survey that do not apply to interview surveys. Even for those tasks or attributes that apply to both types of surveys, most deserve considerably more or markedly less emphasis for one type of data collection than for the other. Because of these distinctions, mail surveys are discussed in detail in this chapter, and interview data collection is considered thoroughly in the next. Those who intend to conduct several survey projects may benefit from study of both chapters. On the other hand, those who intend merely to conduct a single study using one type of data collection need only pursue the chapter on data collection covering the method to be used in the project at hand.

The mail survey is self-administered. Interview surveys ordinarily are administered entirely by the field or telephone worker. Thus, the "cosmetic" aspects of the mail survey are much more important. The mailing piece is the only contact that respondents will have with the researcher and the project. Consequently, it must perform effectively and it has to be completely self-contained. It must "stand on its own" and do the entire job winning cooperation, capturing the data, and returning it to the survey headquarters. Once the questionnaire and mailing piece are complete and the survey is mailed, there will be no opportunity to make changes or corrections. At that point, the researcher is "locked into" the instrument and data collection process. Thus, the preparation and mailing of the survey must receive very careful attention, so that every detail will be handled properly and mistakes or inadequacies kept to an absolute minimum. This may require testing and revision or a "pilot" data collection project, to insure the effective performance of the mailing.

MAILING PIECE PRODUCTION

The appearance and quality of the mailing piece and its contents have a very important effect on mail survey response rates. It is always best to plan and create a mailing piece that is consistent in its quality. If some components of the mailing are to be done very inexpensively, it is wasteful to do other components lavishly. On the other hand, if most of the components are of very high quality, one or two parts that are obviously done cheaply will diminish or eliminate any advantages of the higher quality parts. The researcher must assess the budget and estimate the response rate, then decide on the level of quality for the mailing. Most often, the mailing piece is composed almost entirely of printed material. Before considering each individual component of the mailing piece, those aspects that apply to all of the components will be discussed. These include the paper, color, size, print, layout, attachment, and enclosure. Namelist acquisition, labeling, and personalized cover letters will then be discussed in turn.

Paper. The quality of the paper used in a mailing will affect the general impression the recipients have of the project. It is not advisable to use very light paper stock to save postage costs. The paper should be 20 pound stock or heavier, so that printing will not show through the paper. The least expensive paper has a very low cotton fiber content, but it is quite acceptable for the economical survey project. Only the most elegant survey mailing piece would use 100 percent cotton rag bond paper. Paper with a smooth surface is advisable for almost all surveys. Slick surface paper is not advisable for survey mailings. Paper with a textured surface should be used only for very high quality mailings.

It is usually desirable to use matching envelopes and paper stock for a survey mailing. Envelopes that are specially formed and folded are very expensive in lots of less than several thousand. Matching paper and the preformed envelopes for the survey mailing should all be purchased at the same time and from the same source.

Color. The use of bright or unusual colors to gain attention is not recommended because it may have a negative affect. White paper is always acceptable. Off-white or very light grey, beige, olive green, or cream may sometimes be appropriate for high quality mailings. Pink, blue, and yellow paper should be avoided.

Black ink is always acceptable for mail surveys. Two color printings are almost never required. When questionnaire sections must be highlighted or set apart from others, screening or the use of line borders will work as effectively as color coding in most cases. Corporate or institutional letterhead and printed envelopes can be used for the cover letter and mailing, even though it may be multicolor. The return addresses on the envelopes should then also be printed in the same way. When a cover letter is hand signed a dark blue pen should be used, rather than black, to make the hand signature more obvious.

Size. The cover letter and questionnaire for a mail survey should ordinarily present the reader of the material with a standard, 8½ by 11 inch (letter size) sheet. Smaller sizes are seldom advisable, and 8½ by 14 inch (legal size) paper should be avoided. The standard number 10 business letter envelope is quite satisfactory for nearly all surveys. It can contain several sheets of letter size paper. The return envelope should be a number nine, reply envelope, so that it will fit inside the mailing envelope without folding. When the mailing piece is large, a larger envelope is preferable to multiple folding and a thick mailing piece.

Print. The least impressive, and often the least expensive typeface used in a mailing piece is produced by a "dot-matrix" computer printer. The letters are formed by combinations of dots, and they are not very sharp and clear. An electric typewriter with a good, fabric ribbon will produce type that is legible, but not especially attractive. A single strike ribbon provides a sharper, more consistent character image. When the material is typed, 12 pitch size type (12 letters per inch) is usually satisfactory. Ten-pitch type is easier for older people to read, but takes more space. Fifteen-pitch should ordinarily not be used for questions and scales, but can be used effectively for precodes and record formats.

A word processor or computer with a correspondence-quality printer may produce left- and right-justified copy, so that the lines within a paragraph are of exactly equal length and the right margin is straight. These processors may also use proportionally spaced letters, so that the space for a broad letter, such as M, is wider than that for a narrow one, such as an I. When both right justification and proportional spacing are used, the type looks nearly as attractive as if it were professionally typeset. Typesetting has some additional advantages. The range of type size is almost unlimited, and there are many choices of typeface. Bold or italicized type can be used to highlight words and phrases when required.

Everything in the mailing piece, with the possible exception of the cover letter, should ordinarily be printed, rather than using a copy machine, ditto copier, or other method. Individually typed cover letters will be discussed later.

Layout. The appearance or "cosmetic" aspects of a mailing piece are very important for mail surveys because they affect response rate and bias. The first principal is to use conventional style. The address on envelopes should begin at the point about midway between top and bottom and between the sides. All envelopes should have a return address in the upper, left corner, and nothing should be printed on the back. The cover letter should have ample margins and be typed in simple, "block" style without indentation. They should be single-spaced, with a double-space between paragraphs and elements, in typical business style and format. The layout of the questionnaire should also be as simple, clean, and conventional as possible.

It is very important that every page of the questionnaire for a mail survey has an ample amount of white space. The appearance should be clean and simple, rather than dense and cluttered. It is always advisable to use more pages than to fit the content too tightly. Thus, it is best to use one and a half space or double spaced type than single space, and sections should be double or triple spaced, to set them apart. This makes the response task appear much easier and simpler for the respondent, so response rate and the reliability and validity of the data are increased.

Attachment. Most questionnaires require more space than merely the front and back of a single, letter-size page. When multiple pages must be used for the questionnaire, they should be attached to one another so that they will not become separated or the questionnaire completed in the wrong sequence. Ordinarily, the cover letter need not be returned, so it need not be attached to the questionnaire.

Multiple questionnaire pages can be printed on both sides and stapled together in the upper, left corner. This is the least impressive and least expensive method of attachment. A more elegant alternative is to have the questionnaire printed on larger stock and folded down to letter-size pages. Thus, 11 by 17 inch paper stock can be folded once to produce two letter-size sheets on which four pages are printed. It is usually not advisable to use larger stock, folding twice or more, because the sequence of the pages will not be clear to respondents. A six page questionnaire might be constructed by using a folded, 11 by 17 inch sheet for the "covers" and a single, letter-size sheet inserted between them. In that case, no stapling is likely to be necessary.

The most impressive method of attaching a multiple page questionnaire would be to use a "booklet" format. Several 11 by 17 inch sheets

---

GUIDELIST 7–1

For Mailing Piece Construction

Paper

Good: Twenty pound or heavier, 100 percent rag bond.

Fair: Twenty pound or heavier, part cotton rag stock.

Poor: Light paper that is not opaque, so print shows through.

Color

Good: White, off-white, light grey, or beige paper, black ink.

Fair: White paper and black ink.

Poor: Bright, dense, or unusual colors, pink, blue, or yellow.

Size

Good: Letter-size panels, #9 and #10 envelopes, or special sizes.

Fair: Letter-size sheets, #9 and #10 envelopes.

Poor: Legal size or oversize paper, envelopes small or folded.

Print

Good: Typeset, multisize, proportional, justified, bold italics.

Fair: Typed, singlestrike ribbon, 12 pitch.

Poor: Typed, old ribbon, smaller than 12 pitch.

Layout

Good: Ample white space, use of graphics and shading.

Fair: Ample white space, well separated sections.

Poor: Cramped, dense, narrow margins, sections too close.

Attachment

Good: Large, folded stock, saddle stapled multiple pages.

Fair: Single sheets, stapled in upper, left corner.

Poor: Pages not attached or multifolded and complex.

---

are printed and folded together once down the middle. They are "saddle" stapled two or three times in the binding with a special stapler. This creates a small booklet that will not separate, and the sequence of pages is obvious. The entire booklet can then be mailed in a large envelope or if only a few pages, folded twice for insertion into a number 10 envelope.

Enclosure. The manner in which the components are enclosed or inserted into an envelope affects the appearance of the mailing piece when it is received by the recipient. The general principle is to pick an envelope size that is appropriate to the content and to avoid very thick or bulging mailing pieces. For example, the use of number nine reply envelopes was recommended. If the mailing and return envelopes are the same size, the return envelope must be folded twice to insert it, and this produces a thick, bulky mailing piece.

It is usually advisable to fold the cover letter with or into the questionnaire. Both should then be inserted to the front or the back of the envelope, with nothing else inserted into them. When possible, arrange the insertions so that the cover letter is the first thing those who open the mailing will encounter, followed by the questionnaire, itself. When a mailing house or specialist is used to insert and mail the survey, it is *very important* to check the finished pieces before mailing to be sure it is done correctly.

VENDORS AND SERVICES

Everyone has had a great deal of experience preparing and mailing letters in the normal course of organizational or personal life. So, preparing and mailing a survey may not appear, at first glance, to be a difficult or time-consuming task. On the other hand, only a very few organizations or individuals have had the experience of preparing and mailing hundreds or thousands of identical mailing pieces to recipients with whom they have never before communicated. The sheer size of the task and volume of material can come as a surprise for those who have not had such experience. Also, the fact that the mailing pieces are identical creates additional problems. The effect of any mistakes or inadequacies are automatically multiplied by the number of mailing pieces. Consequently, virtually every detail of the task deserves much greater attention and care than would a preparation of a single letter or a small group of mailing pieces.

Not all tasks associated with the preparation and mailing of a survey need be performed by the researcher or sponsoring organization. Fortunately, there are a variety of vendors and external service organizations and individuals who specialize in various products or tasks required for a survey mailing. They tend to vary greatly in many respects, including their range and level of expertise, the quality of their work, the volume they are prepared to handle, the range of goods or services offered, their costs or prices, and the time required for delivery or performance.

Eight different categories of vendors or service firms are identified and discussed below. It is, of course, the researchers responsibility to assess the need for such external assistance, and to check the quality and performance of any such firms that might be used to prepare and mail the survey material.

GUIDELIST 7-2

For Using an In-House Namelist

1. Use the specification of the population and sample frame as a guide standard when selecting a source of names.

2. Use an existing in-house namelist if one is available and it meets the sample frame requirements.

3. If there is no existing list, see if a namelist can be assembled from accounting, personnel or sales records.

4. See if it would be feasible for the survey sponsor to gather a namelist in the process of regular business.

5. Check existing directories and public records to see if a namelist can be composed from available records.

Namelist Sources. The listing of people to whom the survey is to be mailed is known as a "namelist." For some mail survey projects, the researcher or sponsor may already have a namelist. In other cases, internal accounting or personnel records may contain the information necessary to compose a namelist. Such "in-house" lists make it unnecessary to obtain a list from an outside source. For example, a retail store, wishing to survey its credit card customers, could assemble the namelist from credit applications in the accounting department. A political candidate may wish to survey those who have recently volunteered their time and efforts or contributed to the campaign. Again, the sponsor would have the list in-house. In these cases, the namelist may have to be transformed in some way, but there is no necessity to seek a list from an independent source.

There are many mail survey research projects that require mailing to the general public or some subsection of the general public, such as those in a certain geographic area or with certain demographic characteristics. Other projects may require a mail survey of a special population, such as those engaged in a certain occupation, those in a certain position, or those with some particular condition or attribute. In these cases, the sponsors are not likely to have the namelist in advance, and it must be obtained from those who specialize in assembling and providing such lists.

Namelists can often be acquired from firms who specialize in the management and sale of namelists. Some of these firms may have accumulated a namelist as the result of their principal business, such as a magazine that makes its list of subscribers available for sale. For some firms, namelist management and brokerage is their principal business. These firms have elaborate computer facilities and they obtain namelists together with other coded information about those on the list. They may then merge lists, match names and overlay additional information, purge duplicates, make address corrections, and update the list to keep it current and timely. Some firms are strictly namelist brokers. They do not "own" the lists in which they deal. Rather, they merely serve as a source of lists for those who require them. They maintain records and relationships with a wide variety of firms who own and manage namelists. They are often able to locate and provide special lists, and they are paid for doing so on a commission basis.

The principal market for namelists consist of those who use direct mail marketing of products and services. Nevertheless, these firms specializing in namelists provide a rich and varied source of names for mail surveys. Rarely is the population so specialized that a namelist is not available from some commercial source. Namelist brokers and managers are ordinarily listed in the "Yellow Pages" of any metropolitan telephone book. Mailing houses who specialize in doing large mailings are also listed and they are very likely to be brokers or to know of several in the community. Standard Rate and Data Service, Inc., 5201 Old Orchard Road, Skokie, Illinois 60076 publishes a special directory semiannually, called "Direct Mail List Rates and Data." Those seeking very specialized lists or lacking local namelist brokers may refer to that directory for very thorough and complete namelist information.

Namelists ordinarily cost only about $40 to $75 per 1,000 names, but most firms have a minimum order quantity of 5,000 or 10,000 names. This minimum covers the cost of initiating the job and picking the names from the master list, which may contain many millions of names in total. Namelists may contain a much larger number of names than will be used in the actual sample. When it does, some procedure must be used for selecting the sample, such as the "nth name" sampling process described in Chapter 3. Usually, a commercial namelist takes a week or two to acquire, and sometimes it may take several weeks. Namelists vary greatly in quality, measured in terms of recency, proportion of nondeliverable mailing pieces, correctness of names and addresses, and duplication of names on the list. It is best to investigate quality and find a reputable source.

The Post Office. The mail survey is to be delivered by the postal service and the post office personnel are a valuable source of information and assistance. Obviously, they can provide the necessary information about permit fees, postage costs, and mailing restrictions, but they offer much more. Postal authorities are likely to be familiar with details of metered postage, precanceled stamps, formats for printing permit information on mailing and return envelopes, size and shape requirements for mailing pieces, bulk mail regulations and preparation, and mail box facilities for receiving returns.

The major postage considerations are discussed in some detail, later in this chapter. It is important to note here that the researcher anticipating a mail survey should check with the local postal authorities well in advance. All necessary information should be gathered and all required approval should be obtained *before* any component of the mailing piece is finalized and produced. By doing so, potential obstacles and expensive, time-consuming modifications can be avoided.

Stationers and Paper Supply Houses. Stationery stores and suppliers and paper supply houses offer a wide variety of paper and envelope stock. If a printer is to be used, the printing firm may also provide the paper stock, so it may not be necessary for the researcher to purchase paper separately for printing. Nevertheless, it is advisable to compare both cost and availability of paper, between printers and paper suppliers. Printers would, of course, often prefer to provide the stock because they buy at a discount and sell at retail cost, retaining the margin between the two. On the other hand, most will be willing and able to print on stock provided by the customer. Stationers and other paper and office products suppliers are also sources for other materials and supplies that may be required when preparing a mailing. For example, most stationery or graphic arts supply stores carry "dry transfer" lettering sheets, stencils, lining and shading materials, and the like, which can be used in place of typesetting or graphic art services. Simple, inexpensive devices for affixing stamps, sealing envelopes, and other such routine tasks are also readily available from these outlets.

Word Processing Shops. There are several companies that manufacture computer hardware and software specifically designed for text processing, rather than data processing. While this equipment is readily available, it is also very expensive to purchase or lease and requires that the operator be trained and experienced in using the equipment. Thus, several small agencies or shops specializing in word processing have recently appeared. They ordinarily offer word processing service on a fee basis to customers who have only occasional need for such text processing. The fees may be based on an hourly rate, the number of pages or quantity of work, or they may provide a firm estimate or bid for the entire job.

Depending on the type of equipment used, word processing may provide a variety of type styles and sizes, proportionally spaced letters, automatic centering of titles, left and right justification of lines for even margins, and other printing niceties. Perhaps the inherent flexibility is the most important advantage of such services. With word processing devices, the text is keyed to a file on an electronic storage device, such as a diskette. The software permits text to be deleted, inserted, or moved to other locations in the document. Thus, the researcher using such a service can inspect a draft of the document and if it does not appear as it should, modifications can be made quickly, easily, and inexpensively. When the final document meets the approval of the researcher, it is delivered to the printer where it will be photographed and processed to make the printing plate. Word processing shops may also provide form letter services for individually typed cover letters. This process is discussed briefly, later in this chapter.

Form Letter Shops.   Letter shops are similar in many respects to word processing firms. They often differ in only a couple of ways: Letter shops may be devoted mainly or exclusively to letter production, rather than to composition of other text material. Letter shops may also use many correspondence quality printers, rather than just one or two, so they can produce a large quantity of individually typed letters in a relatively short period of time. Letter shops would ordinarily be used by researchers only to produce cover letters, rather than for composition of all mailing piece components. The production of personalized cover letters is discussed more fully later in this chapter. It is only necessary to note here that such service is readily available in any major metropolitan area. As with the use of any external service, it is advisable for the researcher to check quality carefully and to compare prices and time requirements among vendors, before selecting a letter shop to produce the letters.

Graphic Art Services.   Most metropolitan areas will have several graphic art firms or individual graphic artists who provide a variety of services. The majority of customers for these individuals or firms are advertisers and small advertising agencies. Thus, those in the advertising and public relations community can often provide referrals to several graphic art shops. It is often desirable to obtain such referrals, because the expertise and performance quality of graphic artists varies greatly.

Graphic artists may provide illustrations, sketches and drawings, but they are also experts at layout, design, composition, and type specification. Usually, researchers use graphic art services only when a high quality mailing piece is required and the questionnaire is to be photo-typeset, rather than typed or composed with a word processor. The graphic artist does the layout, type specification and final draft for printing.

Printing Companies. Printers often provide a variety of services besides the actual printing of the survey material. Most have a wide variety of paper stock and envelopes available. Many offer layout and typesetting services as well. At times, the entire "package," including paper and envelopes, layout and typesetting, printing and folding may cost less from a printer than when each task is performed separately. In other situations, considerable savings may be realized by using separate vendors. Thus, it is important to check and compare both the cost and the time requirements and also to assess the degree of expertise and quality of the work that might be obtained from various alternatives. There are two very real advantages to using a "full service" printing company: The research staff need not spend as much time and effort delivering, picking up, and dealing with several different vendors. The coordination is also likely to be greater when a single firm does several tasks. Thus, these factors must be balanced against any savings that might be obtained by using several different vendors.

Mailing Houses. Direct mail advertisers and marketing companies are the principal customers of mailing houses. The mailing house may provide only mail preparation and mailing, but most offer a very wide range of services. Some may even provide namelist acquisition, graphics, typesetting, paper stock, envelopes, and printing. The chief service offering of mailing houses is, of course, the preparation of the mailing. Any mailing house has the facility to take the various materials and components of the mailing piece and do the folding, insertion and sealing, and affix the postage. Most also deliver to the post office. Mailing houses are geared for very large mailings of thousands or millions of pieces. Thus, their use may not be practical for "small" mailings of less than 1,000 pieces. On the other hand, it may be advisable to use a mailing house for a large survey mailing. Lacking special equipment, folding, inserting, sealing, metering, stamp affixing and label affixing by hand may require many person-hours of labor.

MAILING PIECE COMPONENTS

The mailing piece for the typical survey ordinarily consists of four or five different components: the mailing envelope, the cover letter, the questionnaire, the return envelope, and perhaps an inducement. Each of these components are discussed in turn, below. It is important to note here that decisions concerning any one component cannot be made independently of the other components. The mailing piece must be an integrated package and the components must be consistent and compatible with one another. Thus, the researcher must be constantly aware of the effects of a decision about one component on the requirements for the others.

The Mailing Envelope

The typical survey questionnaire would be mailed in a standard business envelope. Nothing should be printed on the back of the envelope, and the front should contain only three elements: the name and address, the return address, and the stamp or postage information.

The Address. The mailing envelope can be addressed either by typing or printing directly on the envelope, or by affixing labels containing the names and addresses of the potential respondents. When personalized letters are to be used for the survey, "window" envelopes can also be used. They contain a transparent window through which the name and address typed on the letter can be seen.

When an "in-house" namelist is to be used, the names and addresses may be typed directly onto envelopes from the source documents, such as a manufacturer's file of completed warranty cards. They may also be typed onto preprinted, letter-size sheets and then transferred to pressure-sensitive label sheets in a copy machine that will accommodate the special forms. This is often useful when the same list is to be used two or more times. With the wider availability of computers of all sizes, namelists may also be keyed or transferred to a computer file and envelopes or labels printed with either a dot-matrix or correspondence-quality printer.

Commercially obtained mailing lists are most often provided on "four-up" Cheshire labels. This merely means there are four names and addresses in each row. The labels arrive printed on a sheaf of computer paper, and they are then fit into a machine that cuts them into individual labels, applies adhesive, and attaches them to envelopes. "One-up" pressure sensitive labels are also common. Adhesive has already been applied and the labels stick to a long strip of special, coated paper. Labels can easily be removed by hand or machine and attached to the envelopes merely by applying pressure. For small mailings of less than 1,000, it is usually advisable to hand affix pressure-sensitive labels. Cheshire labels are best for very large mailings.

The Return Address.   The mailing envelope must always contain a return address. Postal regulations require it, and without it the researcher would not be able to determine the number of mailing pieces that were not deliverable. The return address should be printed in the upper, right corner of the envelope. The printing of the envelope is relatively inexpensive, and labels should never be used for the return address. In most cases, the return address on the mailing envelope should be the same as the address and return address on the reply envelope. The exception would be the case where the sponsor's letterhead and envelopes are used, but the survey is to be returned to an independent researcher for analysis, to maintain the anonymity of respondents.

GUIDELIST 7–3

For Selecting Postage for Mailing

1.   Regular, first class postage stamps on the mailing envelope will result in the highest response rate.

2.   Precanceled stamps at the bulk mail rate are second most effective in obtaining response.

3.   Metered postage on a mailing, even though first class, provides lower response rates than do postage stamps.

4.   Use of a bulk mail permit printed on mailing envelopes obtains the lowest response rate.

5.   Bulk mailing is less expensive and allows for heavier mailing pieces than first class mailing.

The Postage. The type and amount of postage will affect the response rate. The response rate will be greatest when first class postage stamps are affixed. Response rate is least with a bulk mail permit, and metered postage falls somewhere in between. Bulk mailing requires a bulk mail permit from the post office. The permit number and required indication are then to be printed directly on the mailing envelope. An alternative is to acquire a bulk mail permit and purchase "precanceled" stamps, to enhance response rate a little. Bulk mail is slower than first class mail, but it costs just over half as much per piece and each can be over three ounces without extra cost. For large mailings with many pieces going to the same ZIP code, bulk mail preparation provides additional savings. This requires sorting by ZIP code and bundling the mailing pieces for each ZIP code or state. The researcher should check with postal authorities *well in advance,* to allow time for printing and production.

The Cover Letter

The letter that introduces a mail survey or other self-administered questionnaire to respondents is usually known as a "cover" letter. The technical name for it is a "letter of transmittal." In the absence of personal contact and interaction, the cover letter must explain the project and win the cooperation of the recipient, and it must do so entirely on its own. Thus, it must contain several elements and accomplish multiple goals.

Figure 7–1 lists a dozen questions that will ordinarily be in the mind of the recipient of a mail survey. The items are listed in the same sequence that they are likely to arise in the mind of the person who receives the letter. Consequently, it is often advisable to include the answers to each in the same order within the actual cover letter. Example 7–1 includes the answers to each of the 12, in this same sequence. Briefly study the list of questions and the sample cover letter together. Notice that Questions 1 and 2 are answered in the first sentence of Paragraph A in the example. Question 3 is answered in part by the fact that the survey was sponsored by a manufacturer, and the exact reason why is contained in the letter part of Paragraph D. The second sentence of Paragraph A answers Questions 4 and 5. The answers to Question 6, 7, and 8 are contained in Paragraph B of the letter, and the response to Questions 9 and 10 are contained in Paragraph C. Questions 11 and 12 are answered in Paragraphs D and E, respectively. Thus, each and every one of the dozen most likely questions that might arise in the mind of the recipient are anticipated and answered within the model cover letter.

FIGURE 7–1

Questions a Cover Letter Must Answer

1. What is this about?
2. Who wants to know?
3. Why do they want this?
4. Why was I picked?
5. How important is this?
6. Will this be difficult?
7. How long will this take?
8. Will it cost me anything?
9. Will I be identified?
10. How will this be used?
11. What is in it for me?
12. When should I do it?

EXAMPLE 7–1

The Mail Survey Cover Letter

Dear Respondent:

A. The manufacturers have asked us to conduct a brief survey of a sample of hot tub owners. You were selected from those who have purchased a hot tub, and it is very important to learn your opinions because you represent many other owners who have similar experiences.

B. The questionnaire has been designed so that you can complete it very quickly and easily. It takes only a few minutes, and you need only check off your answers or jot down a number. A postpaid return envelope has been included for your convenience.

C. You can be absolutely sure that all of the information you provide is strictly confidential, and no individual hot tub owners will be identified. Your answers will be combined with those of many others and used only for statistical analysis.

D. As a token of the company's appreciation, we have included a gift to enhance your enjoyment of the hot tub. We genuinely appreciate your

EXAMPLE 7–1 (concluded)

valuable assistance. Your honest impressions and opinions, whether favorable or unfavorable, are very necessary to be sure that the company serves the public as effectively as possible. We do appreciate your candid opinions.

E. Please complete and return the form right away. Again, thank you for your help.

Aside from the information content of the cover letter, the form and style are also important. The letter should be geared to the nature of the responding sample. The same general rules concerning vocabulary, grammar, and style that apply to question composition also apply here, with one exception. Survey questions should be as "conversational" as possible, but a cover letter can be too informal. People hold certain expectations about how a business letter should read, and they should not be disappointed. Thus, the general conventions for a business letter should be observed. This does *not* mean that it is advisable or appropriate to use such trite phrases as "Herein enclose please find . . ." or "With your kind permission, . . ." It does require that a conventional format and a slightly more formal style be used in the cover letter than in the questionnaire, itself.

A good cover letter should not be too stiff, formal and demanding. Neither should it beg the recipient to respond. It should not be "over the head" of the least sophisticated respondents, but it should not appear to be patronizing or condescending to the most sophisticated respondents.

Bulk Printed Cover Letters. The type of cover letter that is least expensive and most easily produced is the bulk printed cover letter. The letter has been written and typed in final form, with a salutation such as "Dear Respondent:". It is then printed on letterhead stock. Each letter is identical, and respondents are not individually addressed on the letter.

Personalized Cover Letters. When the cover letter for each respondent is individually typed, including the individuals name and address, and a salutation that greets the person by name, they are called "personalized" letters. The basic principles that apply to the creation of an effective cover letter have been discussed above. These principles and recommendations apply equally to cover letters that are printed in bulk and to personalized letters. Personalized cover

---

GUIDELIST 7–4

For Composing a Cover Letter

1. Remember that the respondent is likely to accept or reject the response task within the first few seconds.

2. Anticipate the 12 questions that recipients might ask and answer them in the cover letter.

3. Use a conventional business letter style and format for the cover letter, to meet respondent expectations.

4. Avoid an overly formal style and trite or hackneyed words and phrases in the cover letter.

5. Keep the vocabulary and sentence structure within the limits of comprehension of the least sophisticated reader.

6. Show respect for the readers, their time and effort, and avoid being overly demanding or presumptuous.

7. Do not beg the reader to respond or grossly overstate the importance of the information.

8. Keep the letter friendly and cordial and be confident that nearly all recipients are likable, cooperative people.

---

letters require additional tasks and decisions. Respondents are more likely to read a letter that is addressed directly to them and appears to be hand typed and signed than they are to a "general" letter that is unaddressed and obviously printed. They are also more likely to do what the "personalized" letter requests. Thus, the researcher can increase the response rate by including a personalized letter. The disadvantage of such a strategy is the cost of the letters.

Personalized letters are created by first composing the body of the letter itself. When it has been edited thoroughly, it is keyed to a word processor or computer file. This is often called a "boiler plate" or "shell document." It contains everything except the name, address, and the salutation. When personalized letters are to be used, the names and addresses must also be keyed or transferred to a namelist file on the same processor or computer system. The letter and the names may have to be coded in a certain manner to indicate what portions of the name and address are to be printed in particular locations in the shell document. These codes depend on the processing system being used to produce the letters. During processing, the program performs a routine called a "list/merge" function. The program typically takes the first name on the list, inserts it into a copy of the letter, and then routes it to another file or to a printer. The result is a letter for each name that includes the name and address of the individual and a salutation using the person's name, followed by the letter itself. Personalized letters should always be produced with a correspondence-quality printer, rather than a dot-matrix printer. Any advantage to the personalization would be lost by the knowledge that the letter was produced in bulk.

There are many firms that specialize in production of personalized letters in every major metropolitan area. Researchers who lack the equipment and wish to consider personalized letters are advised to check the telephone directory or other sources of information in the community and contact some of these firms. It is always advisable to get cost and timing estimates from several sources, because they vary widely from one to the next. An alternative to such a commercial service might be the firm or organization sponsoring the survey. Businesses, schools, hospitals, and government departments often have both the computer capability and the necessary printing equipment to produce personalized letters. This may require a few conversations with those responsible for the computer system in the organization, but the use of such letters may prove to be both feasible and economical.

The Questionnaire

When potential respondents receive the mailing, the first thing they are likely to do is read the cover letter. The second thing (and sometimes the first) is likely to be a quick examination of the questionnaire itself. The more professional and important the questionnaire appears to be, the more likely the respondents will complete and return it. The easier and quicker they perceive the task to be, the more likely they will begin answering the questions. Thus, the "cosmetic" aspects of the questionnaire and its appearance to recipients at first glance are vitally important to an adequate response rate.

The questionnaire is the core of the mailing. It is the instrument that will both present the questions and capture the responses. While the quality of the survey depends in part on every aspect of the mailing, the questionnaire itself, is clearly the most important component. The need to examine every aspect of the final questionnaire draft cannot be overstated. With interview surveys, the researcher can often make modifications in the questionnaire, provide additional instruction for field workers, or extra coaching for respondents, after data collection begins, if such changes are absolutely necessary. When the data are collected by mail, there is no opportunity for any form of modification after the questionnaire has been mailed to the respondents. If there is any uncertainty about the questionnaire's effectiveness, then additional testing and trial are certainly warranted.

Some of the key aspects and essential elements of the questionnaire discussed earlier deserve reiteration here. The questionnaire should be inserted into the mailing envelope so that it will be first thing the recipient views after reading the cover letter. The first page or front of the questionnaire should be especially attractive. It should appear to be very quick and easy to complete. If the questionnaire has several pages, the sheets should be attached. It is ordinarily advisable to print the page number in the upper, right corner of each page. A note in parentheses at the very bottom of each page should be worded, "Please continue on page . . .", with the subsequent page noted.

The questionnaire should have a title printed at the top of the first page, or at the top of each page. It should also have a note at the end of the last page, thanking the respondents for completing the task and urging them to return the questionnaire promptly. The entire questionnaire should comprise an integrated "package" that is obviously one document. If one part of the questionnaire must be modified, the change will often require changes in several other parts of the questionnaire as well. This may discourage the researcher from making what might be viewed as minor changes. The temptation to ignore modifications that tend to "cascade" into several changes must be resisted vigorously. The ultimate criteria for deciding whether a modification is required or not consist of clarity and ease of response, not the convenience of the researcher. Additional time spent on the final preparation and checking of a questionnaire often pays for itself many times over when the data has been received and processing begins.

The internal part of the questionnaire should consist of clearly defined sections. That way, the total response task is divided into a series of short, simple subtasks. This facilitates response, since the recipient is not faced with one, large and time-consuming task. It is very important that the pages do not look crowded or overly dense with type. Ample blank or white space makes the task appear simpler and easier. Any layout or construction that would further simplify and clarify the response task should be sought and examined thoroughly. When a questionnaire draft is to be prepared by a typesetter or graphic artist, the work must be checked very carefully. Those who perform such technical services may be experts at their work, but they seldom compose survey questionnaires. Consequently, they are apt to make decisions on the basis of criteria other than easy and simplicity of response. If aesthetic or artistic principles are at odds

---

CHECKLIST 7-1

To Finalize the Questionnaire

1. Does the questionnaire appear, at first.glance, as though it will be quick and easy to complete?

2. Does the first page of the questionnaire contain only easy, non-threatening questions?

3. Is there any uncertainty about the questionnaire's effectiveness that might be reduced by testing?

4. Will the questionnaire be the first thing recipients see after reading the cover letter?

5. Are the pages attached so they will not be lost or separated from one another?

6. Are all of the pages clearly numbered and arranged so respondents can follow the sequence easily?

7. Does each page have a note at the bottom, directing respondents to the next page?

8. Is there a title at the beginning of the questionnaire and a note of thanks, urging quick reply, at the end?

9. Do the sections within the questionnaire form simple steps or subtasks to be completed one at a time?

10. Does the questionnaire have ample white space, to avoid a dense, cramped or cluttered appearance?

11. Has all work by others been checked thoroughly?

---

with the requirements for clarity and simplicity, they must give way and the latter must take precedence. The researcher must *never* fail to examine the "proofs" and drafts of the work of others. Failure to do so is the single most common source of errors in questionnaires that receive final preparation from others.

There are some special situations where the researcher may want to identify individual subsamples of respondents to whom the survey will be sent, without asking respondents to identify themselves as group members within the questionnaire. They may not know the group or subsample to which they belong, or the question may be threatening to them. In such cases, the questionnaire should be "coded" to indicate group membership, and the code value used as data during analysis. The respondents need not even be aware of such codes, and in any event, the subsample codes have no meaning to respondents.

To produce two or more different questionnaires with the separate codes adds significantly to printing costs. The simplest and most economical way to code the groups is to print an odd number of asterisks, centered, with a few spaces between them, at the very end of the questionnaire. The printer must then be instructed to stop the press after the appropriate number copies of that page has been printed, and "wipe out" one asterisk on each end of the line. This is often required and printers are likely to be familiar with the process. The respondents would not know that their questionnaire contained a different number of asterisks, a different code, than others. When the data are keyed to file, the operator must be instructed to count the asterisks and key in the number that remain on each questionnaire. This number serves as an indication of the group membership when the data is processed and analyzed.

The Return Envelope

As noted earlier, the return envelope should be smaller than the mailing envelope so that it can be inserted into the mailing without folding. Nothing should be printed on the back of the envelope, and the front contains the same three elements as those on the mailing envelope. The return address should contain *both* an address and a return address, even though they will ordinarily be the same. Both should be printed, rather than on labels which are affixed.

GUIDELIST 7-5

For Selecting Postage for the Reply

1. Use of postage stamps on return envelopes *encourages*, rather than discourages response.

2. Metered postage on return envelopes is inadvisable because it is both too expensive and ineffective.

3. Business reply permits printed on return envelopes should ordinarily be used for most mail surveys.

The manner in which postage is attached to the return envelope will affect response rate significantly. Affixing regular, first class postage stamps results in the highest response rate. Some might question the use of a postage stamp on the return envelope, because some respondents will remove the stamps, use them for their own mail, and fail to return the questionnaire, but that rarely happens. The typical recipient is reluctant to either remove the stamp or to discard it, because of its obvious value. Many feel almost obligated to return the questionnaire. The use of first class postage stamps on return envelopes is a costly technique. It is not recommended unless it is important to maximize response rate *in every way possible*. A business reply permit is an alternative. With a business reply permit and indication on the return envelope, postage is charged for only those surveys that are returned. On the other hand, the fees per return are almost twice the rate for first class mail. So if the response rate is expected to be very high, a business reply permit may not accomplish appreciable savings. On the other hand, if a relatively low response rate is anticipated, the business reply permit would be the most economical choice, and that is usually the case.

INDUCEMENTS TO RESPOND

Ordinarily, response rates for mail surveys are rather low. This has two negative effects: It increases costs because the number of mailing pieces must be several times the number of respondents required. It also increases the likelihood of nonresponse bias, reducing the validity. Mail surveys often include a gift or premium for the recipients; an inducement to respond to the survey. Inducements to respond to a survey need not be of great value, so that they "pay" recipients to respond. Rather, they are merely a token of appreciation. The inducement shows goodwill on the part of the sponsor. Inducements tend to catch the recipients' attention and put them in a more positive mood. For some, they can also create a sense of obligation to respond, providing the inducement is sent with the original mailing.

Inducements that are contingent on receipt of a completed questionnaire are rarely recommended. There are several reasons: First, a second mailing or later delivery will be required for all those who respond. Second, such an inducement will much more often be perceived by recipients as "pay" for completing the questionnaire, and so the inducement must be of considerable value. Third, the inducement is more likely to influence the *manner* in which people respond, introducing a serious source of bias. For example, some may feel they must be positive toward the issues in order to receive their gift. Thus, except for the very specialized case, inducements should not be contingent on response, and should be sent with the original mailing, if possible. The range of premiums or gifts that might be used for a survey is practically limitless. Yet, all such alternative inducements will not be equal in their effect on response rate. Six major criteria for

---

GUIDELIST 7-6

For Including an Inducement to Respond

1. Send the inducement with the original mailing, rather than later delivery.

2. Do *not* make the gift contingent on respondents completing and returning their questionnaires.

3. Be sure respondents perceive the gift as a token of appreciation, rather than meager pay for helping.

4. Avoid any form of inducement that might influence the *way* people answer questions, introducing a bias.

5. Evaluate potential inducements using the eight criteria as *flexible* standards for judgment.

6. Do not use money as an inducement unless it is perfectly clear that it will be effective.

---

selecting an inducement are listed below. Obviously, an effective inducement need not necessarily meet all the criteria perfectly, but the closer it conforms to the criteria, the more effective it is likely to be.

Economy.   When hundreds, or even thousands of people are to be included in the mailing, the cost of an inducement becomes a very important factor. It is important to select an inexpensive item.

Nonreactivity.   The inducement should not influence the nature of the responses to the survey questions. It should not be directly associated with the topics, issues or sponsor, so that recipients "react" to the items in a certain way. To the degree that an inducement affects the *way* that people respond, it will create bias. For example, if the survey dealt with the way people evaluate a particular brand or product, it would be extremely inadvisable to use a sample of the same brand or product as an inducement.

Uniqueness.   Inducements that are not otherwise obtainable by the respondents tend to be more attractive. Such gifts may be relatively inexpensive, but they may be perceived by recipients as quite valuable because they cannot be readily purchased or acquired in some other way.

Value.   Even as a token of appreciation for cooperating, an inducement must be of sufficient value so that it does not demean the importance of the survey. Giving something obviously worth only a few cents for a respondent task that requires considerable time and effort might serve to diminish, rather than enhance goodwill and cooperation.

Luxuriousness.   Gifts which the respondents would not be likely to purchase for themselves are the most potent and effective inducements. As with any gift, utilitarian items are less welcome or valued than are little luxuries or treats the recipients would not otherwise obtain for themselves.

Individualization.   While they may be expensive to obtain or produce, gifts and premiums that are individualized are more effective. If the inducement is "personalized" with the individual's name or otherwise directly related to the individual, such as referring to their occupation or some other attribute or characteristic the recipient is known to have, it tends to have greater value. The use of cash as an inducement fails to meet most of the criteria listed above, yet it is often used as an inducement to respond to mail surveys. The disadvantages of using money are several, but the most important is the fact that it "disappears" into the individual's pocket without a trace. In other words, currency is homogeneous, and so the recipient is likely to forget about the gift very quickly. Also, with the use of money as an inducement, there is danger it may appear the person is being "paid" for participation, yet the amount is not likely to compensate them very adequately for their time and effort.

The disadvantages of using money as an inducement do *not* preclude the use of a cash inducement. As with any potential inducement under consideration, much depends on how creatively the researcher communicates with potential respondents. Even money can be used very effectively, with a clever approach. One recent, national mail survey arrived with a cover letter that began with the words, "Let us buy you a hot cup of coffee . . ." and below it a shiny new quarter was attached to the paper. Below the 25 cent piece, the letter continued, ". . . and perhaps while your sipping it, you will take just a couple minutes to answer a few brief questions." Many respondents undoubtedly did just that. When an inducement to respond is to be used with a mail survey, the search for a suitable gift should begin several weeks before the mailing date. There are several specialized companies that deal exclusively with premiums, sales promotional items, and the like. They often carry a very large selection of inexpensive items and they can provide many hundreds or thousands of units. These goods are ordinarily not available in retail stores, but delivery may take a few weeks or more.

MAILING AND RECEIPT

There are still a few tasks and decisions concerning the mailing that remain, even after all components have been prepared and the mailing piece is complete and ready. These factors deserve no less attention than the earlier preparation.

Timing the Mailing.   The timing of the mailing will make a significant difference in the response rate in some cases. Obviously, a lower response rate will result from mailing during a holiday period or some other time of year when respondents are likely to receive large quantities of mail or be extremely busy and pressed for time. Such timing may also induce bias and decrease the validity of the survey. When the survey is addressed to businesses or organizations, a higher response rate can be expected if recipients receive the questionnaire during the middle of the month than if it arrives just before, at, or just after the end of the month. When choosing a time to mail, the researcher should also be aware of any external event that might influence either the response rate or the response itself. For example, a survey of political opinions would obtain different results immediately after a domestic or international crisis than it would before it or a few weeks later.

The "Cutoff" Date.   Ordinarily, over 95 percent of all returns that will eventually be returned will be received within a period of three or four weeks. Rather than waiting for an extended period of time to begin analysis, the researcher is advised to monitor the number of returns received per day and to decide on a cutoff date. Usually, a large number of surveys will be returned within a few days after mailing. Then, fewer and fewer returns arrive each day until the point where the "yield" of additional surveys each day is not worth the wait. A few more returns will be received, and sometimes an occasional questionnaire will be returned many months later. It is usually advisable to ignore this additional data.

Recording Nondeliverables.   Some mailing pieces will be returned to the sender because they cannot be delivered to the addressee, and the number of nondeliverable pieces should be recorded. The percent of nondeliverable mail is an indicator of the quality of the mailing list.

If the list is very current, few addressees will have moved without a forwarding address or be deceased. If the list is accurate, there will be very few mistakes in the addresses. Poor quality namelists will result in a significant number of nondeliverable mailing pieces.

Response Rate Computation. The raw response rate can be computed by dividing the number of returns by the number of pieces mailed, less the number of nondeliverables. This is the gross response rate because some of those returned will prove to be incomplete or unusable. The net rate can be computed in the same way, after editing and data transfer, based on only the number of usable responses.

Re-Mailing and Re-Dropping. When the response rate is difficult or impossible to forecast, it may be necessary to follow the initial mailing with another, after computing the initial rate. This is called "re-mailing" because the same mailing piece is used, although it is sent to different individuals. An example may clarify this procedure. Suppose 300 completed responses are required. If an initial mailing of 2,000 questionnaires provided 200, the response rate would be 10 percent. An additional mailing of 1,000 questionnaires would be very likely to provide the extra 100 returns that are required.

There may be some special situations where it would be useful to remind survey recipients to respond. This is called "re-dropping," and it can be accomplished in two different ways. One method is to send a post card or note, identifying the questionnaire sent earlier and urging those who have not done so to complete and return it. The other procedure is used when it seems likely that many respondents no longer have the questionnaire. In that case, they are merely sent a duplicate mailing. This should not be done, however, unless the researcher can identify duplicate *responses* from the same individuals. If the respondents are not anonymous, then another copy of the questionnaire can safely be sent only to those who did not respond to the first mailing. Only a very few will then return both copies, and duplicates can be identified by key number in the file. If response is anonymous, however, then re-dropping a duplicate questionnaire is prohibited because it is likely to result in many duplicate responses.

Sight-Editing. As the returns are received, the research staff should open and discard the return envelopes, sorting the completed questionnaires and preparing them for data transfer and processing. When doing so, the questionnaires should be sight-edited, or examined to eliminate those that are not usable. Additional editing and post-coding may be required, but the initial sight-edit permits computation of the net response rate and indicates the overall effectiveness of the instrument and quality of response.

SUMMARY

Mail Data Collection Procedures

A. Coordinate the production. Make the decisions about any one component in the light of their effects on the others and on the mailing piece as a whole.

B. Make production consistent. Select paper, color, size, print, layout, attachments, and enclosures that are consistent among the components of the mailing piece.

C. Use external services. Contact namelist sources, the post office, stationers, word processing and form letter shops, graphic artists, printers, and mailing houses.

D. Evaluate vendors carefully. Obtain referrals or samples of work or products, and compare cost and time requirements among several outside sources.

E. Use appropriate envelopes. Follow the principles and recommendations for addressing, return address, and for selection and affixing of postage.

F. Create an effective cover letter. Use the example and be sure that all 12 questions recipients might ask are clearly answered in the letter.

G. Select an effective inducement. Examine many alternatives and evaluate them using the six major criteria for selection.

H. Practice timing and follow-up. Select an appropriate mailing date, allow sufficient time for response, and monitor returns as recommended.

8

Interview Data Collection

ROLE OF THE INTERVIEWER

When a mail survey is to be conducted, the mailing piece in general and the questionnaire, in particular, is the media through which the researcher holds a "conversation" with respondents. With an interview survey, the questionnaire plays an important role, but it is not the key element. Instead, the interviewers are the medium of communication between the researcher and the respondent.

Once a mail survey questionnaire has been finalized and produced, it is an inert and invariable medium. Every mail questionnaire is identical to all of the others, and in effect, exactly the same message reaches every respondent in exactly the same way. Interviewers, on the other hand, are neither inert nor invariable. Thus, the messages that reach respondents through interviews always vary to some degree, both from one interviewer to another and from one interview to the next. This fact creates several very important problems for the researcher conducting an interview survey.

The reliability and validity of a study depend, in a large measure, on consistency. The more variation there is among interviewers and interviews, the greater the introduction of random error and systematic bias, and the lower the reliability and validity of the data. Consequently, the researcher must strive for consistency and control of the interview process in order to obtain reliable, valid results.

Mode of Interviewing

When conducting an interview survey, the researcher has a choice between two basic modes of data collection: contract the interviewing to an external data collection agency, or manage an in-house data collection crew. Each mode has its own set of capabilities and limitations.

Agency Capabilities and Limitations. Perhaps the most important advantage of using a data collection agency for an interview survey is the fact that these agencies are spread across the country. Every major metropolitan area is likely to have several such data collection agencies. When an interview survey requires collecting data over a wide geographic area, it may be almost impossible to field an in-house interviewer crew to conduct personal interviews. Even when the interviews are to be done by telephone, toll charges may be prohibitively expensive. When data collection agencies are used to conduct telephone interviews from widely dispersed areas, several calling locations can be used, so that each is closer to area respondents and toll charges are reduced.

When external data collection agencies are used to collect the survey data, the task can often be accomplished more quickly than through an in-house crew of interviewers. This is because the data collection agencies are already "in place," and have trained interviewers on call. When it is essential to collect the data quickly, the data collection agency can often assign more interviewers to the project than would be available for an in-house crew, so the collection process can be completed more rapidly.

There may be significant economy in using data collection agencies. It would be costly to recruit, select, and train a large, in-house crew of interviewers to conduct a single project that may take only a few days to complete. In effect, only one project must bear the entire development cost for an in-house crew. On the other hand, data collection agencies use their interviewers for many data collection projects. Thus, the recruitment, selection, and training costs for both field workers and supervisors can be "spread" over many such projects. To the degree that these savings are passed on to the client, there may be significant savings.

There are two major disadvantages to the use of data collection agencies: the lack of quality assurance and the lack of control. While some data collection agencies are well managed and maintain high standards of service quality, many others do not. To make matters worse, it is difficult to distinguish between the more capable and the less capable agencies before contracting the data collection project to them. In fact, it may be difficult to detect poor quality work, even after the data have been collected and analyzed. It is also difficult for the agency's client to maintain control of the data collection process, especially from afar. There are frequently communications problems between agency and client. Even when directions and specifications are clearly stipulated by the client and thoroughly understood by the agency, there is no necessity that the agency or its interviewers follow them closely. Thus, contracting with an agency to collect the data for an interview survey certainly does not offer an easy, automatic solution to the data collection process. Using a data collection agency instead of an in-house crew of interviewers only changes the nature of the decisions, tasks and responsibilities of the researcher.

Advantages and Disadvantages of In-House Interviewers.   When a crew of interviewers are hired and trained by those conducting a research survey, the researchers have significantly more control over the data collection process. Because the interviewers are recruited, selected, trained, supervised, and compensated by the individual or organization conducting the survey, they are directly responsible to the researcher. Then those conducting the research have a much wider range of choice, authority, and control over every aspect of the data collection process. There is more direct focus and concentration of effort on the project at hand. Thus, quality control and assurance may be significantly greater.

There are some significant disadvantages to using in-house interviewers that accompany the advantages. With an in-house interviewer crew, the researcher has a much larger burden of responsibility. It requires more expertise and effort on the part of the researcher to recruit, select, train, supervise, and compensate interviewers. There may also be diseconomies of scale for data collection projects that can be completed in a short period of time. The entire cost of obtaining and training the interviewers must be born by the single, short-term project. If the project offers employment for only a few days, it may be difficult to recruit qualified people for interviewing. Thus, for most interview surveys, there is no single, clear-cut choice of the mode of data collection. Rather, the researcher must weight the "pro's and con's" of the two modes. Before making a choice between an independent data collection agency and an in-house interviewer crew, the researcher must be thoroughly familiar with the responsibilities and tasks associated with each mode. While the more seasoned researchers may have gained considerable insight from experience, those with less experience are well advised to study the description of the process for *both* modes, before making a final choice.

DATA COLLECTION AGENCIES

Before taking a close look at the process of collecting interview data through a data collection agency, it may be useful to describe the typical agency itself. Data collection agencies are most often locally owned firms, often run by women who began with a very small business run from their homes. Even the larger, older such firms are typically entrepreneurships that remain under the direction of the individual who began the business. These entrepreneurs have typically obtained their knowledge and expertise through experience. Most have little or no formal training in survey research, and their skills are ordinarily specialized in data collection, rather than the survey process as a whole.

Data collection agencies ordinarily have a small, permanent staff of supervisors and office workers who are full-time employees. The typical agency will have a fairly large number of interviewers who are temporary, part-time workers. Most often, they are middle-aged women whose predominant role is that of a homemaker, but who supplement their family income by doing interviewing. These data collection agencies form a loose network that covers most metropolitan areas of the country and they can reach many nearby towns and rural areas as well. There are, however, many remote and sparsely populated areas that are very difficult to reach through data collection agencies, and coverage is far from complete. In smaller cities, there may be only one or a very few data collection agencies, while the largest metropolitan areas of the country have over 100 such firms.

These agencies almost all belong to an industry association, called The Market Research Association, or M.R.A. Their membership and affiliation permit them to work together and allows client firms to employ several agencies in order to cover the required geographic area when conducting a regional or national survey.

The quality of data collection service varies dramatically from one agency to the next, and often from one time to the next for any given agency. For example, if an agency is very busy at a given time, they may use interviewers that are marginal or inexperienced, and they may take less time and effort to train and instruct them. Also during busy periods, they may be more lax or careless about field supervision and verification than they would otherwise be.

Facilities and services offered by data collection agencies also vary greatly. Some are very small, operating from the owner's home, with very limited physical facilities. Others may have several locations, including shopping center storefronts for intercept and central location data collection. Facilities might also include test kitchens and dining areas for food preparation and taste testing, focus group facilities for observation during conferences with respondents, mobile field units, audio and video equipment for both recording and presentation to interviewees, and a host of other facilities. Despite this variation, virtually all of them will ordinarily *claim* to be able to provide almost any service to the potential client. Consequently, it is

---

GUIDELIST 8-1

For Locating Data Collection Agencies

1. Obtain an M.R.A. directory or membership roster.

2. Visit an M.R.A. national and regional conference.

3. Check other conferences or directories, such as the American Marketing Association (A.M.A.) or the Academy of Marketing Science (A.M.S.)

4. Look for advertisements in trade publications, such as the A.M.A. Marketing News, etc.

5. Refer to the Yellow Pages and local business directories.

---

the researcher's responsibility to check very carefully to be sure the claims are, in fact, reasonably accurate.

Agency Data Collection Process

When a data collection agency is to be used, the process can be divided into six steps or phases: (1) Initial contact and cost estimation. (2) Agency selection, notification, and alert. (3) Delivery of materials and acknowledgement of receipt. (4) Training, instruction, and initiation. (5) Monitoring, control, and supervision. (6) Receipt, verification, and payment. Each of the six phases will be discussed briefly below.

Initial Contact and Cost Estimation. The initial contact with a prospective agency might be made by mail or personal visit to the facility, but most often it is done by telephone. The project and sample requirements, the nature and length of the questionnaire, the anticipated initiation date and expected duration of data collection, and any other relevant details or requirements are described to the agency, and they would inquire about any additional information they might need. It might take a day or two for the agency to assess availability and compute a cost *estimate*. Data collection agencies almost never provide a fixed bid or firm contract. In most cases, the only contract between the sponsor and the agency is a telephone conversation, perhaps followed by a letter of agreement.

Agency Selection, Notification, and Alert. After obtaining the information on availability, timing, and costs from potential data collection agencies, the researcher must compare and contrast them, eliminating those that are not acceptable. It is best to obtain references from the agencies, including the names and telephone numbers of former clients, rather than merely a client list. Before making the final selection of the agency to be used, it is advisable to contact these people to get their recommendations and comments. The agency selected should be notified of the decision when it is final, and the researcher should also alert the agency a week or so before sending the materials for a small project, and perhaps a month or more beforehand for a very large project, to allow the agency to obtain the required interviewers, schedule the project, and make any other preparations for the project.

Delivery and Acknowledgement. At the time of the agency alert or shortly thereafter, the agency should be sent a precise list of what materials will be sent, how they are being shipped, and when they can expect to receive them. It is important to assign a name to the project, by which both the client and the agency will refer to the job. All materials should be clearly labeled with this name. The project name and description of contents should be listed on the outside of each parcel of materials shipped to the data collection agency, together with instructions on when and how the contents should be handled, stored, and opened. This is important because data collection agencies will often have many containers of materials from various clients. Not infrequently, materials or supplies for a data collection project are lost or misplaced, either during shipping or after receipt by the agency.

GUIDELIST 8-2

For Shipping Materials to Agencies

1. Indicate on the outside of each container:
   A. The project name.
   B. The number of the container.
   C. The number of containers in the lot.
   D. The nature of the contents.
   E. Special instructions for storage.
   F. When the container is to be opened.
   G. How the container is to be opened.
2. Notify agency in advance of:
   A. The project name to be used.

GUIDELIST 8–2 (concluded)

    B. The number of parcels shipped.

    C. How the materials were sent.

    D. Where they were sent.

    E. When they were shipped.

    F. When they will be received.

3. Include in each parcel or container:

    A. A detailed packing list of contents.

    B. Complete inventory instructions.

    C. A check-off list for acknowledgement.

4. Instruct the data collection agency *not* to open packages when they arrive, but wait until instructed to open them.

5. Telephone the data collection agency if the proper acknowledgements are not received within a day or so of when they are expected.

6. Retain copies of all materials sent, so that replacements can be produced if required in an emergency.

It is usually advisable to instruct the agency to inspect the outside of any parcels for damage, and then to acknowledge their receipt intact. If the acknowledgement is not received shortly after the expected date of receipt, the researcher must call the agency to be sure the materials have arrived in good order. The agency should be instructed *not* to open containers of materials until just prior to the beginning of data collection. If such containers are opened and inventoried in advance, there is a greater chance that some of the contents will be misplaced, destroyed, or used for another project. An itemized packing list should be included in each container, so that when it is opened, the contents can be inventoried, checked off on a copy of the list, and the acknowledgement of contents returned to the client.

Training and Initiation. It is ordinarily advisable for the researcher or a member of the research staff to visit the data collection agency and help instruct and train the agency staff when the data collection is to be initiated. This may not be practical if several data collection agencies are used, if the agency is very distant from the researchers' project headquarters, or if the data collection task is very simple and straightforward. In such cases, written instructions must be included. When no agency visit is planned, a telephone conversation or a telephone conference among all agencies may be both feasible and helpful.

When a member of the research staff visits an agency at initiation, all materials and supplies for the project should be inspected and inventoried to be sure everything required is present and in good order. The researcher may then instruct and train either the agency supervisors, or both supervisors and field workers. The researcher should provide a general introduction to the project and its purposes. This is followed by a listing of any special, verbal instructions. The trainees should then be given a copy of the materials that will be used, including the questionnaire, written instructions, rating cards, and the like. (Such equipment as pens and clipboards are ordinarily provided by the interviewers or the agency, rather than by the client.) When interviewers are being trained, it is usually advisable to first "walk through" the complete questionnaire, noting each question, instruction, branch, and recording detail. This is ordinarily followed by a "trial run" with the trainer conducting a mock interview of an interviewer. If any questions or problems arise, they are discussed and solved. The interviewers then should each conduct one or two interviews among themselves, to become completely familiar with every aspect of the instrument.

GUIDELIST 8–3

For Training Interviewers

1. Train both supervisors and interviewers if possible.

2. Provide an overview of the project and its purposes.

3. Distribute a copy of all the materials for interviewing.

4. "Walk through" the instrument and other materials, describing each element and its use.

5. Do a "trial run" by conducting a mock interview of one of the supervisors or interviewers.

6. Answer any questions or solve any problems that arise.

7. Question supervisors and interviewers to be sure they understand each aspect of the interview task.

8. Have each interviewer conduct one or two interviews with one another, while monitoring the interviews and the recording of the data.

9. Distribute the necessary materials and supplies for the actual field or telephone work.

When interviewer training is to be done only by a data collection agency supervisor, they should be instructed to proceed with the process *exactly* as it has been described above. Data collection agencies will often try to abbreviate the training process, because they can cut their own costs and make their work easier by doing so.

Monitoring and Control. It is always advisable to monitor the process during the actual data collection. Waiting until the project is to have been completed and the completed records and materials returned may result in unexpected problems or delays. The data collection agency should be provided with the name and telephone number of a research staff member, and be encouraged to call for information or direction whenever a problem or question arises. Typically, researchers who often use data collection agencies find it necessary to take the initiative to telephone the agency daily or a few times a week, to insure that the process is going smoothly and the agency is on schedule with the data collection. The researcher should maintain a log of the number or proportion of interviews completed at each point in time.

When personal interviews are to be conducted at a certain place, when only certain respondents are to be selected, or when quota requirements are based on qualifying questions, it is usually necessary to monitor the respondent selection process, as well as the mere degree of completion. These special selection options and specifications are discussed in more detail later in this chapter. It is important to note here, however, that data collection agencies are much less likely to cut corners or deviate from the selection instructions if they clearly understand they will be monitored and will not be paid if they do not adhere to instructions.

When interviewees are to be selected from a specific list of respondents, provided by the researcher, it may also be advisable to "salt" the list with auditors. These may be members of the research staff or sponsoring organization. Interviewers who telephone or visit such auditors believe them to be naive respondents. Thus, they are likely to conduct the interview and record the responses as they would others. Any cheating, skipping, or false recording would then be revealed easily and quickly.

Receipt, Verification, and Payment. When the completed survey instruments are received from the data collection agency, they must be sightedited for completion and proper recording. Any questionnaires that are not usable should be separated, and the reason for their removal clearly noted. They should not be discarded until later, because it may be necessary to refer to them when renegotiating final payment with the agency. The complete, usable questionnaires should then be numbered, counted, and prepared for final edit, post-coding, and data entry.

A sample of some proportion of the completed questionnaires should be used for verification of response. A questionnaire may appear to be complete, accurate, and quite satisfactory, but it may prove to be invalid on verification. The interviewer may have merely filled out the form him- or herself, rather than actually conducting an interview. This is sometimes called "arm-chairing" in the industry, and the term is an apt metaphor. Other, less blatant forms of cheating or misconduct on the part of the interviewers or agency include skipping parts of the interview, cutting it short or terminating the interview early, or completing sections to which the interviewee refused to respond. The interview may also have been conducted at the wrong time or place, or the wrong respondents or those unqualified to respond may have been included. While incidents of blatant cheating are probably much more rare than are honest mistakes or errors from carelessness, the effect may well be to introduce substantial bias and jeopardize the validity of results.

Verification requires that respondents be identified by first name and telephone number. A sample is then called and asked a few brief questions to reveal if any of the forms of cheating described above have occurred. When such discrepancies are discovered, the individual questionnaire, all those from that interviewer, or all from the agency may be disqualified.

An itemized statement, in considerable detail, should always be required of the agency. When the invoice for payment is received, the amount will virtually always be greater than the original estimate. Each item should be examined closely for accuracy, and each cost compared to that provided on the estimate. Each deviation must then be noted. It is the agency's responsibility to justify each exception or cost overrun. Renegotiation of the final amount is quite common. To save time and effort, such discussions should always be held, from the very beginning, with an officer of the agency who has the authority to make and approve adjustments or modifications.

INTERVIEWER MANAGEMENT FUNCTIONS

The alternative to the use of a data collection agency is the in-house interviewing crew. Some relatively small data collection projects may require only a single interviewer. Ordinarily, unless the data collection process can be extended over a very substantial period of time, several interviewers will be required. The data collection and interviewing often requires hiring temporary, part-time employees to conduct the interviewing. Even those organizations that do interviewing continuously will typically use part-time, rather than full-time interviewers. Thus, it is usually necessary to *recruit* applicants for the interviewing, *select* those that meet the requirements, *train* them to do the job, *supervise* their work, and *compensate* them on the basis of their productivity or time, plus any expenses they incur in their work.

Interviewer Recruitment.   In most communities, there are two basic "pools" of temporary, part-time employment prospects: students and homemakers. Their composition obviously differs markedly by both age and sex, and these characteristics also affect the type and degree of interviewer bias that is likely to be introduced. The major sources of interviewer bias are identified and discussed in some detail later in this chapter. It need only be noted here that the decision to recruit applicants from the student or homemaker populations, or both, should be governed in part by the "match" between the age and sex of interviewers and prospective respondents.

Ideally, a much larger number of interviewer applicants than will actually be needed should be recruited. This permits the selection of only the most qualified, and it provides a list of qualified applicants from which to hire any replacements or additional interviewers, if needed. Ordinarily, recruitment requires only an advertisement or so in the "help wanted" section of the classified ads in the newspapers. The advertisement need be only a few lines, but it should indicate that temporary, part-time employees are being sought. It should state the qualifications that must be met, and indicate when, where, and how the prospects should apply. To have prospects apply in person and to interview them when they first apply often saves time.

Selection of Interviewers.   The interviewers should be selected from the group of applicants partly on the basis of the correspondence between their demographic characteristics and those of the population from which the sample was or will be selected. In other words, it is ordinarily advisable to use interviewers of the same sex, age range, and socioeconomic status as that of the majority of people they will be interviewing.

Aside from correspondence with respondent characteristics, the principal consideration when selecting interviewers is their reliability. Their effectiveness depends on two factors: the degree to which they are *able* to follow instructions and adhere to directions and the degree to which they are *willing* to do so. In other words, both *skill* and *motivation* are prime factors, and both are absolutely necessary.

GUIDELIST 8–4

For Hiring In-House Interviewers

1. Recruit from among those of the same sex, age group, and socioeconomic status as most respondents.
2. Recruit a much larger number of applicants than will actually be needed, to provide sufficient choice.
3. Request applicants to visit the office, complete an application, and be interviewed.
4. Check former employment and references very carefully.
5. Seek indications of personal responsibility, honesty, and integrity above all else.
6. Expect those who are relatively outgoing and gregarious to be most effective at the interviewing task.
7. Give preference to those with interviewing experience only if they are flexible and have been well-trained.

The task of interviewing respondents consists almost entirely of communication. Thus, capable interviewers are those who can both interrogate people effectively, and also listen carefully to responses, perceive and interpret them correctly, and record them accurately. While it is usually desirable that interviewers are gregarious, extroverted, or outgoing personalities who welcome and enjoy contact with others, they must not be too animated. If they are extremely verbose and talkative, they will not be able to pause, listen, and perceive the respondents answers and comments accurately. In other words, they may not give the interviewee sufficient opportunity to respond completely and thoroughly, nor pick up the more subtle verbal or nonverbal cues that constitute a part of the response.

Typically, interviewers are paid only minimum wage or slightly more than minimum, and they are paid for their direct expenses. The job is usually temporary and only part-time, so the pay does not represent a substantial proportion of their present or future income. Thus, the monetary considerations are not at all sufficient to insure that they will not cheat, cut corners, or take the route of least resistance, at the expense of the validity of the data.

Interviewers almost always come to believe that the risk of such behavior being detected is extremely small. In fact, it is difficult to detect it. So, the temptations to cheat can be quite strong. The morals and personal ethics of the interviewers are the strongest and most potent prohibitions against cheating. It is, then, very necessary to accept only those applicants who show every indication of complete honesty and diligence. Checking with previous employers about their experience with the applicant, including the applicants record of absenteeism, is certainly recommended. It is also advisable to obtain personal references and to ask about affiliations, community involvement, and other indicators of personal and social responsibility. It would be far better to select an interviewer who is completely honest and trustworthy, even though the person may be lacking a little in skill or ability, than vice versa.

Whether or not it is advisable to select experienced versus inexperienced interviewers is an open question. There are both "pro's" and "con's" to using experienced interviewers. Obviously, if the researcher has used the interviewers for previous projects and they performed well, they should be hired again. On the other hand, experienced interviewers who worked for some other researcher or data collection agency in the past may not have been well-trained, and they may have acquired many bad habits or practices that will be difficult to correct. The inexperienced require more training, but it is often easier to "begin from scratch" than to dispel inaccurate or inappropriate beliefs and habits. Experienced applicants must be evaluated just as thoroughly as the inexperienced, and perhaps more so.

Interviewer Training. The interviewers who are working more or less continuously for a data collection agency receive some initial training when they begin, and get additional training in the field through actual experience with many surveys. Thus, they ordinarily need only be introduced to the project at hand and to become familiar with the particular questionnaire and materials being used. Interviewers who are hired by the researcher must be trained in both the general nature of interviewing and the particulars of the task for the project at hand. There are two broad classes of information that new recruits must have to be effective interviewers: the "how" and the "why." First, they must know *how* to (1) locate, (2) identify, (3) contact, (4) greet, (5) qualify, (6) interrogate, (7) record, and (8) terminate. Second, they must know *why* it is important to follow the instructions and procedures for interviewing. Most interviewer training programs are much more effective at conveying how to do it than why it must be done that way. Yet, it is very important to provide new interviewers with both, because there are usually many ways to do each of the eight interviewer tasks listed above. Often the way the interviewers are instructed to perform each of the tasks is more difficult for the interviewers than several alternatives they, themselves could find for doing the job. The reasons for doing each task in the prescribed manner will not usually be obvious to new interviewers. Thus, it is important to identify the reasons for the procedures and make clear to new interviewers the consequences of deviating from them.

When the new interviewers have received their instruction and training on survey interviewing procedures in general, they must be given additional instruction in using the particular questionnaire for the survey they are to conduct. The same procedure should be used at this point as that described earlier, for training interviewers from a data collection agency.

Supervising the Interviews. There are two aspects to interview supervision: monitoring the process and checking the results. The interview process can be done overtly or covertly. For example, supervisors should accompany those conducting personal interviews during their first few trials and periodically throughout the process. It is important to see that they get off to a good start with the project. It is also necessary to return to the field to be sure interviewers have not become lax, picked up bad habits, or devised improper short-cuts. When the interviewing is done by telephone, the first few calls should be done in the presence of a supervisor who might help or direct the placement of the calls and listen to the conversations on an extension beside the interviewer. Interviewing can also be monitored covertly, although doing so may not be necessary or desirable if the interviewers are both well-trained and well-motivated and there are no signs of cheating or other misconduct. If there is any possibility that covert monitoring might be used during a project, it is absolutely necessary to inform the interviewers in advance that this might take place. Good business and personal ethics demand this notification, and interviewers might be expected to be justly resentful if they were not informed and discovered it later.

The basic reason for covert, rather than overt monitoring, is because interviewers are likely to behave differently when they know they are being monitored. This difference need not necessarily be intentional or deliberate. Covert monitoring of interviews can be accomplished in two ways: include accomplices unknown to the interviewers on the list or at the location where interviews take place, and have them record the interview or report back to the supervisor, or listen to or record telephone or personal interview conversations without the knowledge of the interviewer.

While some deviations or discrepancies from required procedure or good practice can only be detected by observing the process of interviewing, others can be detected in the results. Thus, effective supervision also requires that the results be checked as early and as frequently as feasible. Daily checking is advisable in most cases if it is feasible to do so that often. Each interviewer may be required to report to a supervisor at the end of the day and submit their finished work. The completed questionnaires are then counted and recorded in the day-log of finished work. In that way, there is a "running record" of progress, and the researcher can tell if the interviewing is on schedule or if additional interviewers will be required. It is also desirable for the supervisor to sight-edit the questionnaires to be sure they are complete and the data has been recorded correctly while the interviewer is present. This permits the supervisor to check with the interviewer about any unusual cases and to make any corrections that are necessary while the interview is still fresh in the memory of the interviewer.

There is a very strong tendency for supervision to focus on any aspect of the interviewing that is wrongly or poorly done. This is equivalent to counting the number wrong, rather than the number right when testing, and it is a drastic mistake. In the first place, it is much easier for those teaching or coaching others to instill knowledge than it is to stamp out ignorance. Secondly, concentrating on the negative, rather than the positive only discourages and demotivates those being supervised. It is very important for supervisors to express praise lavishly and to compliment interviewers sincerely and often for what they do correctly. Interviewers should never be blamed or insulted, and it is only necessary to identify errors and show how they can be corrected. Interviewing can be difficult, but confident, well-motivated interviewers always do superior work.

GUIDELIST 8–5

For Supervising Interviewers

1. Monitor the process and also check the finished results.
2. Have a supervisor present during the first few interviews by each person, to get them off to a good start.
3. Supervisors should return to the field or the phone room periodically to detect problems that might creep in.
4. Use covert monitoring only when necessary and always tell interviewers in advance that it might be used.
5. Require completed work to be submitted in person to the supervisor daily when it is feasible to do so.

6. Finished work should be checked for completion, counted and recorded in the day-log at the time it is submitted.

7. Check the day-log of finished work against the schedule to determine if more interviewers will be required.

8. Have supervisors sight-edit the questionnaires submitted while the interviewer is still present.

9. Provide coaching and make changes on work submitted while the case is fresh in the interviewer's mind.

10. Treat errors or problems in a matter-of-fact manner and never blame, deride, or insult the interviewers.

11. Compliment and praise the interviewers lavishly to enhance their confidence and motivation.

Compensating the Interviewers. Interviewers are ordinarily paid either by interview or by hour. Rarely, if ever are they paid a monthly salary or on a fee basis for the entire job. Each of the two most common forms of compensation have their "pro's" and "con's." Whichever method is chosen, interviewers must also be compensated for any direct expenses that they might incur.

Paying interviewers a set amount for each interview they complete has several advantages. One of the main ones is the fact that those who are most productive receive the most pay. The interviewers who work very quickly, those who are more effective in getting the cooperation of respondents, or who work longer hours will receive more for their efforts, so all are encouraged to do so. That benefits both the interviewers and the researcher. At the same time, this formula also discourages sloppy work, because the interviewers are paid only for completed questionnaires that are complete and usable. This method of payment permits the researcher to compute the cost of the data collection quite precisely, based on the number of responses that are required. Also, the interviewers know exactly what they must accomplish to earn a certain amount and they can easily compute how much they have earned at any given point during collection.

There are also some notable disadvantages to paying a set amount per interview to field or telephone workers. Doing so may encourage cheating. It may also cause the interviewers to hurry respondents or record responses too hastily, or to avoid respondents who should be included because they appear to the interviewer to be too risky or too slow. When interviewers are paid per interview, the researcher must also assess the length and difficulty of the task quite accurately in advance, in order to arrive at an amount that is equitable to both the interviewers and the sponsor. There may be some cases when the interviewing task differs from one interview or interviewer to another. For example, quota requirements may differ, or some respondents may have to complete several sections of the questionnaire that others do not. Paying interviewers a set amount per interview would be appropriate only when the interviewing task is roughly equivalent or when any differences would almost certainly "average out."

GUIDELIST 8 – 6

For Compensating Interviewers

1. Interviewers should be paid for their direct expenses, such as travel and other such costs.

2. Interviewers might be paid either by hour or per interview completed.

3. Payment per interview requires the task to be roughly equal per interview or among interviewers.

4. Payment per interview may encourage cheating, hurrying respondents, or avoiding people who should be included.

5. Payment per interview is more equitable if circumstances permit and it makes cost estimation more accurate.

6. An hourly wage requires more supervision because such workers may be prone to waste time.

7. Hourly wages are usually more equitable when different interviewers work at different times or places.

The advantages of paying interviewers per hour are the same as the disadvantages of paying per interview. Paying an hourly rate is appropriate when interviewers might otherwise be tempted to avoid certain types of respondents that ought to be included or to cut corners to make it easier to get interviews. With hourly pay, there is little or no incentive to misbehave in such ways. This method of compensation is also recommended when the task differs appreciably from one interview or interviewer to the next. Thus, if field workers are stationed at different locations or telephone workers are assigned different calling times, some may be much more productive than others, more because of the time and place than because of ability and effort.

When interviewers receive an hourly wage, it is ordinarily much more difficult for the researcher to arrive at an accurate estimate of total cost. An advanced estimate of the *average* cost per interview must still be made, in order to forecast data collection costs and make financial plans. It is important to note that paying an hourly wage will also require much more rigorous supervision than when interviewers are paid per completed interview. Just as any hourly workers, interviewers paid in this way are more prone to be idle on the job, to chatter with one another, take long lunch and coffee breaks, and generally waste time, because they are still being paid for it.

INTERVIEWING ERROR

Random error reduces the reliability of the survey data, while systematic bias diminishes the validity of the results. These concepts were described and discussed in some detail in Chapter 3. The sources of error and bias resulting from sampling were also noted there. The error and the bias that might arise as the result of interviewing and the methods of controlling them are also major concerns.

Instruction Error.   If interviewers do not present the instructions in precisely the way they are listed on the questionnaire, the deviations will introduce error. Deviating from the written instructions is very common. After reading them a few dozen times, the interviewers may automatically memorize them. Interviewers are likely to repeat the instructions from memory without reading them directly. After doing so several times, without reference to the written instructions, they are likely to repeat them differently. After many such small changes in wording, the memorized instructions may be very dissimilar from the written form.

Interrogation Error.   If questions are expressed differently from one respondent to the next, this will cause error. Even when asking for strictly factual information, people respond differently to different wording. For example, asking "What is your age?" will result in an older age, on the average, than asking, "How old are you?" Merely using the word "old" tends to cause some to report a younger age. Interviewers will not realize how much even subtle differences in the wording affect respondents' answers.

Response Option Error.   Interviewers may be instructed either to read or not to read the response options to the respondents. If interviewers read the alternative answers to respondents when they should not do so, or fail to do so when they should, this will introduce error into the results.

Scale Interpretation Error.   When scale cards are used, errors may result. Suppose a Likert Scale card listed the option "Strongly agree" as number one, "Agree" as number two, etc. Some respondents may reply with the numbers and others with the words. If both the numbers and the options are not listed together on the questionnaire, there is likely to be error. In this example, some interviewers might record the number five for a response of "Strongly agree," rather than number one, as they should.

Recording Error.   The more the interviewers are required to write, the greater the recording errors. There is a much greater likelihood of error when verbatim responses are to be recorded than when interviewers need only jot down a number or letter. Interviewers tend to abbreviate verbal responses, often by necessity. The average respondent speaks at a rate of 150 words a minute. Thus, even a 10-second response may require the interviewer to write a 25-word, verbatim answer.

Interpretation Error.   When interviewers are asked to interpret responses during the interview, errors are likely. For example, interviewers may be instructed not to read the response options listed on the questionnaire to respondents. Instead, the interviewer may be asked to listen to the answers and then choose an option and circle it. Rarely will respondents use exactly the same words as those of the response options. Thus, the interviewers must make judgments about the meaning of the response, and then record them. Such judgments are very prone to error when they must be made in the field or while on the telephone.

Controlling Interviewer Error.   The interview process must be monitored carefully, both at the beginning and periodically during the data collection process, to detect errors by interviewers. The supervisor should follow the conversation while reading a copy of the questionnaire. Any differences between the questionnaire and the interviewers' presentations of instructions, questions or response options should be noted carefully. Simple observation of the interviewers at work in the field or at the telephone may also reveal whether they are reading the material precisely, or merely speaking from memory. To reduce response option errors, a note in parentheses on the questionnaire should indicate if the options are or are not to be read to respondents, unless it is very obvious. If scale cards are used, the numbers and words should also be listed on the questionnaire just as they appear on the scale card, to reduce errors in scale interpretation.

GUIDELIST 8-7

For Controlling Interviewer Error

1. Monitor the interview process to detect instruction, interrogation, and response option error.

2. List both the scale card numbers and the words on the questionnaire to avoid scale interpretation error.

3. Use structured questions and avoid recording verbatim answers to control recording error.

4. Do not require interviewers to select response options based on verbatim answers to avoid interpretation error.

Merely monitoring the interviewing will not detect recording error. The supervisor must monitor the conversation and also record some of the answers, and then compare the record with that recorded on the actual questionnaire by the interviewer. It is important to *prevent* such errors in advance by composing questions and constructing a questionnaire so that recording is quick, simple and easy. It is usually not advisable to ask unstructured questions, where options are not read to respondents, and then require the interviewers to interpret the answers and check an option. If such items must be used, the interviewers should be trained and instructed very thoroughly on the criteria for choosing the response option. They must also be monitored carefully at the beginning and throughout the data collection, to be sure they interpret answers consistently and correctly.

Interviewing Bias

The sources of interviewing error, discussed in the preceding section, affect survey results randomly. The effect of those sources of error is just as likely to "push" the results in one direction as another. Random error reduces the reliability of the data, and it also reduces the validity of the data indirectly, by reducing the reliability. There are also several sources of systematic bias associated with interviewing. Bias reduces the validity of the data directly, by consistently "pushing" the results in one particular direction. Because of this, bias is the more serious problem.

When the validity of the survey results is reduced by bias, it is very difficult to detect after the fact. There is a danger that the researcher and sponsor will base decisions on the data, assuming that it is quite valid, when in fact, it is not. Consequently, it is important to control interviewing bias as much as possible, before and during data collection. In other words, it is always advisable to exert more effort on the prevention of interviewing bias than on trying to detect it or correct it after the data has been collected.

Amplification of Response Bias.   Twelve major sources of bias are identified within Chapter 4, in Figure 4–1. These sources apply both to self-administered questionnaires and to interviewing. It is important to note, however, that the very presence of interviewers is likely to create or increase additional response bias. With a self-administered questionnaire, respondents feel greater anonymity. When they are interacting with an interviewer, either by telephone or in person, any tendencies toward response bias are likely to be amplified, rather than reduced. Thus, it is important to guard against such response bias with even more effort when interviews are to be used to collect the data.

Creation of Response Bias.   Aside from the effect of the mere presence of an interviewer, the telephone or field workers *performance* can create or increase response bias. For example, if the verbal or nonverbal actions of an interviewer are seen as intimidating by the respondents, this would create *threat* bias. If the interviewers were rude or overly pushy, *hostility* bias could be expected to affect the answers to questions, and so forth. To the degree that interviewers are well-trained, well-motivated, and closely monitored, they are less likely to become a source of response bias in and of themselves. When training and monitoring interviewers, the trainer or supervisor should be especially aware of each source of response bias and must watch for signs that the interviewers' actions are creating or amplifying one or more types of bias.

THE INTERVIEW QUESTIONNAIRE

Most of the principles for composing the survey questions and constructing the questionnaire apply equally, whether the data are to be collected by mail, by telephone interviewing, or through personal interviews. Nonetheless, there are some elements of the questionnaire and the other survey materials that differ, depending on whether the questionnaire is to be self-administered or administered by an interviewer. The principles and elements that do apply only to questionnaires administered by interviewers but not to those that are self-administered are identified and discussed below.

The Interview Greeting. The introduction for an interview survey differs markedly from a cover letter used in a mail survey. The most effective interview greeting is very short. This is because the interviewer can interact with the respondent, whether the interviews are conducted by telephone or in person.

Four typical greetings are shown in Example 8–1. The two in the top section ask a question to determine if the individual is "qualified" to respond. A greeting with qualification questions would be used when only certain types of people are to be interviewed and they cannot be identified in advance. The two greetings in the bottom section of the example do not ask qualifying questions. They merely introduce the survey and move quickly and directly to the actual survey questions. Such greetings as these would be used when those who qualify to respond can be identified in advance.

EXAMPLE 8–1

The Interview Survey Greeting

With Qualification

1. Good morning [afternoon—evening]. My name is _____ [first name only] and we are conducting a brief survey of registered voters here in the county. Are you registered to vote? [If YES, continue. If NO, ask for others and continue or terminate if none available.]

2. Good morning [afternoon—evening]. My name is _____ [first name only] and I'm with Expert Research Company. I have a few quick survey questions for those who own certain kinds of automobiles. Is your car an American make or an import? [If at least one American, continue. If foreign or none, terminate.]

Without Qualification

3. Good morning [afternoon—evening]. My name is _____ [first name only] and I'm calling for Field Research, Inc. I'd like to ask you some quick survey questions about your favorite candidate for mayor. [Ask first question immediately.]

4. Good morning [afternoon—evening]. My name is _____ [first name only]. I have some survey questions to ask about your preferences and opinions concerning supermarkets. [Ask first question immediately.]

Notice that mail survey cover letters are much longer than interview survey greetings. Cover letters contain a fairly substantial amount of information, but greetings by interviewers say practically nothing about the survey. At first glance, this may seem to be inconsistent, and those with little or no survey research experience may be tempted to compose a greeting that is much longer, containing more information. Avoid that temptation. The general rule is to keep the greeting and introduction by interviewers as short as possible. The objective here is to get the respondent to begin answering questions immediately. As long as the person's mind is engaged in answering the survey questions, the respondent's thoughts will not turn to consideration of whether or not they should participate.

There is a cardinal rule about interview greetings: *Never, ever ask permission!* Beginning with such questions as, "Do you have a few minutes to answer some questions?" or "Will you take a little while to participate in this survey?" provides potential respondents with an open invitation to decline. The refusal rate will be much, much greater than it would be when using a more correct and effective greeting that does not ask for permission. Remember, the sooner respondents start answering, the better.

Qualification Criteria.   The sample frame for an interview survey identifies the population from which the sample is to be selected. In some cases, the survey research staff may be able to select individual names and addresses or telephone numbers from the sample frame, according to the sampling design, prior to data collection. In such cases, the namelists provided to the interviewers would constitute the sample. It would, of course, be necessary to include a substantially larger number of names than the actual sample size needed, because the interviewers may not be able to contact or obtain responses from all of those listed. When all individuals identified on such a sample list are qualified to respond, the interviewers need not "qualify" respondents with preliminary questions. In that case, a greeting such as those listed in the lower portion of Example 8–1 would be used.

For most interview surveys, it is impractical or impossible to select individual names and addresses or telephone numbers in advance. Consequently, interviewers are provided with a set of general directions concerning who and when to call on the telephone or when and where to go to conduct personal interviews. They are then instructed to interview only those who are qualified to respond and to ignore those who are not qualified. To do so, they must be given a set of criteria by which to judge whether or not those they contact are qualified.

In some cases, qualification criteria for selecting respondents may

---

GUIDELIST 8-8

For Composing Interview Greetings

1. Keep the greeting as short and simple as possible, rather than including a lot of information about the survey.

2. Ask a question very quickly, to engage the respondents' attention and get them started right away.

3. *Never* ask the potential respondents if they have the time or for permission to ask questions.

4. Ask questions to determine if respondents are qualified to respond if that cannot be determined in advance.

5. Remember, anyone has the right to refuse, but the vast majority are friendly and cooperative and will not decline.

6. Be confident that once respondents begin the response task, they will only rarely stop before completion.

---

be based on factors that the interviewers can judge merely by seeing or hearing potential respondents. For example, if only women were qualified, there would be no need to ask potential respondents any questions to ascertain their qualification. Simply observing the person or hearing their voice on the telephone would be sufficient to determine if they should be interviewed. In most cases, however, it will be necessary for interviewers to greet potential respondents and ask them one or more preliminary, qualifying questions. In that case, a greeting such as those listed in the upper portion of Example 8-1 would be used. When the qualification of respondents must be judged by interviewers before they are actually interviewed, it is important to provide clear, concise criteria concerning who is and is not to be included. When qualification is based on such factors as sex, age, or employment status, there is very little ambiguity about who qualifies to respond. When the criteria are based on less concrete or quantifiable factors, such as occupation, mode of dress, or respondent experience or history, the interviewers must be given a complete set of rules for determining who are qualified and who are not.

In order for the respondent qualification process to yield reliable, valid results, two requirements must be met: consistency and accuracy. The actual selection of respondents will be consistent if precisely the same individuals are included or excluded, from one time to the next and from one interviewer to the next. The selection process will be accurate if: (1) *all* those who are, in fact, qualified are included and (2) *only* those who are qualified are included. Thus, the consistency and accuracy of the selection process depends very heavily on providing interviewers with clear-cut, unambiguous criteria.

Quota Specification. When a quota sampling design is to be used, quota specification is a special case of stating qualification criteria. Without a quota, each interviewer uses the same qualification criteria for every respondent interviewed. When a quota sample is required, the qualification criteria differ from one interviewer to the next or from one potential respondent to the next. Aside from this difference, the same principles concerning the specification of qualification criteria apply to quota specification. There are, however, some other factors that must be considered when a quota is used. An example of a typical quota may clarify the discussion.

Suppose an interview survey sampling design specified a quota based on the age, sex, and marital status of respondents, with a total sample size of 240. The quotas for all interviewers might be specified in two different ways, as shown in Example 8–2. Each variable might be considered independently of the others, as in the upper section of the example. If so, it will be relatively easy for interviewers to fulfill the quota, but there is a "catch" to specifying the quota in this way. Because the three variables are considered independently of one another, it would be permissible for interviewers to fulfill this quota with all married men and all unmarried women, providing there were 80 from each age group. This is, of course, an extreme case, but if the quota variables are treated independently, interviewers are not likely to provide closely proportional numbers of one category for each category of the other variables. Quota sampling is usually used to be sure the sample *proportionally* represents the various groups in the population. Thus, if the quota is based on more than one variable, the quota variables are ordinarily treated as interdependent and the quotas would be specified as they are in the lower section of the Example 8–2.

The quota specifications shown in the example above are for the total sample or all interviewers. If more than one interviewer is required, it is also necessary to specify individual quotas for each interviewer. Suppose four interviewers were required to collect the data for the quotas listed in Example 8–2, and they are to be treated as interdependent quotas, as shown in the lower section of the example. There are three basic ways the quotas for individual interviewers might be specified. Each one is identified below, and the advantages and disadvantages of each are noted in turn.

The first method might be called "progressive exclusion." With this

---

EXAMPLE 8-2

The Quota Specification Sheet

	Variable	Independent Quotas Groups	Number
1.	Marital	Married	120
		Not married	120
2.	Sex	Men	120
		Women	120
3.	Age	20–34	80
		35–49	80
		50–99	80

	Marital	Interdependent Quotas Sex	Age	Number
1.	Married	Men	20–34	20
2.	Married	Men	35–49	20
3.	Married	Men	50–99	20
4.	Married	Women	20–34	20
5.	Married	Women	35–49	20
6.	Married	Women	50–99	20
7.	Not Married	Men	20–34	20
8.	Not Married	Men	35–49	20
9.	Not Married	Men	50–99	20
10.	Not Married	Women	20–34	20
11.	Not Married	Women	35–49	20
12.	Not Married	Women	50–99	20

---

method, all interviewers would first be instructed only that those 20 years of age and over are qualified. During the early phase of the interviewing, no additional quotas would be needed, and the interviewers would accept those of different sex, age, and marital status, as they occurred in the population. The supervisor would keep a constant record of the number of respondents in each category that had been obtained on a tally sheet. When a sufficient number had been obtained from any one quota category, all interviewers would be instructed to qualify respondents and to reject any who fell into that group, because no more would be required. As each quota category was progressively fulfilled, additional respondents fitting that quota category would be excluded.

CHECKLIST 8–1

To Choose Qualification Criteria

1. Does the sample frame permit selection of only qualified names in advance? If so, provide interviewers with a list of prequalified individuals to contact that is substantially larger than the actual sample size required.
2. Can qualified respondents be identified only by interviewers observing them after making contact? Then the precise, observable characteristics must be listed clearly and unambiguously for the interviewers.
3. Can qualified respondents be identified only by asking one or more preliminary questions? If so, the questions should be included in the greeting and the selection or rejection based on the answers, so that no judgments by the interviewers are required.

The disadvantage to this method is that it requires close supervision and a constant record of the number of respondents of each type. That may be practical for telephone interviewing from a central location. It may not be feasible for widely dispersed personal interviewing in the field, because it would require each interviewer to call the supervisor after each interview. When practical, this method is the most efficient, because the fewest number of people would need to be contacted and then disqualified and rejected.

The second method of quota specification for individual interviewers is to assign each one an equal portion of each quota. In the example, each of the four interviewers would be assigned a quota of five interviews for each from each group. This technique does not require a running record of the number of interviews completed in each group, but it is likely to require more interviewer time than the first method. This method is less efficient because one interviewer may be seeking a respondent for a particular group while another has fulfilled the quota for that category. Thus, some interviewers would reject potential respondents after contact while others are still seeking such respondents.

The third method of specifying individual interviewer quotas would be to assign the first three categories to the first interviewer, the next three to the second, etc. This technique is temptingly simple, but it is *not* ordinarily acceptable. The reason for avoiding it is a little complex, but quite compelling. No matter how well-trained and motivated the interviewers are, they are likely to introduce *some* systematic bias. In other words, some of the differences in the answers will be attributable to the individual interviewers, themselves. Chances are, when the data are analyzed, the groups resulting from the quotas will be compared with one another. Suppose all married men are interviewed by one interviewer, all married women by another, and the analysis showed significant differences in the answers between these two groups. Such differences might be attributed to either the sex of the respondents *or* to differences between the interviewers, or both. In other words, the analyst would not be able to tell if the sex of the respondent affected the answers or not. In technical terms, this is called a "confound" between individual interviewers and different groups. Thus, the other methods of individual quota specification are markedly superior.

CHECKLIST 8–2

To Select a Quota System

1. Is the quota based on more than one attribute or variable? If so, then it is advisable to treat them as "interdependent," to maintain proportionality.

2. Will more than one interviewer be required? If so, the quota for the entire sample must be divided among them.

3. Is it practical to maintain a continuous record of all interviews completed for each quota category? If so, the "progressive exclusion" method of implementing the quota should be used.

4. Does the dispersion or lack of contact with interviewers preclude the use of progressive exclusion? If so, then each quota category should be divided among the individual interviewers in roughly equal proportions.

Interviewer Instructions. The interview questionnaire contains two very different types of content: that which is to be read to respondents and that which is intended for the interviewers, only. It is very important to distinguish the two types of content very clearly and distinctly. Common means of doing so include the use of parentheses, brackets, underlining, indentation, and all uppercase letters. Different typeface is seldom used because there is ordinarily no necessity to have interview questionnaires typeset before printing. The most conventional method for identifying the questionnaire content that is *not* to be read to respondents is to enclose it in brackets or parentheses. The questionnaire writer should establish one convention, and then use it *consistently* throughout.

Interview Questionnaire Format.   The appearance and cosmetic aspects of a self-administered, mail questionnaire are extremely important because they affect both response quality and response rate. Ordinarily, interview questionnaires are read and handled only by the interviewers, and so they need not be especially attractive to the eye. On the other hand, it is important that they be constructed in a format that makes them easy to use. If the interviewer must take time to study the questionnaire or hunt for the next item while conducting the interview, this may jeopardize the success of the interview. Thus, those composing the questionnaire must anticipate and appreciate the conditions under which the interviewing will be done. Any format or compositional device that will assist the telephone or field workers to conduct the interview quickly and smoothly, with a minimum of hesitation or pause, should be employed when writing the questionnaire.

The Personal Interviewing Process

There are several aspects of personal interviewing that do not apply to telephone interviews, and vice versa. Those things that are of particular concern when personal interviewing is used to collect the data are discussed in this section, and those related to telephone interviewing are considered in the following section.

Timing.   It is very important to recognize that the time of day and day of the week when the interviews are conducted are likely to affect both the refusal or response rate and the nature of the answers to the questions. For example, it is advisable to conduct in-home interviews between the hours of nine o'clock in the morning and nine at night. It may also be advisable to avoid meal times when possible. When interviews are conducted during daytime hours on weekdays, homemakers and those who are retired are likely to be overrepresented, while those employed outside the home will be represented in smaller proportions than in the population as a whole. Thus, it is often desirable to conduct a substantial proportion of the interviews during evenings and weekends. Field workers must be instructed and monitored carefully to be sure they conduct the interviews at the times specified. They ordinarily have a strong tendency to work when it is convenient for them, rather than for the respondents or as directed by the supervisor.

The Interview Location.   The locations at which the interviews are to be conducted must be carefully specified by the researcher, and the field workers must be monitored to be sure they adhere to the locational requirements. The interviewers are not likely to realize that the location of the interview will affect the responses. In Figure 8–1, the most frequently used locations are identified and described. When the interviews require more than a few minutes and they are to be conducted at the home of respondents, it is advisable for the field workers to seek permission to enter the home and perhaps to sit at a table with the respondent. Most people will extend that courtesy, and doing so will facilitate accurate interrogation and recording.

FIGURE 8–1

Common Personal Interview Locations

1. In-Home:
The interviews are conducted at the residence of the respondents. They may be inside the home, at the door, or outside, on the property.

2. Job Site:
The interviews are conducted at the shop or office of the respondents. This location is ordinarily used *only* when the employer is the survey sponsor.

3. Traffic Intercepts:
One or more areas of pedestrian traffic are identified for field workers. They then intercept all qualified respondents as they move through the area. "Shopper" intercepts are the most common. [It is ordinarily necessary to obtain permission to interview at proprietary locations, such as within a store, mall, or at a shopping center.]

4. Mall Intercepts:
These are similar to traffic intercepts, except that the data collection agency may have an interviewing facility permanently located within the mall. Interviews may be conducted outside or inside the facility.

5. Stationary Concentrations:
Those attending or waiting at meetings, sports or entertainment events, and the like may be interviewed where they have congregated.

It is important to note that even when certain areas appear to be "public," in the sense that anyone is welcome to enter, they may, in fact, be proprietary to some company or organization. For example, most shopping malls, stadiums, and the like will not permit interviewing without prior, written permission. If it has not been obtained in advance from someone authorized to approve it, the field workers may be detected and ejected from the site. When such permission has been obtained, each interviewer should be given a copy of the written authorization, so that no misunderstandings or delays result if they are accosted by authorities at the location.

Distractions and Interruptions.   Field workers should be instructed concerning how to handle the most common types of distractions or interruptions that are likely to occur during the interviews. For example, it is important to indicate whether or not the interviewing may be done if one or more other people are present during the interview, so that they could listen to the questions and answers (and/or contribute to the response). The directions given to field workers should also indicate whether or not the interview should be continued if it is interrupted, and if so, how long an interval is acceptable. Ordinarily, interruptions of more than a few minutes require termination and rejection of the incomplete response. It is important to note, too, whether or not respondents can or should refer to other people or to records or other materials, in order to respond to the questions.

Rating Cards and Visual Aids.   When personal interview surveys make use of rating cards or other visual or physical materials that are to be examined by respondents, the field worker instructions clearly indicate how they are to be handled. For example, interviewers must know if they may hand the item to the respondent or merely show them the material, and they must also be told when such visual aids are to be withdrawn or removed. The appearance of such visual materials is very important, because they are viewed by respondents and their perceptions may affect the response. Thus, ordinarily the same such items are used again and again with each interview. It is important to provide two or more "sets" of such material, in case some are lost, destroyed, or defaced. It is also advisable to include a very prominent instruction at the end of the questionnaire, to remind field workers to reclaim any such visual materials from the respondent before leaving. This is important because interviewers are extremely likely to forget such things, fail to retrieve them, and then be unable to continue with the interviewing.

Recording Observations and Responses.   When field workers must record data they observe, they must be given firm criteria by which to classify or categorize the observational data. The same requirements for consistency and accuracy apply to these observations as to the qualification criteria, noted earlier. When recording responses from the interviewees, it is advisable to compose the questionnaire in such a way that items need only be checked or circled or a number recorded, whenever possible. When unstructured or "open-ended" questions are included, field workers should be instructed on what to record, such as whether they should record the complete, verbatim response, word for word, or only key words and phrases. Usually, field workers must also record the time and location of the interview, and provide an indication to identify themselves as the interviewer. The instructions for recording such data should be listed clearly and prominently at the end of the questionnaire.

The Telephone Interview Process

Telephone interviewing can be done either from a central location, such as the research headquarters, or from the interviewers homes. It is always advisable to require interviewing from a central location when it does not add significantly to toll charges or data collection costs to do so. A central calling location greatly facilitates the supervision and monitoring of the data collection. When the telephone workers do call from their own homes or other locations, they must be selected and trained very carefully, and their work supervised as closely as possible.

The Namelist or Directory.   Telephone interviewing is often done directly from a telephone directory. Ordinarily, telephone workers are provided with directions concerning which names and numbers to select. Such instructions must be very clearly *written* and provided to each interviewer for reference when a question arises. It is never sufficient merely to require that interviewers call every *n*th number. Rather, they must be instructed concerning where to start in the volume, where to begin the count on the page and column, etc. They must also be told how to handle listings that are clearly not qualified, such as business listings when only residential listings are to be included.

Timing.   With telephone interviewing, just as with personal interviewing, the time of day and days of the week during which calls are placed will affect the type of respondents that are obtained. It is especially important to supervise and monitor the timing of calls, because telephone workers are much more likely to deviate from the prescribed timing than are field workers conducting personal interviews. Respondents who are called after nine in the evening or before nine in the morning may agree to respond, but if the task is an unwelcome interruption or intrusion, this would certainly affect their answers to the questions.

The duration of the interview constitutes another important timing factor. Field workers conducting personal interviews are ordinarily able to hold the attention and interest of respondents for substantially longer periods than are telephone interviewers. There is ordinarily little or no resistance or premature termination when telephone interviews are less than five minutes, and telephone workers experienced at building and maintaining rapport with the respondents may conduct interviews of 10 minutes or so in duration with few refusals or terminations. Telephone interviews of more than 15 minutes are likely to result in a very substantial number of refusals or premature terminations by the respondents.

Call Results and Options.   The telephone workers must be provided with directions concerning how to respond to the various outcomes that might result when a number from the list has been called. The eight possible outcomes and the five common options that are open to the interviewer are identified in Figure 8–2. Based on the sampling design and requirements, the researcher must compose instructions that indicate which of the five options should be pursued in case of each of the possible call results.

FIGURE 8–2

Telephone Call Results and Options

Possible Call Results

1. Call answered by a qualified respondent.
2. Call answered by an unqualified person.
3. Number proves to be wrong location or subscriber.
4. Call is not answered after 6 to 10 rings.
5. Busy signal is received for the number called.
6. Call answered by an answering service or device.
7. Number has been changed and new number is listed.
8. Number not in service and no new number is listed.

Telephone Interviewer Options

1. Interview respondent and place next call.
2. Ask if a qualified respondent is present.
3. Terminate and place call to next number.
4. Terminate and call back in a few minutes.
5. Terminate and call at different day and time.

Telephone workers should be instructed to record the telephone number of the respondent, the date, time of the call, and their own identity. These instructions should be clearly listed at the end of the questionnaire.

SUMMARY

Interview Data Collection Procedures

A. Understand the interviewer's role. The telephone or field workers should be perceived as part of the measurement instrument, with the potential to create error and bias.

B. Consider the data collection agency. Study the agency data collection process and check on agency cost and availability, and quality carefully.

C. Appreciate the interviewer management task. Study the interviewer management functions and weigh the advantages and disadvantages of an in-house crew.

D. Choose the mode of interviewing. Evaluate the capabilities and limitations of data collection agencies, compared to an in-house interviewing crew.

E. Reduce potential interviewing error. Consider instruction, interrogation, response, scaling, recording, and interpretation as possible sources of error.

F. Control interviewing and response bias. Check each element of the questionnaire and process for each of the major sources of bias.

G. Handle instrumentation carefully. Compose the greeting, qualification and quota criteria, interviewer instructions, and questionnaire format to avoid error and bias.

H. Identify the unique aspects of each process. Recognize the distinctions between personal and telephone interviewing, making required adjustments for the mode selected.

9

Data Processing

RECEIPT OF QUESTIONNAIRES

Data processing should be thoroughly planned at a much earlier stage in the survey process, but the work actually begins with the receipt of the first completed questionnaires from the field. The final preparation and testing of the computer programs can be done while the survey is still in the field and the data are being collected. With mail surveys and with interviewing done by a data collection agency or a separate interviewer team, the researcher will often have a few weeks during data collection when there is little else to do with the survey except to prepare the processing mechanism. This gives the researcher a "head start" on the processing phase. By completing a few blank questionnaires with fictitious data, the researcher can begin constructing files, writing or obtaining analysis programs, and specifying the tasks that will be needed for data analysis.

Data Receipt.   It is usually necessary for the researcher to monitor the collection of the data very carefully. With interview surveys, reports may be obtained from the field on a daily basis, or at least two or three times per week, from each interviewer or agency working on the survey. In that way, adjustments can be made and extra effort exerted when it is required to avoid delays or procrastination on the part of the field workers and supervisors. With mail surveys, it is always advisable to collect the mail daily or with each delivery. Any "nondeliverable" pieces should be checked to ascertain why they were not received by the intended recipient. By doing so, the researcher can assess the quality of the mailing list and the organization or system that provided it. When there are many nondeliverable pieces marked with a notation such as "no such address," this indicates that the list is inaccurate. If a substantial amount of non-deliverable mail results because many have moved and there is no forwarding address, that usually shows that the list is "dated," so that the names were acquired for the list many months or years before the list was obtained or the list has not been kept current. This information is not only useful to assess the namelist quality, but it is also valuable to judge the potential quality and accuracy of the survey results and the degree to which the sample will be representative of the population as a whole.

It is advisable to open mail returns and record the date the questionnaire was received on the back, at the end of the questionnaire. Similarly, interview questionnaires that are returned from the field should be checked to be sure the interviewer has recorded the date of the interview, and perhaps also to record when it was received in the office. It may be necessary later to compare results from the earlier data collection period with that from the later period. With mail data collection, this comparison indicates differences between those who were most motivated and willing to complete the task and those who tended to delay for some time. When the data are collected in interviews, the comparison can show what affect inexperience versus experience on the part of the interviewers may have had on the answers that were obtained.

During this period when the completed returns are received, it is always wise to keep a complete record of how many surveys were sent into the field, how many are still out at any given point, and how many have been completed and returned. This running record of data collection allows the researcher to anticipate the "cut-off" point, when collection can be terminated and additional responses ignored. It also shows whether the data collection process is on schedule and going according to plan. If there are serious delays, it may be necessary to initiate appropriate changes or to allocate additional effort to the data collection.

Handling Source Documents.   The completed questionnaires are the source documents from which files of survey data will be created. This period, during receipt of data, is usually the first time that the researcher will actually experience the volume of data and documents created by the survey. Of course, with surveys of very limited scope, there will be few surprises and little confusion. On the other hand, except for mail surveys where the researcher has done much of the preparation and mailing, larger survey projects are likely to produce more documentation than the inexperienced researcher anticipates or for which the researcher has prepared. The physical volume can be considerable. Thus, it is absolutely necessary to devise a system for handling the source documents and to stick by it throughout the receipt period.

The first step is ordinarily to open mail returns or materials received from interviewers and record the date of receipt, as suggested above. After doing so, the extra materials that might be returned, such as copies of the cover letter, envelopes, rating cards, interviewer instructions, and the like can be discarded or filed for later use on another project, if needed. For some mail surveys, it may be advisable to record the location from which the piece was sent from the postmark on the return envelope, before the envelopes are separated from the completed questionnaires.

Experienced researchers find it very useful to record consecutive numbers at the end of the questionnaire as they are received. This unique code value can then be recorded in the data file, together with the data, so that the researcher can refer back to the source document at any time to make corrections or to inspect it, if necessary. These document identification numbers can be listed by hand or with a special consecutive number stamp. It is important always to note the *last* number used, to avoid duplication.

When the data are to be sight-edited and transferred to data files by one or more people other than the researcher, it will be necessary to devise and maintain a systematic record to indicate which individuals have which source documents. This is especially useful when the documents are to be removed from the survey office or headquarters by those working with them. These documents are, of course, quite valuable and they are not replaceable. Those who work with them are much more likely to handle them with care and to avoid misplacing or losing them if they must "check them out" before taking them and know they will be held accountable for the documents they have. Another advantage to keeping such records is the fact that they automatically indicate which individuals performed the various tasks that are required. If problems, difficulties or mistakes are discovered later in the process, they can be attributed to those responsible. In addition, the individuals who worked on the documents and files can be questioned for clarification, and all of the documents or cases that they processed can be checked for similar discrepancies or treated in the same way. The degree of control that is achieved from a record of source document possession is well worth any extra time and effort required to maintain such records.

Sight-Editing Documents

Once the completed questionnaires have been received, recorded, and sorted, the actual processing begins with a sight-edit of each document. Each one must be examined to ascertain if it is acceptable for processing and to make any corrections or notations that might be required. The initial sight-edit of the early returns can also indicate whether or not the field workers have been instructed properly with interview data collection. Thus, additional instruction or supervision can be arranged if it is required.

GUIDELIST 9–1

For Initiating Data Processing

1. Plan and obtain data processing facilities, files, records, and programs while the survey is in the field.
2. Prepare the physical setting when a large number of questionnaires are to be received, so that there is a place for each group or set.
3. Monitor collection and receipt of data carefully, obtaining daily reports of completion and receipt.
4. Record nondeliverable mail surveys by reason for failure to gauge the quality of the namelist and representativeness of the sample.
5. Record the date of collection and/or receipt at the end of the completed questionnaires, so that comparisons of early and later returns can be made during analysis.
6. Maintain a record of the number of surveys sent into the field, the number remaining, and the number returned.
7. Record a unique, consecutive identification number on each source document returned from the field.
8. Keep a record of precisely who has what source documents, by number, when others are to sight-edit and postcode documents and transfer data to files.
9. Be sure that those who assist or perform the processing tasks know they will be held accountable for both the loss of any documents and the quality of their work.

Judging Completeness. Some questionnaires that are returned from the field, especially with mail data collection, will obviously not have been completed at all. There may be a note or comment by the recipient or interviewer, and if so, it is advisable to keep a brief record of them as a sketch of the reasons for failure to complete the instrument. Aside from that, these documents can be eliminated from the collection of forms to be processed. (Save several blank questionnaires if none were retained earlier, to use as scratch working forms during coding and processing.)

Each document that appears at a glance to be completed must be checked thoroughly. The editor should examine each page and section of the questionnaire to be sure the respondent followed instructions and recorded answers in the proper place. The researcher should establish fixed criteria concerning how much of the questionnaire must be completed to make the case acceptable. This is especially important when others will be assisting with the sight-editing. The editors are not likely to have the ability to make judgments on their own, so they should be given guidelines concerning what to accept and what to eliminate. Ordinarily, it is advisable to have editors form three groups of documents: those that are obviously acceptable, those that are obviously rejects, and those for which there is a question about acceptability. Thus, the researcher can examine the questionable documents and make a more informed decision about them.

There will inevitably be individual items that respondents fail to complete. Some missing data can be tolerated, so if the document is substantially complete, with only an occasional missing answer, it should be retained. On the other hand, if entire sections are incomplete or the respondent has completed only the beginning of the questionnaire and then terminated prematurely, the case must usually be rejected.

Multiple Questionnaire Forms.   Occasionally, a single survey project will require different forms of the questionnaire for different respondent groups. For example, some interviews may be conducted in person and others, to obtain only the most essential data, may be conducted by telephone. Thus, two forms would be required. In such cases, it is advisable to segregate the instruments of each type into separate groups and treat them individually during the initial phase of data processing. The more standard the task, the more efficient the editors and those who transfer data to files are likely to become. Of course, if multiple questionnaire forms are used, the researcher must establish separate criteria for editing and accepting each form of the instrument.

Editing, Branching, and Exclusions.   Some survey questionnaires may require a considerable amount of branching or many items that have exclusionary conditions. For example, the respondent or interviewer may be instructed to skip an entire section or go to a later point in the questionnaire, based on the response to a key item, or there may be several that are conditioned on the previous question, such as a question that begins, "If so, then . . ." If there are many such branches or exclusions in the instrument, the sight-editing becomes more laborious and also more demanding. It is important for the editors to examine such items and to make corrections where necessary, if respondents have completed items they should have disregarded or ignored. It is almost never advisable to transfer such inappropriate items or section responses to the data file for processing, in the hope that they will be detected and eliminated later. Experience indicates that one of the most effective ways to edit such questionnaires is to provide each editor with a blank questionnaire with those items or sections that should sometimes be excluded marked boldly with a red marking pen. This will serve as a "key" against which to check each completed document. The "criterion" question or item,

---

GUIDELIST 9-2

For Sight-Editing Documents

1. Early returns should be sight-edited promptly to detect data collection problems that might be remedied.

2. The objective of editing is to determine the data and cases to be accepted and those to be rejected.

3. Establish firm criteria for editors concerning the degree of completeness required to accept a case.

4. Instruct editors to set aside questionable documents to be examined by the researcher for an informed judgment.

5. Ordinarily, some missing data from an occasional item can be tolerated, and the remaining data are valuable.

6. Usually, cases where entire sections are incomplete or only the first part has been completed must be rejected.

7. When multiple forms of a questionnaire are used, they should be segregated and treated individually.

8. With many branches or exclusions in the questionnaire, editors should be given a key to indicate their location and the conditions when items should not be answered.

9. When respondents or interviewers have mistakenly recorded answers to questions where they should not, the superfluous data should be marked out by the editors.

10. Inappropriate or superfluous data do not usually require that the case be rejected.

---

the one that indicates whether or not the following item or section should be completed, can also be marked clearly on the key, together with an indication of the answers that include or exclude the following section or item. The editors can then compare each page of the completed document with this key or guide, to be sure that there are no inappropriate answers recorded. This is especially important for each editor to do for the first dozen or so questionnaires, until each person is thoroughly familiar with the sections or items that might be excluded and the criteria for completing or excluding them.

When a respondent has failed to complete an item or section of the questionnaire because of a mistake concerning branching or exclusion, the editors should use the same criteria for completion to accept or reject the case as they would for other items or sections. On the other hand, when a respondent has completed an item or section to which they should not have responded, this ordinarily does not necessitate rejecting the case. Often those answers can be safely ignored and the remainder of the data will be acceptable. For such cases, the editors should cross out the superfluous data for the item or section very clearly, using a red marker or writing instrument that is very different from what was used to record the data on the questionnaire. Thus, when the case is transferred to a data file, those recording it will not become confused.

POSTCODING THE DATA

If the questionnaire has been composed and constructed properly, most questions will be "structured" so that almost all of the responses will fall within predetermined categories, or the responses to most of the items will be scale values recorded by the interviewer or respondent. In addition, the questionnaire should have been precoded with the values for each answer printed on the questionnaire and the record format for the data file indicated on the far right margin. Even if the questionnaire was prepared in that way, it will ordinarily be necessary to do a substantial amount of postcoding of responses. Postcoding a document consists of assigning a code value to any response that does not already have such a code. For example, an item may list several alternative response categories, followed by an "other" category and a note to specify what other response. Obviously, such responses could not be anticipated and so they have no precoded value associated with them. Consequently, the editors must postcode such responses before the response codes can be transferred to the data file for processing.

The postcoding can be done either simultaneously with the sight-editing, or as a separate task. Usually, if the postcoding requirements are not very elaborate and it can be done fairly quickly, it is advisable to do both the sight-editing and the postcoding at the same time for each document. To do so would not delay the sight-editing substantially, and it would only require the editors to handle each document one time. When the postcoding process is more demanding and time-consuming, it should probably be done after the sight-editing has been completed. That allows the editors postcoding the questionnaires to devote all of their attention to this single, more complex task and it does not delay the sight-editing and recording of documents.

It is usually advisable to provide the editors who will postcode the questionnaires with a blank, "key" questionnaire indicating the items that should be examined and coded where necessary, similar to that used for the sight-editing. If the same key is used to sight-edit and to postcode the questionnaires, the two types of indicators on the key must be distinct from one another, such as in different colors, and they should both be *very* prominent and easily recognized.

When postcoding the questionnaires, the editors must record two things: the new codes for the answers that have none must be recorded on the questionnaire to be transferred to the data file *and* the answers, themselves, or some abbreviated phrase must be recorded in the codebook or codelist, together with the code value. An example may clarify the process of coding and recording. Suppose a survey question asks, "What is your racial or ethnic identification?" The response alternatives printed on the questionnaire might include: [1] White, [2] Black, [3] Oriental, [4] Hispanic, and [5] Other. There may be an instruction to specify what other is included with the item. Assume that the editor finds that a respondent has checked the "Other" category and written in "Filipino." The editor would then check the codelist for that item to see if that response had already been encountered and recorded with a code on the codelist. If not, the editor would assign the next code value, in sequence, to that answer, record the value and the word, "Filipino" at the bottom of the codelist for the item, and also record the code value prominently in the assigned place on the questionnaire, to be transferred to the data file.

As the example indicates, there must be a codelist for each item that may require postcoding. It is usually advisable to make a codebook containing one or more *separate pages* for each such item, with the item number or questionnaire location clearly indicated at the top of the page. This is because the researcher cannot ordinarily tell how many new codes and answers will result from any one item and there must be room to enter new ones until all completed questionnaires have been coded.

Postcoding is a relatively simple, easy process when only one editor does the coding on any given day or at any one time. Thus, it is almost always advisable for the researcher to arrange it so, either by assigning only one person to the task, or by "staggering" the times and/or days when different editors will code the completed questionnaires. When neither option is feasible, then the editors must all work at the same place when they are coding simultaneously. The reason is evident. If two or more editors are coding the same questionnaire at the same time and in different locations, they will not know what new codes the others have listed in their codebooks. Thus, there is a great likelihood that a single code value will be assigned to two or more *different* answers. The objective of the coding process is to provide a *unique* code for each acceptable answer. Less experienced researchers may be tempted to minimize the importance of this potential difficulty and ignore the recommendation, in order to "save time." Experience clearly indicates that it is very dangerous to permit editors to work independently from different codebooks in separate locations. Serious errors and data problems will almost certainly result.

Criteria for Postcoding.   The researcher should specify the criteria for identifying and categorizing answers and assigning codes to them. The editors must have guidelines concerning how "fine-grained" the categories should be and how to group individual answers into categories. For instance, in the example of the question regarding racial or ethnic identity noted earlier, how should those who check the "Other" category and list "Jewish" be treated? Most respondents of that ethnicity are likely to check the category for White, so in that case, the researcher would probably elect to have the editors *recode* the item to number one, rather than establishing a new category for those few who list their ethnicity as Jewish.

Lacking some fairly concrete guidelines and criteria for coding, editors who are not especially experienced or who lack familiarity with the survey process are likely to error markedly in one of two directions: Some will assign a new code to virtually every new alternative, based on the precise, verbatim word or phrase noted on the questionnaire. This will produce many more codes and categories than are desirable, and probably there will be only one or two cases for each such code. Other editors are likely to simplify their task by "lumping" all of the responses that are even vaguely similar to one another into the same, large category. That would, in effect, discard distinctions and data that might be regarded by the researcher as useful. Thus, the editors must be given the necessary guidelines and ordinarily, they should be monitored during the initial phase of the work to be sure they are doing it correctly.

When deciding on the level of detail, or how "fine-grained" the new categories should be, the researcher is well-advised to be too narrow, rather than too broad. If too much detail is recorded, this will result in a few extra code values that are not required. That is not a serious penalty, and during the analysis, the data can be regrouped into larger categories. This is especially easy to do if computer survey analysis programs will be used to process the data. By contrast, if the data to be coded are grouped into individual categories that are too large and too broad, there is virtually no recourse except to return to the source documents, edit them again, and transfer the data to file a second time. Once distinctions have been lost by grouping into broad categories, they cannot be regained without reference to the source documents. Thus, most experienced researchers would prefer that those who edit and postcode the questionnaires create a new category and code if they are seriously in doubt about its fitting into an existing category.

Maintaining the Codebook.   It is very important to be sure the entries in the codebook are very neatly and legibly made. This point will seem trivial to the less experienced researcher, until it is time to use the information during the analysis and reporting phase. It is far better to avoid a potential catastrophe than to spend hours trying to remedy one. Often the editors will be "clerical help" who are not particularly interested in the survey results or familiar with the process. When there are several editors doing the postcoding, each will be making entries on the codelists. Thus, there is a high potential for error, redundancy, and failure. This potential increases markedly if the codelists are not kept in a neat, orderly fashion. For example, editors will typically make "margin notes" when a sheet is full, rather than creating a new page. If they do, they or others may fail to notice the last entry and assign the same code to a different response. The necessity for neatness in the codebook is more than cosmetic.

If the codelists become disordered or confusing, it is well-worth the time and effort to rewrite them from the originals, creating a more orderly codebook. It is important to note that the entries must *not* be changed in any way, and the same codes must apply to the same answers and categories. When categories must be combined, that should be done after the codes have been transferred to the data file, and not during the coding process.

The most common and detrimental error when coding completed questionnaires and making entries in the codebook is to fail to list a new code and category in the book. If that happens, the same code will be assigned to two different answers, and this must be avoided. On the other hand, if editors fail to note that a particular response

---

GUIDELIST 9–3

For Postcoding the Questionnaires

1. Postcoding is almost always required because any answer that does not have a code value must be assigned one.

2. New codes should be listed on the questionnaire so they can easily be recognized when transferring data to file.

3. A codelist page for the codebook should be created for each questionnaire item that might require postcoding.

4. It is vital that editors record every new code category they create on the codelist, so that others do not use the same code value for a different answer.

5. If more than one editor does postcoding, they must all work from the *same* codebook, either at different times or simultaneously, at the same place.

6. Simple coding can be done together with sight-editing, but substantial coding tasks should be done afterward.

7. Coding editors should be given a "key" questionnaire with the items to be postcoded clearly marked.

8. The researcher should provide the guidelines for when and how to create new codes and group answers.

9. It is better for editors to create too many, small categories than too few, very broad ones.

10. The codebook must be maintained neatly and clearly and should be recopied if it becomes disorderly.

---

has been coded and entered on a codelist and create a new code for the same answer, the two can be recoded to a single value during processing and little, if anything, is lost.

Transferring the Data

When all of the completed questionnaires to be included in the data have been sorted, sight-edited and postcoded, it is time to transfer the data to a file to be tabulated or processed. If the pre- and post-coding have been done properly, the process of data transfer should consist only of reading the codes for each item and recording them in the file, according to the record format to be used. The type of file to which the data will be transferred depends on the type of processing that is selected. The two basic options are either hand tabulation or ͜ computer processing of the data. When the data are to be hand tabulated, the codes on the source documents must be recorded on summary data sheets, before the actual tabulation begins. It is far too cumbersome and time-consuming to page through all of the source documents to tabulate each survey item.

Data to be processed with computer programs must first be transferred from the source documents to a computer file or to punch cards that can be read by machine. If the mode of processing was anticipated and the data record format printed on the questionnaire, as suggested earlier, then the data need only be keyed to file in precisely that format. If the data record format has not been specified and printed on the forms, it will be necessary to design the record and list the format on a blank "key" questionnaire so those who key the data to cards or to file know where each data point is to appear on the record.

The process of designing a record format and listing it on a questionnaire is discussed in some detail in Chapter 6. If that task has yet to be done, the researcher should refer to the section on "Precoding and Formatting" in that chapter for instruction.

Often the survey data are keyed to cards or to a computer file on a disk or diskette by "key operators" who specialize in such work. When more than one person is to key the data to file, each must have a copy of the record format to guide them, if it is not printed on the questionnaire in advance. They should also be provided with any instructions about the task that they require. It is usually advisable for the researcher to be present or readily available while the first few cases are being keyed to file, so that the operators can ask questions and obtain additional direction if they need it. Inexperienced researchers often make the mistake of assuming too much of the operators. The researcher sometimes feels that because the operators are familiar with the keying equipment, they are also knowledgeable about computer operations and data processing, and perhaps even the details of the project at hand. This is seldom, if ever, the case. Ordinarily, key operators can be compared to typists who may be very fast and accurate at their particular task, but know little about the content of the material or data they are transferring or its ultimate purpose or destination, once it leaves their hands.

If the survey data are keyed to file by those who specialize in such work, they may ask if the data are to be "verified." Verification is simply a method to insure a high degree of accuracy. It requires that each case be keyed twice. The first time is to create the original record in the file. The second time, the values that are keyed into the device are compared with the original, to be sure it is identical. If not, the original is carefully changed to conform to the source document. The verification process assumes, and ordinarily, rightly so, that operators will seldom make precisely the same mistake in precisely the same place in the file. Of course, verification usually almost doubles the cost and time requirements for data transfer. Thus, most researchers do not require the data transfer to be verified unless there is a very serious need for a high degree of accuracy. Usually, those keying services that offer verification employ key operators that are quite accurate at their work, and so many, serious errors are unlikely. On the other hand, when inexperienced people key the data to file, there are likely to be a significant amount of errors. One way to assess the accuracy without the cost and delay of verification is to "spot check" several source documents against the listing of the data files. If few errors are detected, the file need not be modified. If many errors appear, it may be necessary to verify the file or create a new one with more accurate key operators.

Process Editing

Once the data have been keyed to file, it is always advisable to edit the data by machine to be sure it is acceptable for analysis. This is *far more important* than it might seem. If the data is not "clean" and in the proper condition for analysis, two serious problems can result: First, it is very likely that the analysis routines will fail to execute or "run" properly, and if they do, they are likely to generate reports with obviously invalid values. Second, and even worse, the programs may execute and generate erroneous results that escape the notice of the researcher. Those who use computers are familiar with a well-recognized principle of operations, called simply "GIGO." It means, "garbage in, garbage out." Process editing can help the researcher to avoid an unpleasant encounter with the GIGO principle.

When data are edited during processing, the objective is to identify two kinds of errors: records that deviate from their format and data fields that are outside of their permissible range. There are a variety of methods for checking each, depending on the processing devices and programs, but it is always advisable to first check record format, and then examine the data fields.

Checking Deviations from Record Format. The data for each record will ordinarily begin and end in a given column, specified by the record format. If there is more than one record (line of data) for each questionnaire (case), they may not all end at the same point on the line, but the same record in each case should begin and end at the same place. It is usually advisable to have operators key a zero in the record if no data are present, rather than leave columns blank in the data file, so that the data will extend to exactly the same place for each similar record. To check the record format, the data can be listed and the ends of the lines at the right inspected to be sure each ends where it is supposed to. Lines that extend beyond their format limit or are too short should be identified by case number and checked against the source document. Similarly, those that are too short should also be checked. This usually indicates that the operator has "skipped" a column or more, failed to enter some data points for the field, or entered some data twice in the same record.

Errors of this nature are particularly troublesome and often create serious problems. If the data deviates from the format and the error was "early" in the record, toward the beginning or left side, this will result in not only the particular field that was miskeyed to be in error, but probably all of the data on the remaining part of the record. Thus, all such records should be corrected in the file before beginning the check of the field range.

Checking Deviations from Field Range.   Each individual response to a survey item has been keyed to a "field" of one or more columns in the record. Each such field has an acceptable range of data. For example, if the item used a six point scale, the range would be from one to six, and if missing data were tolerable for the item, zero would also be acceptable. Similarly, if only adults were to be accepted as respondents, then no age keyed as a continuous, numeric item, should be below 18, 21, or whatever age was used to qualify young respondents. This aspect of process editing should check each data field, by record and column, to be sure the data are within the permissible range.

There are a variety of ways to check the range, by field, depending on the devices and programs being used. If a text editor program is available, it may have the ability to select certain columns, or to select and print only one particular record from each case, so that the fields could be identified vertically and inspected. If the researcher or computer operator is able to write simple computer programs, it would also be a simple task to create a program that "picks" a field from each record, one variable at a time, and prints its numeric value or checks it for range.

When the analysis routines can quickly and inexpensively generate frequency tables, described in some detail in the following chapter, the researcher may elect simply to generate such a table for each survey item and inspect the results to be sure each table contains only acceptable values. The disadvantage to this process is the fact that when invalid values are found, there is no indication of the case number from which it was derived. The researcher may then examine all of the cases in the file for that field. Another option may be to instruct the program to select only cases with the *illegitimate* value and print the case or case number.

GUIDELIST 9–4

For Process Editing the Data

1. Process editing is required to be sure the data analysis will *not* produce erroneous results, and especially errors which are not apparent in the reports.

2. The editing should seek out two types of errors: deviations from record format and deviations from data field range, in that order.

3. Format deviations ordinarily result from one or more pieces of data being skipped over or punched twice.

4. Editing should examine the ends of each record or line of data to be sure it is neither too short nor too long.

5. Format errors are more serious than field range errors because they cause all the items in the remainder of the record to be "off" the correct columns or in error.

6. Establish the "permissible range" of data for each item on the questionnaire, to establish data field range.

7. Each data field in each record of each case should then be checked to be sure it is within proper range.

8. Text editor programs or special editing programs can be used to check values within given fields or frequency tables can be generated and the values examined.

9. When errors are detected during process editing, refer to the source document by case number to make the required corrections in the data file.

DATA PROCESSING

When the term "data processing" is used here, this implies *electronic* data processing and the use of computers. The data from surveys of limited scope can be hand tabulated to obtain valuable information, but electronic data processing has many advantages. Computers allow the researcher to handle the data more quickly and easily. When a computer is used to process the data, the programs contain the instructions for handling the data and writing reports. More importantly, the programs also include the mathematical formulas to do the statistical computations. This means that, contrary to common belief, the researcher need *not* know the formulas and need *not* learn how to do the computations.

Nobody would suggest that a person must be an aeronautical engineer or a licensed pilot in order to fly to a distant city. Most airline passengers have little or no idea what makes the airplane fly and would certainly not be able to calculate such things as thrust, drag, lift, and velocity. Yet, they are ordinarily able to take a flight and reach their destination quickly and safely. This is because all of the highly technical work has been performed in advance by specialists and incorporated into the machines and the air transportation system, and there are highly trained personnel present to assist the passengers and to run the system. The passengers must have a different type of knowledge or information. They must know where they are going, what airlines and flights to use, how to reach the airport, and when they must be there to take the flight. Of course, they must also have the funds to pay the air fare and purchase a ticket. They are *not* required to know how to build an airplane or even how to fly it.

The researcher is in exactly the same position as the airline passenger, in this respect. The researcher does not have to be an expert at statistical computation nor does the researcher have to know a great deal about computers. The computer devices and programs have been designed and created by experts in that area. The computational formulas have been created by mathematicians and statisticians who are also specialists. So, despite what many people believe, survey data processing and analysis can be performed by virtually anyone who has the need for it and enough interest and confidence to learn some very basic and easily understood facts and principles.

During the early part of the century, when automobiles were first introduced to the public, those who owned them had to be quite knowledgeable about them; they had to be both their own mechanics and their own driving instructors as well. The same was true with airplanes when they were first introduced, and this holds true for a wide variety of technical innovations, including computers. Fortunately, those days are in the past, and today computers and computer programs are readily available and they are designed to be used by ordinary individuals. Since the computations are, in effect, "built into" the system, the researcher need not know the formulas or do the computations. Yet there are many who do not recognize this, and so they feel that those who need to do data processing and analysis must learn about the design of computer systems or the mathematical computations for analysis. They tend to proclaim that the researcher must know these technical details in order to understand what they are doing. This notion probably persisted for some time after automobiles and airplanes became available to the average person as well, and unfortunately, it probably discouraged some people from using them.

This brief, introductory discussion of data processing and analysis should make one conclusion crystal clear: *any person with average intelligence and education can learn to do data processing and analysis!* A great deal of experience clearly indicates that the major road block for an inexperienced researcher is certainly not a lack of intelligence or understanding, it is merely their own anxiety and lack of self-confidence. In most cases, such people are perfectly justified in feeling as they do, because of their previous training and experience with computers or with mathematics.

Happily, those who feel some degree of uncertainty about their ability to understand and do data processing and analysis can relax precisely at this point. The remaining discussion of these tasks and procedures provide instruction only on what contemporary researchers need to know and do, without reference to highly technical principles. The concepts and procedures can all be understood quite readily, because they are often intuitive, based on simple logic and common sense. The inexperienced researcher need only approach the material with confidence and handle perplexity with some degree of interest and curiosity, rather than anxiety. Most researchers will find that when they feel tension or stress, the best approach is simply to laugh at themselves a little and then go on with the task, but with a "lighter hand," rather than with greater effort and concentration.

Data processing can be done in two basic modes: by hand tabulation or by computer. Fairly small surveys, with relatively few questions or items and only 100 or so respondents, may not actually *require* computer processing. Even so, hand tabulation requires much more time and the extent and type of analyses are strictly limited. This should not be taken to preclude hand tabulation. It is important to note that when computer services are not available, small surveys that are well-planned and conducted may still provide very valuable information to those who require it. Even though hand tabulation is usually limited to computation of fairly simple, straightforward descriptions of the data, the averages and distributions that result may be pregnant with valuable meaning to researchers. In many situations, it is better to base decisions on such survey results than merely on existing information, intuition, common conjecture, or conventional wisdom. After all, computer analysis has only been available for the past couple of decades, but survey research has a history that extends back for centuries. The discussion that follows will assume that computer data processing will be used.

Purpose of Data Processing

Surveys generate a very large volume of "raw" data, but these are of little or no use to those who seek survey information. It would be extremely impractical for researchers to examine each such datum for each item on each completed questionnaire, and even if they did, it would be virtually impossible to glean any meaning from them as a whole. Thus, the difference between data and information is that data is meaningless on inspection, while those who examine information can understand it and obtain meaning from it. The primary purpose of data processing is to *summarize* the data into information. The objective of data processing and analysis is to *suppress* the detail and to reveal the important and meaningful patterns and relationships contained in the data.

SCALE AND DATA TYPES

The various statistical tools and procedures that are described in the following chapter require the data to meet certain conditions or be in a particular form. The type of scale and data dictate, in part, which statistical techniques are appropriate and which are inappropriate. Thus, before actually beginning the statistical analysis, the researcher should identify the scale and data types for each questionnaire item in advance. That way, the appropriate method of analysis and statistical tool will be more easily and more accurately selected.

Four different types of scales are identified below: nominal, ordinal, interval, and ratio. The researcher should first study the description of the scale types, and then identify each item on the questionnaire as one of the four scale types. This can most readily be done by using a blank, "key" questionnaire, noting the item or variable number and the scale type at each item or in each section of similar items. After examining the descriptions of categorical and continuous data, following the descriptions of scale types below, each item should also be designated as either categorical, continuous, or in some cases, both. This key can then be retained and conveniently used to identify the scale and data type for any given item when selecting statistical tools, without the necessity to reassess each item several times.

Nominal Scale Data. Computers usually handle numbers better than letters or words. When assigning codes to various responses to a survey question, the researcher will ordinarily use numbers, rather than letters. For example, respondents might check the word "male" or "female" to indicate their sex. Male could then be assigned the code of "1" and female the code value of "2" when the survey instrument is coded. The number one would be keyed to the data file at the correct place in the record for all the men respondents and the number two would be keyed for women respondents. The scale range would be from one to two and the data from such a scale would be called "nominal" data. This is because the numbers actually have no meaning as numeric values. They are only *names* of categories.

Other examples of nominal data might be the ZIP code of respondents, or a person's telephone number, or social security number. Nominal scale data can only be used as names and the numeric values have no real meaning. In the example above, the assignment of the numbers one and two to men and women, respectively, was completely arbitrary. In other words, it would make no difference, whatsoever, if the numbers had been reversed for the two sexes, or if the numbers 20 and 80 had been used. One and two would probably be preferable only because they are smaller numbers and people usually begin counting things with the number one. Because these numbers or scale values are arbitrary, their numeric relationships have no meaning. Men are not primary and women secondary, and the only purpose for different numeric values is to show the distinction between one category and the next with these numeric names. Consequently, none of the arithmetic operations, addition, subtraction, multiplication, or division, can even be applied to nominal data. It would make no sense whatever to compute the average ZIP code value for a sample.

Ordinal Scale Data. A typical example of an ordinal scale would be the ranking of a set of things. For example, if respondents ranked several brands of a product, these rankings could constitute an ordinal scale. Another example would be a person's "ordinal position" in the family; whether they were born to the family first, second, third, etc. Ordinal numeric values show the *order* in which things occur within the range of the scale. That is, for an ordinal scale ranging from 1 to 10, an ordinal value of four indicates that there are three things that come before and six things that come after, or three that are lesser and six that are greater.

When an ordinal scale is used, the numeric values have more meaning than they do for a nominal scale, described above. With a nominal scale, the numbers are only names that make one category *distinct* from another, but do not indicate any *relationship*, whatsoever.

Ordinal scale values do show the relationship, in terms of *sequence* or *order*, so the numbers have more meaning than nominal values. On the other hand, the values of ordinal data have less meaning than do those of the two other types of scales, to be described below. This is because the ordinal values show order or sequence, but they do not show the *interval* between the values. For example, if a person's ordinal position in the family is third, that would not indicate how many years younger the person was than their older siblings. The value of three shows that two others were born to the family earlier in time, but it does not show how much time elapsed between the first and the third or the second and the third. If two people from different families each had an ordinal position of two, the ordinal values would be identical, but one may have a sibling who is 20 years older and another, a sibling who is only a year older. Thus, some "information" is lost when only ordinal values are used, and ordinal data cannot be used in mathematical equations.

Interval Scale Data. A scale with numeric values that are equidistant from one another is an interval scale. This simply means that the distance from one integer (whole number) value to the next is the same at any point in the scale. Interval scales are sometimes called "equal interval" scales because the interval between each integer on the scale is the same. Interval scales may not include the value of zero, or when they do, the zero value does not really indicate the complete absence of whatever is measured. In mathematical terms, the zero does not represent the "null set" or a set with nothing in it. A typical example of an interval scale is the fahrenheit scale of temperature. It takes as much energy (one B.T.U.) to heat pure water from 40° to 41°F as it does to heat it from 80° to 81°F. In other words, the interval between each degree is the same as between any other. On the other hand, the zero does not represent the absence of heat. Absolute zero would be a very large, negative number on the Fahrenheit scale. Zero was merely the number assigned to the temperature that resulted from mixing equal amounts of snow and salt, by weight, under standard atmospheric pressure.

Because the zero may be absent from an interval scale, or it does not stand for the absence of the thing measured when it is present, the arithmetic operation of division is not appropriate for such data. For example, if the lowest temperature last night was 40°F and the high temperature today is 80°F, this does not imply that last night was half as warm as today, and such a statement would have no meaning or validity. In short, the ratio (pronounced ray-she-oh) of one value to another has no meaning for interval scale data. On the other hand, interval scales used to obtain survey data, such as the linear, horizontal scale, permit use of most common statistical manipulations. Thus, little is lost by the fact that zero is not absolute.

The Ratio Scale. There is only one difference between an interval scale and a ratio scale: zero is absolute on the ratio scale. For example, distance in miles or age in years would be ratio scales. In this society, at the instant of birth, the infant's age would be zero, and if an object stays in the same place, it would have traveled zero distance. In both cases, the zero is absolute; it stands for no age or no distance. Because zero actually means nothing of what is being measured and the distance between any two points on a ratio scale is always equal to that between any other two, ratio scales impose the least amount of restrictions on the mathematics or statistics that can be used. They are called ratio scales because ratios of one value to another have meaning. For example, if one person travels 20 miles and another travels 40, the first has traveled half as far (1:2 or 1/2) as the second, or the second has traveled twice as far as the first (2:1 or 2/1). Thus, arithmetic operations of division and multiplication are permissible with ratio scale data and the "quotient" or "product" that result from them, respectively, are meaningful values.

Ratio scale data is least restrictive, regarding the types of statistics that can be used. Yet, it is important to note that many things measured on a survey questionnaire do not lend themselves to the use of a ratio scale. Thus, interval scales are much more commonly used. There are ordinarily very few differences between interval and ratio scales, in terms of the ability to manipulate the data with statistical tools, so little if anything is lost by using an interval scale, rather than a ratio scale. On the other hand, a substantial amount of information or meaning is "lost" or unmeasured by using an ordinal scale in place of an interval scale, and a nominal scale strictly limits the use of statistical manipulation. These characteristics of scale data are summarized in Figure 9–1.

FIGURE 9–1

Scale Data Types

Nominal Scales

1. The numeric values are merely the names of categories.
2. The numbers are used only to make categories distinct.
3. The values do not indicate any magnitudes.

4. The values do not indicate any relationships.

5. No arithmetic operations can be used on the numbers.

6. Statistical manipulation is extremely limited.

Ordinal Scales

1. The numeric values show the order or sequence.

2. The values are not a measure of magnitude.

3. The interval between values does not indicate magnitude.

4. The values do show relationships by order or sequence.

5. The values cannot be used in mathematical equations.

6. Statistical manipulation is somewhat limited.

Interval Scales

1. The numeric values show both order and magnitude.

2. The interval between integer values is equal.

3. A zero value does not indicate absolute zero.

4. The values show relationships by order and magnitude.

5. The values cannot be used to form ratios.

6. Statistical manipulation is not very limited.

Ratio Scales

1. The numeric values show both order and magnitude.

2. The interval between integer values is equal.

3. A zero value does indicate absence of the thing measured.

4. The values show relationships by order and magnitude.

5. The values can be used to form ratios.

6. Statistical manipulation is not limited.

Categorical and Continuous Data. Earlier in the chapter, scales were identified as yielding nominal, ordinal, interval, or ratio data. In this section, the selection of a statistical tool is based only on two types of data: categorical or continuous. Categorical data is sometimes called "discrete" data, because the data points identify individual categories that are discrete from one another. In other words, categorical data is simply the *nominal* data type identified earlier. The categories are not related to one another, and there are no "points" between categories. Continuous data includes ordinal, interval, and ratio data. It is merely numeric data that is arrayed or distributed on some continuum. With continuous data, there may be individual scale points or integer (whole number) values, but there are potential or theoretical intermediate points on the scale as well. In short, the underlying scale is a continuous one, rather than being broken into categories.

CHECKLIST 9-1

To Identify the Scale Data Type

1. Are the values only names to designate independent categories? If so, and the categories do not represent some order of magnitude, the data from the scale is *nominal*.

2. Do the values indicate only sequence or order of magnitude? If so, and they do not indicate the actual magnitude or interval between values, the scale is *ordinal*.

3. Do the values indicate actual magnitudes with equal intervals between the scale points? If so, but a value of zero does not represent absolute zero or complete absence of the thing measured, the scale is *interval*.

4. Do the values indicate actual magnitudes with equal intervals between the scale points? If so, and a value of zero does represent absolute zero or complete absence of the thing measured, the scale is *ratio*.

It is important to note that data cannot be viewed as categorical or continuous based on the number of categories, values, or scale points. Some categorical variables may have a fairly large number of categories, and some continuous scales may have only a few scale points or values. The important question is whether the values of the variable identify a *place* or *position* on some continuum, or it specifies some discrete *category* or *unit* that is separate from the other such categories, with no actual or theoretical points or values between them. Thus, there may be a large number of such things as different respondent telephone numbers or ZIP codes and these are designated by fairly large numbers. This type of data is categorical. They do not form a continuum and there are no "in between" points. Certainly it would be impossible to perceive a telephone number with a fractional value, such as 123–4567½. Categorical data is either one category or another, and there is no such thing as a half way point between categories. Similarly, a survey item that yields continuous data may have only a very few scale points. If something were rated on a three point scale with extremes labeled "good" and "bad," this would still

GUIDELIST 9-5

For Determining Data Type

1. Each variable must be identified as continuous data or categorical data, to select the proper statistical measure of association.
2. The number of scale points or values does *not* determine the data type for a variable.
3. Data *must* be treated as categorical if the values represent discrete categories, so that any points or fractional values between integer values are meaningless.
4. The variable may be treated as continuous if the values represent a "position" along some spectrum or continuum, with the theoretical possibility of meaningful positions between integer values.
5. Variables that "qualify" as continuous may also be treated as discrete, provided there are only a small number of data points.

be continuous data because some opinion could and probably will be between points on the continuum, and respondents would then be forced to choose the nearest value.

It is important to note that categorical variables can never be treated by the researcher as though they are continuous. Computer programs only recognize numeric values and do not "know" their meaning, and so they will do computations and generate results, regardless of whether or not the data are continuous or discrete. Such results would have no meaning whatsoever and the whole process would be erroneous. On the other hand, it is both permissible and convenient to treat continuous data with a limited number of scale points as categorical data or as both continuous and categorical, for analysis. When there are more than 8 or 10 scale points on a variable that is to be treated as both continuous and categorical, the data can be recoded into fewer categories of equal interval or size, allowing the variable to be treated as categorical while maintaining its continuous nature as well.

RECLASSIFYING AND RECODING

There are two situations when the researcher may find it necessary or desirable to classify data into different categories for analysis than those used to collect the data. The first such situation is when the data were gathered in one form because of the ease of collecting it that way, but different categories would have more meaning to those interpreting the data or seeking the information. In this case, the data would be recoded into the new categories so that it had more meaning or was more interpretable. The second situation that may require recoding is when the researcher would like to "show" or portray the data in a limited number of categories, but it has been collected in continuous, numeric form and there are too many scale points or values to portray readily. In that case, the necessity for recoding lies more in the limitations on data portrayal, and the researcher may want to preserve the original, continuous variable while creating a new one for recoding, or merely regroup the continuous, numeric data into larger categories that would retain the same scale type. The process for each situation will be discussed in some detail below.

Recoding into More Meaningful Categories.　The variable shown in Example 10–1, shown in the following chapter, can be used as an example. The data were actually collected by asking the respondents, "What was the last year of formal education that you completed? (For example, high school graduate = 12)." Respondents then recorded the number of years. Notice that this original scale was a *ratio* scale. The "raw" data from this item ranged from a low of 9 years to a high of 26 years, so there were originally 18 scale points; too many to show readily in a frequency table or bar chart. Even more importantly, the individual number of years are not as meaningful as the categories shown in Example 10–1. Consequently, the data were recoded or reclassified into new categories or scale points. Reference to Checklist 9–1 will show that the scale data become *ordinal*, rather than *ratio*, after reclassification into the new categories.

There are three rules to follow when forming a new classification system and recoding a variable into new categories: (1) The categories must be all-inclusive. (2) The categories must be mutually exclusive. (3) There must be more variation in the thing being measured *between* categories than *within* categories. All-inclusive categories simply means that there must be a new category for every data point. Often when data are recoded, the upper and/or lower category will be an "open-ended" category. In the example, all those with more than 16 years of education were classified as postgraduates. If, for example, age were to be converted from years to 10 year groups, there are likely to be only a few people in their 80s or 90s. It is best to form an upper category of "70 and over" so that all ages are included and the rule concerning all-inclusive categories is respected.

Mutually exclusive categories are obtained by being sure that there is no "overlap" between categories. In the example, the first category, labeled "some high school," includes only those with 9, 10, or 11 years but not those with 12 years of education. Consequently, the first and second categories are mutually exclusive, and all respondents who went to high school would be classified into one or the other category, but *not both*. If the first category was simply "high school" and the second "high school graduate," those with 12 years of high school might be classified into *either* category because they would overlap. That would violate the rule of mutual exclusivity.

When new categories are formed and the data recoded into them, it is very important that the categories are *meaningful* ones. Thus, the thing being measured and the underlying conditions should show more variation *between* categories than within them. For instance, the behavior and opportunities resulting from education would not be expected to differ as much between those who dropped out of high school in their sophomore year and those who dropped out in their junior year. On the other hand, there is likely to be a substantial difference between those who dropped out and those who graduated. Consequently, in the example, those with 9, 10, and 11 years are grouped together, and similarly, those with 13, 14, and 15 years are all in one category. Those with 12 years and those with 16 years of education had presumably graduated from high school or college, respectively, and so they were grouped into a separate category from those who had attended but not finished.

When forming new categories that are more meaningful and re-coding the data into them, it is important to examine two things: the expected variation in the factors that are being measured or that underlie the variable and the number and percentage of cases or respondents that are likely to be in each category. Assume that opinions about some issue were being measured on a nine-point scale, from strongly positive to strongly negative. If only three groups were desired, rather than nine, it would not make sense to group the first three scale points into one category, the second three into the next, and the third trio of points into the last category. That would be very inadvisable because the middle category would contain some who were slightly positive, some who were, in effect, neutral, and some who were negative on the issue. There would be too much variation in the second newly formed category because it contains people with different orientations or valences, rather than merely with different strength of opinions in the same direction. To adhere to the rule of more variance between than within categories in this case, one option would be to form three groups: positive, neutral, and negative. Suppose it was very important to distinguish between strong and moderate opinions, while keeping a very small number of categories. Another alternative would be to recode the data into four groups, rather than three: strongly positive, moderately positive, moderately negative, and strongly negative. Those who were neutral might then be treated as "missing values," a topic to be discussed later. The result of the four group classification would not group positive and negative opinions into the same category, and the rule for maintaining more variance between than within categories would have been observed.

When variables are to be recoded into new categories, it is also important to specify categories that will each contain a substantial number of respondents. For example, it is seldom advisable to have one category that contains over half the responses and others that have only a very small percentage of responses. There are a couple of reasons why such a classification system would not be advisable: First, categories that contain only a few cases or respondents are seldom useful or meaningful to those seeking the information, simply because they represent such a small proportion of the population. Second, the statistics used to measure the relationships between categories, which are to be discussed in the following chapter, often require some minimum number of respondents in the smallest category, in order to be valid or interpretable.

Assume that respondents were asked to list their destination after they leave some particular location, such as a store or a sports event. Substantial proportions might indicate they are going to their home, to a restaurant, to a friend's home, etc. But, there are likely to be many other destinations that are listed by only one or a very few respondents. It would not be advisable to list each of these categories with only a few cases for each one. Ordinarily, the specification of only a few of the most popular categories will capture about 90 percent of the cases or respondents. The many other categories, which represent only an extremely small percentage of respondents, are routinely grouped into a miscellaneous "other" category that would be of sufficient size to be meaningful and have enough cases to be statistically analyzed.

Recoding Data into Fewer, Larger Categories.   When there are more than about a dozen categories, it becomes extremely difficult to interpret the frequency tables or bar charts. When that is the case, and the researcher wishes to portray the data rather than describe it with statistical coefficients, it may be necessary to combine categories or regroup the data into fewer and "larger" categories. Assume, for example, that the age of the respondents is the distribution to be described. If respondents have simply recorded their age in years, the range of the scale might be from 20 to 89, so there may be as many as 70 different scale points in that case. That would be too many points for a meaningful portrayal. Thus, the researcher may recode the ages into 10 year categories: 20s, 30s, 40s, etc. There would then be only seven scale points and they could be nicely portrayed in a frequency table or bar chart. It is important to note that some information will be lost in the process of forming larger categories because all those in each category would all be treated as identical.

When the data are analyzed with computer programs that allow for recoding of data and generation of frequency tables or bar charts, it may be quite practical to analyze and report the continuous, numeric data in this way. Notice, however, that some information is "lost" in the process of recoding ordinal, interval, and ratio scale data into categories, especially if there are a very large number of scale points or values for the variable. For such distributions, respondents actually do differ from one another if they report different values, even though the differences might be relatively small. When the data are regrouped into categories, all of the cases that are recoded to the same category are treated as identical on that variable. Thus, the small differences are lost. This is the principal disadvantage of recoding continuous data into categories.

In many cases, the loss of information by recoding data into fewer, larger categories is negligible. There are times when it is most efficient or practical to collect the data in continuous form, simply because it is quick and easy for respondents to jot down a number. On the other hand, the small differences between respondents may not be meaningful or relevant. In other words, the scale is practical for data collection but it is "overly sensitive" for analysis and interpretation. For instance, in the case of educational level used in Example 10–1, in the following chapter, the researcher may place little or no importance on the difference between those who have 10 years of formal education and those who have 11 years. Thus, there is no significant loss of information.

There may be cases when the relatively small differences between respondents on a continuous, numeric scale are regarded as important and meaningful, but the researcher would also like to portray the distribution in the form of a frequency table or bar chart. In such situations, the variable can be treated in both ways. This is most feasible when computer analysis is used. Ordinarily, the researcher would simply create a "new" variable that is identical to the original. The original, continuous variable would remain in that form and be treated as such. The new variable would then be recoded into categories, named, and labeled appropriately. If the recoding and reporting of the variable can be done quickly and easily, the researcher is also able to use trial and error to determine the appropriate number and boundaries for the groupings or categories. This is accomplished by recoding the new variable and generating a table or chart. If, on

CHECKLIST 9-2

To Reclassify and Recode Data

1. Would different categories be more meaningful for analysis and interpretation than those in which the data were gathered? If so, devise a new classification scheme.

2. Are the new categories "all-inclusive," so that every original value can be recoded into a new category? If not, change the classifications or include a miscellaneous category for "other" responses.

3. Are the new categories "mutually exclusive," so that each original value can be recoded into only *one* new category? If not, change the classification to eliminate the overlap.

4. Is there more variation in the underlying meaning of the variable *between* the new categories than *within* them? If not, select new classifications that have greater meaning.

5. Do any of the new categories have a very large proportion of the data within them or do any have an insufficient number of cases? If so, divide the larger and/or combine the smaller categories.

6. Is there a need to portray continuous, numeric data with a large number of values in frequency tables or bar charts? If so, recode the data into a dozen or fewer, larger categories with equal intervals and no overlap.

7. Is there a need to portray continuous, numeric data and also to use statistical coefficients to describe the distribution? If so, form a new variable identical to the original and recode the new one into categories.

examination, the categories do not appear to be appropriate because they are too small, too large, containing either too high or too low a percentage of cases, a new classification scheme can be devised and the effort repeated.

When a survey variable has been transformed, recoded, or used to create a new variable in a different form, the researcher is well-advised to note these changes on the blank, key questionnaire that is used as a working document or index of the actual data file. While it may appear to be fairly easy to keep these changes and modifications in mind, that seldom proves to be the case. If the work extends over several days or working sessions, as it normally does, there is a tendency for the researcher to forget modifications or changes in the data file or programs that are used. On the other hand, if a brief record of these changes is diligently maintained, there is less danger that confusion will result.

Subsample Selection

Some analysis programs allow the researcher to select only certain cases from the entire data file, for particular tasks or analyses. Thus, the cases that are selected form a "subsample" of data from which the reports are generated. When the analysis routine does not contain such a provision and there is a need to select only certain groups or categories of respondents, such as only males or only those in a certain occupation, etc., these cases may also be singled out and segregated into a separate data file for analysis. When such subsample selections are used to generate reports, it is important that the subsamples are recorded and the details noted on the report, so that researchers can clearly tell that the results are based on only a certain portion of the entire sample and represent only a specific group within the population from which the sample was drawn.

Report Labeling

Many survey analysis routines do not contain provisions for labeling the reports to indicate the tasks or procedures used, the variables included, or the meaning of the values. Often such programs merely list or report the variables in the sequence of the data format used for a particular task, such as "Variable 1." When that is the case, the variable listed by the routine as number one may or may not be the first variable on the questionnaire. For example, if a task used only the 13th and the 65th variable of the questionnaire, only those may be "specified" in the format statement for the program, and so the routine would "see" them only as first and second. In short, the analysis program may not "know" about all of the variables, and may number or label only those that it has been instructed to recognize or analyze. With such routines, it is vitally important that the researcher clearly label the print output from the programs after *each* report is generated, while it is still perfectly clear which survey variables were processed. Otherwise, the researcher may be faced with the unpleasant task of trying to determine which of hundreds of pages report which variables and procedures.

For those analysis routines that allow the researcher to label the variables in the analysis, the values of the variables, and/or the tasks or procedures used, it is always advisable to take the time and effort to use this facility. This labeling information must be composed and keyed to an instruction program for the analysis routine to use. Each such routine should have its own manuals and documentation, indicating the syntax and format for such labeling information, and these directions must be followed "to the letter." Some researchers may be reluctant to take the necessary time to learn the instructions, compose and key such labeling information, preferring to rush ahead to the actual processing and analysis. This is false economy of effort, indeed. Having written and incorporated the label information one time, the researcher is then relieved of the responsibility for labeling each report printed by the analysis routine, and in effect, after the initial effort by the researcher, the computer does the rest.

SUMMARY

Processing the Data

A. Get a head start. Arrange for processing while the questionnaires are still in the field.

B. Expect a large volume of paperwork. Surveys generate more material than many researchers anticipate.

C. Keep it neat and orderly. Have a place for everything and keep everything in its place.

D. Maintain adequate records. Record things promptly and make notes, rather than depending on recollection.

E. Sight-edit documents thoroughly. Establish criteria for acceptance or rejection of completed questionnaires and use them consistently.

F. Postcode questionnaires carefully. Every item that is not precoded must be assigned a value and recorded.

G. Monitor data transfer. Be sure the data are keyed or recorded in files promptly and accurately.

H. Process-edit the data. Check to be sure the records conform to the format and the data is within range.

I. Identify scale and data types. Record the designations on a "key" questionnaire to use as a working guide.

J. Reclassify data with care. Select categories that are more meaningful and recode continuous items with many values into fewer, but larger categories.

PART FOUR
ANALYSIS AND REPORTING

10

Statistical Analysis

STATISTICAL TOOL SELECTION

Data analysis requires the use of a set of statistical tools that reduce the amount of detail in the data, summarizing it and making the most important facts and relationships apparent. The researcher need not know a great deal about the internal workings of the statistical tools in order to use them effectively. On the other hand, the researcher must be able to select the correct statistical tool to generate the information required, based on the source data. As with any tool, there are two types of things that dictate what statistical tool should be used or would work best: the nature of the data, the "material" to which the tool is applied, and the nature of the report, or the "product" that is to be created. In other words, the researcher must know what tool would work best for a particular type of data and a particular type of report. Ironically, those who learn a great deal about the tools, themselves, are often still in a quandary about which to use in a given situation. This is because they lack information about the types of data that each statistical tool requires and the type of information that can be obtained from each of the statistical procedures.

The various types of scales and data were defined and described in some detail in the previous chapter. This chapter is devoted to a description of the statistical tools, themselves. There are two basic types of statistical tools, each designed to serve a different purpose: either to portray or describe data, or to measure associations or relationships among survey items. There are several statistical tools of each type, and the selection of the proper tool depends primarily on the type of data to be analyzed. To assist the researcher to select the proper tool for portraying or describing data and for measuring relationships between items, the appropriate statistical tool will be identified according to the type of data it is designed to use and analyze.

It is ordinarily not appropriate to use the same statistical tool for every survey item, because some scales are different from others and they require different tools for their analysis. Nominal, ordinal, interval, and ratio scales, as well as categorical and continuous data were defined and described in the previous chapter. The researcher must be completely familiar with these terms and be able to identify the type of scales and data in order to select the proper statistical tools described in the chapter.

The data that is generated by each survey item or that from each individual "data point" on a questionnaire is ordinarily referred to as a "variable" because it will vary from one respondent to the next. When a statistical tool is used, the report may, then, include the analysis of a single variable, it may include two variables and show the relationship between them, or it may include several variables and show the pattern of relationships among them. When a statistical tool reports on one variable at a time, it is called a "univariate" (one variable) statistic. When it includes only two, showing the relationship between them, is called a "bivariate" (two variable) statistic, and when it reports the pattern of relationships among several variables that are all analyzed simultaneously, it is called a "multivariate" (many variable) statistic. The analysis of virtually all survey data will require the use of univariate statistics. Almost all surveys also use bivariate statistical tools. Only a small minority of the more elaborate survey analyses would use multivariate statistical analysis. Consequently, this chapter will include univariate and bivariate analysis, but it will exclude a discussion of multivariate statistics. If and when multivariate statistical analysis is required, the researcher should seek the assistance of a specialist familiar with the techniques or refer to one of the many textbooks or computer program manuals for guidance and instruction.

Description of Categorical Distributions

Survey questionnaire items or variables form "distributions." In other words, the choices or values that respondents provide for any item are *distributed* across some range of values or options. Usually, the first thing that the researcher does when processing data is to describe the distributions for each variable. Frequency tables can often be used to actually show the entire distribution. When they are not appropriate, the distributions must be described using other statistics.

Frequency Tables. When there are a relatively small number of values for a variable, the researcher can describe the distribution by indicating the number and/or percent of respondents who indicated each value. These tabular descriptions of the distribution are called "frequency and percentage distributions of response," or just "frequency tables," for short. The use of frequency tables provides a very complete picture of the distribution of data for the variable. Their use is limited mainly by the number of scale points or categories that can be shown. When there are a dozen or less categories or scale points, frequency tables are ordinarily practical and meaningful to researchers.

Example 10–1 shows both the frequency and percentage of respondents at five levels of education. This example will be used to

---

EXAMPLE 10-1

The Frequency Table

No Missing Values Specified					
Category	Code	Freq.	Pct.	Adj.	Cum.
Some high school	1.	28	4.2	4.2	4.2
High school graduate	2.	191	28.5	28.5	32.7
Some college	3.	141	21.0	21.0	53.7
College graduate	4.	136	20.3	20.3	74.0
Post graduate	5.	118	17.6	17.6	91.5
Refused	6.	57	8.5	8.5	100.0
Total		671	100.0	100.0	100.0

Zero Specified as Missing Value					
Category	Code	Freq.	Pct.	Adj.	Cum.
Some high school	1.	28	4.2	4.6	4.6
High school graduate	2.	191	28.5	31.1	35.7
Some college	3.	141	21.0	23.0	58.6
College graduate	4.	136	20.3	22.1	80.8
Post graduate	5.	118	17.6	19.2	100.0
Refused	0.	57	8.5	---	---
Total		671	100.0	100.0	100.0

describe in detail the meaning of the columns, the way they are computed, the nature of the data that can be described this way, and the methods for handling and portraying the data. The tables in the example are very typical of those that would be generated by several different computer programs for analyzing survey data, but such tables can also be formed with hand tabulation. The computations will be obvious from the description of the tables that follows.

Frequency Table Columns.   Example 10–1 shows a format that is very common for reporting such tables. Starting from the left, the first column ordinarily shows the labels for the various categories that are represented. When only numbers with a limited range are being reported, such as "trips to the bank in the past week" or "number of coffee breaks taken yesterday," no labels may be required and the column would be blank, or only the "# or more" label for the highest group listed.

The second column of the frequency table usually shows the code value. This is merely the pre- or postcode that was assigned to the alternative or answer and keyed to the computer file or checked on the coding sheet. In many cases, it would not be necessary to list the code values, especially within the final report of the data; however, they are almost always printed by computer programs to analyze survey data and they can be useful for checking and editing the data to be sure it is correct.

The third column from the left, labeled "Freq." or "Frequency," is merely the number of respondents that indicated that particular response. In some situations, this may be very useful to researchers. In most situations, it is not especially useful and the percentages would be more easily interpreted. When only percentage distributions are listed in a final report, it is important for the researcher to include the "n-size" or total number responding to the item, on which the percentages are based.

The fourth column of the frequency table in the example is the percentage of all respondents to the survey or to that section of the questionnaire who indicated each of the various alternatives. In other words, this is the percentage distribution, rather than the frequency distribution. The percentages are computed by dividing the frequency for each category by the total number of respondents to the survey or section and moving the decimal point two places to the right. The percentage distributions are often more easily interpreted and of more interest than are the frequency distributions. This is because percentages can be compared from one item or survey to the next, even though they may be based on different total frequencies. More importantly, the sample percentages can be used directly as an estimate of the percentages of the total population that might indicate each alternative response. Thus, the percentage distribution is often the most important column on the frequency table for those interpreting the survey results.

The next to the last column in the example is labeled "Adj." and that stands for "*adjusted* percentages." The "adjustment" is based on the missing values or data for the variable being reported. This is not the same as those who failed to respond to the survey. Ordinarily there will be some respondents who participate in the survey and provide completed questionnaires that are sufficiently complete to be included in the survey data base, but who fail to respond to some individual items. For example, they may refuse to list their education or income, they may simply skip the item by mistake, or they may fail to complete it for some other reason. It is seldom ever advisable to discard all questionnaires that are not 100 percent complete, and to do so would often eliminate a substantial proportion of the responding sample. So, the adjusted percentages are computed in the same way as the previous ones, except that they are based on only those who responded to that particular item.

Notice that in the upper proportion of Example 10–1 the percentages and the adjusted percentages are identical. Note, also, that those who refused to indicate their educational level were assigned a code value of six and were not specified as "missing values," because they are included in the adjusted percentage column. By contrast, in the lower section of that example, those who refused were assigned a code of zero and zero was listed in the program that generated the table as a missing value for that item. Thus, the 8½ percent of the respondents who failed or refused to answer the item is listed in the percentage column, but nothing is listed in the adjusted percentage column. The dashed line indicates the percentage is not zero, but that the percentage for this alternative is not applicable. In this table, the adjusted percentages differ from the unadjusted, and of course they are slightly larger because they are based on a smaller total.

The last column, at the far right of the frequency table in the example, is labeled "Cum." to designate that it contains cumulative percentages. The percentage for the first row of the table will always be the same as the adjusted percentage for that row. The cumulative frequency for the second row is the sum of the adjusted percentages for the first and second rows, etc. So each cumulative percentage is the total of the adjusted percentages for that row and those above it. Cumulative percentages have little meaning or value for nominal data, where the categories are not related to one another in any fashion. They are meaningful and useful, however, for ordinal, interval, and ratio data. In the lower section of Example 10–1, the reader of the table can easily see that nearly 59 percent of those responding have less than a college education. When the rows are ordered from "lowest" to "highest," the value of the column for any row shows the percentage of respondents who are in that category or "less," and 100 minus the value shows what percentage were "greater." The cumulative percentages also indicate the approximate point or value on the scale at which those in the 50th or some other percentile reside. "Percentile" merely means those who rank at some place, out of 100 typical cases.

Some statistical analysis routines have the capability to describe categorical data in graphic, rather than or in addition to frequency tables. For example, the researcher may be able to request the printing of histograms, which are merely horizontal bar charts showing the percentages of respondents in each category. Other routines may offer vertical plots, pie charts that show proportions, or other graphic displays of the categories in the distribution. These graphic descriptions of variables are often very useful when reporting the survey results to those seeking the information. They will be discussed in more detail in the following chapter, devoted to interpretation and reporting. It is only necessary to note here that if such graphic reports are readily available, it is advisable to generate them.

Description of Continuous Distributions

Frequency tables cannot be used to describe continuous, numeric distributions with a large number of values, but there are a variety of ways they can be described by statistics. Different types of scales require different types of statistics. There are three different characteristics of the distribution that researchers ordinarily measure and describe: (1) the most typical value; (2) the amount of deviation from it; and (3) the form of the distribution. The coefficients that indicate the most typical value are often called measures of "central tendency." They will be referred to here simply as "averages." The technical term for the amount of deviation from the average is "dispersion" or "variance" and the term "spread" will be used here to indicate the amount of deviation from the central point or average. The form of the distribution will be called its "shape" in the discussion that follows. The statistics to describe distributions of the four different types of data are shown in Figure 10–1.

In order to select the most appropriate statistical tool, the researcher need only identify which of the four types of scale data the variable represents. When more than one tool might be used, the most common and most often appropriate is listed first, follow by

FIGURE 10–1

Tool Selection for Descriptive Statistics

Scale Type	Average	Spread	Shape
Nominal	Mode		
Ordinal	Median	Range	
	Mode	Maximum	
		Minimum	
Interval	Mean	Std. Dev.	Skewness
	Median	Range	Kurtosis
	Mode	Maximum	
		Minimum	
Ratio	Mean	Std. Dev.	Skewness
	Median	Range	Kurtosis
	Mode	Maximum	
		Minimum	

the next most likely, and so forth. In general, any tool that is appropriate for a "lower level" of scale data would be acceptable for the scales of a higher level, although it may not be the most preferable. If no statistic is listed in the table, as in the case of spread or shape for nominal or ordinal data, this means no common statistical coefficient is appropriate to describe them, and the distributions may have to be described in frequency tables.

Central Tendency and Averages

In most cases, the use of the term, "average," refers to the arithmetic mean, but this is only one of several averages that can be used. Three different averages will be described here, each with different characteristics that make it more appropriate for some distributions and less for others. Figure 10–1 and the following discussion will guide the researcher in selecting the most appropriate average to use in a given situation, as well as the most appropriate measures of spread and shape. The choice is often based on the type of scale data that actually forms the distribution.

The average of a distribution is usually reported because it represents the most typical response, or the researchers "best guess" of how a new or unknown respondent would answer. The arithmetic mean, often referred to simply as "the mean," is the most common average used in most situations to indicate the most typical response. While the median and mode can also be used to describe central tendency for interval or ratio data, the mean is usually the most meaningful statistic. It is computed simply by dividing the sum of the values by the number of values or cases.

While the mean is the most commonly used average, it has some limitations that make other averages more appropriate in certain cases. First, it is not valid to use the mean for nominal data because the values are merely names. If unmarried respondents were assigned a code value of one and married respondents a value of two, it would not make sense to compute the mean marital status. If half the respondents were married, the mean would have the fractional value of 1.5, but that would be meaningless because respondents are either married or they are not. Consequently, it would be completely invalid to say that the most typical respondent was "half single and half married," since that is impossible.

The mean is usually not used for ordinal data, such as that obtained from an ordinal scale or a set of rankings. This is because with ordinal data, the code values indicate only that each sequential value is greater than those with a lower value and less than those with a higher value. Consequently, the intervals between code values on the ordinal scale are not equal, and a fractional value would have little meaning. Thus, other averages are usually more appropriate for ordinal data.

Even with distributions of interval or ratio data, the mean has some limitations that sometimes make other averages more appropriate and meaningful as a measure of the most typical case. The mean tends to be overly sensitive to influence by only one or a few *extreme* values in the distribution. An example may clarify this tendency. Suppose there is a distribution of ratio data, such as sales revenues for retail companies handling a certain type of goods. The vast majority of respondents are likely to be firms with a single retail store, who report revenues in tens or hundreds of thousands of dollars. There may also be a very few, large chain store companies with revenues in the hundreds of millions of dollars. The few, with extremely large figures that are very far from the majority, are sometimes called "outliers," because they are on the far extreme. The mean will be very sensitive to this outlier effect. The mean value in such a case would probably be several million dollars. Yet, this is certainly not *typical* of such retail firms, since the vast majority are much smaller and only a very few are extremely large. Consequently, another average, the median, would be more appropriate for distributions of data that are "asymmetrical" or where there are a few outliers on the far extreme, even though the data is from interval or ratio scales. The symmetry and asymmetry of distributions will be discussed more fully below, when the measures of the shape of distributions are explained.

The median value for a distribution is another form of average or indication of the "most typical" case. The median can be computed, but it is more easily understood intuitively or logically. Suppose all of the cases in the sample are arrayed in order, beginning with that with the lowest value for the variable, extending to that with the highest value. The median would be the value for the "middle" case in the array. Thus, if 75 such sample cases were arrayed from lowest to highest value, the 38th case would be the median value for the distribution. In other words, the median value is the value of the variable for the case in the 50th percentile, or 50 percent of the way through the array. Given this explanation, it should be easy to see that the median is not particularly subject to extreme values or outliers. The cases at the upper end of the array in the example of retail companies, used in the preceding paragraph, might report a revenue of 12 million or 12 billion, but in either case, that would not affect the value of the respondent in the middle of the array. To put it another way, the middle value or median will be the same, no matter how much greater or lesser the values on the extreme turn out to be. Consequently, the median is likely to be more typical of the majority of cases in the distribution and a better average to use than the mean would be in such cases. The median is also preferable for use when the distribution is composed of ordinal data.

The third measure of central tendency or average to be discussed here is the mode. The mode is simply the most typical case, and it is the only acceptable indicator of the most typical case for distributions of nominal data. For such distributions, the mode is simply the code value for the category that contains the largest proportion of respondents. In frequency distribution tables shown earlier in Example 10–1, the modal category has a code value of two, labeled "High school graduate." This category has the highest frequency and percentage, and it would be the "best guess" when predicting the education for a new or unknown case. Distributions of ordinal, interval, and ratio data also have at least one modal value, and perhaps more than one. If the data for such distributions were shown in a graph or chart, with the value of the variable on the horizontal axis and the number of cases reporting the value on the vertical axis, the mode would be the "peak" of the distribution or the high point, where the line tapers off toward a lower frequency in either direction. Often there will be just one such point, but those cases where there are more than one will be discussed more fully below, when measures of the shape of the distribution are explained.

Measures of Dispersion or Spread

Just as distributions tend to have a value that might be regarded as "most typical," they also tend to be spread out around that value in both directions. The minimum value indicates how far the spread extends toward the lower direction and the maximum value shows the extent of spread toward the upper direction from the average. The range is simply the maximum minus the minimum, showing the total spread. While these values may certainly be of interest for many distributions, they are often lacking in one important respect. The minimum, maximum, and range are defined only in terms of the extreme values. They say little or nothing about the spread of the cases within those boundaries.

Fortunately, there is a measure of spread or dispersion that permits the researcher to estimate and report the proportion of respondents or cases within certain ranges in the center part of the distribution, as well as toward the extremes, providing that the distribution does not deviate very markedly from the normal, bell-shaped curve. It is the *standard deviation,* and it is a measure of the deviation or spread away from the mean. The standard deviation is a single value that indicates the amount of spread in a distribution and it is routinely computed by most statistical analysis computer programs. It can be computed manually as well, but the process is a little laborious.

The standard deviation can be computed for any distribution, regardless of its shape, but when a distribution conforms closely to the

---

FIGURE 10-2

The Normal Curve

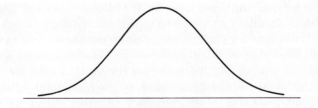

standard, normal distribution or "bell-shaped" curve, shown in Figure 10–2, a given proportion of the survey cases will always fall within certain ranges that are determined by the standard deviation (S.D.) of the distribution. Thus, the standard deviation is an excellent indicator of spread, and its interpretation will be discussed more fully in the following chapter.

SHAPE OF THE DISTRIBUTION

The shape of a continuous, numeric distribution can be described by two statistical coefficients that indicate how much the curve deviates from a normal, bell-shaped distribution. They are used for variables that are measured with interval or ratio scales and have a very large number of scale points or values. As noted in Figure 10–1, the coefficients of *skewness* and *kurtosis* (pronounced ker-*toe*-sis) describe the shape of a distribution. While most people are not at all familiar with these terms and their meaning, they can be explained very easily and understood intuitively. They are ordinarily computed only with computer data analysis routines and most analysis programs can generate them. They can be computed by hand, but the computational process is quite complex. It is ordinarily too tedious, time-consuming and error-prone to be practical to compute either the coefficients of skewness or kurtosis manually.

The *skewness* of a distribution is a measure of the degree and direction of its asymmetry. If a distribution is symmetrical, such as the normal, bell-shaped curve, one side of the distribution is precisely the "mirror-image" of the other. Often the distributions of data for survey variables are somewhat asymmetrical; that is, they "lean" toward one direction or the other. If the distribution is exactly symmetrical, the coefficient of skewness will be zero. If the cases are clustered mostly toward the left side, with many extreme values trailing off quite far toward the right side, the distribution is said to be "skewed to the left" and the coefficient of skewness will have a positive value. A negative coefficient of skewness indicates just the opposite, with most cases clustered toward the right and the tail of extreme values extending further toward the left. The more asymmetrical the distribution is, the further the coefficient of skewness will depart from zero.

Figure 10–3 shows both positive and negative skewness. It is often important to measure the degree of skewness in a continuous, numeric distribution with many values when the data are analyzed to provide data description. This is because the standard deviation as a description of spread provides a close estimate of the proportion of

---

FIGURE 10-3

The Skewness of Distributions

Positive skewness

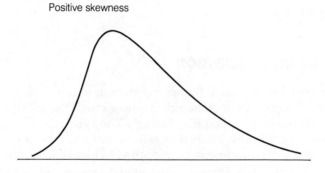

Negative skewness

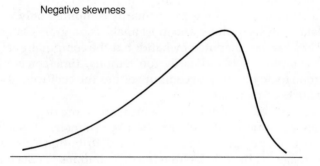

---

cases within a given range around the mean *only* if the distribution is symmetrical, as with the normal curve. Thus, the sign and the value of skewness indicates the degree of accuracy with which the standard deviation can be used to estimate the amount of spread in the distribution.

The *kurtosis* of a distribution is an indication of how peaked or flat it is, compared to the normal curve. If the distribution conforms exactly to the normal curve, having the same shape, the value of the coefficient of kurtosis will be zero. If the distribution has a higher, more narrow peak, with the tails extending out in each direction at a low level, the coefficient of kurtosis will be positive. By contrast, a negative value of kurtosis would indicate a curve with a broad, low

FIGURE 10-4

The Kurtosis of Distributions

Positive kurtosis

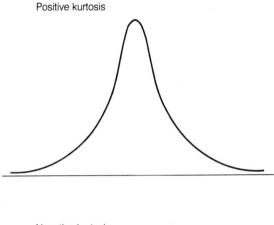

Negative kurtosis

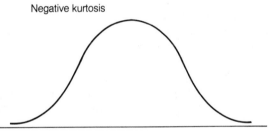

peak, below that of a normal curve. Figure 10–4 shows both positive and negative kurtosis.

The coefficient of kurtosis is usually obtained only with computer analysis. Kurtosis is even more laborious to calculate by hand than is skewness. It is often advisable to measure kurtosis when using computer data processing. If the coefficient of kurtosis departs markedly from zero, this affects the use of the standard deviation as a measure of spread. The interpretation of skewness, kurtosis, and the standard deviation are discussed more fully in the following chapter. It is only necessary to note here that they should always be obtained for continuous, numeric distributions with a large number of values, if they are readily available.

Actual survey data for a continuous, numeric variable from an

EXAMPLE 10-2

Descriptive Statistics

Descriptive Statistics

Mean	6.175	Median	6.729	Mode	9.000
Std. Dev.	2.930	Variance	8.586	Std. Err.	0.147
Sum	2,470	Kurtosis	−0.811	Skewness	−0.505
Minimum	0.000	Maximum	10.000	Range	10.000
95% Confidence interval =			5.887	to	6.463

interval scale is described in Example 10–2. Notice that the distribution tends to be more flat than normal, since the coefficient of kurtosis is negative. This indicates there are probably several percentages in the middle range of the scale that are very similar. The modal scale point is nine, so the data are skewed toward the high side of the scale and the coefficient of skewness is negative. As noted earlier, the mean is sensitive to extreme values in the tail, so it is *lower* than the mode and the median.

The descriptive statistics include some coefficients that were not discussed eariler. The variance is simply the square of the standard deviation. The Standard Error of the Estimate (Std. Err.) and the 95% confidence interval derived from it will be explained in the following chapter.

It is important to note that the values of skewness and kurtosis for this variable indicate the distribution departs markedly from the normal curve. Consequently, it will not be possible to use the standard deviation as an indicator of spread, showing what proportion of the respondents will be within a given range. Since the range includes less than a dozen values, it would be advisable to show the distribution in a frequency table and examine the spread and shape. If the variable had a very large number of numeric values, the researcher is well-advised to recode it to fewer, larger categories with equal intervals and generate a frequency table to assess shape and spread more effectively.

RELATIONSHIPS BETWEEN VARIABLES

The statistical tools and analyses discussed eariler allow the researcher to portray or to describe individual variables. Doing so will often satisfy many of the information requirements. Ordinarily, though, the researcher will not only want to know the nature of individual variables, but also want to learn about the relationship between pairs of variables. There may be substantial meaning in the description of each of a couple of survey items. There may also be substantial interest in how they might be related to one another. For example, when the information requirement is to determine whether or not men and women hold different opinions on a particular issue, this requires assessment of the relationship between the two variables: sex of respondent and opinion on the issue.

When the responses to a pair of survey items or variables are compared to one another, over the individual respondents, there are two possible results: either the answers to the two items may vary or "move" together, indicating they are significantly related to one another, or they may be completely independent of one another, indicating there is no relationship between the two. The statistical tools to measure association (relationships) between variables are designed to indicate precisely that: are they systematically related or are they completely independent.

When two variables are associated with one another, they may have one of two types of relationships: one can be regarded as partially causing or determining the value of the other or they may be viewed simply as varying or changing together, without any causal implications. It is important to note that the statistics to measure associations do *not* indicate whether or not one is causing another. That must be determined by the researcher, based on knowledge about the meaning of the items or variables, themselves. The statistics only measure the presence and degree of relationship between items. The existence and direction of causality must be inferred by the researcher, in advance, because the choice of an appropriate statistical tool often depends on whether or not causal relationship is implied.

The selection of the proper statistical tool for the task at hand is just as important for measurement of association between variables as it is for portraying or describing individual items. When individual items were being analyzed, the choice of the proper statistical tools depended on the type of variable to be described or portrayed. The choice of the right statistical tool to measure association also depends on the types of variables being analyzed, but it also depends on whether or not causality is implied and if so, which item is being affected by the other. Thus, to choose the proper statistical tool to measure a relationship between two items, the researcher must only determine two things: what type of variable is each item and which item will be viewed as "dependent" and which as "independent." The dependent variable is the one being caused or affected, and the independent variable is the one causing or affecting the other.

The researcher need only determine the variable types and direction of causality, and then refer to a simple matrix to select the proper statistical measure of association. The categorical and continuous data types were identified and defined in the previous chapter. The researcher must be familiar with the definitions and be able to identify the data as categorical or continuous, in order to select the proper statistical tool to measure association.

Dependent and Independent Variables

With some statistical measures of association, it makes no difference whether or not one item is causing or affecting the other, and if so, which is affecting the other. Some statistical tools for measuring the association between variables do require the researcher to decide ahead of time which one is likely to affect the other. In the discussion that follows, the variable that the researcher decides is causing the other to vary or affecting the other is called the *independent* variable. The variable that is being affected or that is likely to vary because of the value of another is called the *dependent* variable. The direction of causality is from independent to dependent variable; the independent variable is viewed as affecting the dependent variable.

Merely knowing the name of a variable or what it represents does not necessarily indicate whether it will be a dependent or an independent variable for some measure of association. The researcher must know more than that about the meaning of the variables and the possible relationships or dynamics between them. Thus, the researcher must study the nature of the two items and determine which, if either, is likely to cause or affect the other. At first glance, it might seem that such survey items as demographic characteristics will always be independent variables, while opinions or attitudes are nearly always dependent variables. While that is usually the case, it is certainly not always so in every conceivable situation.

Some survey items may be treated as independent variables for some measure of association or in relation to one set of other variables, and then be treated as dependent variables for another measure of relationships with another set of items. Thus, the researcher must identify a variable as dependent or independent for each analysis or "pairing," rather than merely identifying each survey item as dependent or independent for all measures.

STATISTICS TO MEASURE ASSOCIATION

The statistical tools to measure the relationship between two survey variables are listed in Figure 10–5. To identify the proper statistical tool to measure the relationship between two survey variables, the researcher must identify the variables as *categorical* or *continuous,* and determine which is to be treated as the *independent* variable and which the *dependent* variable. Where no causality is implied and the focus is merely on the degree of association between the two variables, it does not matter which is regarded as independent and which dependent, but only certain statistics listed in Figure 10–5 are appropriate in those cases. The researcher can now refer to the appropriate row and column of the matrix to find the proper statistical tool(s). An example of the use of the matrix for selecting a statistical tool may prove helpful.

Suppose one survey item to be analyzed is the marital status of the respondents and it is a categorical variable, married or not married.

FIGURE 10–5

Statistical Measures of Association

	INDEPENDENT	
	Categorical	Continuous
D E P E N D E N T Categorical	Cross-Tabulation (Contingency) [Chi-Square]	Discriminant Analysis [F ratio]
D E P E N D E N T Continuous	Analysis of Variance [F ratio]	Regression Analysis [F ratio]
	Paired T Test [Value of t]	Correlation Analysis [Prob. of r]

Another survey item might be a simple, yes/no item to some question. Assume the sponsor wishes to know if the sex of the respondent affects the answer to the yes/no survey item. Sex would be the independent variable and it is categorical, indicating the *first column* of the matrix. The yes/no item is the dependent variable, defining the rows of the matrix, and it is categorical also, indicating the *top row*. Thus, to measure this relationship, the researcher would use cross-tabulation of the two items as proper procedure because it is listed in the first column, top row. Cross-tabulation is sometimes called "contingency table analysis" so that term is also listed. The significance of the relationship would be indicated by the chi-square (pronounced *kie-square*) statistic. Thus, selection of the proper statistical tool is mostly a matter of finding the correct cell of the matrix by row and column.

Cross-tabulation is by far the most common measure of association between survey variables, and it is used much more frequently than all of the other techniques combined. Cross-tabulation is common and so popular in part because the method is effective, it can easily be understood and interpreted, it can be tabulated by hand and there are many analysis programs to perform cross-tabulation, and it is a very flexible method. Very often, survey items that are continuous are obtained from scales that have only a few scale points or values, so these variables can be treated as categorical and used in cross-tabulation. Even when continuous survey variables have a wide-ranging scale with many values, the data can often be recoded into meaningful categories to provide categorical data for cross-tabulation with other items. This technique will be discussed in some detail below, together with examples of crosstabulation tables of actual survey data.

The other procedures and statistics that are listed in Figure 10–5 will be identified and their use discussed briefly in this chapter. The interpretation of these other methods will be described in the following chapter. Those researchers who require additional information about these methods are advised to refer to one of the many texts and manuals describing bivariate and multivariate statistics.

Cross-Tabulation

Cross-tabulation tables, or simply "crosstabs," indicate the relationship between two categorical variables. The procedure does not require that one variable be identified as dependent and the other independent, although that is often the case when crosstabs are used. Two such tables are shown in Example 10–3. Both of the tables shown in the example contain actual survey data, and the tables, together with the chi-square statistic associated with them, were generated by

EXAMPLE 10-3

Cross-Tabulation Tables

Number Row Pct Col Pct		Married 1.	Not Married 2.	Row Total
Larks	1.	47	73	120
		39.2	60.8	42.4
		31.8	54.1	
Owls	3.	101	62	163
		62.0	38.0	57.6
		68.2	45.9	
Column		148	135	283
Total		52.3	47.7	100.0

Chi-square = 14.40   d.f. = 1   Prob. = 0.0002

Number Col Pct		Under 35 1.	35 to 49 2.	Over 49 3.	Row Total
Larks	1.	69	17	34	120
		44.5	20.0	21.2	30.0
Wrens	2.	42	26	49	117
		27.1	30.6	30.6	29.2
Owls	3.	44	42	77	163
		28.4	49.4	48.1	42.4
Column		155	85	160	400
Total		38.7	21.2	40.0	100.0

Chi-square = 27.72   d.f. = 4   Prob. = 0.0000

a computer program for analysis of survey data. The purpose of this form of analysis and the components of the tables will be discussed in some detail here. The interpretation of chi-square and statistical significance is described in the following chapter of the handbook.

When crosstabs are used, the values of one of the variables in the analysis are listed on the rows and the values of the other are listed on the columns. Thus, there will be as many rows and as many columns as there are values for each of the variables. The upper section of Example 10–3 shows a "two by two" table and the lower section, a "three by three" table. When one or both variables have more than six or eight values, the tables become quite difficult to interpret, so data for cross-tabulation is often recoded into only a few categories. The data for both tables in the example are for the same survey and respondents. Scores on a brief test were recoded into three categories: larks, wrens, and owls, indicating if the person was most active and energetic in the morning, at midday, or in the evening.

The "wrens" were excluded in the first table, and only the "larks" and "owls" were cross-tabulated against marital status. In the second table, the age variable was recoded into three categories and cross-tabulated against all three groups.

There are three values in each "cell" of the first table. The top one is the number or frequency. For example, 47 married respondents proved to be larks and 101 were owls. The second value in each cell is the row percentage, as indicated by the key at the upper, left of the matrix. The row percentage is merely the number in the cell, divided by the total number for that row. In the upper table of the example, 39.2 percent was obtained by dividing the 47 in the upper, left cell by 120, the number in the top row, and moving the decimal two places to the left for percentage. The third number in each cell is the column percentage, and it is the number divided by the total for the column. Thus, row percentages will total to 100 percent across the rows, while column percentages total to 100 down the columns. The totals and percentages for each row and each column are shown at the right and lower margins.

The object of cross-tabulation is to show whether or not the distributions for one variable differ significantly for each value or level of the other variable. If the two variables are not related to one another, then the row percentages in each row will be nearly the same as the percentages at the bottom of the table and the column percentages in each cell will be nearly equal to the percentages at the far right. In the example, if marital status did not affect the tendency to be a lark or an owl, or vice versa, then about the same proportion of married people would be larks as would those who are not married. In the lower table of Example 10–3, only the column percentages were requested and listed on the table. Age can be considered the independent variable and time of day preferences the dependent. Thus, if age did not affect preference for time of day, about 30 percent of those in *each* column would be larks, about 29 percent would be wrens, and about 42 percent would be owls.

The actual interpretation of the cross-tabulation and the statistics will be discussed fully in the following chapter, but it is interesting to note here that both marital status and age of respondents are significantly related to preference for morning, midday, or evening. For example, the lower table indicated that younger respondents are significantly more often larks and significantly less often owls than are middle-aged or older respondents, while age does not seem to have much affect on the frequency of preference for midday. These conclusions were reached by noting that 44½ percent of those under 35 were larks, while only 30 percent of all age groups were so, and only about 28 percent of that age group were owls, while about 42 percent of the entire sample were in that category. Similarly, all of the percentages in the wren category were approximately the same as one another and the total for all groups. Notice that the same sort of analysis can be done by row, rather than by column, if the row percentages had been listed on the table.

Cross-tabulation tables can be generated with hand tabulation, as well as by computer data analysis routines. The process is not especially complex or difficult to understand, but it is rather time-consuming and tedious.

Row, Column, and Table Percentages.   Whether the crosstabs are to be done by hand or by computer programs, it is usually advisable to compute either row percentages or column percentages, as well as the frequencies or numbers of cases in the cell. Many computer analysis routines permit the researcher to obtain row, column, and table percentages within the cell, as well as the frequencies. As noted earlier, row percentages are merely the percentage of all cases in the row that fall within a given column. They total to 100 percent across the rows. Column percentages are the percentage of all the column totals that fall within a given row, and they total to 100 percent down the columns. Table percentages are just the percentage of all the cases in the table that fall within a given cell, and so the sum of the table percentages for all cells total to 100.

Row or column percentages are ordinarily required because it is extremely difficult to interpret the distributions shown in the cross-tabulation table based only on the frequency or cases in each cell. Ordinarily, there will be different numbers of cases in each row and in each column, as there are in the example. Thus, the proportions and relationships are difficult to gauge, based only on the frequencies. Table percentages are only rarely useful for some special situations where the researcher would like to infer the percentage in the population who answer each of two survey questions in a certain way. In the majority of cases, the researcher will use either the row or the column percentages for the bulk of the analysis and interpretation.

Minimum Cell Frequencies. There will almost always be some difference in the distributions of a cross-tabulation table from row to row or from column to column, even if there would be no difference whatsoever if the whole population were surveyed. In other words, some of the differences will be due purely to sampling error; just happening by chance to pick a group that shows some difference. The chi-square statistic that can be computed from the cross-tabulation table will indicate the probability that there would be as much difference in the distributions, by row or by column, even if there were no differences for the whole population. The interpretation of the significance of chi-square for cross-tabulations will be discussed more fully in the following chapter. There is one important point that must be noted here, however. The chi-square statistic will not be a valid or accurate indication of significance if one or more of the *expected* cell frequencies is too small. In other words, there must be a sufficient number of cases in the rows and columns in order for the statistic to work properly and indicate significance.

Most computer programs for cross-tabulation of data and computation of the chi-square statistic will produce a table and a statistic, regardless of whether or not the expected cell frequencies are of adequate size. In other words, the routines will do what they are told and they, themselves, do *not* require a certain, minimum cell frequency. On the other hand, the statistic they generate and the assessment of statistical significance that is based on it will not be valid. Thus, the researcher must check cell frequency "by hand."

The smallest expected cell frequency for the chi-square statistic to be valid is five cases. If there are fewer than five for the cell of the table with the smallest expected cell frequency, the researcher should then recode the variable to combine rows or combine columns, until an adequate expected cell frequency is achieved. Notice that this requirement refers to *expected* cell frequency, not the actual or observed cell frequency or number of cases that are actually in the cell. Inexperienced or untrained researchers commonly make the error of inspecting the table to see if the smallest actual cell frequency is five or greater. It does not matter if the actual cell frequency is *zero*, so long as the *expected* cell frequency is five or more. The expected frequency must almost always be computed by hand, after the researcher sees the table that has been generated. Fortunately, it is easy to identify the cell that will have the smallest expected frequency and the value can be computed very quickly by hand or with a pocket calculator.

The cell of a cross-tabulation table that will have the smallest expected cell frequency is the one on the *row* with the smallest total and the *column* with the smallest total. Thus, the process of checking the smallest expected cell frequency does not require calculation of all of the expected values. The researcher need only do three things: (1) Find the smallest row total, usually listed on the right margin of each row. (2) Divide it by the total for the table. (3) Multiply this value by the smallest column total, usually listed at the bottom of each column. The result is the smallest expected cell frequency, and if it is less than five, the researcher must either recode the variable defining the rows to obtain a larger row total, or recode the variable listed on the columns to obtain a larger column total. Either one will generate a larger expected cell frequency, but the process must be repeated after generating a new table, to be sure the value for other cells are not too small.

The lower table of Example 10–3 can be used to demonstrate the computation of lowest expected cell frequency. The smallest row total is 117. The total number of cases included in the table is 400, so 117 divided by 400 equals 0.2925. The smallest column total is 85, and 0.2925 times 85 equals 24.8625. Thus, the smallest expected cell frequency for that cross-tabulation table is well-above the required value of five. This procedure is outlined in brief in Guidelist 10–1.

GUIDELIST 10–1

For Computing Expected Cell Frequencies

1. Find the smallest row total in the table, usually listed to the right of the row.
2. Divide it by the total number of cases included in the table, usually listed at the lower, right.
3. Find the smallest column total in the table, usually listed below the columns.
4. Multiply it by the fractional value obtained above to determine the minimum expected cell frequency.
5. If less than five, recode one of the variables to obtain a larger row or column total.
6. Generate another table and follow the same procedure to check the minimum expected cell frequency.
7. Remember, the smallest *actual* cell frequency may be as low as zero or it may be five or greater, but it is the *expected* cell frequency that must still be checked.

Multiple Crosstabs in Banners. Often, survey data analysis will require the cross-tabulation of one particular variable with many others, all of which are similar to one another. For example, a demographic characteristic, such as sex of respondent, may be cross-tabulated against a dozen or so ratings, all with the same scale values. When the cross-tabulation tables are generated one at a time, this would require a dozen or so tables, one for each crosstab. Some analysis routines permit the researcher to specify several such cross-tabulations in what is called a "banner" format. In that case, the cross-tabulation itself is basically the same as that described above; however, the report or print output is condensed to save space and to allow the researcher to view several crosstabs at a time. For example, the scale values may be listed on the left side, defining the rows of the banner. Several pairs of columns would be listed to the right, each containing the frequencies and/or column percentages for the men and for the women. Of course, each such pair is labeled at the top or bottom to indicate which item was being rated by the men and women. In short, the cross-tabulations are generated just as they are for only a single table, but the banner format is more condensed, containing less information about any single crosstab but more information on a single page of print output.

Crosstabs and Other Measures of Relationship. Cross-tabulations are by far the most popular and commonly used measure of the relationships between survey variables. Researchers often have a strong preference for this method over others, even though they may be completely familiar with the other statistical techniques for measuring relationships between items. This is because sponsors are usually more familiar with crosstabs than other statistics. Because of their utility and popularity, crosstabs were described more thoroughly above than are the other measures that follow.

GUIDELIST 10-2

For Using Cross-Tabulation

1. The objective is to determine if the distributions of one variable differ for each category of the other.

2. The variables to be cross-tabulated must *both* be derived from categorical scales.

3. One variable may be identified as independent and the other dependent, but they need not be.

4. The chi-square statistic and its probability are used to measure the statistical significance of the relationship.

5. The minimum *expected* cell frequency must be computed to be sure it is five or greater for chi-square to be valid.

6. Either column or row percentages are most useful for interpretation, but table percentages are rarely needed.

7. It is best to list the categories of the *dependent* variable on rows and use column percentages for interpretation.

Analysis of Variance

When the independent variable is categorical and the dependent variable is continuous, the appropriate technique to measure the relationship between the two is analysis of variance, sometimes referred to by the acronym, ANOVA. Analysis of variance is a technique to measure the statistical significance of the differences between means. When the difference between only two mean values is to be assessed, a statistical t-test can also be used. The t-test is merely a "special case" of analysis of variance that applies to only two distributions. Analysis of variance can actually be used to measure the association for two *or more* values. An example may demonstrate the use of analysis of variance.

Suppose customers of a certain store were surveyed to learn the dollar value of their purchases over a certain period, and respondents also indicated their sex. The researcher might wish to determine not only the average value of the purchases for the entire sample, but also for men and for women. The researcher might simply obtain the average for the entire sample, the average for men, and the average for women. If the average for one was somewhat greater than for the other sex, the researcher would not be able to tell if this difference was because the entire population of men and women differed, or if it was merely due to the fact that the sample happened by chance to select those of one sex with larger purchases. Analysis of variance could be used to determine the statistical significance of the differences in mean values. In this example, the independent variable would be the sex of the respondent and it would be categorical. The dependent variable would then be the dollar volume of purchases and it would be continuous. Reference to Figure 10–5 will indicate that analysis of variance is the appropriate technique to measure the significance of the relationship.

Most computer programs for analysis of variance have the ability to report the mean values by category (men and women in the example) and for the entire sample, since they must compute these means during the procedure. The analysis of variance routines will typically generate an F-ratio value and an indication of the "degrees of freedom" associated with it. If the program did not compute and report the significance of the differences in mean values by category in the form of a probability, the researcher could determine the significance by checking a table of the F-distribution, using the value of the F-ratio and degrees of freedom that were computed. Such tables are commonly appended to basic statistics or research texts.

GUIDELIST 10-3

For Using Analysis of Variance

1. The objective is to determine if the mean values of the dependent variable for each category of the independent variable are significantly different from one another.

2. The independent variable must be categorical and the dependent variable must be continuous.

3. The dependent variable must be derived from either an interval or a ratio scale, but *not* an ordinal scale.

4. The variance in the dependent variable must be about the same within each category of the independent variable.

5. The independent variable may have two *or more* categories for analysis of variance, but only two for a t-test.

6. The values of the dependent variable must be obtained from different respondents, so they are completely independent of one another.

7. When two values of a continuous, dependent measure are obtained from the *same* respondents and their means are to be compared for significant differences, a *paired t-test* should be used in place of analysis of variance.

It is important to note that analysis of variance *requires* data with two characteristics: First, the data must be from interval or ratio scales. Second, the variance or spread in the distributions of the dependent variable for *each* category of the independent variable must be approximately the same. There is also a third requirement that relates to the manner in which the data is collected. Each case must be independent of the others. That simply means that each value of the dependent variable must be from a different person, responding independently of the others. Some analysis routines allow the researcher to specify a test to be sure the variances mentioned in the first requirement above are not significantly different. It is important to note, however, that analysis of variance can be conducted regardless of whether or not the requirements are met. If they are not, there is, of course, a great likelihood that the results would be competely erroneous.

GUIDELIST 10-4

For Using Correlation Analysis

1. The objective is to determine the degree to which two variables move or vary together from one respondent or case to the next and the significance of the relationship.

2. Both variables must be continuous, but they need not be identified as dependent and independent.

3. Product-moment correlation requires *both* variables be from interval or ratio scales, but rank correlation can be used when one or both are derived from ordinal scales.

4. The correlation coefficient ranges from zero, no relationship, to plus or minus one, a perfect relationship.

5. When the coefficient is positive, the variables move together in the same direction, and when it is negative, they move together in *opposite* directions.

6. The percentage of all possible shared variance or movement together is indicated by the *square* of the correlation coefficient, the coefficient of *determination*.

Occasionally, a survey will obtain ratings or other continuous data for two or more variables from the *same* respondents, and the researcher may wish to determine if the mean value for one was significantly greater or lesser than the other. In that case, the values would not be "independent" of one another, as noted in the third requirement, above. Analysis of variance could not be used to measure the significance of differences. In such cases, the researcher might use the "paired t-test" noted in Figure 10–5. If so, only one pair, or two variables could be compared with each analysis, and the independent variable would simply be the first versus the second variable from the same case.

Regression and Correlation Analysis

When the relationship between two continuous variables is to be measured for significance of association, the appropriate technique is either regression or correlation analysis. Regression requires that one variable be identified as independent and the other dependent. Correlation analysis measures only the degree to which the two are related, or tend to move together, but there is no assumption that one is causing or determining the other with correlation analysis. Correlation will be considered first because it is less complex than regression.

Correlation Analysis. A correlation between two continuous variables is just what the word implies, "co-relation," and it is based on covariance, or movement together. Correlation analysis generates a single value, the correlation coefficient, that shows how much the two variables move together. The coefficient of correlation is often designated in statistics and research books simply as the letter, r. The correlation coefficient ranges from a value of zero, indicating there is virtually no relationship between the variables, to a plus or a minus one, indicating a perfect, linear relationship. If the value of the correlation coefficient was one, this would indicate a "lockstep" relationship between the two variables. In other words, if the value of one of the items increased by one unit from one case to the next, the value of the other item would always move by a given amount, although it need not necessarily be the same value.

The plus or minus sign on the correlation coefficient indicates the *direction* of the correlation. If the correlation is positive, the two move in the same direction. If it is negative, they move in the opposite direction. In other words, the plus or minus indicate a *direct* or an *inverse* relationship between the two variables. The absolute value (ignoring the plus or minus sign) shows how much the two items are correlated or moving together. The closer to zero, the less the relationship, and the closer to one, the greater the relationship. Thus, both the sign and the value of the correlation coefficient provide information about the relationship between items.

Interpreting the "degree" or strength of the relationship between two variables using the correlation coefficient can be a little misleading, because this coefficient does *not* show what proportion of a "perfect" relationship the two variables have. The proportion of "shared variance" is actually indicated by the *square* of the correlation coefficient, and that is called the coefficient of *determination*. Some examples might clarify this relationship. Suppose two survey items are submitted to correlation analysis and the coefficient of correlation is .50. This does *not* mean that they are "half" as closely related as they might be if they were perfectly associated with one another. If the correlation coefficient has a value of .50, the coefficient of determination is the square of that value, or .25, and only about 25 percent of the variance in the two items would be "shared" between them. Similarly, if the correlation coefficient was .90, they would share 81 percent of the variance, not 90 percent. It is important to note this relationship, because inexperienced researchers sometimes gain the impression that relatively weak relationships are much stronger than they actually are. Thus, a correlation coefficient of .20 appears to be a fairly pronounced relationship, but actually only 4 percent of the total variance in the variables is shared between them.

The researcher will not only want to know the size and direction of a correlation, but also whether or not it is statistically significant, in terms of the probability that such a relationship would result purely by chance from the sampling if the two items were uncorrelated in the population. Many statistical analysis routines will report the significance. If this probability is not reported, the significance can be checked by reference to standard statistical tables ordinarily appended to many statistics and research texts. The researcher need only know the value of the correlation coefficient and number of cases or "degrees of freedom" reported by the routine.

There are two kinds of correlation analysis and statistical routines that are often used by researchers. The most common requires that the data be from either *interval* or *ratio* scales, and it is called "Pearson Product-Moment Correlation," or sometimes just "Product-Moment" or "PM" correlation. When researchers or statisticians simply use the term, "correlation," they are referring to this most common method. The other method of correlation is appropriate for data from ranking scales or other *ordinal* data, and it is called "Spearman Rank Correlation," or just "Rank Correlation." Rank correlations can also be used for interval or ratio data, but it is not advisable because this method is less sensitive and powerful. It is ordinarily not advisable to use product-moment correlation for rankings or ordinal data, because the results are likely to be interpreted erroneously.

Regression Analysis. When one continuous variable can be identified as an independent variable and another continuous variable as the dependent variable, regression analysis is the appropriate technique to measure the relationship between them and assess its significance. When the analysis includes just one independent variable, the more precise term for the statistical method is "simple, linear regression," or just "linear regression." This is the technique described here, but there are extensions of the method, called "multiple regression," when there is a single dependent variable and more than one independent variable.

There are two potential objectives of regression analysis: One is to measure the degree and direction of the influence of the independent on the dependent variable, and of course, to assess the statistical significance of the relationship. Another is to obtain a formula so that an unknown value for the dependent variable can be predicted or computed within a specified range of accuracy, if the value of the independent variable is known. A brief example may demonstrate the two objectives.

Suppose a clothing shop sponsors a survey to determine the age of their customers and the dollar value of their purchases during the recent past. Both age in years and purchases in dollars are continuous, ratio scale variables. The researcher might also safely assume that the age of the customer would affect the volume of purchases, but not vice versa. Thus, age would be the independent variable, purchases the dependent variable, and regression analysis the appropriate method for assessing the relationship, as indicated in Figure 10–5.

The first objective of the researcher would be to determine if age did, in fact, have a statistically significant influence on purchase behavior, and if so, how much it affected the amount purchased and in what direction. (If the researcher wanted only to measure the significance of a relationship, correlation analysis might be used, rather than regression.) If a significant relationship was detected, the researcher might then want to know how to predict the purchase level of customers of a certain age, and also to determine how much accuracy could be expected of such predictions. If purchases could be predicted with a reasonable degree of accuracy, the shop sponsoring the survey might then adjust their merchandising and promotional policies to obtain the age group with greatest potential sales volume, or use the information to forecast sales based on the age distribution of those visiting the store or shopping center.

Regression analysis produces a coefficient that is virtually parallel to the coefficient of determination for correlation analysis, and it is ordinarily referred to as r^2 (r-square) or abbreviated RSQ. Some statistical programs also compute and report the significance of r-square, but if not, the researcher must refer to statistical tables to determine the significance. With correlation analysis, the square of the coefficient indicates the proportion of variance in the two variables that is "shared" between them. With regression analysis, the r-square value indicates the percentage of variance in the dependent variable that is "explained" by the values of the independent variable. Thus, the r-square value is an indication of how much influence the independent variable has on the dependent variable.

While the correlation coefficient is either positive or negative, indicating the direction of the relationship, the r-square value obtained by regression is always positive. (With correlation analysis, the coefficient of determination is always positive as well, because the product of numbers with like signs is always a positive value.) The value of r-square ranges from zero to one. A value of zero indicates the independent variable has no influence whatsoever on the dependent variable. A value of one indicates that the value of the dependent variable could be predicted exactly if the value of the independent variable is known. In other words, just as with correlation, the variables are in a perfect, linear, "lockstep" relationship with one another from one case or respondent to the next.

Regression analysis generates a "regression equation," as well as the r-square value. The regression equation is the formula for computing a predicted value for the dependent variable, based on the value of the independent variable. Actually the regression equation is a very simple one when there is only one independent variable because only two values are required: a constant and a regression coefficient. To predict the value of the dependent variable for a given case when only the value of the independent variable is known, the researcher need only multiply the regression coefficient by the value of the independent variable and add the constant. Assume, for example, that the regression analysis generated a constant of 5 and a regression coefficient of 2. If the value of the independent variable was known to be 8 for a given case but the value of the dependent variable was unknown, it could be predicted to be 2 times 8, plus five, or 21. (Those with a mathematics background will recognize the equation for a straight line: $Y = a + bX$, where a is the constant Y intercept and b is the regression coefficient or slope of the line.)

Figure 10–6 shows the pattern that would be obtained if each data point were plotted on a graph with the scale for the independent variable on the horizontal axis and the scale for the dependent variable on the vertical axis. The fact that the points are very close to the regression line also indicates that the r-square value would be very high, and the researcher in this case could make very accurate predictions of unknown values for the dependent variable if the values of the independent variable were known. On the other hand, when the data points on a scatterplot "splay" widely from the regression line, the r-square value and the ability to predict will be low.

The regression line intersects the vertical axis just a little above the lower level of the plot. The constant in the regression equation is simply the value of the dependent variable scale when the independent variable is a zero. The regression line in Figure 10–6 slopes upward, to the right, indicating that as the value of the independent

FIGURE 10-6

A Linear Regression Scatterplot

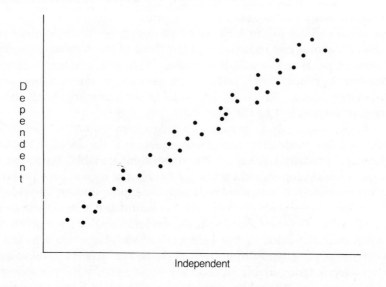

variable increases, so does the value of the dependent variable. If the independent and dependent variables stood in an *inverse*, rather than a *direct* relationship to one another, the line would slope downward, to the right. The regression coefficient is simply the slope of the regression line; it is the "rise" of the line divided by the "run" of the line to the right. Thus, when the regression coefficient is positive, the line slopes upward and the relationship is direct; when the value of one variable increases, so does the other. When the coefficient is negative, the line slopes downward and the relationship is inverse; when one value increases, the other decreases. Just as the positive or negative sign of the correlation coefficient indicates the direction of the relationship between variables, so too, does the sign of the regression coefficient.

Regression analysis requires that certain conditions of the data be met in order for the results to be valid or legitimate. Both the independent and the dependent variables must be derived from interval or ratio scales. Each pair of values must come from a different or independent case or respondent. In addition, the relationship between the variables must be "linear." That means simply that if the cases were

GUIDELIST 10-5

For Using Regression Analysis

1. One objective is to measure the degree and direction of influence the independent variable has on the dependent variable.

2. Another objective is to obtain an equation to predict an unknown value of the dependent variable, based on the known value of the independent variable.

3. One variable must be identified as independent and one dependent, and both must be derived from interval or ratio scales.

4. The strength of the influence of the independent on the dependent variable is indicated by r-square, ranging from zero, indicating no influence, to one, indicating the dependent variable is completely determined.

5. The regression equation consists of a constant and the regression coefficient, indicating the direction and amount of influence, or slope of the regression line.

6. When the regression coefficient is positive, the relationship is *direct* and the slope is upward to the right, and when it is negative, the relationship is inverse and the slope is downward to the right.

7. Regression analysis requires that the relationship be linear, rather than curved or kinked, and that the spread around the regression line be approximately the same from one end of the line to the other, both of which can be checked by inspecting a scatterplot of data points.

plotted, the points on the plot must be arrayed approximately in a straight line. Figure 10–7 shows a case where the corridor of data points are sharply curved, rather than linear. If these data were used for regression analysis, the r-square value would be deflated, and predictions for the dependent variable would be too high for high and low values of the independent variable and too low for medium levels. There are statistical tests available with some statistical analysis routines that will indicate whether or not the scatterplot departs from linearity. The most commonly used such test is called a "runs test." Lacking a test such as that, the researcher is well-advised to obtain a plot of the data points or to tabulate a plot using a random sample of the actual data. As with most statistical requirements, the analysis routines will compute the statistics regardless of whether or not the plot is linear, but the results are very likely to be grossly misleading or completely erroneous.

FIGURE 10-7

A Curvilinear Scatterplot Pattern

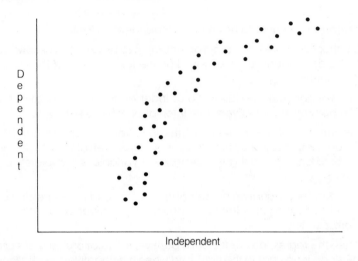

Another requirement of regression analysis is that the spread or variance around the regression line be approximately equal. If not, erroneous results will be generated. Figure 10–8 shows a pattern that is very common for survey data. Notice that the data points are closely clustered around the regression line for the lower values of the variables, but they splay outward quite widely for the higher values.

Discriminant Analysis

When the independent variable is continuous and the dependent variable is categorical, the appropriate statistical method to measure the relationship is discriminant analysis. The technical term for the procedure is "analysis of the linear, discriminant function," or "discriminatory analysis," and it is sometimes called simply "discrimination." If the researcher wishes to measure the relationship between two variables that need not or cannot be identified as independent and dependent, analysis of variance is recommended, rather than discriminant analysis. Analysis of variance is preferable because it is much more common, more readily understood, and programs for doing the statistical computations are much more prevalent. The results of discriminant analysis are often complex and extremely diffi-

FIGURE 10-8

A Funnel-Shaped Scatterplot

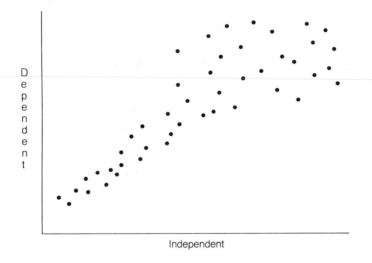

Independent

cult to interpret. Thus, those who lack training and experience with statistics are well-advised to use analysis of variance to measure the relationship between a continuous and a categorical variable. Experienced researchers commonly prefer analysis of variance if there is no compelling reason to use discriminant analysis.

The objectives of discriminant analysis are to measure the degree and direction of influence the independent variable has on the dependent variable, and to obtain an equation that would permit the rsearcher to predict the category of the dependent variable when it is not known, based on the known value of the independent variable. Thus, discriminant analysis is analogous to regression, except that the dependent item is in categories or groups, rather than in continuous, numeric form. The statistical significance of the relationship may be computed by the analysis routine in the form of a probability, or an F-ratio may be generated so that the researcher can refer to the appropriate statistical tables to assess significance.

Discriminant analysis also provides the coefficient of the linear, discriminant function, somewhat similar to a regression equation, as well as a "critical value." The category of the dependent variable when it is not known can be predicted by multiplying the known value of the independent variable by this coefficient. If the product is less than the critical value, the case would be predicted to be in the "lower" group, and if it is greater than the critical value, to be in the "upper" group.

Discriminant analysis as it is described here, assumes there is only one independent variable and also that the dependent variable contains *only two categories* or groups. If there are more than two groups, a discriminant function will be generated for every possible pair of categories, and the analysis and interpretation become exceedingly complex. Even with just one function, additional values and coefficients generated by the program make it difficult to interpret. Discriminant analysis requires that the dependent variable be categorical while the independent variable must be continuous and derived from an interval or ratio scale. The spread in the independent variable must be approximately the same within each category of the dependent variable, much as the similar requirement for analysis of variance.

GUIDELIST 10–6

For Using Discriminant Analysis

1. One objective is to measure the degree of influence of a continuous independent variable on the category value of a dependent variable, together with the statistical significance of the relationship.

2. Another objective is to obtain a coefficient and critical value, so the unknown category of the dependent variable can be predicted, based on the known value of the independent variable.

3. The procedure as described here requires a continuous, independent variable derived from an interval or ratio scale and a dependent variable with only two categories.

4. Both the statistical procedure and the results it generates are complex and difficult to interpret, so analysis of variance is ordinarily preferable unless discriminant analysis is absolutely necessary.

ANALYSIS VERSUS INTERPRETATION

The discussion of statistical analysis will help the researcher to choose the appropriate tools. For those who are not very familiar with the methods and statistics described, many questions concerning interpretation are likely to remain. The interpretation of the results and the response to information requirements are the topic of the next chapter. Those with a background in statistics may find the discussion elementary because many of the complexities and niceties of the statistical methods are absent. Ample reference materials on statistics are readily available where needed, and the level of discussion here will be adequate for the vast majority of survey data analysis.

SUMMARY

Statistical Analysis of Data

A. Remember the objectives. Statistics are designed to suppress detail and reveal *important* findings.

B. Provide data description first. Treat individual variables for the entire sample before examining relationships.

C. Always identify the scale types. The nature of the scale determines, in part, the proper descriptive measures.

D. Treat variables both ways. Continuous items with only a few scale values can be treated as categorical.

E. Portray information when feasible. Showing the entire distribution is more effective than describing it.

F. Describe data with care. The shape of the distribution affects the choice and interpretation of descriptors.

G. Determine the data type. Continuous and categorical data require different statistical measures of association.

H. Show relationships with crosstabs. The cross-tabulation tables are more easily understood than other statistics.

I. Assess causality carefully. Choice of independent and dependent variables depends on their underlying meaning.

J. Select the simplest tool. The simplest method used well is far more effective than a complex method that is used incorrectly or misunderstood.

11

Interpreting Results

DESCRIPTIVE STATISTICS

The statistics used to analyze survey data fall into two broad categories: those that describe individual variables and distributions and those that measure the relationships between variables. Complete data descriptions, for both continuous and categorical data, are ordinarily generated and studied by the researcher before turning to measures of association between variables. Thus, the first portion of this chapter will discuss the interpretation of statistical descriptions of categorical and continuous data, and the remaining portion will be devoted to the various statistics for measuring relationships among survey items.

Frequency and percentage distributions are the most common and practical method for describing categorical survey variables. The format and content of frequency tables were described and exemplified in some detail in the previous chapter. When the variable being analyzed can only be considered as categorical, so that there is really no continuum or relationship between categories, the only statistic that is appropriate to describe the distribution is the mode, the category with the largest frequency. Aside from that, the frequency table is largely self-explanatory.

The interpretation of continuous, numeric survey data with a large number of values is considerably more complex and difficult than for categorical data. When continuous ordinal, interval, or ratio data are obtained from scales with a limited number of scale points or values, this type of variable can be treated *both* as continuous and as categorical data. Each scale point can be treated as a separate category, even though they are on a continuum, and doing so is not only permissible, it is advisable. Of course, the conventional descriptive statistics, such as averages, measures of spread, and shape of the distribution can also be computed for such items.

When continuous variables have too many values to be listed in a frequency table, it is often advisable either to recode the variable into fewer, larger categories, or to generate a "duplicate" variable and recode it into categories, as suggested in the previous chapter. The range of the interval for each category should be identical, and there should be no more than a dozen categories, and preferably only six or eight. When a continuous variable has been recoded into categories in this fashion, it can be treated as *either* continuous or categorical, providing certain conditions are met. For example, if age in years resulted in 40 or 50 different values, the variable might be recoded into five or six, 10 year categories. There are then two options: One is to create a duplicate variable, recode it into categories with equal intervals, and list the categories in frequency tables and perhaps use them for cross-tabulation later, when relationships between variables are analyzed. The duplicate age variable that was retained in continuous form might also be described with the statistics appropriate for continuous distributions.

Another option is to recode the original variable only into categories with equal intervals. If no duplicate, continuous variable is retained, then each category should be coded with the value of the *midpoint* of the interval. For example, if age was reclassified into 10-year categories: 20s, 30s, 40s, etc., then each category should be recoded with the values: 25, 35, 45, etc. In that way, the descriptive statistics for continuous distributions can be used along with the frequency tables. These statistics would be interpreted in the same way as they would when a strictly continuous variable was analyzed, except that all of the values and coefficients will be slightly different because all those in one group or category will be treated as identical during the computations.

While it may take some time and effort to recode continuous survey variables in this way, it is usually well-worth it. The statistics for both describing the data and for measuring the relationships between items are much more complex and difficult to interpret for continuous variables than for categorical ones. Probably well over 90 percent of all survey data is reported with the use of frequency tables for description and crosstabs for measuring association with other items. These statistics and reports are readily understood, while those for continuous measures are often more obscure and less meaningful. Some information is "lost" when recoding continuous data into categories, but the loss is usually negligible, compared to the clarity and simplicity that is gained from the process.

EXAMPLE 11-1

Frequencies and Descriptive Statistics

Frequency and Percentage Table

Code	Freq.	Pct.	Adj.	Cum.
0.	20	5.0	5.0	5.0
1.	14	3.5	3.5	8.5
2.	19	4.7	4.7	13.2
3.	34	8.5	8.5	21.7
4.	33	8.2	8.2	30.0
5.	30	7.5	7.5	37.5
6.	39	9.7	9.7	47.2
7.	48	12.0	12.0	59.2
8.	51	12.7	12.7	72.0
9.	64	16.0	16.0	88.0
10.	48	12.0	12.0	100.0
Total	400	100.0	100.0	100.0

Descriptive Statistics

Mean	6.175	Median	6.729	Mode	9.000
Std. Dev.	2.930	Variance	8.586	Std. Err.	0.147
Sum	2.470	Kurtosis	− 0.811	Skewness	− 0.505
Minimum	0.000	Maximum	10.000	Range	10.000
95%	Confidence interval =		5.887	to	6.463

In Example 11–1, the lower portion of the example shows the same statistics as those shown in the previous chapter, in Example 10–2. The upper portion of Example 11–1 shows the frequency table of the distribution from which the statistics listed below were computed. If the distribution had conformed closely to a normal, bell-shaped curve, it would not have been necessary to show the distribution. The mean and the standard deviation would have indicated the approximate proportions of respondents along the scale continuum. In this case, however, the coefficients of skewness and of kurtosis indicate the distribution departed markedly from the normal curve. Thus, showing the distribution in a frequency table reveals very clearly the shape of the distribution. In addition, the percentages of respondents at each point on the scale are indicated in the adjusted percentage column. The column containing the cumulative percentage distribution also shows the proportion of respondents at each place on the scale continuum or below. An explanation of the averages, measures of spread, and of shape may be helpful for interpreting such continuous data.

Interpreting Central Tendency

The three most commonly used averages, the mean, the median, and the mode, were identified in the previous chapter. Often, all three are computed, leaving the researcher to decide which would be the "best"indicator of the most typical case. If the data were obtained from an ordinal scale, the median is usually preferable. If the data were derived from an interval or ratio scale, the choice depends on the *shape* of the distribution. If the coefficient of skewness is very near zero, indicating the distribution is symmetrical, the mean, median, and mode will all be the same value or nearly identical to one another, as shown in Figure 11–1. If the distribution is skewed to the left or the right, as shown in Figure 11–2, the mean, median, and mode depart from one another.

FIGURE 11–1

Averages for a Normal Distribution

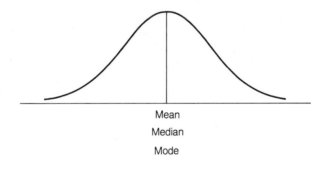

Mean
Median
Mode

Notice that in Figure 11–2, the mean is sensitive to extreme values on the high side, off to the right, for positive skewness. Similarly, the mean tends to be "pulled" toward the extreme values on the low side, toward the left, when the distribution is negatively skewed. This characteristic of the mean was discussed earlier, in the previous chapter, but it can be seen graphically here. This fact indicates the greater the amount of skewness in a distribution, the *less* appropriate the mean is likely to be as a measure of the most typical case.

The mode was described earlier as the only proper measure of the most typical case for categorical data, where the modal category is merely the one with the largest percentage of responses. For con-

FIGURE 11-2

Averages for Skewed Distributions

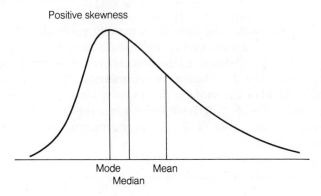

Positive skewness

Mode   Mean
Median

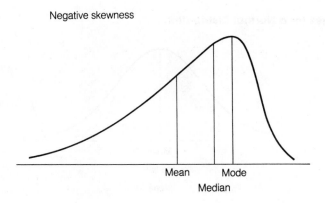

Negative skewness

Mean   Mode
Median

tinuous data, the mode is the "high point" in the distribution. If the value of the scale from which the data were obtained were listed along the horizontal axis of the plot in Figure 11-2, the mode would be the scale value where the distribution has reached its peak. Thus, it is often used as the best indicator of the most typical case when a distribution is highly skewed to one side or the other. The mode is an especially appropriate average to use if the distribution is both skewed to one side and also has a high peak, indicated by a positive value for the coefficient of kurtosis. This is because a large portion of the cases will be very close to the mode, to be discussed in the next section.

The median is the approximate value of the case that would be in the middle, if all cases were arrayed from low to high value on the variable. It is *not* the center point on the horizontal axis of the plot shown in Figure 11–2, because this is merely the midpoint of the scale. In the figure, the number of cases is represented by the *area* under the curve, rather than the horizontal distance on the scale. When the distribution is slightly skewed, when it is relatively flat so that the value or kurtosis is negative, or when it is near normal with only a few very extreme values far to one side, the median is the most appropriate average to indicate the most typical case. Note that the median is only influenced by the *number* of cases with higher values and with lower values, but it is *not* sensitive to *how much* the values are higher or lower.

GUIDELIST 11–1

For Choosing the Best Average

1. If the data is from an *ordinal* scale, the median should be used.

2. If the skewness is zero or very nearly so, the distribution is symmetrical and the mean, median, and mode will all be the same or nearly identical.

3. If the skewness is positive, the mode or peak will be to the left of center, the median greater, and the mean the highest.

4. If the skewness is negative, the mode will be to the right, toward the high side, the median will be a lower value and the mean, the lowest value.

5. If the distribution is nearly normal but there are a few *very* small or *very* large values, these are "outliers" and the median is the best indicator of the most typical case.

6. If the distribution is skewed and the kurtosis is zero or negative, indicating a flat curve, the median is the best average to show the most typical case.

7. If the distribution is skewed and the kurtosis has a high, positive value, the distribution has a high peak with many cases round the mode and it is the best average.

To check the affect of skewness on the relationship between the mean, the mode, and the median, the researcher might refer back to the descriptive statistics listed in Example 11–1. Note the coefficient of skewness has a negative value, indicating the peak of the curve leans toward the high side of the scale and the values tail off to the left. That can be verified by examining the frequency and percentage table just above it in the example. Low scale values have lower percentages of respondents than do the higher ones. Notice also that of the three averages listed in the descriptive statistics, the mean is the lowest, the median next, and the mode of nine is the largest value. The coefficient of kurtosis is negative, indicating the distribution is relatively flat, rather than normal or highly peaked. That, too, can be verified by noting in the frequency table that the mode of nine has only a slightly larger percentage of respondents in that category than do those around it. Thus, in this case, with a sharply skewed distribution and a fairly flat curve, the best choice of an average to show the most typical case is likely to be the median. If the coefficient of kurtosis had been a substantial, positive value, the modal category would probably contain a much higher proportion of cases than the other categories. In that case, a researcher might be better advised to use the mode as the average indicating the most likely or single, most typical case for the population.

Interpreting Spread of Distributions

When a distribution conforms closely to the standard, normal curve, a given proportion of the cases will always fall within certain ranges that are determined by the standard deviation (S.D.) of the distribution. About 68 percent of the cases will be within ±1 S.D. of the mean, 95 percent within ±2 S.D., and 99 percent within ±3 S.D., as shown in Figure 11–3.

Suppose the survey data for a certain variable is normally distrib-

FIGURE 11-3

Spread for a Normal Distribution

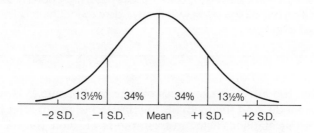

uted and there are 100 cases. If the mean value was computed to be 30 and the standard deviation was five, this would mean that 34 cases would have values between 25 and 30 and another 34 cases would have a value between 30 and 35, so 68 cases would be between 25 and 35. This is within one standard deviation above and below the mean. Similarly, 95 cases would be within two standard deviations of the mean, or have values between 20 and 40. Only about one case would have a value of less than 15 or more than 45, because about 99 would be within three standard deviations of the mean. In this way, the researcher can see the range and describe the spread of the distribution for the variable, simply by knowing the mean and standard deviation, *providing the "shape" of the distribution is approximately normal.*

FIGURE 11-4

Spread and Skewness of Distributions

Positive skewness

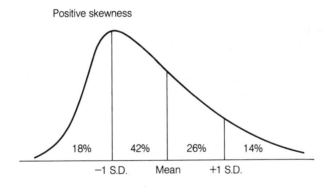

Negative skewness

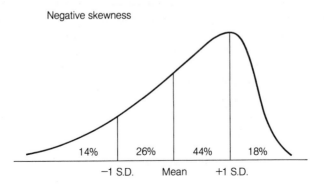

The standard deviation provides a close estimate of the proportion of cases within a given range around the mean *only* if the distribution is symmetrical. In Figure 11–4, the mean and the range from ±1 S.D. are shown in the diagram. The percentages are approximate, and they represent the *area* under the curve for each section, which corresponds to the *proportion* of cases within each range along the horizontal scale. Notice that when the coefficient of skewness is positive and the distribution is skewed sharply to the left, there will be many more cases within one standard deviation to the left of the mean than there will be within one standard deviation to the right of it. Conversely, when the coefficient of skewness is negative and the data are skewed sharply to the right, there will be fewer cases within one standard deviation to the left than there are to the right of the mean. Thus, the sign and the value of skewness indicates the degree of accuracy with which the standard deviation can be used to estimate the amount of spread in the distribution.

Nor can the standard deviation be used to show the range within which a given percentage of cases will fall if the coefficient of kurtosis departs markedly from zero in either a positive or negative direction, as shown in figure 11–5. If the value of kurtosis is positive, indicating a more peaked distribution than normal, a *larger* number of cases than 68 percent will fall within ±1 S.D. of the mean. On the other hand, if the distribution is flatter than normal, indicated by a kurtosis value that is negative, then fewer than two thirds of the cases will be within ±1 S.D. of the mean.

In summary, it is important to note that it is still possible to compute the standard deviation for a distribution, even though it may be skewed radically in one direction and even though it may be much more peaked or flat than a normal distribution. The point is simply that if either or both of these conditions are present, the standard deviation still indicates the degree of spread but *not* the proportion of data within a given range of standard deviations from the mean. If the distribution is not fairly symmetrical, and the data are skewed to one side, there will be more or less cases above the mean value than below it, depending on the direction in which the data are skewed. Similarly, if the distribution is much more peaked than a normal distribution, more than two thirds of the cases will be within one standard deviation from the mean value, and if it is much flatter than normal, less than 68 percent of the cases will fall within plus or minus one standard deviation from the mean. Thus, when using the standard deviation to gauge the proportion of cases that will be within some range around the mean, it is important for the researcher to check the skewness and kurtosis.

If the statistical analysis results in coefficients of skewness and kurtosis that are zero or very nearly so, the standard deviation can be

FIGURE 11-5

Spread and Kurtosis of Distributions

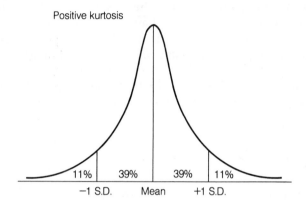

Positive kurtosis

11%	39%	39%	11%
−1 S.D.	Mean	+1 S.D.	

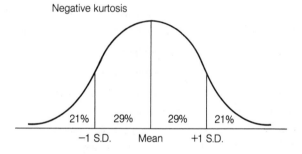

Negative kurtosis

21%	29%	29%	21%
−1 S.D.	Mean	+1 S.D.	

GUIDELIST 11-2

For Spread of Nonnormal Distributions

1. If either skewness or kurtosis depart significantly from zero, the distribution is not normal and S.D. will not indicate the proportion of data in a given range.

2. If the scale has only a few values, obtain a frequency table and use the percentages and cumulative percentages to show proportions within ranges and above and below points on the scale.

3. If the scale has a large number of values, recode it or a new variable identical to it into fewer, larger categories each of equal interval and obtain a frequency table.

used to indicate that about two thirds of the cases are within ±1 S.D. of the mean, about 95 percent within ±2 S.D., and over 99 percent within ±3 S.D. In addition, these proportions can be manipulated in other ways. For example, the normal curve is symmetrical, so half the cases will have a value less than the mean and half greater. Thus, about 84 percent of the cases will have a value of less than the point 1 S.D. *above* the mean, etc. This is merely the 50 percent below the mean plus the 34 percent within 1 S.D. above it. Similarly, 50 percent minus 34 percent, minus 17½ percent, or only 2½ percent of cases will have a value less than −2 S.D. from the mean, etc. These computations are based on the proportions shown in Guidelist 11–3.

GUIDELIST 11–3

For Using Standard Deviation with Normal Curves

1. About 34 percent of cases are between the mean and +1 S.D.

2. About 34 percent of cases are between the mean and −1 S.D.

3. About 68 percent of cases are within ±1 S.D. of the mean.

4. About 95 percent of cases are within ±2 S.D. of the mean.

5. About 99 percent of cases are within ±3 S.D. of the mean.

6. About 50 percent of cases will be above the mean.

7. About 50 percent of cases will be below the mean.

8. The percentage of cases above and below other points on the scale, defined by the standard deviation, can be determined by adding and subtracting these percentages.

When the statistical analysis indicates that a continuous distribution with a large number of scale values has a skewness and/or kurtosis value that departs significantly from zero, this indicates the data are *not* normally distributed. In that case, the researcher cannot determine the proportion of cases within a given range of scale values, expressed in terms of the standard deviation. It would be advisable to recode the item or create a "new" variable equal to the continuous variable, and then recode it into fewer, larger categories, each with an equal interval. For example, if a variable indicating the age of respondents had 60 or 70 values, they might be recoded into age decades; 20s, 30s, 40s, etc. The spread and shape of the distribution could then be examined with the use of a frequency table or bar chart and the cumulative percentages used to indicate the proportion of respondents (and by inference, the population) above or below a certain age.

Continuous, numeric survey data distributions are very often asymmetrical or skewed to one side. This is often due to what are sometimes called "ceiling" or "floor" effects. For example, there is a floor effect on such items as personal income, because nobody reports negative income and almost everyone has a few thousand dollars per year of income, while most report many thousands. On the high side, a few respondents may report income in the hundreds of thousands of dollars or more, so there is virtually no ceiling. This causes the distribution to be skewed positively, toward the left or low side of the distribution. In effect, the "floor" of zero cuts off the distribution on the left, but it can extend far toward the right extreme.

The same tendency in reverse occurs when there are ceiling effects on the scale for the variable or item. For example, suppose respondents were asked to indicate how many days per month, on the average, they drive their automobile for any purpose at all. Some may report only a few days, but many are likely to report they use the car every day. Since there is a maximum of 31 days per month, nobody could report more than that ceiling value, and the distribution would be negatively skewed toward the right or high side of the distribution. With such distributions, it is usually advisable to recode the data into fewer, larger categories and then show the distribution in a frequency table or portray it graphically.

The presence of such skewness, due to floor or ceiling effects, is often encountered with rating scales with only a few points or values as well. This is especially true when respondents' evaluations are sought concerning some topic or issue. The majority are likely to feel quite positive or quite negative, and move toward the extremes of the scale, while only a small minority may take an opposite or more moderate view. This, too, will yield an asymmetrical or skewed distribution. When there are only a few scale points, it is almost always advisable to use frequency tables or graphic presentations to show the entire distribution.

Ordinarily, a significant coefficient of skewness for a continuous, numeric distribution indicates that the mode leans toward one side or the other, but this is not always the case. Occasionally, the skewness will result from only a few, very extreme outliers. In other words, the vast majority of the cases will form a fairly normal distribution, but a very few cases will be far toward one extreme. These outliers are, of course, atypical of the majority because they are so extreme and they represent very few people in the population. Yet, the presence of their responses causes the skewness. This can be detected by comparing the maximum, minimum, and range for the distribution with the mean and standard deviation. These values are often reported by analysis routines, as shown in the lower section of Example 11–1. For example, the researcher might note that the maximum or the minimum is six or eight standard deviations away from the mean. That means simply that the range from the mean to the maximum or the minimum, as the case may be, is several times greater than the value of the standard deviation. In such cases, it is ordinarily advisable to determine how many such outliers there are in the data for the distribution. If there are only a few and they are far from the mean, with few if any data points between them and the main body of the distribution, the researcher may elect to eliminate those cases and again compute the descriptive statistics. This often results in a fairly normal distribution that is generally more representative and more readily interpreted. If such outlying cases are eliminated or recoded, it is, of course, necessary to note this in the report, so that those seeking the information understand the modification and the reason for it.

The Meaning of Bimodality. The distributions that have been shown in this and the previous chapter were all "unimodal" (one mode) distributions. This is not always the case. Sometimes a distribution will have two or more modes or peaks, such as those shown in Figure 11–6. For continuous, numerical data such as that shown in the upper section of the figure, the coefficient of kurtosis would be quite negative, indicating a very flat curve, because that is the way the computational routine would "see" the distribution. In fact, the distribution dips sharply downward in the middle and then rises to a second mode on the right. When the data are categorical, the bimodality can easily be observed on inspection.

A bimodal distribution usually indicates that there are two, fairly distinct "populations" or groups of respondents. If so, each group might provide a fairly normal distribution of response for the item, but when they are combined into one sample and the curves are, in effect, overlayed on one another, a bimodal distribution results. A bimodal distribution is a clue that some factor or characteristic serves to distinguish one group from the other. The important question is *what* characteristic? The content of the survey question or item may suggest what may separate the two groups, causing each to range around a different point on the scale. The researcher is well-advised to note any bimodal distributions that are detected, to examine the item or question generating the distribution, and perhaps to analyze the relationship between the variable and others in the survey, such as the demographic items. Often, such demographic characteristics will prove to be strongly related to items with bimodality. For exam-

FIGURE 11-6

Bimodal Distributions

Continuous distribution

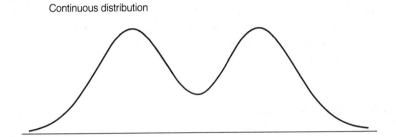

Categorical distribution

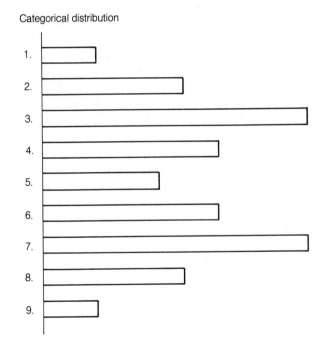

ple, a bimodal distribution of frequency of air travel may be strongly related to occupational groups, indicating higher frequencies for business travelers and lower frequency of travel by those in occupations that do not require it. This may be of major importance to those seeking the information because the average amount of travel for the whole sample would not be typical of *either* group, but the average for each separate population might be highly typical. Similarly, men and women often respond in systematically different ways, as do married and unmarried respondents, those with children in the family and those without, those who are and those who are not employed outside the home, those with college degrees and those with less education, or those in blue-collar and those in white-collar jobs. There may be no way to explain bimodality based on the survey results, but more often it can be.

STATISTICAL INFERENCE

Ordinarily, a researcher is not really interested merely in the results obtained from a sample. For nearly all surveys, the researcher wants to "estimate" the parameters of the population, based on the statistics obtained from a sample. This process of making inferences about the population from sample statistics is called "statistical inference." It must be based on a *random* sample, or at least close approximation to random selection. With a random sample, the respondents to be included in the sample are randomly selected and each individual's probability of being picked is exactly equal to that for any other person. This discussion of statistical inference and reliability is based on random sampling.

Suppose a researcher wants to learn the average age of those in a particular population, such as those living in a well-defined geographical area. A sample of some portion of the people within the area might be surveyed to learn the age of each, and the average age of the people in the sample could be computed. If the sample were selected at random from among all those in the population, the average age for the sample would be an unbiased estimate of the average age of all the people in the area. The average age of the population would be *inferred* from the sample. If, on the other hand, the sample were picked only from among those living in the part of the area closest to the survey headquarters, that would not be a random sample and the sample results would not be representative of the entire population. It would be a biased estimate of the population, and no legitimate inferences could be made about the population as a whole. Thus, statistical inference is based on random sampling, but the more the sample design deviates from random selection, the less legitimate any such inferences about the whole population would be.

Standard Error of the Estimate.   The fact that no sample is likely to be perfectly representative of the entire population was noted earlier. In other words, no sample survey data is perfectly reliable. In the example above, the average age of the people in the sample is likely to be slightly different than the actual average age of everybody in the population. Those who seek survey data would often like to know just how "good" the estimate really is. In other words, they want to know about the reliability of the estimate. Most statistical analysis routines can compute and report the *standard error of the estimate,* usually called simply the standard error or abbreviated as S.E. The standard error is actually the standard deviation of a "would be" distribution of the mean values computed from many different samples of exactly the same size from precisely the same population. Such a distribution is usually a normal curve or very nearly so. Consequently, the standard error indicates how far off any one sample mean might be from the population mean at a given level of probability. Thus, there is a 68 percent chance the population mean will be within one standard error, a 95 percent chance it will be within two standard errors, and a 99 percent probability it will be within three standard errors. (The researcher may recognize these probability levels as the "cases" within the ranges of one, two, and three standard deviations from the mean of a normal curve.)

The standard error of the estimate is *directly* related to the variation in the population. In other words, the more the respondents tend to differ from one another or vary in their response to the item, the higher the standard error will be. The standard error is *inversely* related to sample size. The larger the sample, the more representative of the entire population it is likely to be. Thus, the mean from a large sample is less likely to be different from that for the whole population than the mean from a small sample.

Confidence Interval.   The confidence interval is a range around the sample mean based on the standard error. Thus, the 68 percent confidence interval is the range from -1 S.E. below the mean to $+1$ S.E. above the mean. Similarly, the 95 percent confidence interval is the range within ± 2 S.E., and the 99 percent confidence interval is the range within ± 3 S.E. Notice that the descriptive statistics listed in the lower portion of Example 11–1 lists a mean of 6.175, a standard error of 0.147 and the 95 percent confidence interval from 5.887 to 6.463. In this case, the analysis routine computed the confidence interval by subtracting two times the value of S.E. from the mean for the lower value and by adding two times the value of S.E. to the mean for the higher value. When only the standard error is computed and reported, the researcher can quickly compute the confidence interval in the same way.

To interpret the confidence interval to sponsors, the researcher need only indicate that there is a 68 percent chance, a 95 percent chance, or a 99 percent chance that the mean for the whole population is within that range, depending on whether ±1 S.E., ±2 S.E., or ±3 S.E. is used to compute the confidence interval. Actually, all three confidence intervals might be reported for key variables. Reporting the confidence interval around a mean value provides those seeking the survey information with a sense of the reliability of the estimate and the confidence they may have when making inferences about the whole population.

GUIDELIST 11–4

For Interpreting Confidence Intervals

1. Confidence intervals are based on the *standard error of the estimate*, often called S.E.

2. Confidence intervals apply only to continuous, numerical variables.

3. A confidence interval is always based on a given level or probability, usually 95 percent or 99 percent.

4. The 68 percent confidence interval is the range from −1 S.E. below the mean to +1 S.E. above the mean.

5. The 95 percent confidence interval is the range from −2 S.E. below the mean to +2 S.E. above the mean.

6. The 99 percent confidence interval is the range from −3 S.E. below the mean to +3 S.E. above the mean.

7. Confidence intervals are used to indicate the probability that the actual *population* mean is within a given range around the sample mean.

8. The standard error and the range of the confidence intervals are measures of reliability.

9. The larger the sample, the greater the reliability and the smaller the standard error and confidence intervals.

It is important to note here that the standard error of the estimate and the confidence intervals computed from it can be used for *both* normal distributions, as well as those that depart from normality. In other words, the distribution need not have a skewness and kurtosis value of near zero for the standard error to be used validly. There is no equivalent to S.E. for categorical data. That is why it may be desirable to retain the continuous form of a numeric variable, creating a new, identical one to be recoded when it is necessary to inspect shape and spread because of skewness or kurtosis.

MEASURES OF ASSOCIATION

The statistics discussed earlier in this chapter provide a description of individual variables. When the researcher studies the relationships between variables, other statistics are required and these, too, must be interpreted so that their meaning can be conveyed to those seeking the information. The previous chapter identified the statistical procedures used to measure relationships between pairs of variables. The objective here is to identify the most relevant statistical values and coefficients that are generated by those procedures and to explain their meaning and interpretation.

Virtually all of the measures of relationships between variables are designed not only to show the *degree* of association between them, but also to report the *statistical significance* of the relationship. The word, "significance," has a very special and consistent meaning when used in this context. It does not mean importance! If a relationship between two variables is statistically significant, this simply means that it *signifies* or signals that the variables are quite likely to actually be related to one another in the population. Thus, significance is required in order to make a statistical *inference* about the population, based on the sample. An example may clarify the meaning and interpretation of statistical significance.

Suppose a survey were conducted to measure the age of respondents as well as their sex. The sponsor may want to know if the men in the *population* tend to be older, the same age, or younger than the women surveyed. Thus, the researcher will need to assess the *relationship* between two variables: age and sex of respondents. The age of the men could be compared to that of women by computing the average age of those of each sex. Suppose the average age of all respondents proved to be 40 and that half of the respondents were of each sex. The men may have an average age of 41 and the women an average age of 39. At first glance, it may then appear that the men in the population are about two years older than the women. That may or may *not* be true.

The earlier discussion of reliability and confidence intervals noted that the values computed from a sample are not likely to be precisely accurate estimate of the values for the entire population. The same holds true for the values computed for subsamples, such as men or women respondents. Thus, the average age of 41 for men is only an estimate of the age of all of the men, and the same holds true for the average age of women. Put differently, there is always some chance that the sample "happened," purely by chance, to include a group of men who were somewhat older than the actual average age for all men in the population. There is also some chance that the sample contained a disproportionate number of younger women from the population, also purely by chance. Because of this possibility, there is some chance that the average age of men and of women in the population as a whole is exactly the same; 40 years of age. Yet the sample seemed to indicate that men were older. The researcher needs a way to determine the *probability* that the sample would produce such differences between men and women, if, in fact, the average age of all men in the population were the same as that for all women. Fortunately, there is a way to determine that probability. If it is sufficiently small, the differences in age would be said to be "statistically significant." If the probability of obtaining such differences in the sample, even when they did not exist in the population, were too large, the differences in the sample values would *not* be treated as significant. In other words, they would not "signify" or signal a difference in the population. They would be attributed only to sampling error, rather than to actual differences between the two groups in the whole population.

It is important to note here that significance is related to the importance of a relationship between variables, but the two are not the same thing. In technical terms, significance is *necessary*, but not *sufficient* for importance. That simply means that if a relationship or difference is not statistically significant, it cannot be regarded as important. On the other hand, simply because it is significant does not imply that it will necessarily prove important. In the example above, if the differences between the average age of men and of women were not significant, the difference would be attributed to sampling error and it would not make good sense to treat the two groups in the population as though they were different in that respect. On the other hand, differences may prove to be significant, indicating that the two groups in the population are very likely to differ from one another, yet the two year difference may not be of much importance to the sponsor. Statistical significance depends on computation. It is a function of the size of the sample and subsamples or groups, the actual differences that exist in the population, and the value of the probability below which the results will be viewed as significant. The importance of a relationship depends on the meaning of the variables and relationships to the sponsor. It depends on the actions that are implied or the consequences.

Statistical significance is always interpreted in this way, regardless of the statistical measure of association on which it is based. For example, the significance of a relationship measured with cross-tabulation has exactly the same meaning and should be interpreted in precisely the same way as the significance of a relationship measured by correlation, regression, analysis of variance, or discriminant analysis. Significance is determined by *the probability that such a relation-*

ship would exist in the sample if, in fact, there were no such relationship in the population as a whole.

The researcher and/or the sponsors must decide what relationships will be regarded as significant, based on probability that the sample would show such a relationship even if it did not exist in the whole population. (In technical terms, they must decide on the *alpha* level.) Often, if there is less than one chance in 20 that the sample would show a relationship between variables when it did not exist in the population, the relationship will be regarded as significant. It would then be significant at the .05 level of probability. Thus, any statistical measure of a relationship that resulted in a probability of .05 or less would be viewed as significant. If so, the assumption is merely that this particular sample is *not* the one in 20, and so the inference is that the two variables are actually related in the population. When it would be costly to make a mistake by viewing a relationship as significant if it did not actually exist in the population, the researcher or sponsor may want to be more sure. In that case, a *smaller* probability would be required before a relationship was seen as significant. Often, one chance in 100, or the .01 level of significance is used in that case, and sometimes when it is necessary to be extremely sure the relationship exists in the population, the .001 level, or one chance in 1,000, is used. Again, these probabilities simply mean that there is only one chance in 100 or one chance in 1,000 that such a relationship would exist in the sample data if, in fact, it did not exist in the population. Again, the assumption is that this is *not* that one time, and therefore, the two items are systematically related in the population as a whole.

GUIDELIST 11–5

For Assessing Statistical Significance

1. Significance is determined by the probability that a sample would show such a relationship if it did *not* exist in the population as a whole.

2. If a relationship between variables is regarded as significant, it is taken by *inference* to exist in the population as a whole.

3. A relationship *cannot* be viewed as important if it is not significant, because there is too great a chance it resulted only from sampling error.

4. A relationship that is statistically significant *may* or *may not* be important, because importance depends on the strength and meaning of the relationship.

5. The researcher or sponsor must determine the *critical value* of proba-

GUIDELIST 11–5 (concluded)

bility below which the relationship will be viewed as significant and above which it will be attributed only to sampling error.

6. If the probability or significance value generated by an analysis routine is .05, this means there is only a 5 percent chance of such a relationship in the sample if it did *not* actually exist in the population.

7. If the probability or significance value is not reported by the analysis routine, the researcher must refer to statistical reference tables to determine if the probability is above or below the critical value, .05, .01, or .001, because these are the values most often listed in tables.

Note that significance is related to statistical inference and the computation of these probabilities assumes a *random sample*. To the degree that the sampling design deviates from random, such interpretations will be invalid and are likely to be in error.

Interpreting Cross-Tabulation

Assessment of the relationship between two categorical variables is accomplished with the use of crosstabs, such as those shown in Example 11–2. It does not matter which variable is regarded as dependent and which as independent, or even if causality is assumed, for the use of this method. It is important to note that when ordinal, interval, or ratio scales have only a limited number of scale points, they, too, can be cross-tabulated with other similar items or with nominal scale variables. The researcher must be careful to check the minimum expected cell frequency in each such table, as instructed in the previous chapter, to be sure that the interpretation of significance is valid.

The statistic to assess significance is the chi-square value. The more the two variables are related to one another, the larger the chi-square value will be. If the analysis routine does not show the probability or significance value, the researcher must check the value of chi-square for the cross-tabulation in a statistical reference table for the chi-square distribution. To check such tables, the researcher must also know the number of *degrees of freedom*, abbreviated simply as d.f. If the d.f. value is not reported by the analysis routine, it can be computed very easily. The value of d.f. is merely the number of rows in the table minus one, times the number of columns in the table, minus one. In the example, there are three rows and three columns, and the d.f. value is three minus one, or two, times three minus one, or two, for a d.f. value of four. If the value of chi-square for the crosstab is *greater* than the value printed in the reference table for the appropriate num-

EXAMPLE 11–2

Cross-Tabulation Tables

Crosstab of: Time of Day Type by Age Group

Number Col Pct		Under 35 1.	35 to 49 2.	Over 49 3.	Row Total
Larks	1.	69	17	34	120
		44.5	20.0	21.2	30.0
Wrens	2.	42	26	49	117
		27.1	30.6	30.6	29.2
Owls	3.	44	42	77	163
		28.4	49.4	48.1	42.4
Column Total		155 38.7	85 21.2	160 40.0	400 100.0

Chi-square = 27.72   d.f. = 4   Prob. = 0.0000

Number Row Pct		Under 35 1.	35 to 49 2.	Over 49 3.	Row Total
Larks	1.	69	17	34	120
		57.5	14.2	28.3	30.0
Wrens	2.	42	26	49	117
		35.9	22.2	41.9	29.2
Owls	3.	44	42	77	163
		27.0	25.8	47.2	42.4
Column Total		155 38.7	85 21.2	160 40.0	400 100.0

Chi-square = 27.72   d.f. = 4   Prob. = 0.0000

ber of degrees of freedom and at a given probability level, such as .05, then the actual probability is *less* than .05 and the relationship would be regarded as statistically significant.

Notice that in the Example 11–2, the probability of the chi-square value is listed as zero. Actually, there is always *some* probability that the relationship is due merely to sampling error, but in the example the analysis routine printed only four significant digits beyond the

---

GUIDELIST 11–6

For Interpreting Crosstabs

1. Check the minimum expected cell frequency as described in the previous chapter to be sure it is five or greater.

2. If *degrees of freedom* and *probability* are not listed, compute d.f. by multiplying number of rows minus one, times number of columns, minus one.

3. In a statistical reference table for the chi-square distribution, look up the value listed for the correct value of d.f.

4. Tables usually list values for only the .05 and the .01, and sometimes for the .001 level of probability.

5. If the chi-square value *from the crosstab* is *larger* than the value in the table, the probability is *smaller* than the probability level listed, and the relationship is *significant.*

6. If the relationship is *not* significant, explain that the variables are probably not related in the population.

7. If the relationship *is* significant, inform sponsors that in the population as a whole, distributions across the rows are likely to differ systematically from column to column, or vice versa.

8. It is usually best to use column percentages consistently, and it does not matter which variable is listed on the rows and which on the columns when doing the computations, so arrange the table the way it can be most easily read and interpreted.

---

decimal point and the probability is so small it registers as zero. This means that there is only an *extremely* small chance that the differences in the distributions by row or by column would result from sampling error if no differences existed in the population as a whole. In other words, the age groups are significantly related to the time of day types. Of course, the researcher would assume in this case that the age of respondents tends to *cause* them to assume a certain time of day preference, rather than the other way around.

In Example 11–2, the column percentages are listed in the table in the upper section and the row percentages are used in the lower section. If the researcher were most interested in assessing how people in different age groups differ in their time of day preferences, the column percentages would be compared across rows in a table such as that in the upper section. Thus, over twice the percentage of young people are "Larks" as are the others, etc. If, on the other hand, the researcher wished to assess how people of different time of day types differ in age, the row percentages would be compared down the columns. For example, only about 28 percent of "Larks" were 50 or older, while nearly 42 percent of "Wrens" and about 47 percent of "Owls" were in the elder group. Note that it would also have been possible to reverse the bottom table so that the time of day patterns were over the rows and the age groups on the columns. The researcher would then have listed column percentages in the table and used them to make the second type of assessment described above. It is usually best to use column percentages consistently and arrange the tables to facilitate the kind of comparison desired.

Interpreting Analysis of Variance

When one variable is assumed to be causing or affecting another and the dependent variable is continuous while the independent variable is categorical, analysis of variance (ANOVA) is the statistical technique for measuring the relationship. In Example 11–3, the dependent variable is listed as test scores and they are a continuous, numeric distribution. The independent variable is categorical, consisting of two groups: married and not married. ANOVA would also be used if there were more than two groups. The object of the analysis is to determine if the *mean* values of the dependent variable (test scores) differs significantly between or among the groups. The mean, standard deviation, variance, and number of cases for each group and for the whole sample are listed in the upper portion of the Example 11–3. Married respondents in the sample have an average score that is higher than the average for those not married. The researcher must know if this difference is likely to be due merely to sampling error;

EXAMPLE 11–3

Analysis of Variance Tables

Dep. Var. =	Test Scores	Groups =	Marital Status	
Group	Mean	S.D.	Var.	N
Married	6.67	2.75	7.56	215
Not married	5.60	3.03	9.21	185
Combined	6.18	2.93	8.59	400

Source	S.S.	d.f.	M.S.	F	Prob.
Between groups	113.80	1	113.80	13.68.	.0002
Within groups	3311.95	398	8.32		
Total	3425.75	399			

---

and if there is a very small probability of that, the researcher can assume those in the population also differ in this direction and intensity.

In the lower portion of Example 11–3, the "S.S." stands for *sum of squares*, and these are merely the squared distances from each data point to some mean value, either for the group or for the whole sample. The d.f. value is also printed, and it is the number of groups minus one for the "numerator" and the number of cases minus two for the "denominator." The "M.S." stands for *mean squares*, and this is simply S.S. divided by d.f. The value of F is also listed, and it is merely the *ratio* of the numerator, M.S. between over the denominator, M.S. within so it is called an F-ratio. The researcher is primarily interested only in the probability, but if it is not computed and listed, the F-ratio value and two d.f. values will be needed.

GUIDELIST 11–7

For Interpreting Analysis of Variance

1. The object is to compute the mean value of the dependent variable for each category of the independent variable and determine if the means for the groups in the analysis are significantly different.

2. If the probability is computed by the analysis routine, it is the probability that as much difference in means would be due merely to sampling error if, in fact, the groups had the same means in the population.

3. The *larger* the F-ratio value, the *smaller* the probability and the *greater* the likelihood of significance. The *smaller* the F-ratio, the less likely the relationship will be significant at a given probability.

4. If the probability is not reported by the analysis routine, significance is judged by comparing the value of the F-ratio with the value in a statistical reference table for the F-distribution.

5. Such tables have rows and columns for various numerator and denominator d.f., and if the value listed there is *smaller* than the F-ratio value from the analysis of variance, this indicates significance.

The probability of .0002, means there is only two chances in 1,000 that this much difference in mean scores between groups would result purely from sampling error. If the analysis routine reports only the F value and does not list the actual probability, the researcher must check a statistical reference table for the F-distribution, at the appropriate level of probability, such as .05 or .01. Usually the researcher must read down the column indicated by the numerator d.f. and across the row indicated by the denominator d.f. If the value listed there in the table is *smaller* than the F-ratio computed in the analysis of variance, the differences in means is significant. If the value in the table is *larger* than the F-ratio from the analysis, the relationship is not significant at the given level of probability. In other words, the *larger* the F-ratio, the *more* likely the differences in means between groups will be statistically significant.

Interpreting a Paired T-Test

There are times when the researcher may want to check the significance of differences between two continuous variables that were both provided by the same respondents. For example, it may be necessary to determine if the mean rating of one topic is significantly different from the mean rating of another, when the same respondents have rated both items on the questionnaire. In that case, the comparisons are "within each case." There are a pair of variables for each respondent, and a paired t-test would be used. The report from such a measure is shown in Example 11–4. The two items are the time of day when respondents would ideally like to rise each morning and the times they actually do so. The objective is to determine if the mean difference between what they would like and what they do is statistically significant or due merely to sampling error. In Example 11–4, the probability is listed as zero, which means that it is actually extremely small and the difference of about − .42 hours, or about 25 minutes, is statistically significant. If the probability were not listed, the researcher would refer to a statistical reference table for the t-distribution and check the value there for the desired level of probability, such as .05 or .01, and for the correct value of d.f., which is the number of cases minus one. The plus or minus sign on the t-value

---

EXAMPLE 11–4

Paired T-Test Printout

Comparison of:	(A)	Actual wake time	with	(B)	Ideal wake time	
(A) Mean	6.78	Std. Dev.	1.316	Std. Err.	0.066
(B) Mean	7.20	Std. Dev.	1.431	Std. Err.	0.072
Dif. Mean	− .42	Std. Dev.	1.059	N of cases	400
T value	− 7.93	d.f.	399	Prob.	0.000

---

indicates which mean is greater. If the *absolute* value of t, ignoring the plus or minus, is *larger* than the value listed in the reference table, the difference between the means is statistically significant.

In Example 11–4, the standard deviations and standard errors of the estimate for each group were listed by the analysis routine. Accept for academic research, ordinarily only the mean values for each variable, the difference, and the significance are of principal interest to the researcher.

GUIDELIST 11–8

For Interpreting a Paired T-Test

1. The objective is to measure the statistical significance of the difference between two means when the variables are "paired" because the same respondents provided both.

2. The probability of as much difference (in either direction) purely by sampling error if those in the population did *not* differ on the two items is based on the t-value.

3. If the probability is not listed, the researcher must refer to a statistical reference table for the t-distribution, using the value of d.f., the number of cases minus one.

4. If the *absolute* value of t, ignoring the plus or minus sign, is *larger* than that listed in the table, the difference is significant at the given level of probability.

5. Only the two means and difference are of major interest.

Interpreting Correlation

Correlation measures the degree, direction, and significance of relationships between two continuous, numeric variables *without* assumption that one is dependent and one independent. Product-moment correlation is used for interval or ratio scale data and rank correlation analysis is appropriate for ordinal scale data. Both are interpreted in the same way. Example 11–5 shows the correlation coefficients for each pair of five variables. When all of the two-way relationships among a group of variables are to be analyzed, many statistical analysis routines report the results in this matrix form. In this example, the probability for assessing significance is printed just below the correlation coefficient. Some routines also report the number of cases for each correlation as well. Notice tht only the upper, right half of the matrix is printed, but some routines print only the lower, left half while others print the full matrix. The two sides of the matrix are identical because no causality is implied, and the correlation of variable one with variable two is precisely the same thing as the correlation of variable two with variable one. In Example 11–5, each variable is "perfectly" correlated with itself so a correlation coefficient of 1.000 is listed. Some routines merely leave the diagonal cells of the matrix blank or do not include it in the matrix.

EXAMPLE 11–5

A Correlation Matrix

	Var. 1	Var. 2	Var. 3	Var. 4	Var. 5
Var. 1	1.000	.303	.011	.164	.094
	—	.001	.402	.001	.018
Var. 2		1.000	− .098	.479	.083
		—	.014	.001	.032
Var. 3			1.000	− .193	.425
			—	.001	.001
Var. 4				1.000	.010
				—	.408
Var .5					1.000
					—

N = 500 for every pair

The researcher will recall from the previous chapter that the correlation coefficient ranges from zero to plus or minus 1, where zero indicates no relationship and plus or minus one indicates a perfect relationship. The plus or minus sign indicates whether the relationship between the variables is *direct,* moving in the same direction from case to case, or *inverse,* moving in opposite directions, respectively.

In Example 11–5, the strongest relationship is between variables two and four. About 23 percent of the variance in the two variables is "shared," because the coefficient of *determination* or proportion of shared variance is the *square* of the correlation coefficient. Most relationships are positive, but two are negative or inverse. It is important to note that a significant relationship does *not* imply that one variable is *causing* the other. If two variables, A and B, are correlated with one other, this only shows they are systematically related. A may cause B, B may cause A, A and B may be interacting, or another variable, C may cause both A and B.

GUIDELIST 11-9

For Interpreting Correlations

1. The object is to measure the direction, degree, and statistical significance of relationships between two continuous variables when no causality is implied.

2. Product-moment correlation analysis is used for interval and ratio scale data, and rank correlation analysis is used for ordinal data.

3. The correlation coefficient ranges from zero, indicating no relationship, to plus or minus one, indicating a perfect, linear (lockstep) relationship.

4. The plus or minus sign on the correlation coefficient shows whether the variables are directly or inversely related (moving in the same or different directions).

5. The probability for assessing significance is the chance that such a relationship would result purely by sampling error if the variables were not related in the population.

6. If the probability for assessing significance is not listed, the researcher must refer to a statistical reference table for significance of correlation coefficients.

7. If the absolute value of the correlation coefficient, ignoring the plus or minus sign, is *larger* than that listed in the reference table, the relationship is significant.

8. Correlation does *not* imply that one variable is causing the other, because A may cause B, B may cause A, A and B may interact, or C may cause A and B.

The probability listed indicates the chance that a relationship of this strength would result purely from sampling error if the two variables were not related in the population. If it is not listed by the analysis routine, the researcher must check a statistical reference table for significance of correlation coefficients, using the number of cases to indicate the proper row or column of the table. If the absolute value of the correlation coefficient, ignoring the plus or minus sign, is *larger* than that listed in the reference table, it is significant at the given level of probability.

Interpreting Regression Analysis

Linear regression analysis is used to measure the effect of one continuous variable on another, so one must be regarded as the independent variable and the other, the dependent variable. Both variables must be from either interval or ratio scales. The other conditions and assumptions required for the legitimate use of regression analysis are discussed in the previous chapter. Example 11–6 shows a typical report of a regression computed by a statistical analysis routine.

EXAMPLE 11–6

Regression Analysis Printout

Regression of: Actual time (Y) on Estimated time (X)

R-Squared	.62892	N of cases	400	Missing values	0
Correlation (R)	.79304	Std. Err. of Est.	1.06966	Significance R	.00001
Intercept (A)	2.26852	Std. Err. of A	.54467	Significance A	.00002
Slope (B)	.87842	Std. Err. of B	.03382	Significance B	.00001

The first line of the report simply identifies the variables in the analysis. The X and Y show which is dependent and which independent. When a regression is plotted, the dependent item is shown on the vertical or Y axis and the independent variable on the horizontal or X axis, by convention. The second line of the report indicates the r-square value, which is analogous to the coefficient of determination for correlation analysis. In other words, it is the *percentage of variance* in the dependent variable that is *explained* by the independent variable. In effect, this coefficient indicates how well the dependent variable could be predicted, if it were not known, with knowledge of the value of the independent variable. An example, based on Figure 11–7 may clarify the use of r-square.

Suppose the researcher wanted to predict the value of the dependent variable for a given case picked at random from the same population that was sampled for the survey, when nothing is known about the new case. The "best" prediction would then be the *mean* for that variable, computed from the sample data. The mean is shown by the horizontal line through the data plots in Figure 11–7. Inspection of the plot in the upper portion of the figure indicates that the researcher could make a much better "guess" or prediction about the value of the dependent variable, if the value of the independent variable was known. That is, if the value of the independent variable was low, toward the right, the value of the dependent variable would be predicted to be low as well, because the relationship is a *direct* one.

FIGURE 11-7

The Strength of Regression Relationships

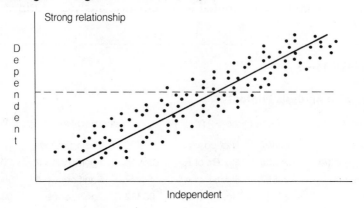

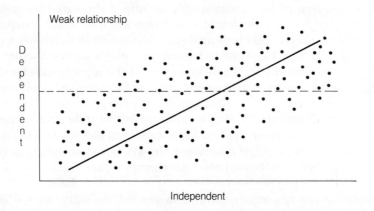

The term, "variance," simply means the distance from each point to some line, squared, and then added up for all data points. So, the variance around the mean value of the dependent variable will be fairly large. Some points are quite close to the horizontal line showing the mean, but those on the far left and the far right are fairly distant from the mean. It is also possible to compute the variance around the sloping regression line. It is merely the horizontal distance in scale values from each data point to the regression line, squared and then added up for all data points. Obviously, this variance around the regression line will be smaller than the variance around the mean, because the data points are much closer to the regression line than to the line of the mean.

With regression analysis, the difference between the variance around the mean and the variance around the regression line is the amount of variance that is "explained" by knowing the value of the independent variable. Notice that in Example 11–6, the r-square value is about .63, and this means that the variance around the mean for the dependent variable in that analysis was *reduced* by about 63 percent by calculating it around the regression line, instead. In other words, about 63 percent of the variance (around the mean) in the dependent variable was *explained* by the regression.

Turning to the plot in the lower section of Figure 11–7, the data points are much further from the regression line than they are above in the figure. Thus it appears that the variance around the regression line in the lower plot would be less than the variance around the mean, but not much less. In other words, when the relationship is weaker, less variance around the mean is *explained* by the regression. When the relationship is strong, the researcher could predict the dependent variable value of the dependent variable by knowing the value of the independent variable much better than if only the mean were known. When the relationship is weak, the prediction based on the independent variable would be only slightly better than if only the mean were known. Thus, if the relationship were perfect, the r-square value would be one, and the prediction would be perfectly accurate. If the value of the independent variable were known, the dependent variable could be predicted exactly. If there were no relationship between the two variables, the r-square value would be zero, and the mean of the dependent variable would be the predicted value for an unknown case. It would not help at all to know the value of the independent variable. Thus, the size of r-square indicates both the strength of the relationship and also how well the regression equation could be used to predict the value of the dependent variable for new cases if the value of the independent variable were known.

Returning now to Example 11–6, the third line of the report shows the correlation coefficient. This is merely the correlation between the two variables. The standard error of the estimate on that line is *not* the S.E. for making inferences about the mean, as it was described earlier in this chapter, but it is interpreted in a similar way. The S.E. for regression is used to compute *confidence intervals* around the regression line, rather than around the mean. Thus, 68 percent of the time, the *predicted* data points for new cases would prove to be within ±1 S.E. of the regression line, 95 precent of the time they will be within ±2 S.E., and 99 percent of the time they will be within ±3 S.E. The standard error here is used the same way for the distribution around the regression line as it was earlier for the distribution around the mean.

The probability for assessing significance for the regression is listed in Example 11–6. If it were not, the researcher could determine statistical significance with reference to a statistical table of values in exactly the same way that the significance of any other correlation coefficient is assessed.

The last two lines of the report in Example 11–6 list the value of the "Intercept" and the "Slope." The intercept is the value of the dependent variable when the dependent variable is zero. In Figure 11–7, it would be the place on the vertical scale of the dependent variable where the regression line crossed or *intercepted* the scale where the horizontal scale for the independent variable was zero. Thus, it is called an intercept, and it is sometimes called a constant because the same value is always added in the regression equation when a prediction is to be made. The slope value is the number of units of the dependent variable that are added for each unit of the independent variable. It is often referred to as "the rise over the run," since it is the number of units the line rises on the vertical scale for each unit the line runs from left to right on the horizontal scale. The actual slope in degrees on a scatterplot or graph depends, of course, on the scale values used for the graph. The value of the slope will be high if the dependent variable increases very rapidly with each "step" or unit of the independent variable. If the slope has a positive value, the line would slope upward and the variables would be *directly* related. If the slope has a negative value, the regression line would slope downward to the right and the variables would have an *inverse* relationship to one another; as one increased, the other would decrease.

The Regression Equation. The intercept is sometimes called the "constant" in a regression equation to predict new cases, and the slope is usually called the "regression coefficient." These are the two terms that are used for prediction. By convention, the dependent variable is called Y, the independent variable X, the intercept A, and the slope or regression coefficient B. To compute a predicted value for the dependent variable, the researcher would use the equation: $Y = A + (B \times X)$, where the multiplication within the parentheses would be done first, and then the constant added. Thus, in the example, if the researcher wanted to predict the actual time that would be required for a new case, given the estimated time of 10 hours, the computation would be: $0.878 \times 10 = 8.78 + 2.27 = 11.05$ hours. This says, in effect, that a job estimated to take 10 hours is quite likely to actually require a little more than 11 hours.

Notice that *both* the intercept and the slope have an influence on the prediction. The intercept seems to indicate here that all jobs (a constant) are estimated to take about 2¼ hours less than they actually do. The slope suggests that once into the job, the work actually takes only about 88 percent as many hours as the estimate. So, for a small 10 hour job such as that used in the example above, the time will be *under* estimated. Notice the result if the job is much larger, such as an estimate of 100 hours: $0.8784 \times 100 = 87.84 + 2.27 = 90.11$, so the estimate was about 10 percent *over* the time required.

The regression equation can be interpreted and used in two ways: (1) to compute estimates of one variable when only the value of the other is known and (2) to obtain some insight or understanding of the relationship between the variables. In the example used here, the researcher or sponsor may actually use the equation to "adjust" time estimates in order to make better predictions of time requirements and plan more effectively. They may also learn about the persistent and systematic errors in the time estimation process and advise those making the estimates, so that they could be made more accurately. The purpose to which the information is put depends on the needs and requirements of the researcher and sponsor.

The relationship between the dependent and independent variable is seldom perfect. There are many random factors or other variables that might affect the value of the dependent variable besides the one independent variable used in the computations. Given that these are, in fact, *random* factors, a standard error value can be computed for the intercept and for the slope of the regression line in much the same manner as that for the mean. The S.E. for the intercept and slope are used in the same way as before. In other words, there is a 68 percent chance that the actual value of the constant or the coefficient for the whole population will be within ± 1 S.E. of the value listed, a 95 percent probability of within ± 2 S.E., and a 99 percent chance of within ± 3 S.E. If the probability for assessing the significance of the intercept and slope are not listed by the analysis program, their significance can be assessed by referring to statistical reference tables for the T-distribution, using the d.f. values reported by the analysis routine and the desired level of probability.

The interpretation of regression has been discussed in some detail here because survey sponsors would often like to obtain a regression equation to gain insight into a relationship or actually to make predictions. While the descriptions may seem rather extensive, compared to that of the other techniques, it is only a very brief sketch. There are, in fact, many other important considerations concerning the appropriate use of regression analysis and prediction with the use of regression equations. For example, considerations of the *range* within which predictions are to be made must always govern the use of a regression equation. These topics are well beyond the scope of the handbook, but researchers and sponsors should be cautioned to refer to the appropriate reference materials where needed, to be sure that the regression technique is being used properly and the resulting regression equation will yield sufficiently accurate results. It is also important to note that only bivariate regression was described here. Multiple regression includes more than one independent variable, and while it is much more complex, it can also be much more powerful.

GUIDELIST 11–10

For Interpreting Regression Analysis

1. Regression is used to determine the degree, direction, and significance of one variable's affect on another *and* to obtain an equation to predict values of the dependent variable based on the values of the independent variable.

2. The r-square value ranges from zero to one and indicates the proportion of variance in the dependent variable that is *explained* by the values of the independent variable.

3. The assessment of significance is determined by the value of r, the correlation coefficient, and significance is checked in the same way as for correlation analysis.

4. The regression equation consists of a coefficient to be multiplied by a known value for the independent variable, plus a constant to be added, to compute a predicted value of the dependent variable for a "new" case.

5. The constant, often designated with the letter A, is the *intercept*, the value of the dependent variable when the independent variable is zero.

6. The regression coefficient, often designated with the letter B, is the *slope* of the regression line, or the rise on the dependent variable scale for each unit of the independent variable.

7. A positive coefficient indicates a *direct* relationship and a regression line sloping upward, toward the right, while a negative coefficient indicates an *inverse* relationship and a line sloping downward, to the right.

Interpreting Discriminant Analysis

Discriminant analysis is the statistical technique for measuring the degree and significance of a relationship between an independent variable that is continuous and a dependent variable that is categorical. The analysis described here assumes that the dependent variable has *only two categories*. Discriminant analysis can be used with multiple independent variables and a dependent variable that has more than two groups, however, the specification and interpretation become too complex for consideration here.

The report of a statistical analysis program is shown in Example 11–7. The upper portion of the example merely identifies the variables and groups included in the analysis. In the case of this example, it consists of the respondents scores on one form of a psychological test to be validated by the researcher. The scores are numeric, and they constitute a continuous variable. The dependent variable in the example consisted of a survey question asking whether they perceived themselves as a "Lark" or an "Owl," based on a description of those who are at their best in the morning or in the evening. The groups, then, are defined by those who answered *Lark* to that question and those who answered *Owl*. The analysis was performed to determine if the test form scores could "predict" the category in which respondents perceived themselves. If the researcher was to determine whether self-perceptions would affect test scores, the dependent and independent variables would be reversed. In that case, analysis of variance would be appropriate to determine if the average test scores of those in one group was significantly different from that for those in the other group. In this case, however, the researcher seeks a prediction of group identification by scores, rather than an explanation of the level of scores, themselves. The first three lines in the second section of the report show the mean values, standard deviations, and the number of cases for each group and for the entire sample. The fourth line lists the value of the Wilks Lambda statistic, from which an approximate F-ratio value was computed by the routine. The probability for assessing the statistical significance of the relationship between the variables is listed next to the F-value. If it were not, the significance of this F-value could be determined in exactly the same way as for an F-ratio from analysis of variance, with reference to statistical tables for the F-distribution. If it were necessary for the researcher to refer to such a table, the degrees of freedom for both the numerator and the denominator of the F-ratio would be used to find the proper row and column of the table. Though they are not listed here, the d.f. for the numerator is simply the number of groups minus one, and since discriminant analysis is always computed for one pair at a time, the d.f. for the numerator will *always* be one. The d.f. for the denominator of the F-ratio is the number of cases minus two, so for this analysis, it would be 398.

Discriminant analysis is similar in many respects to regression analysis. Both generate an equation that can be used to "predict" values of the dependent variable for new cases if the values of the

EXAMPLE 11–7

Discriminant Analysis Printout

Groups defined by: Are you a Lark or an Owl?
Groups designated by: (A) Lark   (B) Owl
Discrimination variable: Test Form R Score

(A) Mean	22.35	Std. Dev.	0.947	N of cases	178
(B) Mean	23.61	Std. Dev.	1.246	N of cases	222
Combined Mean	23.05	Std. Dev.	1.284	N of cases	400
Wilks Lambda	.76276	Value of F	123.8	Probability	.000
Coefficient	.89055	Constant	− 20.52619	d.f.	399
Chi-Square	107.65	d.f.	1	Probability	.000

Classification matrix . . .

Actual Groups	Number Percent	Predicted Groups		Total
		Lark 1.	Owl 2.	
Lark	1.	111	67	178
		62.4	37.6	
Owl	2.	46	176	222
		20.7	79.3	

Percent of cases classified correctly = 71.75

independent variable are known. With regression analysis, the *prediction* is in terms of a numeric value for the dependent variable, because that variable is continuous. With discriminant analysis, however, the value of the prediction is a category or group because the dependent variable is a categorical variable, rather than a continuous, numeric one. In this example where there are just two groups, the analysis provides one coefficient and one constant, just as in regression, and they are listed in the center section on the fifth line of the report. Using this equation to "compute" a prediction for a new case, based on the value of the independent variable, is exactly the same as for regression. The value of the independent variable is first multiplied by the coefficient, then the constant added. If the result is negative, the case would be classified into the first group, and if positive, into the second group.

Assume, for example, that the researcher had received the test score of some individual, and it ʼs 24. If the researcher may wish to predict the person's own self-perceived time of day preference. The coefficient of 0.89055 would first be multiplied by 24.00, and the product would be 21.37. The constant would then be added, but in this case it is a negative value, so the resulting value would be 21.37 minus 20.52619, or +0.84. Since this is a positive value, the new case would be predicted to belong to the second group. The analysis routine actually made such predictions for each case in the analysis and reported the results. Each case was *predicted* to be in one group or the other, and each was *actually* in one group or the other. Thus, they could be listed in a two by two table called a "classification matrix" shown in the lower section of Example 11–7.

GUIDELIST 11–11

For Interpreting Discriminant Analysis

1. The objective is to measure the degree and significance of the relationship between a continuous independent variable and a dependent variable with only *two* categories.

2. The F-value associated with the Wilks Lambda statistic can be used to assess significance in the same manner as with analysis of variance.

3. The analysis generates a discriminant function similar to a regression equation, with a coefficient and a constant.

4. To "predict" group membership when only the independent variable is know, its value is multiplied by the coefficient, and then the constant added.

5. If the value resulting from use of the function is negative, the case is classified into the first group, and if it is positive, it is predicted to be in the second group.

6. The "Classification Matrix" is a cross-tabulation of predicted categories with actual categories and it shows the percentage and direction of correct and incorrect classification.

If the discrimination had been perfect, then all 178 cases that were actually in the first group would have also been predicted to be in that group, and the same for those in the second group. In other words, all of the cases would have been in the "diagonal" defined by Lark-Lark and Owl-Owl on the table. By studing this classification matrix, the researcher can see the number and direction of error. The table shows that over 62 percent of those who said Lark were classified correctly and a higher percentage, over 79 percent of those who said Owl were classified correctly. About 37½ percent of those who actually said Lark were classified incorrectly into the Owl group, while only about 20½ percent of those who actually said Owl were classified into the Lark group.

The chi-square statistic with one d.f. and the probability for assessing significance, listed in the bottom line of the center section in Example 11–7, were computed from the classification matrix, just as they would be for any cross-tabulation. This indicates the significance of the "improvement" over random assignment when predicting group membership, based on the discriminant analysis. If there were equal numbers of cases in each group, random assignment would prove correct only about half the time. With the use of the discriminant coefficient and constant, the prediction was improved from 50 percent to nearly 72 percent. In one respect, this 22 percent improvement is analogous to the r-square value or percentage of *explained* variance with regression analysis.

SUMMARY

Interpreting the Survey Results

A. Begin with data description. Organize and interpret the descriptions of individual variables before turning to measures of association.

B. Choose the best average. Consider both the type of scale and the shape of the distribution when selecting the best average.

C. Recode data when necessary. Recode continuous variables into fewer, larger categories to use frequency tables and crosstabs.

D. Treat data both ways. Treat continuous variables with only a few scale points as both continuous and categorical data for both description and measures of association.

E. Make inferences carefully. Choose an appropriate level of probability for making inferences about the population and assessing statistical significance.

F. Depend on cross-tabulation. Use crosstabs to measure associations between variables when feasible, rather than more complex measures of relationships.

G. Use prediction cautiously. Be sure that equations for prediction from regression or discriminant analysis are valid and stay within the range of the data base.

H. Check causality carefully. Remember that an association between variables does not automatically imply that one is causing the other.

12

Report Generation

INFORMATION NEEDS SATISFACTION

Report generation is the task of making the survey results respond directly and meaningfully to the information needs. During the instrument composition phase, when the questions, scaling, and questionnaire were composed and constructed, the items were arranged in a sequence that would be meaningful to respondents and that would permit the items using the same scaling techniques to be clustered into sections. During the reporting phase, the survey content must usually be rearranged according to the information requirements. The principal information requirements and the most important items or facts are ordinarily listed first, followed by those that are of lesser importance, regardless of the order in which the questions appeared in the questionnaire.

In the previous chapters, two types of statistical analysis were discussed: data description and measures of association between items. When composing survey reports, the researcher ordinarily presents the information in that sequence, first showing the results for all of the individual survey items or sections, followed by presentation of the *major* relationships between items. The most common method for reporting survey results to sponsors is the composition of a combined narrative and condensed tabular report. In addition, computer print output may be organized, indexed, bound, and delivered to those seeking the information, for reference purposes, but such documents seldom if every serve as the major report vehicle. Graphic materials may also be prepared for display at group conferences, and at times researchers will be called on to present or amplify survey results. These modes of reporting are almost always subordinate to the written report containing condensed tables and graphs and a narrative interpretation and explanation by the researcher.

Report Introduction

Perhaps the most useful and practical form of organization for a survey report is one that might be called the "newspaper" format. With this approach, the results are presented two or three times, rather than just once, but with each presentation, the level of detail increases markedly and the sections are divided and identified.

Executive Summary. The first section would contain an "Executive Summary" of the information. Often no more than two or three pages, this initial section provides only the *major highlights* of the results. It addresses only the most important information needs and presents a very brief sketch of only the most valuable findings. Such executive summaries are best composed in very brief paragraphs of no more than three or four sentences each. Each paragraph should be headed or titled with a key phrase to identify the type of information. The entire executive summary should require no more than a few minutes to read. It should only "hit the high points" of the information acquired in the survey and excite the interest and curiosity of the readers, provoking them to look further to the next section.

Response Summary Questionnaire. When those who will read the report have contributed to the composition of the questionnaire or edited it thoroughly, so that they are quite familiar with the instrument, the questionnaire may be used very effectively in *addition* to the executive summary. Many researchers find it both useful and quite easy to produce a facsimile of the questionnaire, containing brief indications of the distributions of response. This device might be called the "Response Summary Questionnaire." When it is used, it may be appended to the executive summary or included between that and the major part of the report. It is *never* advisable merely to jot in the results on a blank questionnaire form and include it.

While the cosmetic aspects of the report may not seem to be at all important, relevant to the contents and results, the appearance of the report is *always* important, and every experienced researcher should be able to attest to that. The reason is simple: sponsors are seldom experts at judging the technical performance of the survey designer or researcher. They ordinarily have some doubts concerning how accurate, reliable, and valid the results of the survey will be, and they have very few means by which to judge these things. Thus, they will invariably place more confidence and value on any report that is neatly and carefully composed and presented than on a report that is quickly or ineptly composed. Despite what those receiving reports may claim, and regardless of their impatience to receive the information, the researcher can be sure that bad appearance or the discovery of even minor errors or omissions will seriously jeopardize the confidence of those who read the report.

GUIDELIST 12–1

For Writing the Report Introduction

1. Begin with an *executive summary* of two or three pages.
2. Use brief paragraphs of three or four sentences each.
3. Cover only the *major* highlights and information needs.
4. Use headings with key phrases to identify sections.
5. The summary must provoke interest and excite curiosity.
6. Use a *response summary questionnaire,* if appropriate.
7. Delete superfluous content from the response summary.
8. Type all entries and compose the summary very neatly.

When a response summary questionnaire is included, the superfluous record format indications and precoding values should be deleted, together with any instructions or notations that are not relevant to understanding the results or the way the questions were expressed to respondents. The distributions of response to categorical items and the appropriate averages for continuous items can then be *typed* in the proper places, next to the questions or items. The advantage of including a summary response questionnaire is the fact that sponsors can turn to it later to see how the actual questions were phrased, the order in which they were presented, and the nature of the surrounding material. This can be quite helpful because the items must often be abbreviated or presented in a different sequence and context in the narrative and tabular report. The disadvantage of a response summary is the fact that it is organized in a sequence for the convenience of respondents, rather than according to the categories of information needs or by importance of issues. Because it is quick and easy to prepare, the researcher is advised to use a response summary if there is any doubt about whether or not to include it.

THE REPORT NARRATIVE

The executive summary and response summary should serve only as a prelude to the second part of the final survey report. This part, containing well-formed and composed tables and graphs, also includes a complete narrative discussion of the survey results. The text should be divided into major sections, according to the various types of information requirements, topics, or issues that were the focus of the survey. The narrative should refer to the tables or figures by number or letter where appropriate. The tables or figures should *not* appear *before* they are referenced in the text. It is also important for the researcher to avoid technical terms or phrases because sponsors are not likely to be familiar with the jargon associated with survey research, data processing, or statistical analysis. Even the most complex results can usually be expressed in lay terminology with some effort. The objective of the report is to convey information, and not merely to impress the reader. It is far better to violate every rule of grammar in order to say something clearly than to express it "correctly" but obscurely.

Use simple, direct sentences. They are more powerful and concise than long, flowing sentences. They make reading the report easier and more enjoyable for those seeking the information. Be *very* careful about identification of antecedents and object references. Do not use pronouns, such as they, them, its, those, etc. unless their antecedents are perfectly clear. Always use the noun to identify the person or thing being referenced if there might be doubt, even if it must be repeated in the same sentence. Refer to tables, graphs, variables, or items by name or number, even though it might seem obvious. Simply saying "the table indicates . . ." too often leads the reader to ask, "*Which* table?" and that is especially true if the table being referenced gets moved to another page.

The narrative text of the survey report should consist of a verbal description of the major results for each section or category of information needs. Even though those seeking the information may be well able to read and understand the tables or figures, the narrative is virtually always necessary and valuable, for some very good reasons. First, the narrative text is *interpretive,* rather than merely descriptive. Thus, the text indicates the meaning of the values and relationships that are revealed by the survey. Second, virtually everyone can communicate more effectively in words than in numbers or symbols. Those who seek the information constantly deal with concepts and images that are largely verbal and only rarely numeric or symbolic in nature. Consequently, they can often perceive the meaning of facts and relationships expressed verbally much more readily than those expressed numerically or with symbols. Third, the researcher can often provide additional insight, ideas, and information, quite aside from the purely tabular or graphic portrayal of results. By virtue of having worked so closely and intimately with the project, the researcher will inevitably acquire intuitive understanding or a "gut feeling" for certain facts or relationships. These insights cannot be expressed in numeric form, but they can and should be stated verbally in the narrative text. Whenever the researcher offers opinions, suggestions, or recommendations that are based on judgment or intuition, rather than concrete survey results, that must be clearly noted in the text. Lastly, researchers who are knowledgeable about survey research because of their past experience with such work can often provide very helpful and useful perspective on the results. Researchers can draw freely from previous survey experience, provided that they respect the proprietary nature of the actual results of other surveys that were conducted for other sponsors.

For each section of the survey report, the narrative text should provide a brief introduction to the information. This is usually done by citing the information need category or, more simply, by stating the questions in the mind of those seeking the information during the initiation of the survey. It is often advisable to say why the information was sought as well, if that can be expressed easily. For example, the narrative for a new section might begin:

> Survey respondents were questioned with six items to indicate their attitudes toward the issue of new work rules. Their reactions were regarded as important to gauge their potential acceptance of the proposed new policy.

Following this type of introduction to a section, the text would cite the tables or figures where the information was presented, and continue to identify and highlight the most important results. This is most often done by directing the readers attention to the specific facts or relationships, thus:

> Notice that the attitudes of new employees were markedly more positive than the attitudes of those who have been with the company for several years. This is very consistent with employee ratings of several other topics as well.

The researcher must often provide explanation and interpretation of the values that are shown in tabular or graphic form, but this is usually only part of the researcher's responsibility. At the very least, the researcher should be willing and able to identify the most relevant facts and relationships in the narrative text. For those with a grasp of the material being measured by the survey, much more extensive comment may be appropriate.

There may be a question concerning whether or not concrete recommendations should be included, whether merely suggestions would be appropriate, or if only the bare facts should be noted. It is always advisable to ask those seeking the information for their preference, and then abide by their request. When researchers provide concrete recommendations, there are two possibilities for problems: those reading the report may feel the researcher has infringed on their prerogatives as executives or decision makers, or they place too much reliance on such recommendations, in the face of some other information that is contradictory. To avoid either extreme, the researcher should simply provide *suggestions* and identify the data that serves as a basis for the suggestions. Doing so allows those reading the report to contradict when appropriate and to weigh the suggestions against their own background, experience, and body of accumulated information.

Each narrative report section should conclude with a very brief summary of the results for that section. These conclusions are usually only a few sentences, and they are quite similar to the individual entries in the executive summary that heads the report. Thus, the narrative report process can be outlined in three steps for each section: (1) say what results will be presented, (2) present the results, and (3) say what was presented.

GUIDELIST 12–2

For Composing Narrative Text

1. Divide the text into major sections according to the types of information needs, topics, or issues.

2. Include the tables *after* they have been referenced in the text, not before.

3. Avoid technical jargon used in statistics or processing in favor of the simpler, layperson's vocabulary.

4. Use short, simple, direct sentences, rather than long, complex ones.

5. Use nouns repetitively to avoid any confusion about the antecedent of pronouns such as *it, them, they,* etc.

6. Identify tables, figures, and other inclusions by their consecutive number or letter in references to them.

7. Make the text *interpretive,* rather than merely *descriptive* of the results.

8. Introduce each major section by identifying its purpose or the reason for including it.

9. Discuss the *major* facts or relationships contained in each table or figure, but make the text fairly independent, so that it is meaningful without reference to tables.

10. Include additional ideas, conclusions, or suggestions, based on previous experience or intuition, but clearly note when they go beyond the actual results.

It is important to note that the narrative text should not be too "dependent" on the tables and figures. Just as the reader should be able to gather the gist of the results from the tables and figures alone, so, too, should they be able to comprehend the major results by reading only the narrative text.

CONDENSED REPORT TABLES

The tables in the report should be edited versions of those generated by the computations. Only the relevant values and entries should be included. It will often be possible to condense the tables, so that the results for many survey items of a similar type or nature can be contained in a single table or shown graphically on just one figure. The composition of meaningful, easily understood tables and figures is an art that can be cultivated easily and accomplished readily, with some careful attention and effort.

There are two rather basic kinds of things that the researcher must decide on when composing tables or figures: the first is the format and the second is the labeling. When choosing a format, use space as effectively as possible. Arrange rows and columns, as well as sections, so that they contain *similar* material or apply to the same concept or topic. Allow enough "white space" so that the tables or figures do not appear to be glutted with numbers of words. Keeping different types of content separated also helps the reader to recognize what is being presented. While there may be exceptions, it is usually a good policy to show the material on vertical pages, rather than reverting to a horizontal page. While the horizontal format allows for much more information on a single line, it is often cumbersome for the reader who must turn the document to the side to read the contents. Another very practical policy when writing tables is to use a *very consistent* format. This helps the report reader because, once familiar with the format, no further study is required to comprehend those that follow in a similar format. Lastly, it is good to remember that a table can contain too much information. The general rule is that no one table or figure should require more than a very few minutes of study to comprehend.

The second major factor to consider when composing tables or figures is the *labeling*. Each table or figure in the report should be *named* and *titled*. Consecutive numbers or letters usually make better name indicators than Roman numerals or other designations. The title should *say what is in the body of the table or figure*. If the body of a table contains frequencies, the table might be labeled, "Number of Respondents Indicating Each Alternative." If percentages are listed, then they should be identified in the title. If averages are contained in the body of the table, the title must indicate not only the fact that they are averages, but also *what* averages, the means, medians, or modes. For example, the title might be "Average (Mean) Estimates for Four Series." It is essential that the title of the table or figure informs the reader of exactly what the table contains. The reader should be able to understand clearly what is in the table *without* reference to the text or knowledge of any of the other parts of the report.

The columns and rows of tables and the sections or parts of figures should be labeled clearly as well. In order to conserve space, some researchers will attach codes, such as 1, 2, 3, etc. or A, B, C, etc. to the rows or columns and then list a key at the bottom of the table to show the items or concepts to which these codes refer. This is almost never advisable, and it is almost always better to include less information on each table and use as many as are required. The one exception is when it is necessary for the reader to *compare* items, because that can be accomplished more easily within a single table than among multiple tables. Statistical significance can best be shown in tables with the use of asterisks beside the appropriate values, such as 25*, or with letter superscripts, such as 25[a]. The significance can be noted in a footnote to the table.

The following section of this chapter contains a series of examples that might serve as model tables for reporting the results of *practical* survey research. First, the results that might be obtained from each of the various scale types shown in Chapter 5 are shown in a series of condensed tables that provide data description. Next, the data that were analyzed with each of the measures of association that were described in Chapter 10 and that were reported for interpretation in Chapter 11 are presented in a form more suitable for inclusion in final survey reports. These tables are described and many examples of narrative text that might accompany them are also included. There is no one, *correct* way to report results, but these examples are designed to provide researchers with suggestions for table and narrative format and content.

GUIDELIST 12-3

For Composing Tables and Figures

1. Name each table and figure with a consecutive number or letter, preferably not with Roman numerals.

2. Title each one with a brief description of exactly what is contained in the *body* of the table.

3. Label rows, columns, and sections with meaningful words, rather than codes that are labeled below.

4. Use a standard format when possible, so that many tables are quickly recognized once the first is understood.

5. Use space and distance effectively to show relationships or provide identification.

6. Keep similar content in the same columns, rows, or sections, using space to separate distinct content.

7. Allow sufficient "white space" and do not contain too much information in one table or make it too dense.

8. Note statistical significance with an* or letter superscript[a] and note probability *level* in a table footnote.

9. Use vertical, rather than horizontal pages whenever possible, even if more tables or figures are needed.

10. Remember, each table or figure should virtually "stand alone," so that it is meaningful *without* reference to text.

11. Always try to keep it *clean* and *simple*.

Multiple Choice Item Reports

Multiple choice items, such as those shown in Example 5-1, are categorical data and they are usually described by showing the percentage of respondents choosing each category. Example 12-1 shows a variant of the frequency table discussed earlier. In this example, only the percentages are shown because ordinarily these proportions are generalized to the population as a whole, by statistical inference. The number who responded to the item is shown on the table so that if, in rare instances, a reader wished to know the number in the sample responding to a given item, that could easily be estimated or calculated. In Example 12-1, there were 7 percent who indicated some other, miscellaneous newspaper. Because so few indicated some

---

EXAMPLE 12–1

Single Response Item Table

What kind of newspaper do you *most often* read for business news? (Check only *one.*)

[Number = 160]	Percent
Local, morning paper	22%
Local, evening paper	14%
Local, weekly paper	9%
National, daily paper	43%
National, weekly paper	5%
Other, miscellaneous papers	7%
Total	100%

---

other paper and the frequency of listing of any one publication was usually only one person, the others are all grouped into this miscellaneous category. Usually the others that are identified are recorded on a codelist and entered into the data file for processing, but they are not ordinarily listed in a report *unless* a substantial number of respondents select one particular "other" alternative or the sponsors express a strong interest in having these so-called "write-ins" reported. If they were to be reported, they could either be included in the sample table or listed in a separate table with the percentages based only on those who selected and entered some additional, miscellaneous alternative.

Notice that the alternatives were listed in Example 12–1 in the same order as they were listed on the questionnaire item. This sequence was maintained in the table because there is something of a logical order to the alternatives. If there were no inherent sequence, the researcher will often list the modal category first, followed in descending order of percentages, with the "other" category always presented last.

The narrative discussion of such a table is likely to be brief, because the table is largely self-explanatory. It is usually important only to identify the most popular categories, and perhaps to comment on the results if they are not intuitive, thus:

> The national daily newspaper proved to be the single, most often used source of business news for the respondents in this population. The survey questions about subscription, to be shown later, suggest that the Wall Street Journal is by far the most popular and probably four out of five who indicated a national daily paper here were referring to that

newspaper. Nearly all of the others are likely to be referring to Barrons, because there were few other national dailies to which respondents subscribed at home or at work. It is also intersting to note that the local *evening* paper was less popular than was the morning paper, even though the morning paper is generally less often read by business people.

Example 12–1 is a single response item and so it constitutes a single survey variable and the statistical analysis generates only one frequency table, from which the percentages were drawn. In Example 12–2, the respondents could select more than one alternative. Consequently, this single survey question actually generates *six* variables, to which the respondents actually indicate "yes" or "no." Consequently, the analysis will ordinarily generate six frequency tables; one for each alternative that is a variable. Example 12–2 is "condensed" because it lists all six sets of percentages in a single table, to save space and facilitate comparison. In fact, it is often not even necessary to list the percentages in the "No" column, who did not check the alternative, because this is easily recognized by the reader based on the percentage who did check the category. The narrative text to accompany this table would be very similar to that for the previous one, citing major categories and knitting the survey results together.

EXAMPLE 12–2

Multiple Response Item Table

Please check *any* type of newspaper you regularly read for business news:

[Number = 160]	Yes	No
Local, morning paper	38%	68%
Local, evening paper	22%	78%
Local, weekly paper	7%	93%
National, daily paper	41%	59%
National, weekly paper	2%	98%
Other, miscellaneous papers	3%	97%

Likert Scale Item Reports

Survey items such as those shown in Example 5–2 can also be reported in a condensed table in many cases, if the reseacher uses some ingenuity with the tabular format. In Example 12–3, the scale

EXAMPLE 12–3

Condensed Likert Scale Report

How much do you agree or disagree with each statement below?

[Number = 325]

	Strongly Agree	Agree	Neutral	Disagree	Strongly Disagree
A man should never cry in public............	8.4%	11.5%	27.7%	36.5%	15.9%
A woman's place is in the home............	12.9%	16.2%	19.1%	31.5%	20.3%
A man should help a woman in public.......	13.5%	16.4%	21.9%	29.6%	18.6%
Women should always pay their share.......	10.4%	18.0%	16.5%	26.2%	28.9%
Men must take the lead in sex matters.......	16.6%	18.3%	19.0%	22.1%	24.0%
Women should put family before career.....	21.5%	26.4%	18.2%	13.5%	20.4%

categories are shown in slanted lines to conserve space. Those who construct tables may often be tempted merely to list the code values above the columns and print the scale, itself, above or below. This is never advisable in a final report if it can be avoided. To do so often places too much of the burden on the reader, and that is very contrary to the basic objectives of the reporting function.

In Example 12–3, six items are shown in a single table, and actually many more could easily have been listed. This saves a great deal of space and saves time for those reading the reports, but there is a more important reason for using condensed table formats: They allow the reader to make direct comparisons of response distributions quickly and easily among comparable items. Thus, such formats provide more information and enhance the value of the results. They do require more work from those who generate the reports, but they are ordinarily well-worth the extra time and effort.

Showing the entire distributions of response to Likert scale items in the fashion used here has both advantages and disadvantages. Ordinarily, the entire distributions are of interest and should be listed if the content of the items is such that it is useful to compare each *category* with the others. It does require more space and makes the comparisons among *items* more difficult because there are so many values to study. An alternative would be to list only the *median* values for each item. Using the median as a single indicator of the level of agreement is recommended when individual categories need not be compared, to facilitate comparison among *items* and to save space.

Verbal Frequency Scale Reports

Another format for showing the entire percentage distribution of response for several items is shown in Example 12–4. As with the Likert scale, this scale generates a set of *ordinal* data, and the scales are described in Chapter 5 and shown in Example 5–3. The format in Example 12–4 is very similar to the previous one, except that the names of the categories are short enough to be listed on two lines and "staggered" so that the labels appear directly over each column.

EXAMPLE 12–4

Condensed Verbal Frequency Report

How much do you agree or disagree with each statement below?

[Number = 220]	Always	Often	Sometimes	Rarely	Never
Seek information about candidates ..	5.3%	13.9%	22.4%	28.5%	29.9%
Vote in *local* elections..............	3.1%	6.4%	39.5%	17.8%	33.2%
Vote along strict party lines..........	8.4%	17.7%	19.5%	13.2%	41.2%
Contribute money to candidates......	1.3%	3.9%	9.4%	6.3%	79.1%
Volunteer to work on campaigns	0.8%	1.6%	3.3%	16.6%	77.7%

Only five verbal frequency items are shown in the table contained in Example 12–4, but of course many more might have been listed in the table, so that a dozen or so such related items could be reported on a single page. Actually, an analysis routine would probably generate one page of print output for each such item, containing the frequency and percentage table and perhaps the median value as well. Thus, such a table is an excellent way to condense the information and make items very comparable with one another. The items have not been rearranged so that their sequence represents the order of magnitude of the responses. Rather, the original order was retained here because it represented a rough "continuum" from minimal involvement in political issues to rather intensive involvement. This is quite common with well-composed survey items and well-constructed questionnaires. The format and sequence permit the report reader to examine the *change* in the distributions from one item to the next, moving downward in the table to detect patterns as the level of some underlying dimension increases or decreases. Thus, showing the items together enhances the meaning of the information.

Ordinal Scale Reports

Both the Likert scale and the verbal frequency scale generate ordinal data, because the categories are listed in a sequence that represents the increase or decrease in the order of magnitude, although intervals or "steps" between scale points are not necessarily equal to one another. Other things besides the amount of agreement or the frequency of something can be arranged in a fairly large number of such sequential steps as well. When this is the case, the scale is called "ordinal" because it generates ordinal data. Example 5–4 shows a situation where the scale steps are times of day defined not by the hour and minute, but rather, by daily activity patterns of respondents. It is not so important to sponsors to know the exact time of the occurrence according to the clock, because different families perform activities at different times of day. Rather the times, *relative to the families' daily activities,* are of greater importance.

Example 12–5 shows the tabular report of the data from a single variable using this type of scale. Notice that as always, the number of respondents is listed clearly on the table so that readers know the total on which the percentages are based. Rather than merely listing the percentage distribution by category, the *cumulative* percentages are also shown. The cumulative percentages are often very revealing for ordinal scale items. The reader of the report can then obtain two types of information from the table simultaneously: The percentage of people who, in this case, turn on their TV set at a certain time of the day, and also the percentage who have turned on their TV set up to that point in the day. This latter piece of information is obviously very useful, especially given the assumption that some fixed proportion of television sets have remained on once they are originally turned on.

In the narrative interpretation of such a table, it is important both to explain the cumulative percentage distribution, if that has not been done earlier in the report, and also to note the relevant results in terms of both category percentages and cumulative percentages. Notice how a typical narrative also makes suggestions and refers to cross-tabulation to check them:

Respondents indicated the time during a typical weekday when they or someone in the family turned on the television set. They indicated

EXAMPLE 12-5

Ordinal Scale Cumulative Table

Ordinarily, when do you or someone in your family *first* turn on the television set in your home on a weekday?

[Number = 165]	Percent	Cumulative
The first thing in the morning..........................	6.3%	6.3%
A little while after awakening	4.5%	10.8%
Mid-morning..	5.2%	16.0%
Just before lunch	2.1%	18.1%
Right after lunch	11.8%	29.9%
Mid-afternoon	7.6%	37.5%
Early evening, before dinner	18.1%	55.6%
Right after dinner	21.0%	76.6%
Late evening	17.7%	94.3%
Usually don't turn it on...............................	5.7%	100.0%

when they did so according to certain daily activities, rather than by the clock, because daily activity patterns differ widely from family to family. The results are shown in Table 5. The percentages are all based on 165 respondents who answered the question, and the largest percentage turned on their television sets *right after dinner,* but very nearly as many did so in the *early evening before dinner,* and in the *late evening.* The cumulative percentages indicate that less than one family in five had turned on the TV by *lunchtime,* while over a third had done so by *mid-afternoon,* well over half by *early evening, before dinner,* and three quarters *right after dinner.* These results suggest very light morning viewership for this audience, and only moderate afternoon viewing for "soaps," the "game shows," and the "sit-com" reruns. On the other hand, the marked increase in the cumulative percentages just before dinner suggest a youthful audience coming in during late afternoon, perhaps after school, for the "cartoon" and "kid show" programming, as well as the early evening news for some stations and nets. These suggestions will be tested further when this item is broken down by *Family Life Cycle* to measure differences in viewing patterns for those in different stages of the life cycle.

Forced Ranking Scale Reports

The ranking of alternatives creates a variable for each item ranked and they are ordinal level data, just as the three scales described above. In Example 5-5 four brands of cola beverages were ranked according to the respondents degree of preference. Thus, an analysis routine to generate frequency and percentage distributions would produce one table for each item ranked. Such data can be condensed into a single table, such as that shown in Example 12–6 where the percentage distributions for each brand (variable) are shown by row, totaling to 100 percent at the far right. Thus, each row of the table in Example 12–6 was derived from a frequency and percentage table for that particular brand or variable. If the data had not been condensed, it would be necessary for the report reader to refer to four different tables.

EXAMPLE 12–6

Forced Ranking Scale Distributions

Please rank the brands of cola listed below in their order of preference:

[Number = 119)]	Ranking				
	1st	*2nd*	*3rd*	*4th*	*Total*
Coca-Cola	46.5%	4.0%	6.7%	2.8%	100.0%
Pepsi-Cola	31.2%	51.6%	11.3%	5.9%	100.0%
Royal Crown Cola.	19.1%	3.1%	67.5%	10.3%	100.0%
Like Cola.	3.2%	1.3%	14.5%	81.0%	100.0%
Total	100.0%	100.0%	100.0%	100.0%	

Aside from saving report space and reader time, there is another advantage to condensing tabular reports of rankings such as those shown in Example 12–6. Each respondent must rank each item, and no two items can be ranked the same. This is why the scale is called a *forced* ranking. If the data are edited properly, the rows should also total to 100 percent. Thus, checking both column and row totals provides an indication of accuracy.

Taken in total, the table in Example 12–6 provides those seeking the information with an entire "picture" of the *pattern* of preference or choice, rather than merely information about individual items. Thus, patterns are revealed merely by the choice and composition of the report format, rather than dependence on multivariate statistical procedures. It is also important to note that this table does *not* show how those who ranked a particular item a certain way ranked the other items, but that can be clearly revealed with a set of cross-tabulation tables for each pair.

Paired Comparison Scale Reports

Paired comparison scales are used only rarely in surveys because the data from them are difficult to analyze, as noted in Chapter 5. The items used in Example 5–6 are cola brands that were also used in Example 5–5. The object was to demonstrate the greater ease of alternative scales to the paired comparison scale. On the other hand, there are some situations where the researcher wishes to measure paired comparisons because the scales actually mirror "real-world" choices the respondents must sometimes make. Thus, in Example 12–7, only three items and thus three pairs are measured. The items to be compared are the meats of three animals and there was an explicit reason for the choice of a paired comparison scale. Both personal preference and the dietary laws of some religions dictate certain choices, while respondents are often placed in a position of making a choice between such pairs.

EXAMPLE 12–7

Condensed Table of Paired Comparisons

If given the choice of only *one* from *each pair* listed below, which type of meat would you most likely choose? (Please check only *one* from *each pair.*)

[Number = 120]*	Beef	82%	versus	18%	Pork
	Beef	96%	versus	4%	Lamb
	Pork	88%	versus	12%	Lamb

* Transitivity. forced by deleting intransitivity cases.

In Example 12–7, there is a footnote indicating that transitivity was forced by the elimination of intransitive cases. Since only three items and three pairs were used, there were probably very few such cases. *Intransitivity* results when a respondent indicates they prefer: A over B, B over C, and C over A. This is, of course, a logical impossibility, but it occurs very frequently with paired comparisons when many items and pairs are used in a survey. It is one of the principal reasons paired comparisons do *not* substitute for ranking of many items, while *rating* of the items does work effectively in those cases. When paired comparisons are used in surveys and reported in tables such as that in Example 12–7, either the coefficient of transitivity must be reported or the fact that such cases were eliminated must be noted.

The narrative should also briefly explain transitivity, at least the first time the term is referenced in the report, as well as explaining the meaning of the results, thus:

> Respondents rated their preference for beef, pork, and lamb when each was paired with one other variety of meat. There were two respondents who indicated they preferred beef to pork, lamb to beef, and pork to lamb, so their choices were intransitive and the data from these two cases were disregarded for this section. The results indicate: (1) A strong general preference for beef, as might be expected. (2) A fairly pronounced dislike for lamb. (3) A preference for lamb over pork by more than one in 10 people. The results suggest that if only two varieties were to be offered, beef and pork or beef and lamb would be much more acceptable than would pork and lamb. The choices seem to be governed by both preferences and *prohibitions;* by both "likes" and "dislikes" of respondents. Comparisons of these results with religious preference and affiliation may provide more evidence for this conclusion.

Comparative Scale Reports

When an absolute reference is lacking or inadequate and comparisons or relative measures are required, there is no necessity to use *paired* comparisons. Example 5–7 shows a method for obtaining interval scale data based on a relative frame of reference, rather than on an absolute standard. This scale can be used for singular or multiple comparisons. Example 12–8 reports the results of comparisons between the sponsors retail store and six other shops. As in Example 5–7, a five point scale was used, but instead of scale values ranging from one to five, they were oriented around zero and ranged from a negative two to a positive two. The table in Example 12–8 lists both the entire percentage distributions of response and also, since the scale is interval level, the average (mean) values.

When the percentage distributions are listed as they are in Example 12–8, those who read the table can easily make comparisons of *categories* or response across the rows. For a quick comparison of the *items* among one another, the averages can be compared more readily than the entire distributions. Finally, the averages also provide a quick and fairly indicative measure of the relationship between each competing shop and the "standard," the sponsor's own shop. The plus or minus sign provides a very visible indication of whether the other shop is regarded more or less favorably than the standard for comparison when the scale pivots on zero. The magnitude of the average value shows clearly how much more or less favorably the other shops were perceived by respondents. Thus, this form of table provides a wealth of information to those seeking it and it conveys it quickly and clearly. The content of the table was obtained from an analysis program that

EXAMPLE 12-8

Condensed Multiple Comparative Scale Table

How would you rate *each* of the shops listed below, compared to *this shop*?

[Number = 175]	Very Inferior − 2	− 1	Very Similar 0	+ 1	Very Superior + 2	Average
Abbot's............	11.5	16.4	35.3	20.1	16.7	+ 0.14
Baker's	44.0	16.7	14.5	14.2	10.6	− 0.69
Clark's............	20.0	22.9	35.4	14.5	7.2	− 0.34
Drake's	58.8	31.3	7.5	1.7	0.7	− 1.46
Evert's............	9.5	16.8	19.9	37.4	16.4	+ 0.34
Frost's	6.6	14.4	40.9	23.1	15.0	+ 0.26

generated six frequency and percentage distribution tables, one for each of the shops that was rated on the comparative scale. The mean values were also requested and listed together with the percentage distributions in the table.

Horizontal, Numeric Scale Reports

Perhaps the most common scale used in survey research for continuous, interval data is the linear, numeric scale, such as that shown in Example 5–8. A report of the results from such a scale, used to rate 14 attributes, is shown in the table in Example 12–9. Because this scale yields interval level variables, the mean values were computed. Rather than listing each distribution, the averages were plotted graphically in the table. Instead of listing the items in the sequence in which they appeared in the questionnaire, they were ordered according to the results of the ratings.

By reordering the items from the most to the least important and using the graphic form of presentation, the table in Example 12–9 shows an easily interpreted *profile* of the things that are important to those shopping for sports equipment. Fourteen individual tables were reduced to a single page, not only saving space, but enhancing the meaning very markedly.

Semantic Differential Scale Reports

Semantic differential scales are widely used in survey research for the measurement of image profiles. This method of scaling is dis-

EXAMPLE 12-9

Horizontal, Numeric Scale of Importance

When choosing a place to buy sports equipment, how *important* is:

[Number = 325]   [Average (mean) values shown]

	Not Important				Very Important
	1	2	3	4	5
Quality of merchandise	:	:	:	:	● :
Selection of brands	:	:	:	:	● :
Variety of products	:	:	:	:	● :
Service after purchase	:	:	:	:	● :
Store guarantees	:	:	:	:	● :
Price of the goods	:	:	:	:	● :
Courtesy of service	:	:	:	● :	:
Help and advice offered	:	:	:	● :	:
Speed of service	:	:	:	● :	:
Store hours	:	:	:	● :	:
Location of store	:	:	: ●	:	:
Size of the store	:	:	● :	:	:
Attractiveness of store	:	:	● :	:	:
Availability of credit	:	: ●	:	:	:
	1	2	3	4	5
	Not Important				Very Important

cussed in Chapter 5 and shown in Example 5–9. The same items are reported in two tables, in Example 12–10 and Example 12–11. The table in Example 12–10 is called a "facsimile" because the items are *exactly* as they appeared in the questionnaire. The comparison of that table with the one in Example 12–11 demonstrates an important objective of survey reporting. When the questionnaire was constructed, the survey items were ordered in a sequence that was dictated by the *response* task. Thus, the items were randomly ordered and some of them were listed with the positive adjective first while others were reversed. Consequently, when the modal values were plotted on the facsimile, they do not actually form a *profile* for interpretation and reporting, and it is difficult and time-consuming to obtain meaning from the facsimile by forming a mental picture of the results.

EXAMPLE 12-10

Semantic Differential Facsimile

Please put a check mark in the space on each line
below to show your opinion of the *pizza* served here.

[Modal positions are plotted]

Hot	.... :	...●... :	.... :	.... :	.... :	.... :	....	Cold
Bland	.... :	.... :	.... :	.... :	.... :	...●... :	....	Spicy
Expensive	.... :	.... :	...●... :	.... :	.... :	.... :	....	Inexpensive
Moist	...●... :	.... :	.... :	.... :	.... :	.... :	....	Dry
Soggy	.... :	.... :	.... :	...●... :	.... :	.... :	....	Crisp
Good	.... :	...●... :	.... :	.... :	.... :	.... :	....	Bad
Unattractive	.... :	.... :	.... :	.... :	.... :	...●... :	....	Attractive
Fresh	...●... :	.... :	.... :	.... :	.... :	.... :	....	Stale
Small	.... :	.... :	.... :	.... :	...●... :	.... :	....	Large
Natural	.... :	.... :	...●... :	.... :	.... :	.... :	....	Artificial

In Example 12–11, the modal values are again shown, but there are two modifications in the table: First, several of the items were "reflected" or reversed so that all of the adjectives regarded by the sponsor and respondents as positive are shown on the left, with their negative counterparts listed on the right. Second, item pairs were reordered so that those receiving the most positive responses were listed first and the less positive items followed in sequence down the page. In the data analysis for this example, the means were also computed, so that when an item had the same modal value as one or more others, the one with the "highest" (most favorable) mean value was listed first for the set, to break the "tie."

A major goal when composing tables for reports is to enhance the information content by facilitating the recognition of patterns and the

EXAMPLE 12-11

Semantic Differential Image Profile

Please put a check mark in the space on each line
below to show your opinion of the *pizza* served here.

[Modal positions are plotted]

Fresh	● : .... : .... : .... : .... : .... :	Stale

Fresh   ● : .... : .... : .... : .... : .... : ....   Stale

Moist   ● : .... : .... : .... : .... : .... : ....   Dry

Good   .... : ● : .... : .... : .... : .... : ....   Bad

Hot   .... : ● : .... : .... : .... : .... : ....   Cold

Spicy   .... : ● : .... : .... : .... : .... : ....   Bland

Attractive   .... : ● : .... : .... : .... : .... : ....   Unattractive

Large   .... : .... : ● : .... : .... : .... : ....   Small

Natural   .... : .... : ● : .... : .... : .... : ....   Artificial

Crisp   .... : .... : .... : ● : .... : .... : ....   Soggy

Inexpensive   .... : .... : .... : .... : ● : .... : ....   Expensive

---

comparisons among items. This often requires reordering and reflecting of items. The table in Example 12–11 much more readily portrays the image *profile*, by comparison with that in Example 12–10. When the table is composed properly, the report reader easily obtains a clear picture of the relationships shown.

Adjective Check List Reports

The most simple and direct way to measure image attributes in a survey, although certainly not the best means in most cases, was shown in Example 5–10. The price of the simplicity is the fact that only categorical, dichotomous data are obtained for each item. Thus, the reports of such items consist only of the proportion of respondents who checked each item. Such a report is shown in Example

12–12. If the data for the entire sample, combined, were to be shown in such a table, they would be obtained by generating an individual frequency table for each item, and then listing only the percentage checking the item in the condensed, tabular report. In Example 12–12, the percentages are shown for each of two departments, using the same items as those shown in Example 5–10. Thus, the data shown are for two individual subsamples, and the proportions checking each item for the entire sample as a whole are not shown because this would be "mixing apples and oranges" from the view of those seeking the information. These percentages could have been obtained by first selecting only one subsample or department and obtaining frequency tables, then repeating the computations for the second subsample or department. This was not the procedure used here, however, because to do so requires doing the same analysis twice and does not provide a measure of the statistical significance of differences between the two departments. Rather than using frequency distributions, these data were submitted to cross-tabulation analysis, so that each table contained the percentages checking and not checking the item for each department. Consequently, Example 12–12 shows a data description report that was actually based on a measure of asso-

---

EXAMPLE 12–12

Adjective Check List Percentages

> Please put a check mark in the space in front of any word or phrase that describes your job.
> [Percentage checking each item for each department*]

Dept. A	Dept. B		Dept. A	Dept. B	
9%	31%	Easy	91%	65%	Safe
88%	7%	Technical	55%	39%	Exhausting
3%	77%	Boring	74%	40%	Difficult
71%	12%	Interesting	62%	8%	Rewarding
12%	55%	Low-paying	41%	70%	Secure
8%	41%	Strenuous	3%	29%	Slow-paced
2%	88%	Routine	62%	17%	Enjoyable
16%	48%	Dead-end	5%	44%	Rigid
91%	12%	Changing	38%	21%	Pleasant
55%	9%	Important	59%	25%	Satisfying
79%	16%	Demanding	1%	14%	Degrading
1%	18%	Temporary	2%	17%	Risky

* Differences between departments are all statistically significant.
Number for Dept. A = 72   Number for Dept. B = 315

ciation: cross-tabulation. Notice that the number in each department and the statistical significance is noted in a footnote.

The original order of the items, used in the questionnaire and shown in Example 5–10, was retained in the report. The items were not resequenced according to the magnitude of the proportions because they differ so widely between departments. The narrative description of these results would point out the differential patterns between the two departments, based on comparisons between both items and departments.

Stapel Scale Reports

Yet another method for measuring image profiles is the Stapel scale, described in Chapter 5 and shown in Example 5–11. Each item on such a profile might be analyzed by generating a separate frequency table, but the variables are actually continuous, interval level variables and so the use of averages and coefficients to describe each distribution can also be used appropriately. In Example 12–13, the results of a series of Stapel scale items listing attributes of a retail outlet are shown. The median value was selected by the researcher as the appropriate average to list, based on the skewness and kurtosis of the distributions. The median is more representative of the most typical rating when the distributions are highly skewed, as they obviously are in Example 12–13, because the mean is overly sensitive to the fairly rare, extreme examples in the "tail" of the distribution furthest from the mode.

In the table shown in Example 12–13, the items were reordered from the sequence used in the questionnaire. As in Example 12–9, the items in Example 12–13 are arranged by order of magnitude of the results, so that those that were most descriptive were listed first, followed in sequence by those that were regarded by respondents as less descriptive. This was also done in Example 12–11 but when a Stapel scale is used to measure an image profile, there is, of course, no necessity to reverse the items. In fact, it would be completely inappropriate to do so, and "negative" items should not be converted to "positive" meaning by reflecting the scale. For example, the last item in the table in Example 12–13 is "Intimidating," and it was least descriptive. If the item had been "Unintimidating," it may or may *not* prove to have an average rating near five on the scale, and to assume so would not be at all permissible.

Fixed Sum Scale Reports

The last method described in Chapter 5 was shown in Example 5–12. Such scales yield as many variables as there are items, but the

EXAMPLE 12−13

Stapel Scale Image Profile Report

How well does each word or phrase describe this shop?

[Number = 325]   [Median values shown]

	Not Descriptive				Very Descriptive
	1	2	3	4	5
High quality products	:	:	:	:	●:
Neat and clean	:	:	:	:	● :
Wide selection	:	:	:	:	● :
Long time in business	:	:	:	:	● :
Helpful staff	:	:	:	: ●	:
Friendly	:	:	:	: ●	:
Large	:	:	:	: ●	:
Ample parking	:	:	:	: ●	:
Fun to shop	:	:	:	:●	:
Convenient hours .	:	:	:	:●	:
Easy to visit	:	:	:	●:	:
Fast counter service	:	:	: ●	:	:
Expensive goods	:	:	● :	:	:
Bad location	:	: ●	:	:	:
Understaffed	:	:●	:	:	:
Hard to find	:	:●	:	:	:
Deliveries often late	:	●:	:	:	:
Short on experience	:	● :	:	:	:
Hard to reach by phone	: ●	:	:	:	:
Unattractive	: ●	:	:	:	:
Intimidating	:●	:	:	:	:
	1	2	3	4	5
	Not Descriptive				Very Descriptive

objective is to show the proportions of each item, based on some given total of incidents. Thus, all items and variables from the scale must be reported in a single table, to indicate the complete meaning of the data, as in Example 12−14. If the items used in Example 5−12 were reported in this way, it would be advisable to reorder them according to the magnitude of the proportions, because those items were merely types of food and do not stand in any logical sequence or relationship to one another. The items reported in Example 12−14 are not the same, and they do form a sequence based on the time of day.

Thus, they were listed in the tabular report in exactly the same way as they originally appeared in the questionnaire. Resequencing such items as these would actually make the table more difficult to comprehend, rather than making the meaning more understandable. Note that when particular times during the day constituted the items in Example 12–5 the cumulative percentages were listed, but they are not shown in Example 12–14. This is because the fixed sum scale items are individual variables and respondents can and usually would respond to many or all of the items. Consequently, there really are no cumulative percentages.

EXAMPLE 12–14

Fixed Sum Scale Summary

Of the last 10 times that you had a meal away from home, how many times did you eat during the times of day listed?

Number = 200   [Average (mean) percentages listed]

In the morning, before 11:00 AM	16.2%
During lunchtime, between 11:00 AM and 2:00 PM	28.4%
During the afternoon, 2:00 PM and 5:00 PM	8.0%
During dinner time, between 5:00 PM and 7:00 PM	24.6%
In the evening, after 7:00 PM	22.8%
Total	100.0%

Despite the fact that the items are individual variables, the data can be converted from whatever fixed sum or given total was used to a base of 100, so that the item *mean* values can be reported as percentages. (Median or modal values would *not* necessarily total to 100 or any other fixed sum.) Thus, the table in Example 12–14 shows a distribution *across* items, based on the percentages of the fixed total for each.

The narrative description of the table reporting a summary of the fixed sum scale should indicate the *actual value* of the given total used in the questionnaire if the proportions have been converted to percentages. They may also have to explain the nature of the scale, if it is the first time such data are shown in a table in the report. Thus, the narrative might begin:

> Survey respondents indicated the number of times they had a meal away from home out of the *last 10 times* they did so, for each of the times listed in Table 14. The average values were then converted to percentages, as shown.

By inserting such clarifications in the narrative text, the researcher can avoid confusion and the possibility that report readers might perceive the inconsistency in the table as an error, reducing the credibility of the survey.

MEASURES OF ASSOCIATION

The statistical survey results to be reported arise from two types of analysis: data description or measures of association between variables. The examples presented earlier and the discussion of report tables and narrative have dealt primarily with the first type; data description for individual variables or for groups of variables from the same type of scale. Thus, each of the basic types of scales exemplified in Chapter 5 were referenced and sample reports for each type of scale were shown. In the following section, the tabular and narrative reports of measures of association will be discussed and exemplified. When the relationship between variables is to be shown, the data reported within one section or table are often derived from different types of scales. The focus is not so much on the description of each variable as on the relationship between the variables.

The most common methods for measuring the relationships between pairs of variables were identified and discussed in Chapter 10 together with instructions about the selection of the proper techniques for data of different types. In Chapter 11, the reports generated by the analysis routines for these major measures of association between variables were shown in a series of examples. In the following section, the tabular and narrative reporting of each of the major measures of association will be discussed and shown in examples. Each of the examples of statistical reports from analysis routines, shown in Chapter 11, will be cited and suggestions concerning what content should be included in the final reports and what might best be excluded will be offered. It is important to note that those conducting and reporting *academic*, rather than *pragmatic* survey research may wish to provide their readers with more comprehensive and detailed reports of results than are suggested here.

Cross-Tabulation Reports

When the relationship between two variables that are both categorical is to be measured, cross-tabulation is the conventional technique for doing so. Two typical analysis routine printouts from this type of procedure are shown in Example 11–2. The data from four such crosstabs are reported in Example 12–15. This format is called a vertical banner because the same categories are listed on the columns for

EXAMPLE 12-15

Cross-Tabulation Vertical Banner Report

Time of Day Preference Types by Demographic Characteristics

[Row percentages are listed. Number = 400]

	Larks	Wrens	Owls	Total	Comb.
*Age Group**					
Under 35	44.5	27.1	28.4	100.0	38.7
35 to 49	20.0	30.6	49.4	100.0	21.2
50 and over	21.2	30.6	48.1	100.0	40.0
Combined	30.0	29.2	40.7	100.0	100.0
*Education**					
No college	24.7	32.5	42.8	100.0	41.5
Some college.	40.0	28.8	31.2	100.0	31.3
College graduate.	26.6	24.8	48.6	100.0	27.2
Combined	30.0	29.2	40.7	100.0	100.0
Sex					
Males	31.4	26.6	42.0	100.0	51.7
Females.	28.5	32.1	39.4	100.0	48.3
Combined	30.0	29.2	40.7	100.0	100.0
Occupational Group					
White collar	43.9	26.7	29.4	100.0	63.8
Blue collar.	31.0	33.8	35.2	100.0	36.2
Combined	30.0	29.2	40.7	100.0	100.0

* Differences by age and education are statistically significant.

all four sections. The data are condensed in the table, both to save space and to facilitate comparison of the measures among the four different demographic variables.

Notice that the table in Example 12–15 clearly identifies what item is being cross-tabulated with what other items in the heading. Row percentages are identified as the numbers within the body of the table, and since the percentages are reported, the number of respondents is listed so that readers know the total on which the percentages are based. In each section of the table, the combined percentages in the last *column* at the right show the percentage of respondents in each category, totaling to 100 percent for the entire sample. The combined percentages in the bottom *row* are the percentages of the entire sample within each column. They are, of course, the same for each section because the columns represent the same categories, but they are listed in each section so that the row percentages for each category of the variable can be compared with the combined total, as well as with one another. All rows total to 100 percent, and the "Total" column is listed in the table so that readers will quickly recognize that the percentages total *across* the rows and *not down* the columns. The first two demographic variables are listed with an asterisk and a footnote indicates the differences in the distributions are statistically significant. The other two cross-tabulations are not.

The narrative text to accompany a table such as that shown in Example 12–15 should *briefly* explain the table for readers if it is the first table of its type or the first use of that format to appear in the report. It would then note the statistical significance and identify the major results:

> There is less than a 5 percent chance that the distributions of Larks, Wrens, and Owls would differ as much as they do among age groups and among educational levels, for a sample such as this, if they actually did not differ in the whole population. Consequently, these differences are statistically significant and we can assume that those in the population really do differ by age and education level in their time of day preferences. The differences between the sexes and occupational groups in this sample are not large enough to assume they exist in the population as well.
>
> The proportion of Larks, Wrens, and Owls differ very little between those who are in the middle and those in the upper age groups. By contrast, a much higher proportion of the youngest group tends to be Larks, a somewhat smaller proportion than the other groups are Wrens, and a markedly lower percentage are Owls.
>
> Educational level also seems to affect time of day preferences. It is interesting to note that those with *no college* and those who are *college graduates* have similar proportions of Larks, Wrens, and Owls, while those with *some college* are much more often Larks and less often Owls. But if education actually affects time of day preferences, and education certainly affects membership in occupational groups, then time of day preferences should also differ between blue and white collar occupations. They do *not*. To check further on this puzzling relationship, age groups were cross-tabulated with educational level. The results indicate that a large proportion of those with *some college* are young students, so the conclusion is that age is the most important determinant and education plays only a small role.

Another format for reporting several crosstabs in the same table is shown in Example 12–16. In this format, the same four ratings define all rows, and each pair of columns shows the percentages for a different variable or brand, in this example. Column percentages are listed in the body of the table, so they total downward to 100 percent. Since there were exactly as many men as women, the researcher did not show the combined percentages for both sexes, so the focus is directed exclusively on the comparison between the ratings of men and

EXAMPLE 12-16

Cross-Tabulation Horizontal Banner Report

Ratings of Four Brands by Sex of Respondent
[Column percentages are listed. Number = 100 men, 100 women]

	Brand A Women	Brand A Men	Brand B Women	Brand B Men	Brand C Women	Brand C Men	Brand D Women	Brand D Men
Excellent	31	19	8	12	17	26	36	44
Good	42	36	21	33	40	38	51	38
Fair	19	26	39	41	32	21	10	22
Poor	8	19	32	14	11	15	3	4
Total	100	100	100	100	100	100	100	100

Differences between sexes for all four brands are statistically significant.

those of women for each brand. By presenting the distributions for all four brands in one banner, the comparison between brands is also facilitated, but it is important to note that measuring *significance* of differences *between brands* would require cross-tabulations between pairs of brands, for each sex, individually.

Analysis of Variance Reports

The statistical method for measuring the significance of differences among *mean* values of a continuous, dependent variable for the categories of an independent variable is analysis of variance. A typical print output from an analysis program is shown in Example 11–3. Reports of academic research ordinarily show the results very much as they are listed in Example 11–3, but the reporting of pragmatic survey research usually contains only the tables of mean values and omits the analysis of variance table, itself. This is the case in Example 12–17. In this format, the researcher was able to list not only the table of means for marital status, the variable shown in Example 11–3, but also those for age groups and for family life cycle.

Notice that in Example 12–17, the actual probability is listed, rather than merely noting statistical significance. This is permissible only when the narrative explains the meaning of the probability or when the report readers are all very likely to know the meaning from an earlier explanation or previous training and experience. The footnote to the table in Example 12–17 indicates that the other demographic variables in the survey did not prove to have significantly different

EXAMPLE 12-17

Condensed Analyses of Variance Report

Breakdowns of: Lark-Owl Test Scores by Demographic Variables*
[Average (mean) values and number of respondents listed]

Item	Group	Probability	Average	Number
Age Group		.0000		
	Under 20.		2.09	11
	20 to 29		5.14	97
	30 to 39		6.18	73
	40 to 49		7.00	59
	50 to 59		6.72	78
	60 to 69		6.90	51
	70 and over.		6.71	31
	Combined		6.18	400
Marital status		.002		
	Married.		6.67	215
	Not married.		5.60	185
	Combined		6.18	400
Family Life Cycle		.0014		
	Young single		5.19	113
	Young couple		6.18	39
	Child under 6		6.77	30
	Child 6 to 15		6.18	44
	Child over 15.		6.72	54
	Elder couple		6.97	74
	Elder single.		6.26	46
	Combined		6.18	400

* Scores not significantly different for other demographic items.

test scores when they were analyzed. Thus, there was no purpose in showing the means for each category of those variables, because they are automatically assumed to be the same for all categories of each in the population.

The narrative text to accompany a tabular report such as that in Example 12-17 would typically identify the highest and lowest mean value for each category, for one variable at a time. Any trends or identifiable relationships among categories, in terms of the mean values, should be noted in the narrative, and the major differences by category discussed as well.

Paired T-Test Reports

When the significance of the difference between means for a pair of continuous variables *both obtained from the same respondents* is to be measured, a *paired* t-test can be used. The report of such an analysis from a statistical program is shown in Example 11–4. In that example, the differences between the time respondents actually arose in the morning and the time they would ideally like to arise was measured. In Example 12–18, the analyses of this pair of times and four others are all reported in the same, condensed table. For academic survey research reports, the table would probably contain most or all of the items shown in Example 11–4. For more pragmatic survey research, the reports usually show only the mean values, just as with analysis of variance. When paired t-tests are reported, it is also advisable to show the direction and magnitude of *differences* in means as well. Of course, there must be some notation of the statistical significance as well. Example 12–18 lists the actual probability for gauging significance.

EXAMPLE 12–18

Condensed Report of Paired T-Tests

Comparisons of: *Actual* versus *Ideal* Times of Day

[Number = 400 Average (mean) values are listed]

Activity	Actual	Ideal	Difference	Probability
Get Up...............	6:47 AM	7:12 AM	− 25 Min.	.000
Start Work	8:16 AM	8:35 AM	− 19 Min.	.000
Finish Work	4:02 PM	4:21 PM	− 19 Min.	.000
Have Dinner..........	6:31 PM	6:30 PM	+ 1 Min.	.598
Go To Bed............	11:00 PM	11:03 PM	− 3 Min.	.126

In many cases, there is no need to list relationships that do *not* prove to be statistically significant. For example, the table in Example 12–17 merely notes that the means for the other demographic variables were not significantly different, and the actual means were not listed. The table shown in Example 12–18 does show the actual and ideal *dinner times* and *bed times*, even though the differences are clearly not statistically significant. This is a case where it is just as important to recognize the *similarity* in the mean values as it is to identify differences. Whenever such similarity in values is as notable or even more remarkable than are differences in values, the similar pairs of means should be listed, even though the differences are not statistically significant.

The inclusion of five-paired t-test analyses in one table, for comparable pairs, as in Example 12–18, allows the researcher to compare similarities and differences between pairs in the narrative text, thus:

> Survey respondents clearly indicated in their listings of actual and ideal times that they would prefer to arise in the morning about a half hour later than they do. The results shown in Table 18 also indicate they would like to start and finish their workday about 20 minutes later. By contrast, the results show that they eat dinner in the evening at almost exactly the time they would like to do so, and also retire for the night at very nearly the ideal time.
>
> These relationships suggest two things: (1) The average individual in the population would like to start and finish work a little later than they are required to do so. (2) The fact that they must start work earlier than they would ideally like causes them to *arise* earlier than they want to, but they *dine* and *retire* in the evening when they would like. Thus, they sacrifice *sleep* time to meet work requirements.

Correlation Analysis Reports

When the *means* of two continuous variables that are both responses from the same respondents are to be compared, the paired t-test is used. When the relationship between such variables is to be measured in terms of their change or variance from one respondent to the next, *correlation* is the appropriate measure. Correlation analysis does *not* assume that one is causing or determining the other. When the data are from interval or ratio level scales, product-moment correlation is used and when the data are from ordinal level scales, rank correlation is appropriate. The results are shown in reports and interpreted in exactly the same way, but when rank correlations are shown, it should be noted in the report table. If the table simply lists correlation coefficients, the assumption would be that the coefficients are product-moment correlations.

In Example 11–5, each pairing of five variables was reported in tabular form by the analysis routine. The variables were only identified by number, and were not labeled to indicate their meaning. The same results are shown in Example 12–19, but the table is labeled to identify the variables by name, the correlations of each variable with itself have been omitted, and the redundant "halves" of the matrix are both shown, so that readers can locate a pair by approaching from the top or the side of the matrix. In Example 12–19, the probabilities for assessing statistical significance are listed, and this assumes the readers are all well-able to understand and interpret them. If that were not

EXAMPLE 12-19

Correlation Matrix Table

Correlations among: Ratings of Self-Image for Five Attributes

[Number = 500 Correlation coefficients (r) and probabilities (p) are shown]

	Creative	Assertive	Patient	Outspoken	Cooperative
Creative		r = +.30 p = .001	r = +.01 p = .402	r = +.16 p = .001	r = +.09 p = .018
Assertive	r = +.30 p = .001		r = −.10 p = .014	r = +.48 p = .001	r = −.08 p = .032
Patient	r = +.01 p = .402	r = −.01 p = .014		r = −.19 p = .001	r = +.43 p = .001
Outspoken . . .	r = +.16 p = .001	r = +.48 p = .001	r = −.19 p = .001		r = +.01 p = .408
Cooperative. .	r = +.09 p = .018	r = −.08 p = .032	r = +.43 p = .001	r = +.01 p = .408	

the case, only the correlation coefficients would be shown and an asterisk would be attached to those that were significant, with a footnote to indicate the fact that they are significantly related. The narrative interpretations would merely identify the direction and intensity of each significant correlation.

Regression Analysis Reports

When the effect of one continuous variable on another is to be measured, regression analysis is the statistical method to do so. In Example 11-6, the relationship between *estimates* and *actual* time requirements is assessed and reported by the analysis routine. The time variables are denominated in hours and fractions of hours. A tabular report of the same data is shown in Example 12-20 only the values have been converted to minutes.

It is always advisable to list the mean, minimum, and maximum values and the ranges for the variable in the analysis in reports of regression analysis. This is because the prediction equation is ordinarily only valid and accurate within or very close to that range. The table in Example 12-20 also lists the difference in means and the probability for assessing the significance of the difference. This measure is the same as a paired t-test, and it is interpreted in the same way. It merely indicates that the actual time requirements are significantly greater than the estimated times, in this case. The correlation

EXAMPLE 12-20

Regression Analysis Report

Regression of: Actual time required on Estimated time required

[Number = 400 Values expressed in minutes]

Variable	Average	Minimum	Maximum	Range
Actual time required	231	30	390	360
Estimated time required	212	30	390	360

Item	Symbol	Value	Std. Err.	Probability
Mean Difference	(D)	19.00		0.00004
Correlation	(R)	0.79		0.00001
Determination	(R^2)	0.63	64.180	0.00001
Coefficient	(B)	0.88	0.034	0.00001
Constant	(A)	136.111	32.680	0.00002

Prediction equation: *Prediction* = 0.88 times *Estimate* plus 136. (In minutes)

coefficient is also listed in the table shown in Example 12–20, along with the probability for assessing its significance. Again, the meaning and interpretation are precisely the same as for product-moment correlation, described and exemplified earlier.

The value of r-square is shown in the regression analysis report to indicate the degree to which the independent variable affects the dependent variable and suggest how accurate any predictions, based on the regression equation, might be. The standard error of the estimate and the standard errors of the constant and the regression coefficient might also be included in the report, if the readers are sufficiently informed or familiar with regression analysis. In Example 12–20, the prediction equation is listed at the bottom of the table in verbal, rather than symbolic form, for those who are not familiar with prediction equations and symbolic notation.

As noted earlier in previous chapters, regression analysis is both quite powerful and useful and also very complex. Consequently, regression analysis report tables often require a fairly complete and elaborate narrative explanation for report readers and sponsors who are not completely familiar with statistical methods. If the focus of the information needs is on *measurement of the existing relationship*, the narrative would deal with that aspect. If *predictions of the dependent variable*, based on the independent variable are required, then the narrative would place more emphasis on prediction, its accuracy, and especially on meeting the requirements for valid application, such as staying within the range of values used to compute the equation. In this example, only the *relationship* is discussed in the narrative:

> Respondents were questioned concerning the written *estimates* they had received from the shop and they also reported the *actual* time required, as listed on their invoices. The results are shown in Table 20, and all of the values there are in minutes, rather than hours. The table indicates that shortest estimated and actual time required was a half hour and the longest estimates and actual times were six hours. The average job took almost 20 minutes longer than was originally estimated. Thus, there seemed to be a significant bias toward *under*estimation of the jobs, but it was not a completely *consistent* bias. That is, it does not apply equally to long and to short jobs.
>
> The regression equation indicates: (1) Over 60 percent of the variance in the amount of time a job requires is "explained" or anticipated by the estimates. Thus, almost 40 percent of the variance in the amount of time required from one job to the next was *not* anticipated or explained by the estimator. (2) The regression also shows that the degree of *under*estimation, nearly 20 minutes on the average, does not apply equally to all jobs, long and short. Rather, there seems to be a tendency to grossly underestimate short jobs, but to underestimate the longer jobs only slightly. These relationships suggest that estimators are able to predict the time requirements for the actual work process fairly well but they may often fail to allow sufficient time for "start-up" and "shutdown" of individual jobs.

In this brief portion of a narrative text discussing the regression relationships shown in Example 12–20, the researcher first cited the differences in mean values, then indicated the strength of the relationship, based on the r-square value. Finally, the researcher based an interpretation of underestimation for jobs of various length on the value of the constant in the regression equation, as well as the slope or regression coefficient. The *constant* indicated that nearly *every* job requires over two hours, minimum.

Discriminant Analysis Reports

If the effect of a continuous, numeric variable on the category membership of a dependent variable is to be assessed, discriminant analysis is the appropriate statistical method. The discussion of this statistical method in previous chapters has been concerned with only a very limited situation, where just one independent variable is specified in the analysis and where the dependent variable has only two categories or groups. Even with these limitations, the technique can be quite complex and difficult to interpret for those not thoroughly familiar with statistical methods.

Example 11–7 contains only a portion of the contents that are ordinarily provided by statistical analysis routines for discriminant analysis. In Example 12–21, only a part of the content of Example 11–7 is shown. The table heading identifies the groups or categories that constitute the dependent variable and the scores that are used to predict category membership. In the upper portion of the table, the classification matrix is listed and the mean values of the scores for each group, together with the number in each group are also shown. The percentages of cases classified correctly is reported to show the strength of the relationship or the effectiveness of the discriminant equation in making predictions. The probability for assessing statistical significance is also listed.

EXAMPLE 12–21

Discriminant Analysis Report

Discrimination of: Self-perceived category by Test scores

Actual	Predicted		Average	Number
	Larks	Owls		
Larks	62.4*	37.6	22.35	178
Owls	20.7	79.3*	23.61	222
Combined			23.05	400

* Percent classified *correctly* = 71.75 Probability = .000

Prediction equation: *Prediction* = 0.891 times *Score* minus 20.526.

Negative = Lark, Positive = Owl category.

The lower portion of the table in Example 12–21 shows the "prediction equation" in words, rather than symbolic notation, much as the regression equation was listed in Example 12–20. (In technical terms, this is the coefficient and constant of the linear, discriminant function.) The narrative text to accompany such a tabular report would deal mainly with explanation of the classification matrix and the use of the prediction equation. As with regression analysis, the focus of discriminant analysis can be primarily on either the strength of the relationship or on actual prediction. In this brief sample narrative, only the relationship is discussed:

> After reading a brief description of Larks (morning people) and Owls (evening people), respondents were asked which phrase best described their own habits. Later, they completed Form R of the assessment test.

Table 21 shows that their self-perceptions of type can be predicted correctly by their test scores over 7 times out of 10. More of those who actually saw themselves as Owls were correctly classified than were those who viewed themselves as Larks, and over a third of the actual Larks were predicted as Owls.

CONCLUDING THE PROJECT

The final report of the results should be carefully edited and a clean copy typed using a dark print that can be copied clearly. Multiple copies are often required for sponsors and those seeking the information. The pragmatic survey research report should be headed with a title page that identifies the sponsor, project, and researcher or organization who conducted the survey. It is important to note on the title page the address and telephone number of the person or office responsible for the project, so that they can be contacted at a later time for clarification, if that should be needed.

All of the pages within a survey report should be consecutively numbered, and the page numbers should appear in the same place on every page. When the report is of substantial size, an index must ordinarily be prepared and included directly following the title page. The major sections of the report should be listed with the page number, and a list of tables or figures should follow the list of contents or index if there are several.

If the final survey report consists only of a few pages, they should be stapled together in the upper, left corner, or attached in a small binder or folio, to keep the document together and intact. When the report consists of many pages, it can either be punched and contained in a ring binder, or it might be punched and comb-bound or spiral-bound by a copy service. Larger reports stay more neat and readable when they are bound within durable covers. Ring binders are available that have covers with a clear plastic "envelope" in which the title page can be inserted, so that it is visible from the outside. When comb-binding or spiral-binding is used for final reports, it is often advisable to use an opaque plastic backing and a clear plastic front cover, so that the title page can be read and the document identified without opening it.

It is always advisable for the researcher to retain data files and documention for a *substantial* period of time, after completing a project. Very often sponsors or those seeking the information will have additional questions after studying the report. These additional information needs can usually be met quickly and inexpensively if the data files, programs, and documents are retained in good order. All of the survey materials, including the source documents, data files, special programs, and other materials obtained specifically for the survey are ordinarily the property of the sponsor. Thus, when these materials are clearly no longer of use to the researcher for the project at hand, the sponsor should indicate which are to be delivered to the sponsor's office and which are to be destroyed. In most cases of commercial survey research, all of the materials are regarded by the sponsor as proprietary information. Consequently, extra copies of the reports or other documents must ordinarily be delivered to the sponsor's care or destroyed, so that they do not fall into the hands of those who are not entitled to the information.

Whether the survey research project was conducted to meet academic requirements or professionally, as the result of employment or a contract, most experienced researchers find one source of "payment" to be very valuable. That is merely the sense of satisfaction and accomplishment that is inevitably achieved at the completion of a job *well done*. No matter how simple or mundane the content of a well-conceived and conducted survey might be, those who do the project can be assured of its value. This society both generates and consumes vast amounts of information and the entire technical system is heavily dependent on it. Consequently, those who use survey research to generate *information* that is both reliable and valid have contributed significantly to the progress and satisfaction of the society.

SUMMARY

Generating the Final Report

A. Spend the time and effort. Avoid the temptation to rush through the report and do it carefully, even though sponsors may be overly anxious.

B. Keep it very neat. The appearance and cosmetic aspects of the report often indicate to readers, rightly or wrongly, the credibility of the survey results.

C. Use an executive summary. Pragmatic survey research reports should begin with a quick summary of the main highlights and major results.

D. Include a response summary. Prepare a blank questionnaire listing the simplest form of data description and removing any superfluous codes or instructions.

E. Compose tables first. Condense the information with clean, simple formats in a single page, so that patterns and relationships can readily be perceived.

F. Write a simple narrative. Avoid jargon and use plain vocabulary to describe the major findings revealed in each table, with introductions and summaries of each section.

G. Keep components independent. Tables should be labeled and the narrative written so that report readers can obtain the major gist of the results from either one.

H. Conclude the project. Edit, copy, and bind the reports, including a title page for identification, and maintain data and documents until directed to deliver or destroy them.

Glossary

Absolute Frequency   The number of cases or respondents appearing in each category of a frequency distribution or in each cell of a cross-tabulation table.

Absolute Value   The value of a number, ignoring the plus or minus sign.

Action Component   One of the three basic components of an attitude, indicating the person's consistent tendency to take action regarding the topic or to remain passive about it.

Accessibility Bias   One type of selection bias during sampling, where some respondents in the population are over- or underrepresented because they are more accessible or are less accessible than others.

Affective Component   One of three components of attitudes, consisting of the persons evaluations or feelings about the object, issue, or topic.

Affiliations   The network of durable, formal, and informal associations an individual has with family, relatives, friends, and acquaintances.

Affinity Bias   A form of interviewer bias resulting from interviewers showing preference for certain types of people, for whom they have an affinity, such as respondents who are similar to them or that they find attractive, and including them in the sample at higher rates than others.

Aided Recall   A form of questioning respondents about what they remember, where their memory is aided by presenting or describing the things they might recall.

Adjective Checklist   A scaling device that lists a series of adjectives which might be used to describe some person, place, or thing and asks the respondent to check any adjective that applies.

Alpha Level   The critical value, or probability level above which a relationship between variables will not be regarded as statistically significant because it is too likely that it could result only by chance from sampling error if the variables were actually not related in the population as a whole, also referring to the probability of a type I error in academic research.

Alternative Hypothesis   The proposition that some condition or relationship exists, accepted in scientific or academic research, if the results fail to support the "null hypothesis" that it does not exist.

Analysis of Variance (ANOVA)   A statistical measure of the association between a categorical, independent variable and a continuous, numerical, dependent variable from an interval or ratio scale, used to assess the significance of differences among means for different groups.

Area Sampling   A form of cluster sampling where the region of the population is first divided into areas, some are randomly selected, and then respondents within those areas are randomly selected.

Attitude   Relatively durable, psychological predispositions of people to respond toward or against an object, person, place, idea, or symbol, consisting of three components: their knowledge or beliefs, their feelings or evaluations, and their tendency toward action or passivity.

Attitude Scale   A scale used to measure attitudes, usually focusing on the respondents' feelings or evaluations toward one or more objects or topics.

Average   A measure of central tendency that represents the most typical case, usually referring to the arithmetic mean, but also applying to the median and the mode.

Banner   A method for showing several cross-tabulations in one, condensed table in order to save space or facilitate comparison, ordinarily used only when one variable is cross-tabulated against several others.

Bar Chart   A graphic portrayal of several quantities, such as frequencies or percentages, where the length of the horizontal or vertical bars represents the relative magnitudes of the values.

Behavior   The actions of people or objects in the past or at the present.

Bias   The tendency for some extraneous factor to affect the answers to survey questions or the survey results in general, in a systematic way, so that results are "pushed" or "pulled" in some specific direction.

Bimodality   The existence of two modes or peaks in a distribution of response, rather than a single modal value, often caused when the sample contains two, distinct populations or groups with differing reactions.

Bipolar Adjectives   A pair of adjectives, such as those used in a semantic differential scale, that represent the polar extremes on one dimension or continuum.

Bivariate Relationship   A relationship between only two variables.

Bivariate Statistics   The statistics used to measure the relationship between only two variables and assess its statistical significance.

Bottle Scale   A pictorial scale showing a series of bottles filled to varying levels, sometimes used when surveying those who may not always understand verbal or numeric scales, such as young children or those with reading impairments.

Breakdowns   A data analysis procedure that computes and reports the mean, standard deviation, and number of cases for a continuous numeric variable for each level of a categorical variable, ordinarily using analysis of variance to measure the statistical significance of differences in mean values.

C.P.U.   Abbreviation for central processing unit, the part of the computer that contains the circuits that control and perform the execution of instructions.

Callbacks   The second and subsequent attempts to contact respondents by telephone or in person when they were not present to respond to the first attempt to contact them.

Case   A set of data obtained from one completed questionnaire or one respondent that serves as a single unit for analysis.

Categorical Data   Nominal data where the values of the variables are merely the names of discrete, independent categories and the numeric magnitudes have no meaning or stand in no fixed relationship, as opposed to continuous data.

Categorical Item   A survey question coded with values that are merely the names of categories, so that the values do not represent magnitudes or stand in any ordered relationship with one another.

Causality   The potential influence or effect that one item or variable has on another.

Ceiling Effects   The truncation or "chopping off" of the high side of a distribution because respondents' answers could go no further up the scale.

Census   Counting or taking measurements from all members of a given population, rather than sampling only a portion to represent the whole.

Central Processing Unit (C.P.U.)   The part of the computer that contains the circuits that control and perform the execution of instructions, as opposed to the peripheral devices for data input, storage, and output.

Central Tendency Measures   Statistical averages that describe the most typical value or case, such as the mean, median, and mode.

Chi-Square   A value, usually obtained from cross-tabulation of two items in survey research, that can be compared with the values of the chi-square distribution to obtain a probability for assessing statistical significance.

Chi-Square Distribution   The particular form of a distribution derived from a set of computations and defined by the number of "degrees of freedom," often listed in statistical reference tables.

Closed-Ended Question   A structured survey question where the alternative answers are listed so that respondents must ordinarily pick only from among them.

Classification Variables   Survey items, such as demographic variables, that are used to classify respondents into groups or categories for comparison.

Cluster   One group of individuals or sampling units that have proximity with one another within the sample frame in some respect, such as those within a given area.

Cluster Bias   A form of selection bias resulting when a cluster sampling design selects respondents who are too closely related to one another within a cluster, so that they tend to give similar responses.

Cluster Sampling   A technique often used in surveys to save travel or long distance toll charges where the population is divided into clusters and a few clusters, each containing many respondents, are randomly selected.

Codebook   The entire set of codelists for several variables from one survey.

Codelist   The list of code values and category labels for a single survey variable that is generated by postcoding and used during analysis and reporting.

Coding   The process of assigning code values to the various alternative answers to survey questions, either when constructing the questionnaire (precoding) or after data collection (postcoding).

Coefficient of Determination   The square of the correlation coefficient, indicating the proportion of "shared" variance for correlation or the proportion of variance in the dependent variable that was "explained" by the independent variable in regression.

Cognitive Component   One of the three basic components of attitudes, consisting of what the individual knows or believes about the topic.

Comparative Scale   A scale using one entity as the standard by which one or more others are judged or evaluated.

Computer Hardware   The physical devices and components of computers, including both the central processing unit and the peripheral devices for inputting, storing, and outputting data.

Computer Software   The programs and coded instructions to the computer, including both the operating system that provides general control and the applications programs that perform specific computations.

Confidence Interval   The range around a numeric statistical value obtained from a sample, within which the actual, corresponding value for the population is likely to fall, at a given level of probability.

Confidence Level   The specific probability of obtaining some result from a sample if it did not exist in the population as a whole, at or below which the relationship will be regarded as statistically significant.

Continuous Variable   A variable that represents a continuum without any breaks or interruptions, so that the numeric values could potentially take on an infinite number of values expressed in whole numbers and fractions.

Construct Validity   The degree to which survey instrumentation conforms to the underlying concepts or makes sense based on what is represented.

Content Validity   The degree to which the survey instrumentation is judged by experts to represent the thing to be measured, based on the content of the questions and scales.

Convenience Sample   A sample selected more on the bias of the researcher or data collection team's convenience than on the requirements for random selection with a known probability of inclusion and representation.

Correlation Analysis   A measure of the relationship or association between two continuous, numeric variables that indicates both the direction and degree to which they covary with one another from case to case, without implying that one is causing the other.

Correlation Coefficient   The value computed with correlation analysis, ranging from zero to indicate no systematic relationship to plus or minus one, indicating a perfect, linear relationship, where the positive or negative value shows if the relationship is direct or inverse, respectively.

Correlation Matrix   The correlation coefficients between each pair, for several variables, arranged so that each variable is identified on each row and on each column, with the coefficient listed in the cells defined by the rows and columns.

Critical Value   The probability level above which a relationship between variables will not be regarded as statistically significant because it is too likely that it could result only by chance from sampling error if the variables were actually not related in the population as a whole.

Cross-Tabulation   Plotting two categorical variables in the form of a matrix so that the values of one variable define the rows and the values of the other, the columns, with the cells containing the frequency of cases with a given value for each of the two items and from which a chi-square value can be computed to assess the statistical significance of the relationship.

Curvilinear   A line or distribution of values that is continuous, but forms an arch, rather than a straight line.

Data   Most often numbers, but also letters, or words that symbolize or represent quantities, entities, or categories of things.

Data Analysis   The manipulation of numbers, letters, or symbols in order to suppress the detail and reveal the relevant facts or relationships.

Data Collection   The process of communicating questions and obtaining a record of responses from a sample, either by mail, telephone, or personal interviewing.

Data Deck   A file or collection of machine-readable punch cards on which the survey data have been keyed.

Data Field   The location and number of columns in a data file record required to contain the largest number of digits for any code value for a particular variable.

Data Point   A datum, or one, single entry of a number, letter, or symbol, usually for one variable and one case or respondent.

Data Processing   Submitting the survey data to computer programs and routines in order to perform the statistical analysis and to generate reports, as opposed to hand tabulation of the data.

Data Tabulation   Condensing the data by accumulating the frequencies and listing them with their identification in tables.

Datum   The singular form of the word "data", and referring to a single data point or one piece of data.

Decisions   The process and/or results of individual evaluations, judgments, and choices among alternatives.

Degrees of Freedom (d.f.)   A parameter most often based on the number of cases or respondents, but slightly reduced to adjust for some earlier computations and used when checking reference tables or computing probability to assess statistical significance.

Demographics   A set of conditions or attributes of people, often including age, sex, marital status, education, employment, occupation, and income, among others, usually measured in surveys to determine the types of people represented by the sample and to make comparisons of other results among demographic groups.

Dependent Variable   The variable that is viewed as being potentially influenced, affected, or determined by some other variable in a cause and effect relationship, based on the logic and meaning of the things represented by the variables.

Descriptive Research   Research that is designed primarily to describe, rather than to explain a set of conditions, characteristics, or attributes of people in a population, based on measurement of a sample.

Descriptive Statistics   Statistics such as averages and measures of spread, used to suppress the detail in data files and to condense and summarize the data to make facts more visible, as well as to indicate the degree to which the sample data are likely to represent the entire population.

Depicted Scale   Any scale that cannot be included within the survey question, so that it must be shown in the form of numbers, words, or pictures representing response alternatives.

Diagrammatic Scale   Any form of scale that uses a diagram to depict the response options or to obtain or collect the answers to survey questions.

Dichotomous Question   A question with only two response alternatives, such as a yes/no question or an item that can either be checked or ignored.

Discrete Variable   A categorical variable yielding nominal data, where all of the answers must fall within a category and the code values stand in no ordered relationship with one other.

Discriminant Analysis   A statistical measure of the relationship between a continuous, numeric, independent variable from an interval or ratio scale and a categorical dependent variable defining two or more groups, used both to assess statistical significance and also to compute the discriminant function, used to predict or classify new cases into groups.

Discriminant Function   The prediction or classification equation obtained from discriminant analysis, used to predict or classify new cases into groups when only the value of the independent variable is known.

Dispersion   The range and degree of spread or variance in the distribution of data for a survey variable.

Editing   The process of examining questionnaires or data against some set of criteria, to be sure the content is correct or appropriate.

Explicit Scale   Any scale that is directly expressed or stated, either verbally or visually, as opposed to those that are only implied by the question.

External Validity   The degree to which survey results can be generalized to represent actual conditions in the whole population.

Extreme Case   A response that is an outlier, with a value so extreme it is far distant from any other response, which may sometimes suggest there has been an error while recording or transferring the data.

Expected Cell Frequency   A value computed during or after cross-tabulation, based on the proportion of the data represented by the entire row and column on which the cell resides.

F-Distribution   The particular form of a distribution derived from a set of computations and defined by two numbers of "degrees of freedom," often listed in statistical reference tables.

F-Ratio   The ratio of a numerator and denominator value consisting of variance expressed as "mean squares," or the "sum of squares" divided by the degrees of freedom for each, usually computed with analysis of variance and compared to the F-distribution in a statistical reference table to assess statistical significance.

Face Validity   The degree to which survey items or results appear to be valid or meaningful, based only on the subjective judgment.

Feeling Component   One of the three main components of attitudes, consisting of the evaluations and judgments of the topic by the individual holding the attitude.

Fixed Sum Scale   A particular type of scale where the respondent is asked to list the number of times each of a set of alternatives occurred or apply, out of a given total, so that the sum of the values must equal the total.

Floor Effects   The truncation or "chopping off" of the low side of a distribution because respondents' answers could go no further lower on the scale.

Forced Ranking Scale   A type of scale, yielding ordinal level data, where the respondents are instructed to rank a series of items in sequential order, with no "ties" or equal rankings allowed.

Formatting   The design or a particular arrangement for words, numbers or symbols, specifying their order or sequence, physical location, relative distance or proximity, and general form, often used in reference to the location of data fields within a file record.

Frequency Distribution   The number of cases that contain each of the scale values for a particular survey item or variable.

Frequency Table   A tabular presentation of the frequency distribution, often including percentage distributions based on the frequencies and the sample size, the number of valid cases, and the cumulative number of valid cases.

Grand Mean   The arithmetic mean of the dependent variable for all of the cases in an analysis of variance, as opposed to the "group means," including only the cases in each category of the independent variable.

Hand Tabulation   The statistical computations and analysis of survey data without the use of computer analysis routines, usually confined to frequency tables, crosstabulation tables, and the statistics that can be obtained from them without the processing of continuous, numeric variables with many scale values.

Happy-Sad Face Scale   One form of pictorial scale showing a series of simple sketches of faces with the mouth of each turned up in a smile to show pleasure or down to show displeasure in varying degrees, often used for surveying young children who may not be able to understand numeric or verbal scales.

Histogram   A horizontal bar chart showing the frequency or percentage distribution of response for a survey item in graphic form, often generated by computer analysis routines if requested.

Homoskedasticity   The required condition of a scatterplot of data for regression analysis, where the data points are spread around the regression line in approximately equal amounts at any given point on the line, forming an even corridor of data, as opposed to heteroskedasticity, such as a "funnel shaped" pattern of data round the regression line.

Horizontal Numeric Scale   One of the most common scaling devices, consisting of a horizontal line of a few sequential numbers for the scale points, with the left and right extremes labeled to indicate some dimension, such as importance, value, or preference.

Hypothesis   A conjectural statement about the value of some variable or the relationship between variables that will be tested and ultimately accepted or rejected on the basis of statistical analysis of survey results, most often used in formal scientific or academic research.

Images   The generalized or synthesized picture representation of some object, person, place, or idea held in the minds of people, based on partial information from previous experiences, perceptions, or evaluations, and often one of the major topics of survey research.

Implicit Scale   Any scale that need not be explicitly stated in the question or presented verbally or visually to respondents because they automatically understand how they are to respond, such as asking one's age with the implicit understanding that it will be expressed in years since birth.

Independence   The conditions between two variables or measurements where information about one gives no indication of the likely value of the other because they are unrelated.

Independent Variable   The variable that is viewed as influencing, affecting, or determining the values of another variable when they are regarded as being in a potential cause and effect relationship.

Inferential Statistics   Any statistical measure that can be used to make inferences or generalizations about a population, with a known level of probability, based on the values or conditions of a sample.

Information Needs   The specific categories of information required by those sponsoring pragmatic survey research, in order to make decisions or choices or to set policy, or required by those conducting academic research, to test theoretical or conceptual hypotheses and enhance some body of knowledge or literature.

Instrumentation   The survey questionnaire and other devices, such as cover letters, rating cards, and the like, used to obtain data from respondents.

Instrumentation Bias   The tendency for some aspect of the survey instruments to cause respondents to answer in a particular way or systematically "push" or "pull" the survey results in some given direction, thus reducing the survey validity.

Instrumentation Error   The tendency for some aspect of the survey instruments to randomly affect the data in such a way that they are not true representations of the respondent opinions or conditions, but there is no specific direction or systematic influence, so that survey reliability is reduced.

Integer   A whole number, as opposed to a fractional or decimal value.

Internal Consistency Reliability   Assessment of reliability based on the comparison of the results for comparable items within the same questionnaire, using a single sample of respondents.

Interval Scale   Any scale where the intervals between scale points are equal, even though there may be no zero value or zero does not represent an complete absence of the thing measured, such as the fahrenheit scale.

Interviewer Error   The tendency for some aspect of the interviewing to randomly affect the data in such a way that they are not true representations of the respondent opinions or conditions, but there is no specific direction or systematic influence, so that survey reliability is reduced.

Interviewing Bias   The tendency for some aspect of the interviewing to cause respondents to answer in a particular way or systematically "push" or "pull" the survey results in some given direction, thus reducing the survey validity.

Judgment Sample A sample selected on the basis of the researcher's judgment about what units or respondents should and should not be included, as opposed to random selection.

Knowledge Component One of the three main components of attitudes, consisting of the facts or beliefs the individual holds about the topic of the attitude.

Kurtosis A statistical measure of the shape of a distribution that indicates whether the curve is more peaked or more flat than a normal, bell-shaped curve and how much so.

Level of Confidence The specific probability of obtaining some result from a sample if it did not exist in the population as a whole, at or below which the relationship will be regarded as statistically significant.

Lifestyle The general pattern of daily behavior, activities, choices, and preferences for an individual or family that might be used to characterize them and distinguish them in meaningful ways from those following a different pattern.

Likert Scale A type of scaling where the respondents are presented with a series of statements, rather than questions, and asked to indicate the degree to which they agree or disagree, usually on a five point scale.

Linear Regression A statistical measure of the effect of one interval or ratio level variable on another, used both to indicate the statistical significance of the relationship and to generate an equation to predict or estimate the value of the dependent variable for a new case, based only on the known value of the independent variable.

Mail Data Collection The mailing of questionnaires and their return by mail by the designated respondents.

Mainframe Computers The larger varieties of computers that are often centrally located, so that many users operate from remote locations or submit "batch" jobs to be executed and printed, as opposed to the smaller, tabletop computers used directly by a single operator.

Maximum The highest value for a variable that was actually obtained from a sample, often reported by analysis routines and used by analysts to assess range and likelihood of outliers or ceiling effects.

Mean The most common average or measure of central tendency, providing an indication of the most typical or representative value for the sample and the population as a whole, within a given confidence level.

Mean Squares A value usually computed for analysis of variance to form an F-ratio to assess statistical significance, consisting of the total of the squared deviations from the mean for each data point, or sums of squares, divided by the number of cases or degrees of freedom.

Measures of Dispersion   Statistical indications of the spread in a distribution of data for one variable, such as the standard deviation.

Measures of Spread   Statistical indications of the dispersion of the data around the central point, such as the standard deviation.

Median   An average or measure of central tendency, consisting of the value the middle case would take on if the cases were arrayed from lowest to highest value for the variable and the scale represented a continuum or could include an infinite number of points, used in preference to the mean for ordinal level data and often preferred to the mean for distributions that are highly skewed to one size or have outlying values.

Microcomputer   A small, tabletop computer with an integrated circuit "microprocessor" as its central processing unit.

Minimum   The lowest value for a variable that was actually obtained from a sample, often reported by analysis routines and used by analysts to asssess range and likelihood of outliers or floor effects.

Minimum Expected Cell Frequency   The lowest expected cell frequency in a cross-tabulation table, that must be at least five for valid use of the chi-square statistic to assess the significance of the relationship, computed by identifying the smallest row frequency and column frequency, multiplying the two, and dividing by the total frequency for the table.

Mode   The only average appropriate to indicate the most typical case for a distribution of nominal data, consisting of the category with the highest frequency, and also representing the location of the peak or high point in a distribution of continuous data with many scale values.

Multiple-Choice Question   A structured survey question that requires the respondent to choose one or more alternatives from a given list.

Multiple Response Question   A multiple-choice question where the respondent can check as many alternatives as apply, rather than only one alternative, so that each alternative becomes a survey item or variable.

Multiple Rating Grid   A survey item format used to save space and response time, designed so that more than one object or topic is rated on several dimensions, all using the same scale.

Multiple Rating Matrix   A survey item format used to facilitate response, designed so that the same scale values are shown opposite each item to be rated, often with the labels for the scale shown at the top of the list.

Multiple Regression   Linear regression that uses a single dependent variable and two or more independent variables in the same analysis, in contrast to simple, linear regression using only one independent variable, so that both the effect of each independent variable and the effects of interactions among independent variables can be gauged.

Multivariate Analysis   Statistical analysis techniques to assess the relationships or patterns among more than two variables simultaneously, including such methods as multiple regression, factorial analysis of variance, analysis of covariance, factor analysis, cluster analysis, multidimensional scaling, and the like.

N-*Size* A commonly used term for the sample size or the number of cases included in an analysis or tabular report.

N*th Name Sampling* A sampling design where the number of units in the sample frame is first divided by the desired sample size to obtain the value of n, a value between one and n is randomly selected as a starting point or first case to be selected, and then every nth name or unit is selected, yielding a random sample.

Namelist A listing of names and addresses, often used for mail surveys, that may be accumulated or acquired from one of many namelist brokerage firms who accumulate and manage such lists for people with particular characteristics or in certain locations.

Nay-Sayer An individual or respondent who persistently tends to respond in the negative more often than others, regardless of the questions.

Nay-Sayer Bias The tendency for a set of survey results to be generally and artifically negative on a series of items because all items are inclined in the same direction, toward the positive or toward the negative, and negative responses to the earlier items were generalized to the remaining ones, thus reducing the validity.

Need In a psychological context, a persistent or fundamental requirement of the individual in order to maintain physical, psychological, or social well-being, often fluctuating over time in its degree of satisfaction.

Nominal Scale A scale that uses numbers, letters, or symbols only as the names of independent categories, so that the scale values do not stand in any ordered relationship to one another.

Nonprobability Sampling Any sampling procedure that deviates from random selection of respondents or some other design where the probability of inclusion of individual sampling units is equal and known, such as a convenience sample or a judgment sample.

Nonrespondents Those in the population who were included in the sample but failed to respond because they refused, could not be reached, or some other reason.

Non-Response Bias A systematic affect on the data reducing validity that results when those with one type of opinion or condition fail to respond to a survey more often than do others with different opinions or conditions.

Non-Response Rate The percentage of all those included in the sample who failed to respond.

Normal Curve A continuous, symmetrical distribution that forms a curve with a particular shape defined by a mathematical equation, often referred to as a "bell-shaped" curve, valuable as a frame of reference because the precise areas under the curve can be computed or obtained from reference tables.

Normal Distribution   Any distribution that conforms exactly or very closely to a normal curve.

Null Hypothesis   The hypothesis stipulating there will be no significant relationship between two variables, which can be tested with survey or other data and rejected in favor of the alternative hypothesis if the relationship proves significant, and most often used in scientific or academic research.

Numeric Item   Any survey item with scale numbers that are meaningful and stand in an ordered relationship to one another, such as those from ordinal, interval, or ratio scales.

Open-Ended Question   An unstructured survey question that does not include a list of alternative answers, so that respondents must answer in their own words.

Order Bias   The tendency for the order in which survey items are listed to effect respondents' answers in some systematic way, reducing validity.

Ordinal Scale   A particular type of scale where the response alternatives define an ordered sequence, so that the first is less than the second, the second less than the third, and so on, yielding ordinal level data where the intervals between scale points are not known or necessarily equal.

Outlier   An extreme case or data point that stands well-above or well-below its nearest neighbor and is highly atypical of the distribution as a whole.

Paired Comparison Scale   A type of scale that presents respondents with one pair of alternatives at a time, instructing them to pick just one from each pair, yielding dichotomous, nominal data.

Panel Study   A survey of a group of preselected respondents who agreed to be panel members on a continuous basis for a given period of time and provided initial demographic data, allowing for selection of special groups and permitting the use of surveys to monitor responses over time.

Parameter   A coefficient or value for the population that corresponds to a particular statistic from a sample, and is often inferred from the sample.

Paired T-Test   A technique for assessing the statistical significance of differences in mean values when both are obtained from the same respondents, and are therefore, paired with one another.

Pearson Product-Moment Correlation   The statistical method of correlation that requires interval or ratio level data and is not appropriate for ordinal scale data, which requires Spearman Rank correlation.

Percentile   An indication of the position of a case or value within a distribution, based on the number of cases with a lesser value out of a total of 100 cases.

Peripheral Devices   Units of computer hardware other than the central processing unit, used to input, store, and output data or information.

Personal Interview   Data collection accomplished with the interviewer in the presence of the respondent, so that they have visual contact, as opposed to telephone interviewing.

Pictorial Scale   Any scale with scale points portrayed as pictures or diagrams, rather than numbers, letters, or words.

Pie Chart   A method for portraying survey results graphically, consisting of a circle divided by lines from the center to the perimeter, so that the angles between the lines, and therefore, the size of the "pieces" represent proportions.

Pilot Survey   A brief preliminary survey, often using a small, convenience sample, conducted to test the survey instruments and data collection method, before the project details are finalized and the larger, formal survey conducted.

Population   The definition of all those people or elements of interest to the information seekers and from among whom the sample will be selected.

Postcode   The process of examining completed survey questionnaires, choosing response categories for items not precoded, assigning code values to them on the documents, and recording codes and categories labels in a codelist.

Precode   Assigning code values to the categories of structured questions and listing them for printing on the questionnaire prior to data collection.

Precision   The range of the confidence interval at a given level of probability, expressed in absolute terms or as a percentage of the mean value.

Pretest   Preliminary trial of some or all aspects of the sampling design, survey instrumentation, and data collection method, to be sure there are no unanticipated difficulties or problems.

Primary Data   Data collected for a particular project to meet specific information needs, as opposed to data that already exists for general use or as the result of inquiries for other purposes.

Probability Sampling   Any sampling design where every element in the population has either an equal probability of selection, as with random sampling, or has a given probability of being selected that is known in advance and used in analysis to assess significance.

Process Editing   Examining survey data with computer processing routines to be sure the data conform to the data file format and that all values are expressed in the proper form and are within the range of the scale for each item.

Qualification   The process of inspecting or interrogating potential respondents to be sure they are qualified to respond or that they fit the quota specifications for a particular interviewer.

Qualitative Research Research obtaining data in the form of words or other indications that do not lend themselves to quantitative analysis and whose analysis and interpretation depend on subjective judgments by experts.

Quantitative Research Research obtaining data in a form that can be represented by numbers, so that quantities and magnitudes can be measured, assessed, and interpreted with the use of mathematical or statistical manipulation.

Questionnaire The basic survey instrument containing instructions, questions or items, response alternatives where appropriate, and specific means for recording responses.

Quota Sample Any sampling design that requires a set number or proportion of respondents with given characteristics or attributes.

Quota Specification The listing of quota requirements for the entire sample or for specific interviewers, including identification of the characteristics that define the quota, the manner in which they are to be ascertained, the method of qualification of respondents, and the number or proportion of respondents who are to have each attribute or combination of attributes.

R-Square (R^2 or RSQ) The coefficient of determination obtained during regression analysis, indicating the proportion of variance in the dependent variable that is "explained" by the values of the independent variable.

Random-Digit Dialing A sampling system for telephone surveys where all telephone numbers in households or all that have one of a given set of three-digit telephone number prefixes are regarded as the sample frame, and seven-digit or four-digit numbers are generated and dialed manually or automatically to obtain the sample.

Random Error The result of extraneous factors, such as sampling error, affecting the survey results in no systematic pattern, so that answers are not consistently pushed or pulled in one specific direction.

Random Sample A sampling design that seeks to select respondents from the population or sample frame in a completely random fashion, so that every respondent has an equal probability of being selected.

Rank Correlation The statistical method of correlation appropriate when one or both of the variables are from only ordinal level scales, sometimes called Spearman Rank correlation.

Rank Order Scale A scale essentially the same as the forced ranking scale.

Range A measure of the spread in the distribution of data for a variable, defined as the maximum minus the minimum, plus one.

Rating Cards A card or sheet containing a rating scale that is handed to or shown to respondents during personal interviews and from which they pick their response alternatives by number or letter.

Rating Scale Any scale from which respondents choose values that represent their responses, ordinarily yielding interval or ratio level data.

Ratio Scale Any scale that has the same characteristics as an equal interval scale, plus the fact that zero represents the complete absence of the thing being measured, so that a ratio of one scale value to another has a meaningful and legitimate interpretation.

Raw Data Data that has not been transformed or processed, although it may have been edited and transferred from one medium to another.

Recode The process of systematically assigning new code values to variables, based on the original values, usually done in order to group data into larger categories to obtain fewer code values.

Record Format The specification of where the data field for each variable are to be keyed or recorded in a data file, including both the column(s) and the record numbers within a single case.

Regression Analysis A statistical measure of the effect of one interval or ratio level variable on another, used both to indicate the statistical significance of the relationship and to generate an equation to predict or estimate the value of the dependent variable for a new case, based only on the known value of the independent variable.

Regression Equation The equation generated by linear regression analysis, expressed as a coefficient that can be multiplied by the value of the independent variable for a new case and a constant to be added, to predict the unknown value of the dependent variable.

Relative Frequency A term that is sometimes used to refer to the percentages listed in a frequency table, indicating the proportion of the sample in each category.

Reliability The degree to which the survey results are free from random error, as opposed to systematic bias, often expressed in terms of confidence intervals or confidence levels.

Report Generation The process of arranging and condensing tabular survey results and expressing the written interpretations of the findings to provide information to those seeking it.

Responding Sample The number of cases with valid responses to the survey or to an individual survey item, as opposed to the total sample size.

Response Bias The tendency for some aspect of the response task, such as annoyance or a desire to please the interviewer, to cause respondents to answer in a particular way or systematically "push" or "pull" the survey results in some given direction, thus reducing the survey validity.

Response Error The tendency for some aspect of the response task, such as boredom, inattention, or fatigue, to randomly affect the data in such a way that they are not true representations of the respondent opinions or conditions, but there is no specific direction or systematic influence, so that survey reliability is reduced.

Response Rate   The percentage of those included in the sample who responded to the survey and provided usable, completed questionnaires.

Runs Test   A statistical process used in connection with regression analysis to determine the probability that the data are actually linear or arrayed evenly around a straight line if the data were plotted, by counting the "runs" of successive data points that are all on one side of the regression line.

Sample   The number and/or identification of respondents in the population who will be or have been included in the survey.

Sample Frame   A listing that should include all those in the population to be sampled and exclude all those who are not in the population.

Sample Selection Bias   Any form of bias resulting from the selection of respondents in a manner that deviates from random selection, so that some types of respondents are over- or underrepresented in the sample.

Sampling Design   The specification of the sample frame, sample size, and the system for selecting and contacting individual respondents from the population.

Sampling Error   The degree to which the results from the sample deviate from those that would be obtained from the entire population, because of random error in the selection of respondent and the corresponding reduction in reliability.

Sampling Unit   The smallest unit of the sample to be surveyed or the unit that will constitute one case for analysis, ordinarily one, individual respondent or questionnaire.

Scatterplot   A graphic plot of the data points for two variables, usually generated on request by analysis routines during regression analysis, so that each data point is plotted horizontally according to the value of the independent variable and vertically according to the value of the dependent variable.

Secondary Data   That that has been acquired for general use or for some purpose other than the information requirements of the project at hand.

Selection Bias   A systematic effect on the data resulting from selection of respondents in a manner that deviates from random selection, so that some types of respondents are over- or underrepresented in the sample.

Self-Selection Bias   A systematic affect on survey results because some respondents voluntarily participate while others decline or refuse, so that those with certain opinions or conditions are under- or overrepresented in the sample.

Semantic Differential Scale   A scaling device that lists several pairs of bipolar adjectives, usually separated by a seven-point scale, and instructs respondents to rate the topic or object on each, ordinarily used to measure image and provide a profile.

Sequential Sample   A sampling design that requires the collection of data in increments with a relatively small sample at each stage, so that analysis can be performed after each stage to determine when the sample is large enough to provide the required level of confidence or reliability.

Sight-Edit   The visual examination of the completed questionnaires immediately after data collection to determine if they are sufficiently complete and usable.

Significance Level   The probability that the magnitude of the relationship might result in a sample of that size purely from sampling error if, in fact, it did *not* exist in the population.

Simple Linear Regression   A statistical measure of the effect of one interval or ratio level variable on another, used both to indicate the statistical significance of the relationship and to generate an equation to predict or estimate the value of the dependent variable for a new case, based only on the known value of the independent variable.

Simple Random Sample   A sampling design that seeks to select respondents from the population or sample frame in a completely random fashion, so that every respondent has an equal probability of being selected, and no clustering or stratification methods are used.

Skewness   A designation of the shape of a distribution, indicating the degree of symmetry or the degree and direction that the mode or peak "leans" toward one side, with only a few values extending well out toward the tail on the other.

Slope   In regression analysis, the "rise over the run" when the dependent variable is plotted on the vertical axis of a scatterplot, or the amount of increase or decrease in the units of the dependent variable for each unit of the independent variable, indicated by the regression coefficient.

Social Desirability   The tendency for respondents to give answers to survey questions that are consistent with what the society believes is right, proper, correct, or acceptable, creating bias in the results whenever the true answers are suppressed to meet social norms.

Spread   The range and degree of dispersion or variance in the distribution of data for a survey variable.

Stair-Step Scale   One type of pictorial scale graphically showing the scale points as a series of steps, appropriate for use with young children or other respondents who might have difficulty understanding a numeric or verbal scale.

Standard Deviation   A computed measure of spread or dispersion in a distribution of data, based on the squared deviations of each point from the mean, that can be used to indicate the proportion of data within certain ranges of scale values when the distribution conforms closely to the normal curve.

Standard Error (of the Mean)   A computed value based on the size of the sample and the standard deviation of the distribution, indicating the range within which the mean of the population is likely to be from the mean of the sample at a given level of probability.

Standard Error of the Estimate   In regression, a computed value that indicates the range within which a value of the dependent variable predicted from the regression equation is likely to be, from the actual value of the case, at a given level of probability.

Stapel Scale   A scaling method listing a series of words or phrases that might be used to describe an object or topic, together with a numeric scale, and instructs respondents to rate the degree to which each item is or is not descriptive, often used to measure image and obtain a profile in much the same manner as the semantic differential scale is used.

Statistic   Some value computed from sample data that may also be used to make inferences about the corresponding value or "parameter" for the whole population.

Statistical Analysis   The process of computation and manipulation of sample data in order to suppress the detail and make relevant facts and relationships more visible and meaningful, and to generate statistics in order to make inferences about the population as a whole.

Statistical Inference   The process of generalizing information from a sample to the population as a whole by estimating population parameters, based on their corresponding statistical values from the sample.

Statistical Significance   An explicit assumption by the analyst that a relationship revealed in the sample data also exists in the population as a whole, based on the relatively small probability that it would result in the sample if it did not exist in the population.

Stratified Sampling   A two-step sampling design where the population or sample frame is divided into various levels, called strata, and random samples of given sizes are selected from each, usually used to insure a certain level of representation for various groups in the population.

Stratum   The singular form of "strata," indicating one level of a stratified sampling design.

Subsample   One part of an entire sample that is singled out for special attention or analysis, often defined in terms of a demographic characteristic.

Sum   The total of a series of values or the process of adding them.

Sum of Squares   A value computed for several forms of statistical analysis, such as computing the standard deviation, analysis of variance, regression analysis, and the like, where some mean is subtracted from each data point, this deviation is squared, and the squared values are added for all the cases.

Survey   A research technique where information requirements are specified, a population is identified, a sample selected and systematically questioned, and the results analyzed, generalized to the population, and reported to meet the information needs.

Systematic   A relationship or effect that is not random, but rather, one that is consistent or in a given "direction."

Systematic Bias   A redundant term, since bias is defined as a systematic effect, but commonly used to emphasize the nonrandom nature of a bias or to distinguish bias from random error.

Systematic Sampling   Another term for *n*th name sampling, where the number of units in the sample frame is first divided by the desired sample size to obtain the value of *n*, a value between one and *n* is randomly selected as a starting point or first case to be selected, and then every *n*th name or unit is selected, yielding a random sample.

T-Test   A statistical method of assessing the significance of differences between two mean values for the same variable, as opposed to a paired t-test of values for two different variables for the same cases, and yielding the same basic information as would analysis of variance with only two categories for the independent variable.

Telephone Interview   Interview data collection using the telephone to contact respondents, as opposed to personal interviewing where respondents are in the presence of the interviewer and have visual contact.

Type I Error   In academic or scientific research (as opposed to pragmatic research), the probability of rejecting the "null hypothesis" that no relationship exists, and therefore, accepting the "alternative hypothesis" that there is a relationship, when, in fact, no relationship exists in the population as a whole.

Type II Error   In academic or scientific research (as opposed to pragmatic research), the probability of not rejecting the "null hypothesis" that no relationship exists, and therefore, rejecting the "alternative hypothesis" that there is a relationship, when, in fact, a relationship does exist in the population as a whole.

Unaided Recall   A form of questioning respondents about what they remember, where the facts, objects, or events are not listed or presented to them to aid their recollection, as with aided recall.

Unbiased   Free of bias or unaffected by any extraneous factor that would systematically affect the values or results.

Unbiased Estimate   A statistical term that indicates the value of a particular statistic, such as the mean, obtained from the sample, will be exactly equal to the corresponding value of the population parameter, on the average over an infinite number of such samples.

Unimodal   Having only one modal value for a distribution of categorical data or only one peak or mode for a continuous distribution.

Univariate Analysis   The statistical description or the analysis of just one variable at a time.

Unstructured Question   An "open-ended" survey question where the alternative answers are not listed, respondents must provide the answers in their own words.

Validation A term commonly but incorrectly used by survey researchers and data collection agencies to indicate "verification" of responses.

Validity The degree to which the survey data or results are free from both systematic bias and random error.

Variable A measurement unit that can take on several different values, usually used to refer to the distribution of data for one survey item.

Variance A statistical term referring to the sum of the squared deviations of each data point from the mean (the sum of squares), divided by the number of cases or degrees of freedom (the mean squares), and also the value from which the standard deviation is computed by extracting the square root.

Verbal Scale Any scale whose points are either expressed in words or whose numeric code values are labeled throughout the scale with words.

Verbal Frequency Scale A particular type of verbal scale where the frequency of an event to be indicated by the respondent is expressed verbally, ordinarily with the words "Always, Often, Sometimes, Rarely, and Never," rather than in numeric quantities.

Verification The process of checking with respondents after they have been interviewed to be sure the person was actually interviewed and that the interview was done correctly and completely when and where it was supposed to be, and commonly but incorrectly called "validation".

Visibility Bias One form of selection bias, where a particular type of respondent is over- or underrepresented in the sample because they are more visible than others with different characteristics.

Yea-Sayer An individual or respondent who persistently tends to respond in the affirmative more often than others, regardless of the questions.

Yea-Sayer Bias The tendency for a set of survey results to be generally and artificially positive on a series of items because all items are inclined in the same direction, toward the positive or toward the negative, and positive responses to the earlier items were generalized to the remaining ones, thus reducing the validity.

Index